W9-BVP-682

INDOMITABLE WILL

LBJ surrounded by well-wishers following his last State of the Union address, January 14, 1969.

INDOMITABLE WILL

LBJ IN THE PRESIDENCY

MARK K. UPDEGROVE

CROWN PUBLISHERS
NEW YORK

Photo credits appear on page 372.

Published in the United States by Crown Publishers, an imprint of the Crown Publishing Group, a division of Random House, Inc., New York.
www.crownpublishing.com

CROWN and the Crown colophon are registered trademarks of Random House, Inc.

Library of Congress Cataloging-in-Publication Data

Updegrove, Mark K.
Indomitable will : LBJ in the presidency / Mark K. Updegrove.—1st ed.
p. cm.
Includes bibliographical references and index.
1. Johnson, Lyndon B. (Lyndon Baines), 1908–1973. 2. Presidents—United States—Biography. 3. United States—Politics and government—1963–1969. I. Title.

E847. U63 2012
973.923092—dc23
[B]
2011037480

ISBN 978-0-307-88771-9
eISBN 978-0-307-88773-3

Printed in the United States of America

Book design by Lauren Dong
Jacket design by Darren Haggar
Jacket photography: LBJ Presidential Library photo by Yoichi Okamoto

10 9 8 7 6 5 4 3 2 1

First Edition

FOR

HARRY MIDDLETON

AND

BOB HARDESTY

Contents

Acknowledgments

Few projects of this scope come from one mind or set of hands. This book is no exception. I owe my deepest gratitude to those who helped me see it through.

First and foremost, my thanks go to my family. As she has with previous projects, my wife, Evie, encouraged me to set pen to paper and write to my heart's content—even though it took away from time spent with her and our beloved children, Charlie and Tallie. Her love and support—and that of Charlie and Tallie—has never wavered.

The same is true of my parents, John and Naomi Updegrove, who have always recognized and nurtured the best in their own children; my faithful siblings and their spouses, Susan and Glenn Crafford; Randall Updegrove; and Stuart and Christine Updegrove; and the Kaskey, Krombach, and Wiewel families. Likewise, I'm thankful to many loyal friends, among them, Don Carelton, David Dunham, Steve Huestis, David Hume Kennerly, Cathy Saypol, Nick Segal, and Ray Walter.

My agent, Stuart Krichevsky, and my editor at Crown, Roger Scholl, provided wise counsel and guidance that made this a better book than it would have been otherwise. At Crown, I'm also grateful to Logan Balestrino, Christopher Brand, Tina Constable, Rachel Rokicki, Annsley Rosner, and Molly Stern.

Helping immeasurably throughout the project was my right hand, Meg Chapin, who became Meg Chapin Haden in its midst. I was also aided by Dolph Briscoe IV, who gave generously of his time to research facts and oral histories that are at the heart of the book. Well before I landed at the Lyndon Baines Johnson Presidential Library and Museum as its director, I gained first-hand appreciation of the institution's reputation for archival excellence as an author of a previous work. This time, I was able to draw on its archivists as colleagues. Claudia Anderson, Tina Houston, and Regina Greenwell, all of whom have devoted nearly their entire careers to the LBJ Library, combed through the book's manuscript and provided their feedback, helping to ensure that my facts were straight and my perspective balanced. Any remaining errors, I can assure the reader, are my own. I also benefited from the expertise of Barbara Biffle, Barbara Cline, Sarah Cunningham, Laura Eggert, Allen Fisher, Nicole Hadad, Margaret Harman, Brian McNerney, and John Wilson. Other people at the Library, as well as at the LBJ Foundation and the National Archives, also contributed to this enterprise: Judy Allen, Renee Bair, Elizabeth Boone, Sandy Cohen, Parker Duffie, Sharon Fawcett, David Ferriero, Mary Herman, Mike MacDonald, Sarah McCracken, Marge Morton, Raine Pipkin, Chris Runkel, Janie Sides, Nancy Smith, and Anne Wheeler.

Throughout the past several years, I have received invaluable input through official interviews or offhanded conversations from many who have deepened my impressions of Lyndon Baines Johnson and his times. They include Ben Barnes, Carl Bernstein, Michael Beschloss, Julian Bond, George H. W. Bush, Joe Califano, Liz Carpenter, Jimmy Carter, Bob Dallek, Marie Fehmer Chiarodo, Gerald R. Ford, Lloyd Hand, Bill Hobby, Jesse Jackson, Edwina Johnson, Jim Jones, Larry Levinson, Bill Little, George McGovern, Harry McPherson, Walter Mondale, Bill Moyers, Lyndon Nugent, Catherine Robb, Chuck Robb, Hugh Sidey, Neal Spelce, Marvin Watson, and Lee White. In particular, I am indebted to Luci Johnson, Tom Johnson, Lynda Johnson Robb, and Larry Temple, who patiently provided unvarnished answers to my questions as I called on them early and often throughout the writing process.

Finally, I owe thanks to Harry Middleton and Bob Hardesty, to whom this volume is dedicated. Harry's fingerprints are all over this book. In thirty plus years at the helm of the LBJ Library, he amassed oral histories from most of the major participants of the administration, which are among the vast volumes of material accessible to scholars. It was Harry who, with the unshrinking Lady Bird Johnson's consent, opened 643 hours of taped telephone conversations from President Johnson to the public despite LBJ's wish that the tapes be sealed for fifty years after his death. All this was in keeping with LBJ's directive to tell the story of his administration "with the bark off," something he was confident Harry would take to heart when he appointed him to the position of LBJ Library director in 1971.

Bob also contributed to this book, not only directly like Harry, but by helping to put together and publishing the proceedings of symposia at the LBJ Library that shed additional light on President Johnson, who Bob has called "a mystery of a man." Harry and Bob's contributions make the enigmatic LBJ a little less mysterious.

I hope this book does, too.

—MKU
Austin, Texas

Index of Voices

Note: Individuals are identified in the context to which they would be most relevant to LBJ

Bess Abell: Lady Bird Johnson's White House social secretary, 1963–69
Carl Albert: U.S. representative, Oklahoma (D), 1947–77
Valerie Anders: wife of Apollo 8 astronaut Bill Anders
Chuck Bailey: Washington correspondent, Cowles Publications
Bobby Baker: secretary to the Senate majority leader, 1955–63
George Ball: undersecretary of state, 1961–66; U.S. representative to the United Nations, 1968
Ben Barnes: speaker of the Texas House of Representatives, 1965–68; lieutenant governor of Texas, 1968–69
Carl Bernstein: metro reporter, *The Washington Post*
Phyllis Bonanno: personal assistant to President Johnson, 1968–69
Susan Borman: wife of Apollo 8 astronaut Frank Borman
John Brademas: U.S. representative, Indiana (D), 1959–81
Jack Brooks: U.S. representative, Texas (D), 1953–95
McGeorge Bundy: special assistant to the president for National Security Affairs (National Security Advisor), 1961–66
William Bundy: assistant secretary of state for East Asian and Pacific Affairs, 1964–69
David Burke: friend of the Kennedy family
Horace Busby: special assistant to the president, secretary of the Cabinet, 1963–65
George H. W. Bush: U.S. representative, Texas (R), 1967–71
Joe Califano: special assistant to the president, 1965–69
Liz Carpenter: Lady Bird Johnson's White House press secretary and staff director, 1963–69
Doug Cater: special assistant to the president, 1964–68
John Chancellor: political correspondent, NBC News, 1962–65; director of Voice of America, 1965–67

Marie Fehmer Chiarodo: personal secretary to the president, 1962–69
George Christian: White House press secretary, 1966–69
Ramsey Clark: assistant attorney general, 1961–65; deputy attorney general, 1965–66; acting attorney general, 1966–67; attorney general, 1967–69
Clark Clifford: member and chairman, President's Foreign Intelligence Advisory Board, 1961–68; secretary of defense, 1968–69
Wilbur Cohen: secretary of health, education and welfare, 1968–69
John Connally: LBJ congressional aide; Texas governor, 1963–69; and LBJ adviser
Chet Cooper: senior member National Security Council staff, 1964–66; special assistant to Ambassador Averell Harriman, 1966–67
Frank Cormier: White House correspondent, Associated Press
Walter Cronkite: CBS News anchor, 1950–81
George Davis: pastor, National City Christian Church, Washington, D.C., and friend of LBJ
James Davis: employee of the Johnson family, 1955–2007
Sid Davis: White House correspondent, Westinghouse Broadcasting Company, 1959–68
Willard Deason: manager, owner, KVET, Austin, 1949–65; college classmate and friend of LBJ
Everett Dirksen: Senate minority leader, Illinois (R), 1959–69
Ervin Duggan: staff assistant to the president, 1965–69
Dwight D. Eisenhower: president of the United States, 1953–61
James Farmer: civil rights activist, national director, Congress of Racial Equality, 1961–65; program director, NAACP, 1959–61; assistant secretary of health, education, and welfare for administration, 1969–70
Myer Feldman: deputy special counsel to the president, 1963–64; special counsel to the president, 1964–65
Gerald R. Ford: U.S. representative, Michigan (R), 1949–73, House minority leader, Michigan (R), 1965–73
Abe Fortas: associate justice, U.S. Supreme Court, 1965–69
Max Frankel: White House correspondent 1966–68, Washington bureau chief 1968–72, and executive director 1986–94, *The New York Times*
Orville Freeman: secretary of agriculture, 1961–69
J. William Fulbright: U.S. senator from Arkansas (D), 1945–74
James C. Gaither: staff assistant to the president in the War on Poverty, 1966–69
John Gardner: secretary of health, education, and welfare, 1965–68
Ernie Goldstein: special assistant to the president, 1967–69
Barry Goldwater: U.S. senator, Arizona (R), 1953–65, 1969–87
Richard Goodwin: speechwriter for John F. Kennedy, 1959–63; special assistant to the president, 1964–66
Billy Graham: evangelist and friend of LBJ

Joe Haggar: president of the Haggar Clothing Company
Fannie Lou Hamer: civil rights activist, vice chair of the Mississippi Freedom Democratic Party
Bob Hardesty: assistant to the president, 1965–69
Bryce Harlow: senior adviser and counselor to Richard Nixon, 1968–71, 1973–74
George Hartzog: director, National Park Service, 1964–72
Betty Hickman: secretary to Senator Johnson; aide to the president
Sarah Hughes: judge, U.S. District Court, Northern District, Texas, 1961–75
Hubert H. Humphrey: U.S. senator, Minnesota (D), 1949–65; vice president, 1965–69
Haynes Johnson: reporter and editor, *Washington Evening Star*, 1957–69
Lady Bird Johnson: wife of LBJ; First Lady of the United States, 1963–69
Luci Johnson: younger daughter of Lyndon and Lady Bird Johnson
Sam Houston Johnson: LBJ's younger brother
Tom Johnson: special assistant to the president, 1965–69
Jim Jones: appointments secretary (chief of staff), 1965–69
Nicholas Katzenbach: U.S. deputy attorney general, 1962–65; U.S. attorney general, 1965–66; undersecretary of state, 1966–69
Jacqueline Kennedy: wife of John F. Kennedy, First Lady of the United States, 1961–63
Rose Kennedy: mother of John F. Kennedy
Ted Kennedy: U.S. senator, Massachusetts (D) 1962–2009
Douglas Kiker: reporter, *New York Herald Tribune*, 1963–66; NBC News correspondent, 1966–91
Martin Luther King Jr.: president, Southern Christian Leadership Conference, 1957–68
Robert Komer: National Security Council, 1961–66; special assistant for Vietnam, 1966; chief of pacification, 1967; General William Westmoreland's deputy for civil operations and revolutionary development and support (CORDS), 1967–68; U.S. ambassador to Turkey, 1968–69
Arthur Krim: chairman, Democratic National Finance Committee, 1966–68
John Lewis: chairman, Student Nonviolent Coordinating Committee, 1963–66
Marilyn Lovell: wife of Apollo 8 astronaut Jim Lovell
Mike Mansfield: U.S. senator, Montana (D), 1953–77
Thurgood Marshall: solicitor general, 1965–67; U.S. Supreme Court justice, 1967–91
John Bartlow Martin: speechwriter for John F. Kennedy, 1960–63; U.S. ambassador to the Dominican Republic, 1962–64; special envoy to the Dominican Republic, 1965
John McCormack: U.S. representative, Massachusetts (D), 1928–71; Speaker of the House of Representatives, 1962–71
George McGovern: U.S. representative, South Dakota (D), 1957–61; U.S. senator, South Dakota (D), 1963–81

Robert McNamara: secretary of defense, 1961–68; president of World Bank Group, 1968–81

Jack McNulty: staff assistant, 1966–68

Harry McPherson: deputy undersecretary of the Army for international affairs, 1963–64; special assistant to the secretary of the army for civil functions, 1963–64; assistant secretary of state in the bureau of educational and cultural affairs, 1964–65; special assistant and counsel to the president 1965–66; special counsel to the president, 1966–69

Marianne Means: White House correspondent and columnist, Hearst Newspapers, 1958–2008

Harry Middleton: staff assistant to the president, 1967–69; director, Lyndon Baines Johnson Library and Museum, 1971–2001

Scooter Miller: political supporter of LBJ

Wilbur Mills: U.S. representative, Arkansas (D), 1939–77; chairman of the committee on ways and means, 1957–74

Walter Mondale: U.S. senator, Minnesota (D), 1964–76

Bill Moyers: special assistant to the president, 1963–67; White House press secretary, 1965–67

Lawrence F. O'Brien: special assistant to the president for congressional relations, 1961–65; postmaster general, 1965–68; chairman, Democratic National Committee, 1968–69 and 1970–72

Kenneth O'Donnell: appointment secretary (chief of staff) to John F. Kennedy, 1961–63; special assistant to the president, 1963–65; executive director, Democratic National Committee, 1964–65

Wright Patman: U.S. representative, Texas (D), 1929–76

Jake Pickle: U.S. representative, Texas (D), 1963–95

W. DeVier Pierson: chief counsel, Joint Committee on the Organization of Congress, 1965–67; special counsel, 1967–69

Phil Potter: city editor, White House and Senate correspondent, and bureau chief in New Delhi and London, *Baltimore Sun*

George Reedy: special assistant to Vice President Johnson, 1961–63; White House press secretary, 1964–66

Lynda Johnson Robb: elder daughter of Lyndon and Lady Bird Johnson

Chuck Roberts: White House correspondent, *Newsweek*, 1951–72

Hugh Robinson: U.S. Army aide to the president, 1965–69

Warren Rogers: bureau chief and chief Washington correspondent, Hearst Newspapers, 1963–66; and Washington editor 1966–69, and Washington bureau chief 1969–70, *Look* magazine

Walt Rostow: special assistant for national security affairs (national security advisor), 1966–69

Dean Rusk: secretary of state, 1961–69

Richard Russell: U.S. senator, Georgia (D), 1933–71

Ray Scherer: White House correspondent, NBC, 1947–75

Sargent Shriver: director, Peace Corps, 1961–66; director, Office of Economic Opportunity, 1964–68

Hugh Sidey: Washington correspondent, *Life* magazine, 1955–57, and *Time* magazine, 1957–96

Robert Strauss: friend of LBJ; lawyer, founder, Akin Gump Strauss Hauer & Feld, 1945–present

James Symington: director, President's Committee on Juvenile Delinquency, 1965–66; chief of protocol, State Department, 1966–68

Larry Temple: special counsel to the president, 1967–69

Helen Thomas: White House correspondent, United Press International, 1943–2000

Bob Thompson: White House correspondent, *The Los Angeles Times*; Washington bureau chief, Hearst Newspapers

Homer Thornberry: U.S. representative, Texas (D), 1949–63; United States district judge for the western district of Texas, 1963–65, circuit judge of the United States Court of Appeals of the Fifth Judicial Circuit, 1965–95

Stewart Udall: U.S. representative, Arizona (D), 1955–61; secretary of the interior, 1961–69

Jack Valenti: special assistant to the president, 1963–66

Richard Valeriani: NBC news correspondent, 1964–88

Earl Warren: chief justice, U.S. Supreme Court, 1953–69; chairman, Warren Commission, 1963–64

Robert C. Weaver: secretary of housing and urban development, 1966–68

Lee C. White: assistant special counsel, 1961–63; associate counsel, 1963–65; special counsel to the president, 1965–66

William S. White: syndicated columnist, United Feature Syndicate, 1958–73

Tom Wicker: Washington Bureau staff 1960–64; bureau chief 1964–68; associate editor 1968–85, *The New York Times*

Roger Wilkins: assistant attorney general, 1965–69

Roy Wilkins: executive secretary 1955–64, and executive director, 1964–77, NAACP

Warren Woodward: Johnson congressional aide, 1948–53; employee of KTBC and friend of LBJ

Andrew Young: administrator Citizen Education Program, 1961–64; executive director 1964–70, Southern Christian Leadership Conference

Introduction

HISTORY, IN ITS MOST CURSORY FORM, IS OFTEN A BEAUTY CONTEST: abbreviated judgments based on imagery and sound bites that commonly have substance yielding to superficiality.

The image of George Washington, the stolid, brave general on horseback, is consistent with the formidable legacy he left (minus legends of wooden teeth). The enigmatic, idealistic Thomas Jefferson—like Washington, tall for his day at over six feet—also cuts a dashing figure in history, reflected in the statue romantically peering from the Jefferson Memorial in the capital's Tidal Basin.

Other presidential founding fathers, while essential to the country's beginning, don't fare so well. John Adams, who had the misfortune of following Washington into the presidency, was further hampered by a portly frame and an irascible, acerbic nature that complemented his physical appearance. The dry and diminutive James Madison, who crafted the Constitution and ruled the White House in a venerable eight-year run, was described by a contemporary as a "withered little Apple John." He followed Jefferson into office and, two hundred years later, remains eclipsed by his predecessor's long shadow. Madison is seldom given his historical due; nor is Adams, though resurrected in recent years through biographical treatment by historian David McCullough and an HBO miniseries.

When it comes to our modern presidents, photographs, broadcast footage, and sound bites have disproportionate influence on how we view our leaders in retrospect, favoring the most graceful, attractive, visionary, and eloquent. History blows a kiss to Franklin Roosevelt, John F. Kennedy, and Ronald Reagan in that regard, while becoming chaste with their immediate successors: Harry Truman, Lyndon Johnson, and George H. W.

Bush. That's not to suggest that the latter presidents should necessarily merit better critical appraisal than the former, or that image isn't a crucial element for public figures, as any K Street consultant will attest, but simply that Truman, Johnson, and Bush are held back by their own relative shortcomings in the image department.

Throughout his presidency, Truman battled public perceptions of himself as a prosaic little man—often a sniping partisan—out of his depth in the Oval Office, particulary when likened to the titanic FDR. Bush had his own image problems. Though boasting patrician good looks, he admitted to falling short on "the vision thing" and, upon leaving office after failing to win a second term, lamented that Americans didn't know his own "heartbeat." Like Truman, Bush came up short when contrasted with his predecessor, Reagan, who radiated heartbeat, which one could practically see thumping beneath the pocket square of his suit jacket. (Both Truman and Bush would fine some measure of vindication during their lifetimes as the public belatedly came to appreciate their steady hands and strength of character.)

But perhaps more than any, Johnson is given short shrift through historical shorthand. Though tall at six foot three, the long-eared, droopy-eyed LBJ would win no beauty contests, especially relative to the graceful Kennedy. Unlike Kennedy, Johnson didn't photograph well. The best-known images of LBJ are born of tragedy, bookending his presidency: a somber former vice president being sworn into the presidency on *Air Force One*, flanked by his wife, Lady Bird, and the newly widowed and shell-shocked first lady, Jacqueline Kennedy; and an emotionally wrought commander-in-chief toward the end of his reign, head down on the White House Cabinet Room table, agonizing over a tape recording from his son-in-law, Chuck Robb, in Vietnam. Other famous photographs from Johnson's White House years are hardly the stuff of presidential greatness, suggesting a cowboy crudeness incongruous in the White House: the president lifting his shirt to reveal his gallbladder scar to members of the press or holding up his beagle by its ears.

Nor did Johnson play well on television. Just as the medium expanded Kennedy and Reagan, it shrank the "bigger-than-life" LBJ, who kept his oversize personality in check when the camera lights were on for the sake of appearing "presidential." Instead, Johnson came off as a neutered version of himself, subduing the dynamism that made him the most effective legislator of his time. "Television never really caught a true picture of the man," recalled Ray Scherer, NBC News's White House correspondent during the Johnson years. "Somehow he was too big for the twenty-one inch tube." Maybe the best-known video clip of Johnson is from his last year in the White House, when the embattled president announced to a shocked nation, "I shall not seek, and I will not accept, the nomination of my party for another term as your president."

And though he was an effective public speaker, Johnson's rhetoric and delivery generally didn't achieve heights beyond the marginal, at least by White House standards.

None of these areas does justice to the thirty-sixth president.

In fact, there are few who knew him who wouldn't describe Lyndon Johnson as a great man. Flawed, yes, and not always good, but great. Moreover, almost anyone who was exposed to him has a story worth telling. When one was in his presence, his kinetic energy, mental intensity, and aura of power were palpable; he was always the biggest man in the room—the most colorful, complex, and enigmatic, too. "Allowing for shades of subtlety," wrote Johnson aide Bob Hardesty, reflecting on his former boss, "there were as many LBJs as there were people who knew him. Each individual had a unique perspective on him—and as often as not these perspectives were contradictory."

Along with almost everyone who knew Johnson, John Connally, an early Johnson campaign manager and friend, who achieved his own political success as governor of Texas, picked up on Hardesty's theme: "There is no adjective in the dictionary to describe [Johnson]," he mused, "He was cruel and kind, generous and greedy, sensitive and insensitive, crafty and naive, ruthless and thoughtful, simple in many ways and yet extremely complex, caring and totally not caring; he could overwhelm people with kindness and turn around and be cruel and petty toward those same people; he knew how to use people in politics in the way nobody else could that I know of. As a matter of fact, it would take every adjective in the dictionary to describe him." Like Shakespeare's King Lear before him, Johnson seemed to ask, "Who is it that can tell me who I am?"

But what is consistent is that all of those qualities added up to a giant of a man, and they help explain Johnson's prodigious achievements, which can't be ignored by history. More than any president since his mentor, Franklin Roosevelt, Johnson got things done. His "Great Society," with its flurry of laws delivering social change, bears testimony to his force of personality and triumph of will. As veteran journalist and president watcher Helen Thomas put it, "I think [Johnson] did monogram our society in his time here. . . . In the first place, I thought he had no peers—maybe FDR—in terms of what he did for the general welfare with the Great Society: Medicare, Head Start, federal aid to education, the Civil Rights Act, the Voting Rights Act, all those things." LBJ's sweeping reform in the areas of civil rights, education, health care, immigration, the arts and humanities, and the environment changed forever the face and heart of America and the way we live.

Still, Johnson gets little credit for it. In the contentious 2008 Democratic presidential primaries that saw party favorite, Hillary Clinton, square off against upstart Barack Obama, Clinton was excoriated when she allowed, "[Martin Luther] King's dream began to be realized when President Lyndon Johnson passed the Civil Rights Act of 1964. It took a president to get it done." A barrage of critics charged that Clinton's comment diminished King and was tinged with racism. But is there any doubt that a president might have an essential role in seeing a landmark law to fruition, particularly the first major piece of civil rights legislation since Reconstruction? As civil rights leader and former lieutenant to Martin Luther King, Andrew Young, put it later, "Martin Luther King understood that we would not have been able to be successful if we didn't have a president with the kind of [political] skill [as Lyndon Johnson], and while [King] loved President Kennedy, and knew that President Kennedy gave his life [for his country], he said, 'I'm not sure President Kennedy could have done this for us.'"

Yet when Barack Obama became president in 2009, maybe the most historic milestone in the nation's long struggle for civil rights, Johnson was generally not among those on the short list of people who came to mind in ensuring that that day would come. As historian Douglas Brinkley wrote in an essay in *Barack Obama: The Official Inauguration Book*, reflecting the sentiments of many, "The baton had been passed from Lincoln to the Roosevelts to the Kennedys and King to this man [Obama]." It likely wouldn't have surprised Johnson, who was given to bouts of self-pity and was particularly thin-skinned over the backseat he had taken to the Kennedy brothers.

In his forward to that same book though, congressman and civil rights hero John Lewis wrote that after the bloody campaign in Selma, Alabama, in 1965, "President Johnson made one of the most meaningful speeches that any American president has made in modern times on the question of voting rights and civil rights. The most powerful nation on the face of the earth had heard the cries of pain and the hymns and protests of an oppressed people, and this government was prepared to act"—resulting in the passage of the Voting Rights Act and transformational political power and social change for people of color. But then, King and Lewis knew Johnson, worked with him, and saw firsthand the difference he made.

In understanding Johnson, *seeing* was believing. Those who witnessed "the Johnson treatment" up close appreciated Johnson's ability to get people who mattered to say yes—even to the most controversial reforms. Leon Jaworski, best known for his stint as Watergate special prosecutor, said of Johnson, "This man makes the greatest, most persuasive talk to a small group of anyone I have ever known. I have never known his equal." Lady Bird Johnson called her husband "the last of the courthouse politicians," those who commanded the attention of a gathering of folks within earshot from the steps of a courthouse, and he was certainly among the best. "People, not TV studios, were adrenaline to him," Liz Carpenter, a longtime Johnson aide, observed. "They were not only his adrenaline, they were his cause, and he wanted to seize his moment and take his chance with them." Those qualities and skills, plus a fierce desire to do right, led to a societal transformation that has not since been achieved by any of his successors.

There, too, was Vietnam, the inherited war Johnson didn't bargain for and never overcame. In the eyes of history, Vietnam dances around Eisenhower, Kennedy, and Nixon, flirting with them, but it attaches itself to Johnson, clinging to him by the light of day. As Helen Thomas quickly added to her accolades for Johnson, "Vietnam, of course, was his great tragedy." For Johnson, who longed for greatness and a place in the pantheon of presidents, Vietnam was indeed a tragedy. "I knew from the start that if I left the woman I love—the Great Society—in order to fight that bitch of a war, then I would lose everything. All my programs. All my hopes. All my dreams," historian Doris Kearns Goodwin recalled Johnson lamenting in his winter years. While the Great Society added immeasurably to the utopian optimism that marked the dawn of the sixties era, Vietnam, an ill-fated war that saw the loss of more than thirty-six thousand American troops by the time Johnson left office—fifty-eight thousand when the war was over in 1975—was the conflict that ultimately divided the nation.

Clare Booth Luce, playwright and wife of *Time* magazine founder Henry Luce, famously lectured incumbent presidents that they would be remembered in one sentence: "Lincoln: He freed the slaves," she would illustrate. If so, Johnson's sentence surely has *Vietnam* in it, and if it's long enough, it may include the prodigious accomplishments of the Great Society—in particular those involving civil rights—as a triumphant counterbalance. Had the Great Society marked the end of his presidency and Vietnam the beginning, and not the other way around, the sentence may have been different. But it was Vietnam that brought Johnson's once-auspicious presidency to an end, punctuating his obstreperous tenure.

Compounding Johnson's challenges in any historical judgment—abbreviated or otherwise—is his protean nature, which makes him an easy mark for historical revisionism. Among the most extreme examples came in 2004, when the History Channel broadcast a special implicating him as a conspirator in the assassination of John F. Kennedy. Never mind that the documentary was based on conspiracy theories that held no water, Johnson, undeniably power hungry and ambitious, could be retrofitted into the implausible storyline. (In the wake of outrage from Presidents Carter and Ford and former Johnson aides, among others, the History Channel issued to Lady Bird Johnson "deepest apologies" over choosing to air the program.)

Even responsible biographers, drawing on the rich tapestry of Johnson's life and personality, can craft an account that is factually accurate but unduly skewed, given the subject's enormous breadth and inherent contradictions. As Connally once told Robert Caro, in response to Caro's celebrated biographies of Johnson's early and Senate years, "Every time you could put a dark twist to something Johnson did, you did it. You never paint the bright side. You never give him credit for anything that's virtuous or noble or reasonable or fair or rational." Walter Cronkite agreed, characterizing Caro's portrait of Johnson as "one-sided." "I don't really believe that [Johnson] was all evil," Cronkite said. "He had an ugly side. Many of us do, I suppose." Johnson used to joke about the Depression-era schoolteacher in desperate need of a job who was asked by the school board whether he taught that the world was round or flat. "I can teach it either way," he replied. Those interpreting Johnson's life and legacy have the same leeway.

After Pablo Picasso painted his now-famous portrait of Gertrude Stein, which was criticized at the time for not accurately capturing his subject, he replied, "It doesn't look like her now, but it will." History's distortions can resonate similarly, becoming conventional wisdom as impressions congeal. It may help to explain the delta in public perceptions of LBJ versus those of presidential scholars. In a 2010 Gallup poll in which Americans were asked to rank the nine presidents of the last fifty years—from Kennedy through George W. Bush—Johnson came in seventh, after Jimmy Carter and just ahead of George W. Bush and Richard Nixon. At the same time, presidential scholars—those who have combed through the record and taken measure beyond the surface—typically rank Johnson in the second quintile of *all* presidents, on a plane with other "near greats" such as Jackson, Theodore Roosevelt, and Truman, and just short of the pantheon reserved for Washington, Lincoln, and FDR.

The essence of Lyndon Johnson cannot be adequately captured through the lens of a camera, behind a microphone, under a klieg light, or by way of any desultory account. He is best remembered up close by those who knew him, and in myriad accounts. Even then, he remains elusive.

This book aims to provide a portrait of Johnson through the stories and recollections of the people who were there with him day in and day out during his presidency—living with him, working alongside him, covering him in the White House press pool—and through Johnson's own recollections and his own words, in phone conversations as history was being made. It is not meant to be a definitive presidential biography, but a collection of impressions illuminating the totality of who he was, what he did, and what it meant. For it is through firsthand narrative more than anything that Lyndon Johnson—who teemed with vitality throughout his sixty-four years and remains enigmatic nearly four decades after his passing—comes to life.

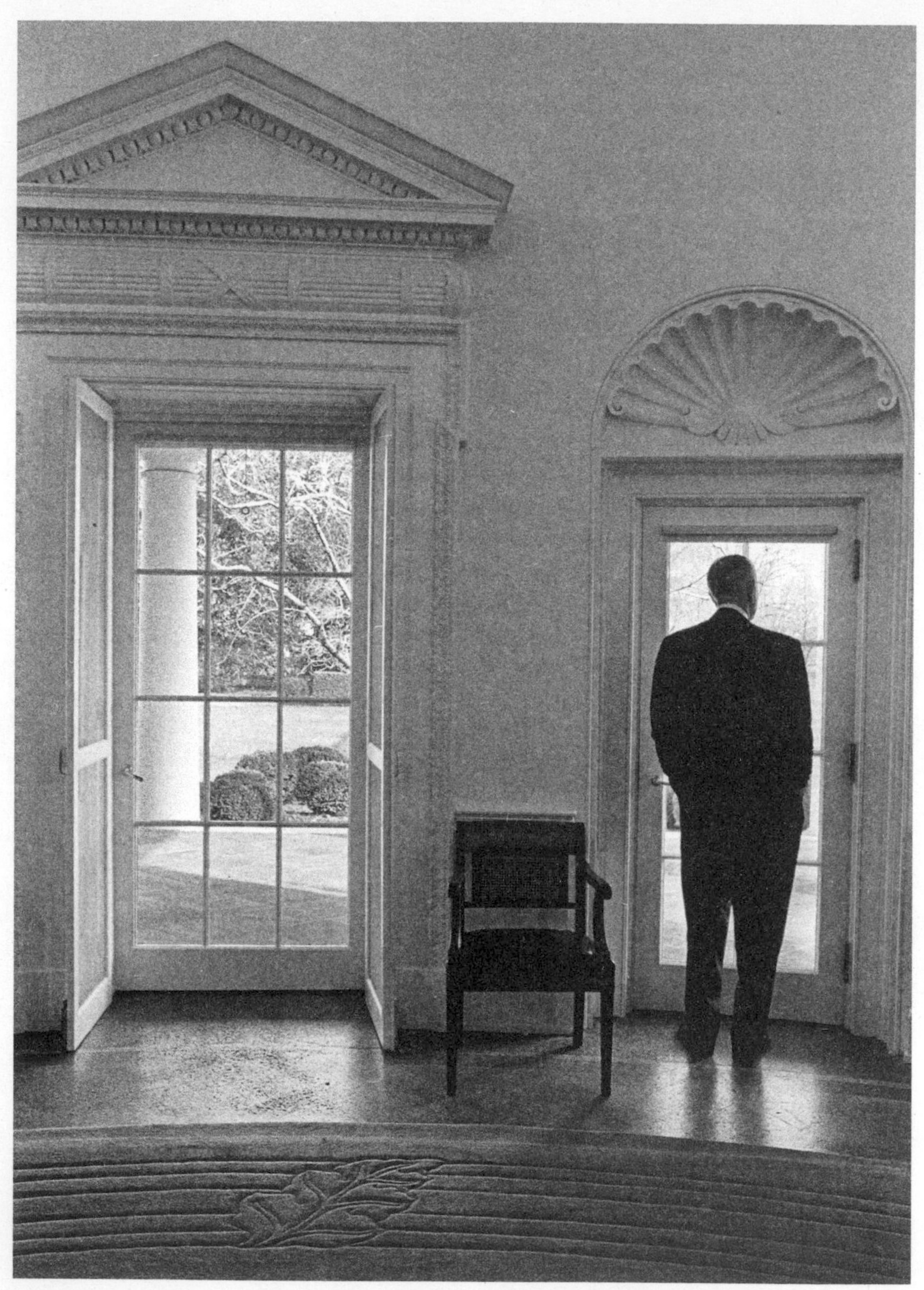

LBJ in the Oval Office, January 24, 1966.

Chapter 1

"A MAN WHO REMAINS A MYSTERY"

"HOW DO YOU CAPTURE THE ESSENCE OF A MAN WHOSE 'ESSENCE' WAS like quicksilver?" Bob Hardesty, a White House speechwriter from 1966 to the end of Johnson's term in 1969, once asked of his former boss. "How can you capture a man who remains a mystery even to those who knew him best?" It is a question that will go unanswered in these pages. Any attempt to answer it in any depth or with any degree of certainty would be pure folly. Though it is a journey worth taking.

JACK VALENTI, special assistant to the president, 1963–66: I frankly didn't understand him. I loved him, and I followed him, but I sure as hell didn't fathom all that made him tick.

[S]ince the first time I met him, my opinions about him never changed. It was like being in the jungle and meeting a magnificent panther, silken, silent, ready to spring, and you are a bit afraid and at the same time fascinated by the animal.

HARRY MIDDLETON, staff assistant to the president, 1967–69; director, Lyndon Baines Johnson Library and Museum, 1971–2001: There have been good books written about LBJ, not great ones. There are just too many nuances in him. It would take a dramatist, not an author, to capture LBJ.

WARREN ROGERS, White House correspondent, Hearst Newspapers and *Look* magazine: I've known or interviewed every president since Harry Truman, and Lyndon Johnson is absolutely the most overwhelming human being I've ever known in my life. Anything you want to say about him: good, bad, compassionate, ruthless; everything.

WILBUR COHEN, secretary of health, education, and welfare, 1968–69: He was a complex, contradictory personality. I have heard him, when we were on the [LBJ] Ranch going by and watching the animals, refer to all sorts of sexual characteristics of the animals and of people, and then five minutes later you could stand on the hillside there watching the sunset and you'd find a man who was a poet describing the sunset and the relationship of the land to the people and his hopes and aspirations for people. And it seems to me that people who talk about his crudity do not understand that this was an earthy man . . . a combination of Boccaccio and Machiavelli and John Keats.

HUGH SIDEY, Washington correspondent, *Time* and *Life* magazines: Lyndon Johnson was the single most fascinating human being I have met in my life and I doubt no matter how extended my years be that the record will be challenged. Within hours of meeting him when he stood astride the U.S. Senate as majority leader, I was ushered into his office and given "the treatment," complete with chest thumping, leg and arm squeezing, LBJ's Texas stories and admonitions to take care of him and he would take care of me. Once he made it to the White House, he was even larger and more important than before, natural grist for a column.

JOHN CONNALLY, LBJ congressional aide, Texas governor, 1963–69, and LBJ adviser: He was an extremely ambitious man. He was dedicated to his career. His whole life was politics. He didn't read books. I don't want to embarrass his family, but I might ask them if they ever remember him reading a book. I don't ever remember him reading a book.

That is not to say he wasn't intelligent, or that he wasn't informed or that he wasn't interested. But he didn't have time to read books. He was committed to succeeding as a politician.

MARIANNE MEANS, White House correspondent, Hearst Newspapers: Johnson got his kicks out of working. He was a workaholic. He enjoyed it all; he didn't want to miss a minute. He wanted to be in charge every second.

JOSEPH CALIFANO, special assistant to the president, 1965–69: The Lyndon Johnson I worked with was brave and brutal, compassionate and cruel, incredibly intelligent and infuriatingly insensitive, with a shrewd and uncanny instinct for the jugular of his adversaries. He could be altruistic and petty, caring and crude, generous and petulant, blatantly honest and calculatingly devious—all within the same few minutes. He had a marvelous, if crude, sense of humor. Once he made up his mind, his determination to succeed usually ran over or around whoever and whatever got in his way. He used his prodigious energy—which produced second, third and fourth winds, as others, allies and adversaries alike, slumped in exhaustion—to mount a social revolution and to control everything and everyone around him. He gave new meaning to the word *Machiavellian*, as he gave new hope to the disadvantaged.

MYER FELDMAN, special counsel to the president, 1964–65: I think Lyndon Johnson had great virtues and great vices, depending on whether that particular day he was emphasizing the vices or the virtues, you liked or disliked him. You couldn't say that you liked Lyndon Johnson all the time. It was equally impossible to say that you disliked Lyndon Johnson all the time—but he was a very strong personality, and he had big swings.

MARIE FEHMER CHIARODO, personal secretary to LBJ, 1962–69: [Johnson] was a man of appetites. He worked too hard, lived too rough, and felt too much. I didn't like him all of the time, but I respected him most of the time.

WILLARD DEASON, Johnson friend and supporter: He was a young man always in a hurry; and then he was a middle-aged man always in a hurry.

I used to say that he could see around a corner. He had an intuitive thing about him. He understood what was happening and what was going to happen, and he could tell you.

WARREN WOODWARD, LBJ congressional aide, 1948–53, and friend: On the question of his ambition to be president. I grew up in a time when our mothers and fathers told us that our highest ambition should be to grow up to be president. So in that sense every American child wanted to be president. But the contention that it was for the power—to be president just for the power—I don't agree with that. If he wanted to be president it was because he saw it as a vehicle to get something done for people. That was his ultimate position. That is why the notion that he was consumed by the lust for power is not entirely accurate. It was necessary to have power to accomplish things.

GEORGE CHRISTIAN, White House press secretary, 1966–69: In my book, President Johnson gave it all he had. He might have been ornery at times, he might have been too tough for folks, he was probably less lovable than he wanted to be. But I have never had one shred of doubt concerning his motivations, and that motivation was to change the lives of people he thought were being shortchanged by the system.

LIZ CARPENTER, Lady Bird Johnson's White House press secretary and staff director, 1963–69: Looking back on LBJ and his problems, I think he makes subsequent presidents seem—well, listless, heartless, certainly colorless, and maybe a little chicken.

LEE C. WHITE, special counsel to the president, 1965–66: It was no secret that Lyndon Johnson was a very complex human being. He could be charming, slightly outrageous, extremely thoughtful and considerate, vindictive, sensitive, profane, sentimental, mean, demanding, overbearing, persuasive, crafty, and shrewd. Above all, he was intelligent and focused. High on his agenda were the issues of racial discrimination and problems of the poor. His empathy for the blacks who had been treated so badly and for the poor, regardless of their color, was deep in him, and he was willing to do what needed to be done to try to solve their fundamental problems.

BILL MOYERS, special assistant to the president; 1963–67, White House press secretary, 1965–67: [A]nyone who knew him knew that he could be abusive, hard, sometimes callous, deceptive, often distrustful. Anybody who knew him knew all of those things about him. And yet from this ugly and mean man came a program, a philosophy, a purpose that transcended what we knew about him. . . .

The seminal moment of the Johnson years came in a press conference when Jim Deakin of the *St. Louis Dispatch* asked him, "Mr. President, I don't understand why for all these years you were either indifferent to or opposed to the advance of civil rights in Texas, and you suddenly turn around and are doing what you're doing in the White House."

The president replied (and this is only a paraphrase), "Isn't it wonderful that after all those years of keeping my hand on the scale, you might say, I have a chance to put right what for so long I helped to keep wrong?"

That is the mystery of Lyndon Johnson. I'm astonished that that much good happened in the world where civilization is but a veneer, where selfishness is exploited and encouraged and people are urged to look out for number one. I'm surprised that anything good and decent occurs. . . .

The question is, why did a man as flawed as any human vessel that was ever made rouse a nation to reach beyond itself in such a time?

Lady Bird and Lyndon Johnson with Jacqueline Kennedy on board Air Force One, *Love Field, Dallas, Texas, November 22, 1963.*

Chapter 2

LOOKING AT THE LIVING, WISHING FOR THE DEAD

THE ASSASSINATION OF JOHN FITZGERALD KENNEDY INHABITS A PLACE deep in America's collective consciousness along with the grainy frames of the home movie taken by Abraham Zapruder from a pedestal in Dealey Plaza in Dallas on November 22, 1963. Those of a certain age can recall in vivid detail where they were, and the shock they felt when they heard the news that the president had fallen prey to assassination. Those who were there in Dallas to witness his murder experienced a horror that was difficult to escape, even years later. "Dallas has always been a nightmare for me," recalled Lyndon Johnson of the tragedy that would heap the burdens of the presidency upon him upon his hearing the words "He's gone," spoken by a Kennedy aide in a hospital waiting room. "I don't want to think about it any more than I have to."

LIZ CARPENTER: [Lyndon Johnson] arrived center stage during a national tragedy. And inevitably, as Lady Bird said so poignantly at the time, "People looked at the living and wished for the dead."

JACK VALENTI: God, how well I remember how it all began. The motorcade moved slowly, confidently, under a sky wiped clear of clouds, before a throng of people who were cheerful and warmly hospitable. Then it happened, a senseless act of mindless malice; a gallant young president slain in the streets of Dallas, a nightmare so unimaginable that you could not believe it, an evil so monstrous you could not contemplate it.

LYNDON BAINES JOHNSON (LBJ): We left Fort Worth [on *Air Force Two*] ahead of the president's *Air Force One*. We landed in Dallas around 11:30. We—Mrs. Johnson and I—got off the plane and shook hands with the group that was there to receive the president, and we moved back with the dignitaries and welcomed the president and Mrs. Kennedy as they came off the plane. He was happy, smiling, and I think he was stimulated by the previous day's Fort Worth experiences. And Mrs. Kennedy was radiant and looked charming and beautiful in that pink hat and pink suit.

They got in a big Lincoln with Governor [John] Connally because the president always rides with the first man of the state when the first man of the nation comes to visit. They got in the big Lincoln and drove away, and Mrs. Johnson and Senator [Ralph] Yarborough and I got in the car that was driven by a patrolman, and Rufus Youngblood was our Secret Service escort. And as we continued to drive, once we heard some sound. Some thought it was a firecracker, some thought it was a gun, some thought it was a muffler on a car backfiring or something. But very shortly after the sound, the first sound, just almost instantaneously, the very competent, cautious Secret Serviceman jumped over the front seat and shoved me to the bottom of the Lincoln. He told Mrs. Johnson and Senator Yarborough to lean over as fast as they could so they could get their head below the back seat. He got on top of me and he put his body between me and the crowd. And he had his knees in my back and his elbows in my back and a good two hundred pounds all over me. And the car was speeding up. He had a microphone from the front seat that he'd pulled over with him as he came over, a two-way radio talking and there was a lot of traffic on the radio and you could hear them talking back and forth, and one of them said: "Let's get out of here quick."

[T]he next thing, we were on our way to the hospital. They just almost shoved us into the hospital, into the first room that they'd come to down the corridor. They pulled all the shades in the room, closed it, and we sat there and endured the agony and waited for reports that came in from time to time.

LADY BIRD JOHNSON: Through it all Lyndon was remarkably calm and quiet. He suggested that the presidential plane be moved to another part of the field. He spoke of going back out to the plane in unmarked cars. Every face that came in [to the hospital waiting room], you searched for the answer. I think the face I kept seeing the answer on was the face of Kenny O'Donnell, who loved President Kennedy so much.

It was Lyndon who spoke of it first, although I knew I would not leave without doing it. He said, "You had better try to see Jackie and Nellie [Connally]." We didn't know what happened to John [Connally].

I asked the Secret Service if I could be taken to them. They began to lead me up one corridor and down another. Suddenly I found myself face to face with Jackie in a small hallway. I believe it was right outside the operating room. You always think of someone like her as being insulated, protected. She was quite alone. I don't think I ever saw anyone so much alone in my life. I went up to her, put my arms around her, and said something to her. I'm sure it was something like "God help us all," because my feelings for her were too tumultuous to put into words.

And then I went to see Nellie. There it was different, because Nellie and I have gone through so many things together since 1938. I hugged her tight and we both cried and I said, "Nellie, John is going to be all right." And Nellie said, "Yes, John's going to be all right."

I turned and went back to the small white room where Lyndon was. Mac Kilduff, the president's pressman on this trip, and Kenny O'Donnell were coming and going. I think it was from Kenny's face that I first knew the truth and from Kenny's voice that I first heard the words, "The President is dead." Mr. Kilduff entered and said to Lyndon, "Mr. President."

JACK BROOKS, U.S. representative, Texas (D), 1953–95: [Johnson] was very sober during this period, very straight-faced, very cautious, thinking, planning; thinking about what needed to be done and what had to be done. There are a lot of changes, you understand, a lot of problems involved, and he was thinking about them. And the Secret Service wanted him to leave, get out of there.

We just stood there and waited a minute and [LBJ] said, "Well, Jack, you go in the car with Bird and take Bird in the second car and I'll take the first car, and we'll have two cars meet us at that side entrance there." So the Secret Service set up a couple cars and we went out and got in them.

LBJ: [S]omewhere in my mind, I knew there might be more. I knew that this conceivably could be part of something even bigger. So I said let's go back to Washington as soon as we can.

We went in an unmarked car and I remember leaning back over the back of the seat, all the way back.

We went on *Air Force One*. Just as they told us to.

I called the Attorney General [Bobby Kennedy] from the plane and I asked him if I should come back to Washington and take the oath. He said he would call me back, but he thought offhand I should take the oath there. He was calm and unexcited. . . .

Everyone was saying, "Let's get this plane off the ground." I said, "No, we'll wait for Mrs. Kennedy." She came on.

HOMER THORNBERRY, U.S. representative, Texas (D), 1949–63: Mrs. Kennedy came on the plane and the other Kennedy people. The president was solicitous of all their concerns and wanted them to be in the room when he was sworn in. He asked if Mrs. Kennedy did not want to be present. They administered the oath. The president was as calm and collected as I believe I have ever seen him.

LBJ: Deputy Attorney General Mr. [Nicholas] Katzenbach dictated the form of the oath to one of the secretaries aboard the plane.

I thought of Sarah Hughes, an old friend who is the judge of the U.S. District Court in Dallas. We telephoned Judge Hughes's office. She was not there, but she returned the call in a few minutes and said she would be at the airplane in ten minutes. I asked that arrangements be made to permit her to have access to the airplane.

A few minutes later Mrs. Kennedy and the president's coffin arrived. Mrs. Johnson and I spoke to her. We tried to comfort her but our words seemed inadequate. She went into the private quarters of the plane.

KENNETH O'DONNELL, special assistant to President Kennedy, 1961–63: We get on this airplane and I'm urging them to take off. We don't know that Johnson's on the plane. [Godfrey] McHugh runs up to the pilot, who's our pilot—and that's the first time we knew we were on *Air Force One*—told him to take off and then somebody said, "Tell O'Donnell he's not the commander-in-chief anymore. President Johnson is on the plane."

So then I went in to see the president. Before I could say anything, he said he'd talked to Bobby and that Bobby told him to be sworn in right there. On the surface it doesn't make any sense, because he's the president of the United States the minute they say "you're dead." You don't even need to be sworn in. I think the man wanted to be sworn in in Texas, and there's nothing really wrong with that except if you've got a crisis and a conspiracy you ought to be up in the airplane, which I thought at the time. But that's not my business, he's president. I was just concerned about Jackie.

I went up to see him get sworn in and I'm trying to get them to get moving. He said to me, "Would you ask Mrs. Kennedy to come stand here?" I said, "You can't do that! The poor kid has had enough for one day, to sit here and hear that oath that she heard a few years ago! You just can't do that, Mr. President!" He said, "Well, she said she wanted to do it." I said, "Well, I just don't believe that."

I was pacing up and down the hall, I was waiting for her to come out. You don't break into a lady's bedroom quite often, and the President of the United States's wife. I paced up and down for five minutes and I'm hysterical myself now, so I finally walked in. I said, "Do you want to go out there?" She said, "Yes, I think I ought to. At least I owe that much to the country." So I said, "Fine."

There's no question in my mind that Lyndon Johnson wanted to be sworn in by Judge Sarah T. Hughes, an old family friend, and he was afraid somebody was going to take this thing away from him if he didn't get it quick.

SARAH HUGHES, judge, U.S. District Court, Northern District, Texas, 1961–75: I walked into the compartment and there were a lot of people there; the Vice President and Mrs. Johnson were there and neither—none of us said anything. I embraced them both and then the Vice President said, "Mrs. Kennedy wants to be here. We'll wait for her." She had come from the hospital and was in the rear of the airplane. So we waited a few minutes and she did come out and he, Vice President Johnson, told her to stand on his left and Mrs. Johnson on his right. And I leaned over to her and said, "I loved your husband very much."

Mrs. Johnson turned to her and told her who I was; that I was a district judge appointed by her husband.

Then I repeated the oath of office and the Vice President repeated it after me, he had his hand up—one hand up, and the other one on this book.

[Then] he immediately leaned over and kissed his wife and Mrs. Kennedy, and I said something to him that the country was behind him and I knew that he would make a great President. He turned around and said to the pilot, "Let's be airborne."

Then I went home.

■ ■ ■

Allegations of Johnson's insensitive behavior toward Mrs. Kennedy and Kennedy aides while on board *Air Force One* have been made repeatedly through the years, though not at the time. They began with the serialization of William Manchester's book *The Death of a President* in *Look* magazine in 1966 and continue to surface periodically, but by almost all credible accounts, Johnson's behavior was exemplary. Johnson believed that Manchester's book was a covert effort on Bobby Kennedy's part to undermine him as Kennedy contemplated his own bid for the presidency in 1968—"No question about it."

BOB HARDESTY, assistant to the president, 1965–69: There weren't any rumors about any hostility or resentment during that whole period. It really didn't start until the Manchester book and if that had been going on, it would have leaked out.

LBJ: If it existed, it was unbelievable hypocrisy [the Kennedys] practiced. Manchester's book was Bobby's announcement for the Presidency [in 1968]. It was part of a calculated effort to destroy me.

CHUCK ROBERTS, White House correspondent, *Newsweek*: Bill Manchester reported an instance in which Johnson was crude, boorish, inconsiderate of Jackie Kennedy and unseemly in his haste to take power. As one of the three reporters who witnessed that takeover when he took the oath of office aboard *Air Force One*, and then one of two who flew back to Washington aboard *Air Force One*, I want to set the record straight.

Far from being crude and inconsiderate, Lyndon Johnson was thoughtful, cool, and compassionate in the terrible four hours from the time President Kennedy died until his plane landed at Andrews. His decision to take the oath of office in Dallas that day and to fly home aboard *Air Force One*, the plane with the best communications gear, was eminently sound considering the uncertain world situation created by the assassination; and equally sound, Manchester notwithstanding, was his decision to fly home with Kennedy's body instead of shipping the dead President home in a backup plane with a corporal's guard of presidential aides.

Even as he took over the reins of government, LBJ couldn't have been more considerate of Jackie and Kennedy's bereaved staff, and in my opinion those were four of his finest hours, at the very start of his presidency.

LBJ: It was a peculiar situation that [the Kennedy aides] sat in the back and never would come up and join us. Afterward [Mrs. Kennedy] joined me in his office and very frankly—I wouldn't want to say this in [my] book, but I thought [the aides] were just wine heads. They were just drinkers, just one drink after another coming to them trying to drown their sorrow, and we weren't drinking, of course. We didn't have anything. They were drinking, and I just thought they didn't want to—they were bereaved and wanted to be there [by themselves] and I went back and asked them to come and join us, tried to talk to them about the arrangements.

■ ■ ■

After taking off from Love Field in Dallas, the Johnsons placed a static-filled call to Rose Kennedy, the fallen president's mother.

Air Force One: *Yes, Mrs. Kennedy. I have, uh, Mr. Johnson for you here.*
Rose Kennedy: *Yes, thank you. Hello?*
LBJ: *Mrs. Kennedy?*
Mrs. Kennedy: *Yes, yes?*
LBJ: *Mrs. Ken—*
Mrs. Kennedy: *—yes, yes, Mr. President. Yes—*
LBJ: *I wish to God there was something I could do, and I wanted to tell you that we were grieving with you.*
Mrs. Kennedy: *Yes. Well, thanks a mil—thanks very much.*
LBJ: *Here's [Lady] Bird.*
Mrs. Kennedy: *Thank you very much. I know. I know you loved Jack, and he loved you. [Unclear]—*
Mrs. Johnson: *Mrs. Kennedy, we feel like we've just had—*
Mrs. Kennedy: *Yes, all right.*
Mrs. Johnson: *We're glad the nation had your son—*
Mrs. Kennedy: *Yes, yes.*
Mrs. Johnson: *—as long as it did.*
Mrs. Kennedy: *Well, thank you, Lady Bird. Thank you very much. Goodbye.*
Mrs. Johnson: *Love—*
Mrs. Kennedy: *Yes.*
Mrs. Johnson: *Love and prayers to all of you.*
Mrs. Kennedy: *Yes. Thank you very much. Goodbye . . . goodbye . . . goodbye.*

■ ■ ■

Air Force One touched down at Andrews Air Force Base at close to 6:00 p.m. Upon landing, a stricken Bobby Kennedy boarded the plane and pushed up the aisle, brushing by the new president without acknowledging him. "Where's Jackie? I need to see Jackie," he said to no one in particular. After waiting for the deceased president's casket to be unloaded, and Bobby and Mrs. Kennedy and the Kennedy aides to discharge the aircraft, President and Mrs. Johnson and their aides descended the ramp to the dark uncertainty the next few weeks would bring.

MARIE FEHMER CHIARODO: [The flight was] uneventful. It was very quick as far as we were concerned. We arrived in Washington, landed at Andrews. There were lots of lights. I remember [Johnson] saying, "Get everybody together." In other words, he didn't want his people to get lost. He was very kind about that. I remember asking the Secret Service agents, "Where do [we] go?" And they said, "I don't know. Do the best you can."

JACK BROOKS: I was a little disappointed in the attitude when we landed. Bobby Kennedy came to the back of the plane there, and they brought the coffin off and they went off, kind of shoving; a little bit of a bad deal. I thought it was in very poor taste on their part and they shouldn't have been doing it that way.

LIZ CARPENTER: It seemed like minutes when we landed in Washington; so much was happening. Your mind was so dull, but one of the thoughts that went through my mind on the plane was "someone is in charge." The words Lady Bird has once used—"Lyndon is a good man in an emergency"—kept going through my mind.

I'd seen this once before in an Arizona hotel when we received a call at 3 a.m. that [Mrs. Johnson's] brother, Tony Taylor, had had a heart attack. I'd awakened them to tell them and I could hear Vice President Johnson just take over and run things. . . . He got on the phone and got [a] plane to fly to Dallas to pick him up while she was getting dressed and packed, and talking to members of the family. I was struck at the time with what a comforting thing it was to have a man who really ran everything for her. Again those words—"a good man to have in an emergency"—kept coming to me.

He was in charge—and as I look back, I think now that the United States was never without a president.

■ ■ ■

Facing the harsh lights and television cameras on the tarmac, President Johnson publicly spoke his first words as president, a fifty-eight-word statement crafted by Liz Carpenter on the plane and edited by Johnson.

> *This is a sad time for all people. We have suffered a loss that cannot be weighed. For me, it is a deep personal tragedy. I know that the world shares the sorrow that Mrs. Kennedy and her family bear. I will do my best. That is all I can do. I ask for your help—and God's.*

JACK VALENTI: Twelve hours later [after the assassination], LBJ was in his home in Spring Valley [which the Johnsons called The Elms, in northwest Washington, D.C.], three trusted friends by his side—the late Cliff Carter, Bill Moyers, and myself. He lay on his huge bed in his pajamas watching television, as the world, holding its breath in anxiety and fear, considered that this alien cowboy [had] suddenly become the leader of the United States. That night he ruminated about the days that lay ahead, sketching out what he planned to do, in almost five hours that we sat there with him. Though none of us who listened realized it at the time, he was revealing the design of the Great Society. He had not yet given it a name, but he knew with stunning precision the mountaintop to which he was going to summon the people. As he said later, "Now that I have the power, I [mean] to use it."

LBJ: What we wanted to do for the country is what we did. It was that simple. I really wanted a country where the Congress and the Government would provide education for every kid from Head Start to adult education by '75, and we got those going—health, conservation, pollution, consumption and on down and that is what we did. This is what I wanted to see done in Civil Rights and this is what we have done about it. We wanted a country where a man could own his own home and we got it and we provided in the last Housing Act the framework where it can be done, where there can be equality in housing. We were a long way from it when I came in.

LBJ addresses a joint session of Congress, November 27, 1963.

Chapter 3

"LET US CONTINUE"

"HE KNEW INSTINCTIVELY WHAT TO DO"

AT 12:30 P.M. ON WEDNESDAY, NOVEMBER 27, 1963, JOHNSON APpeared before a joint session of Congress and quietly, solemnly addressed the nation for the first time since his brief statement after landing at Andrews five days earlier.

All I have I would have given gladly not to be standing here today.

The greatest leader of our time has been struck down by the foulest deed of our time. Today John Fitzgerald Kennedy lives on in the immortal words and works that he left behind. He lives on in the hearts of his countrymen.

No words are sad enough to express our sense of loss. No words are strong enough to express our determination to continue the forward thrust of America that he began . . .

An assassin's bullet has thrust upon me the awesome burden of the presidency. I am here today to say I need your help; I cannot bear this burden alone. I need the help of all Americans, and all America. This nation has experienced a profound shock, and in this critical moment, it is our duty, yours and mine, as the government of the United States, to do away with uncertainty and doubt and delay, and to show that we are capable of decisive action; that from the brutal loss of our leader we will derive not weakness but strength; that we can and will act and act now . . .

On the twentieth day of January, in 1961, John F. Kennedy told his countrymen that our national work would not be finished "in the first thousand days, nor in the lifetime of this administration, not even perhaps in our lifetime on this planet." But, he said, "let us begin."

Today, in this moment of new resolve, I would say to my fellow Americans, let us continue.

In that sentiment, *let us continue*, nearly all Americans, and certainly Congress, were united. But the ground on which Johnson trod as he continued his address was at the core of what began dividing the country even before its founding—and was at the root of its most pronounced contradiction. It portended Johnson's bold legislative agenda even before he had settled into the White House.

First, no memorial oration or eulogy could more eloquently honor President Kennedy's memory than the earliest possible passage of the civil rights bill for which he fought so long. We have talked long enough in this country about equal rights. We have talked for one hundred years or more. It is time now to write the next chapter—and to write it in the books of law.

I urge you again, as I did in 1957 and again in 1960, to enact a civil rights law so that we can move forward to eliminate from this nation every trace of discrimination and oppression that is based upon race or color. There could be no greater source of strength to this nation both at home and abroad.

While a supportive Congress had welcomed Johnson into the House chamber with an eruption of applause before he began his remarks, many, particularly those from the South and from Johnson's own party, met those words with a hard silence.

Johnson then went on to press for a second Kennedy initiative, one that would become another of his immediate priorities.

And second, no act of ours could more fittingly continue the work of President Kennedy than the early passage of the tax bill for which he fought all this long year. This bill is designed to increase our national income and Federal revenues, and to provide insurance against recession . . .

I profoundly hope that the tragedy and the torment of these terrible days will bind us together in new fellowship, making us one people in our hour of sorrow. So let us here highly resolve that John Fitzgerald Kennedy did not live—or die—in vain. And on this Thanksgiving Eve, as we gather to ask the Lord's blessing, and give him our thanks, let us unite in those familiar and cherished words:

America, America
God shed His grace on thee,

And crown thy good with brotherhood
From sea to shining sea.

Unity was much on Johnson's mind as he began his new role. "What I wanted to do more than anything," he wrote later, "was to try to unite the leaders of the administration, the leaders of the two parties, and the leaders of Congress—for a while at least until we could get Congress into action." As with Truman in the wake of the death of his predecessor, Franklin Roosevelt, Johnson asked all the members of Kennedy's Cabinet and top officials to remain in place. True, Johnson was conscious of their loyalties to Kennedy, but that was the point. He believed himself to be "a caretaker of both [Kennedy's] people and policies." Some, such as Secretary of State Dean Rusk, Secretary of Defense Robert McNamara, and Secretary of the Interior Stewart Udall, would remain with Johnson for all or most of his terms in office. Others, such as aides Theodore Sorensen and Kenneth O'Donnell, and the former president's brother, Attorney General Bobby Kennedy, would fall away before Johnson got elected to the presidency in his own right.

BARRY GOLDWATER, U.S. senator, Arizona (R), 1953–65, 1969–87: Many people told him to clean house. I concentrated on my pet subject which was [getting rid of] McNamara, but I know [Senator Everett] Dirksen used to plead with him [to] get rid of this group or that. Dirksen called me one night and said, "If you've got any influence on Lyndon, would you tell him the risk he's running in keeping his group of about four people in these jobs?" I said, "Well, I don't have any effect on him, Ev. I've tried to get him to fire McNamara," which he would never do. I think it was that there again, it would upset the Kennedys.

■ ■ ■

Johnson took the issues before him with great urgency. Exigency was an endemic part of his nature even during relatively placid times; such was his sense of importance in anything he undertook. "Do it now!" he would often demand of his staff. "Not next week. Not tomorrow. Not later today. Now!" But after he took over the presidency, that sense was heightened by his feeling that the tide of goodwill that followed his triumphant speech before Congress would quickly recede. He believed that the East Coast–dominated media—and the eastern establishment in general—would be out to get him.

LBJ: I told [*New York Times* journalist] Scotty Reston I'd have to do it all in six months to eight months. The Eastern media will have the wells so poisoned by that time that that's all the time I have. They'll be peeing on the fire. I said I don't think any man from Johnson City, Texas, can survive that long.

LADY BIRD JOHNSON: One of the things about the White House is that you know from the moment you walk in there that this has a time limitation. You don't know exactly what it is; it may be the four years you were elected for, or death, but you know it's got a time limitation. And that's one reason why you do as much as you can do, because you know that this will never happen again, and you can form up the energy from somewhere within you to go more, do more, for this limited time.

■ ■ ■

That urgency further fueled a prodigious work ethic that would become a hallmark of Johnson's presidency, and he grew frustrated early on in his presidency that those on Capitol Hill didn't share it. In a phone conversation with *Washington Post* publisher Katharine Graham on December 2 (which turned into a monologue by Johnson), the president urged Graham to use the paper to expose Congress's excessive vacation schedules and lack of initiative:

> *[T]here wasn't a human here [in Washington last week]. And they're not here now. And they're not working now. And they're not passing anything. . . . So I'd like for [the* Post*] to be asking these fellows, "Where did you spend your Thanksgiving holidays? Tell me about it, was it warm and nice?" And write a little story about it. . . . [Dick] Russell advocates going home at four-thirty and [Mike] Mansfield's wife says he can't meet after five o'clock. . . . You can't run your business doing that! Now you had better take these broad outlines and give [them] to your people and say . . . I don't care what you cover in the sex route, but let's cover some of these folks' vacations. Not in a mean way, but just point up that . . . these things haven't been done and we've paid 'em to do 'em. . . . Of course, a part of their job [is] at home, and in an election year they'll be at home, but they oughtn't to go home until they do something to go home to talk about.*

■ ■ ■

The shadow of John F. Kennedy hovered over Johnson as he set about his new responsibilities. In many ways it would not recede even after Johnson's own election as president. As the myth of "Camelot" began to grow in the wake of Kennedy's death, strengthening over time, Kennedy set an inevitable, and impossible, standard by which Johnson would be measured. Comparisons between the two men on image, style, and matters of policy, and speculations about the wiser, more prudent course Kennedy would have taken, invariably favored Kennedy. No one was more aware of this than Johnson.

LBJ: I had problems in my conduct of the office being contrasted with President Kennedy's conduct in office, with my manner of dealing with things and his manner, with my accent and his accent, with my background and his background. He was a great public hero and anything that I did that someone didn't approve of, they would always feel that President Kennedy wouldn't have done that—that he wouldn't have done it that way, that he wouldn't have made that mistake.

HUBERT HUMPHREY, vice president, 1965–69: Kennedy became much more of a hero as he became more of a martyr. The fact is that his weakness and flaws were quickly forgotten, particularly by the Democrats. Johnson was constantly compared to Kennedy, and that was like comparing a heavyweight boxer to a ballet dancer.

Of course, every presidency has its own personality. Kennedy's had great grace and charm and class. Johnson's presidency was more like a developer moving into an area that needs rehabilitation, renovation, rebuilding. It isn't pretty at times. There's a lot of debris laying [*sic*] around, but all at once you see new structures coming up, and it may not be all quite finished, but the structures are there.

He was a builder above all. He was a muscular, glandular, political man. Not an intellectual but bright. Not a talker, a doer. Kennedy was more a talker.

But I think when you look back, you will see that with Johnson—he didn't get all the little paintings on the wall, and he didn't get the gold plate on the dome and didn't shine up the doorknobs, but he got the foundation in, got the sidewalks up, got the beams put across. The structure was there.

■ ■ ■

Johnson, the prosaic builder, had an undeniable advantage over Kennedy, the inspiring visionary: He knew how to deal with Congress to get his agenda passed. He was passionate about it—consumed by it—in a way that Kennedy hadn't been. As an ambitious congressman from Texas's Tenth District and, later, in the Senate, where he advanced to become the majority leader during the Eisenhower administration, Johnson knew his way around Washington as well as anyone. "They say Jack Kennedy had style," he said. "But I'm the one who got the bills passed." The tragedy of Kennedy's death also created an opportunity for reform as the martyred president became a vessel for the progressive beliefs he was thought to have held, and the American public became receptive to the fulfillment of its perception of his vision.

SARGENT SHRIVER, director, Peace Corps, 1961–66; director, Office of Economic Opportunity, 1964–68: What would Lyndon Johnson have been without Kennedy? I don't know, nor does anyone else. I only know for a fact that when LBJ became president, he had an overwhelming ambition to pass into legislation the entire agenda which JFK had envisioned. I choose the word *envisioned* on purpose. JFK did not spell out the scope or scale, let alone the details, of the Peace Corps or a War on Poverty or a new civil rights law or federal aid to education or Medicare or a bureaucracy capable of putting a man on the moon, not in ten years or twenty-five years or fifty years but immediately.

HUBERT HUMPHREY: Johnson knew how to woo people. He was a born political lover. Many looked upon Johnson as a heavy-handed man. That's not really true. He wasn't one of those Fifth Avenue, Madison Avenue penthouse lovers. He was from the ranch. But what I mean is he knew how to massage the senators. He knew which ones he could just push aside, he knew which ones he could threaten, and above all he knew which ones he'd have to spend time with and nourish along, to bring along, to make sure that they were coming along.

LIZ CARPENTER: I have always thought that you could describe presidents in almost a word. Kennedy inspired, which Johnson was not capable of doing, and Johnson delivered.

■ ■ ■

Moreover, Johnson's ability to achieve harmony beyond results and to bring people together, often through the mire, gave him the tools to move the nation forward in the wake of tragedy.

HUGH SIDEY: Johnson in my judgment was probably the only man in the United States who could have handled that transition. He'd been in Washington since 1937. As an administrative aide, House representative, senator, he'd lived through virtually every crisis in politics this country had had. He knew instinctively what to do.

BIG AS TEXAS

As the country got to know its new president, some intrinsic truths in his nature were becoming manifest. One was as plain as his drawl: he was a Texan through and through, oozing outsize Lone Star pride in keeping with the state's fixation on bigness. The Texas Hill Country where Lyndon Baines Johnson came into the world on August 27, 1908—with a portentous big entrance at an estimated eleven pounds—was as much a part of him as a knot in an old oak tree. "Now the light came in from the east, bringing a deep stillness," wrote Rebekah Baines Johnson while reflecting upon her son's birth, "a stillness so profound and so pervasive that it seemed as if the earth itself was listening." The newborn would grow to listen, in turn, to the Hill Country earth he trod on, and to its people. Any quest for understanding Johnson must begin there.

While his great-great-grandfather had not fought at the Alamo as Johnson had once claimed (straining his presidential credibility), the boast reflected less about Johnson's tendency toward mendacity than it did his yearning to claim a familial piece of Texas's most consecrated chapter. In fact, the Johnson family was among the earliest white settlers in the state. Johnson's great-uncle Jesse Thomas Johnson and his grandfather Sam Ealy Johnson migrated from Georgia to the Hill Country in the early 1850s, where they established a cattle ranch, driving their herd annually up the famed Chisholm Trail to Abilene, Kansas. The place on the map on which they established their ranch, in South Central Texas, would become known eponymously as Johnson City.

Johnson's father, Sam Ealy Johnson Jr., was born not far from there, in 1877, becoming, as a young man, a jack-of-all-trades: a barber, a teacher, a justice of the peace. Lacking the funds for law school, he set his sights on politics, gaining election, at age twenty-seven, as a member of the Texas legislature. The same year, he met Rebekah Baines, a reporter for the *Blanco County Gazette*, when she interviewed him in Austin on his new position, which had just been vacated by her father. Rebekah, who had attended Baylor Female College, came from a long line of educators and displayed unmistakable pride—some would say snobbery—in the accomplishments of her ancestors. Looking beyond pronounced differences in background and temperament, the couple married in 1907. Sam took his young bride to live in a small farmhouse in the Hill Country, fifty miles from Austin, an arduous two-day journey by dirt road and, with no electricity and running water, another world altogether.

LBJ: My father was outgoing and compassionate and trusting. He never met a stranger. He ran for office six times and was always elected. Mama made him quit. He'd stay out two or three years and then the people would make him go back. He was in the cattle business and cotton. Then the San Francisco earthquake came along and money went high. He went broke. He made a little fortune, two or three hundred thousand dollars, and then went broke again after World War I. And cotton went from forty-four cents down to six cents. But he never bellyached. He never griped. I remember him all through the thirties, through the Depression, as a rugged able man.

■ ■ ■

Rebekah, in the words of Johnson, "came out into the hills unprepared for the rough life there." It was clearly not something she had bargained for. "I was determined to overcome circumstances instead of letting them overwhelm me," she later reflected. "At last I realized that life is real and earnest and not the charming fairy tale of which I had so long dreamed." Compounding any broken illusions she may have had of her married life was her husband's rags-to-riches-to-rags economic fate, leaving the family struggling much of the time—though never as much as Johnson would later imply—and eventually taking a toll on Sam's health.

Lyndon was the couple's first child, arriving a year into their marriage. They would have four more, three daughters and another son, over the next eight years.

LBJ: I was three months old when I was named. My father and mother couldn't agree on a name. The people my father liked were heavy drinkers—pretty rough for a city girl. [My mother] didn't want me named after any of them.

Finally, there was a criminal lawyer—a country lawyer—named W. C. Linden. He would go on a drunk for a week after every case. My father liked him and he wanted to name me after him. My mother didn't care for the idea but she said finally that it was alright, she would go along with it if she could spell the name the way she wanted to. So that is what happened.

I was campaigning for Congress. An old man with a white carnation in his lapel came up and said, "That was a very good speech. I want to vote for you like I always have. The only thing I don't like about you is the way you spell your name." He then identified himself as W. C. Linden.

■ ■ ■

The name Lyndon may have been one of the few things Sam and Rebekah agreed on when it came to their eldest child. Rebekah wanted Lyndon to be cultured and refined. Sam held a decidedly more philistine view.

LBJ: One of the first things I remember was the time he cut my hair. When I was four or five I had long curls. He hated them. "He's a boy!" he'd say to my mother. "And you're making a sissy of him. You've got to cut those curls." My mother refused. Then one Sunday morning when she went off to church, he took the big scissors and cut off all my hair. When my mother came home, she refused to speak to him for a week.

■ ■ ■

Lyndon tended toward his father. "I wanted to copy my father always, emulate him, do the things he did," Johnson said. "He loved the outdoors and I grew to love the outdoors. He loved political life and public service. I followed him as a child and participated in it."

Lyndon began his formal education in a one-room schoolhouse, often riding to school on a donkey. His teacher remembered the young man dressed in oversize cowboy garb, outfitted in his father's Stetson and boots, which he wore over his own shoes. He rejected the cultural enlightenment his mother had hoped for. At age eight, when he declined to take the dance and violin lessons she insisted on, she responded much as she had when his father cut his hair. "For days after I quit those lessons," Johnson recalled, "she walked around pretending I was dead." Johnson would, however, adopt his mother's conditional approach to love.

Though a rebellious youngster and an uninspired though able student, he, like his father before him, had dreams beyond those the Hill Country offered. Starting at a young age, he aimed big. At twelve he boasted to a classmate that he would one day be president of the United States. Two years later he decided, "I was not going to be the victim of a system which would allow the price of a commodity like cotton to drop from forty cents to six cents and destroy the homes of people like my own family."

After graduating high school as president of his six-member class at age fifteen, the young man went west, driving to California with a group of friends in a scaled-down Model T—no windshield, no roof—that they dubbed the Covered Wagon. Once there, Johnson "tramped" restlessly up and down the coast working menial jobs—dishwasher, waiter, farmhand, elevator operator—before becoming a clerk in a cousin's law practice. All the adventure got him was "thinner and more homesick"; maybe a little humbled, too. Within a little over a year, he was back in the Hill Country, where his father got him a job on a road crew. But though he was back home working steadily, he was still the prodigal son. After an arrest citation for disorderly conduct for his role in a brawl during a Saturday night dance, his mother wept at his bedside. "To think that my eldest born would turn out like this," she cried wearily.

LBJ: My mother tried to give me the love of books, tried to interest me in literary matter, dramatics, debating, teaching. I think except for her I might not have made it through high school and certainly not through college.

■ ■ ■

Not surprisingly, it was she who talked him into going to college. Tired of being a disappointment to his parents and dreading the blue-collar monotony that awaited him, Johnson eventually gave in to the idea. In 1927, after borrowing seventy-five dollars, he hitchhiked to San Marcos and enrolled at Southwest Texas State Teachers College. Once there, he would find that his high school, which stopped at eleventh grade, wasn't accredited. In order to gain admittance to the college, he would need to pass tests in English and plane geometry, the latter of which his mother would ensure by coming to San Marcos for three days of intensive coaching. Though he remained an average student, he distinguished himself on the school's debate team, while earning money as a janitor, administrative aide, and serving as editor of the *College Star*, the school's weekly newspaper.

He also found a talent for teaching. Before his junior year, facing financial difficulties, Johnson took a year off from school and went south to Cotulla, a small town of three thousand souls between Laredo and San Antonio. There he became a teacher at Welhausen School, a six-teacher elementary school for largely impoverished children of Mexican descent. The sons and daughters of poor farmhands, Johnson's students were growing up in a segregated society where they were treated by the white population, in Johnson's words, "just worse than you'd treat a dog." Johnson threw himself into the task, pushing his students to achieve beyond the low expectations held for Americans of color in the early twentieth century, organizing a spate of teams and activities—everything from baseball and volleyball to debating and literary societies—to allow them to reach beyond themselves. He also did whatever he could to better their plight. Inexplicably forgetting his parents' modest means, he sent a letter to his mother back in the Hill Country asking her to send two hundred packages of toothpaste. "We will soon have 250 [students] in school," he wrote. "They are rather small and I think they would appreciate it very much."

"[H]e would ask questions about Texas history of us," recalled one of his students years later. "And he would mention the fact that this country is a great big country of great liberties and opportunities for everybody and that any individual by studying hard and working hard would possibly be able to become president of the United States." It was likely not a notion his students had entertained before.

While immersed in his responsibilities at the school, Johnson somehow found time to take correspondence courses for college credit, teach the school's janitor to read, and find his first taste of love in a relationship that didn't last with a "pretty girl," also a teacher, who lived thirty-five miles away. Though he would be gone within a year, back to college, the memory of his students, dirt poor, starved for hope and encouragement, and battling prejudice, would remain with him throughout his life.

After graduating from Southwest Texas State in 1930 as the Depression scourged the country, Johnson found work as a teacher at Sam Houston High School in Houston, earning an annual salary of $1,530. While he plied his trade with the same energy and success as he had in Cotulla, his interests, inevitably, turned to politics. Volunteering for a political friend of his father's in his spare time, Johnson found his prodigious work ethic and sheer competence, earning him a job in Washington as an aide to Congressman Richard Kleberg, who represented Corpus Christi and the surrounding areas.

In Washington, Johnson quickly made himself indispensable to Kleberg, gaining a keen understanding of the byzantine procedures and protocol under the Capitol dome, while seeing that the needs of Kleberg's constituents were tended to. His standout performance was recognized by his peers who, in 1933, elected him speaker of the "Little Congress," an organization of congressional aides. The following year, he met and married Lady Bird Taylor—as different from him in style and temperament as his father had been from his mother—wearing her down in a whirlwind eleven-week courtship that led to the altar. Her wealthy background, equanimity, and easy charm made Mrs. Johnson the perfect political wife, though she dreaded the thought of her husband's pursuit of politics. Earnest pleas urging him to resist the pull of the political arena proved as futile as pushing back the ocean's tide with a broom.

Johnson would seize his chance in 1937, at the tender age of twenty-eight. After an impressive two-year stint as the Texas director of the National Youth Administration, a youth-directed jobs program under President Franklin Roosevelt's New Deal, Johnson won a seat as the U.S. representative of his home district, Texas's Tenth, after the incumbent, James "Ol' Buck" Buchanan, died suddenly. Johnson staged an unlikely underdog's victory to win Ol' Buck's seat, which the young up-and-comer would occupy for twelve years.

JOHN CONNALLY: I think in one sense [Johnson] had an undistinguished career in the [House]: He did not attach his name to a lot of legislation. That didn't alter the fact that he was interested in a great deal of legislation. He understood early on that it wasn't the author of legislation who passed the bill, but the individual who understood it, who was committed to it, dedicated to it, and most effective in pursuing it.

That was his history in both the House and the Senate. He didn't have a long list of bills with his name on them because he didn't operate that way. He was a man who picked his battleground. He did it religiously, he did it intelligently, he did it rationally. And he rarely lost in either the House or the Senate.

■ ■ ■

Three years later, in 1941, another death, this time of Texas senator Morris Sheppard, offered Johnson an opportunity for advancement to the U.S. Senate. A special election pitting the young congressman Johnson against W. Lee "Pappy" O'Daniel, a conservative radio personality turned Texas governor, heavily favored Johnson, who benefited from FDR's long coattails in the Lone Star State. But when the ballots were counted, the election, initially too close to call, fell to O'Daniel by just over 1,300 votes. While voter fraud was alleged in both the Johnson and O'Daniel camps, Pappy took the office.

LBJ: I was elected to the Senate in 1941 when I was thirty-three years old. That election was stolen from me in Dallas; they kept counting votes until W. Lee O'Daniel won. He was a nonentity and a flour salesman.

■ ■ ■

Shortly after the loss, maintaining his House seat, Johnson entered World War II. Already a lieutenant commander in the U.S. Naval Reserve, Johnson became the first congressman to volunteer for active duty, sending President Roosevelt a letter on December 8, the day after the bombing of Pearl Harbor, requesting "active duty with the Fleet," and conducting inspections on the West Coast in the Pacific theater. He earned a Silver Star, pinned on him by Douglas MacArthur, when the only bombing mission he participated in drew intensive enemy fire. Released from active duty in July 1942, Johnson returned to the House, where he soldiered on for the better part of the decade, twice becoming a father when Lynda Bird and Luci Baines were born in 1944 and 1947 respectively. (The additions of his daughters would bring the number of Johnson household inhabitants bearing the initials LBJ to four, a figure that would later increase to five when the family dog, Little Beagle Johnson, was included.)

In 1948 a second chance to win a Senate seat came when Senator O'Daniel stepped down. But another Texas governor waited in the wings. The popular former governor Coke Stevenson also had his eyes on the seat. Conscious of his narrow defeat for the office seven years earlier, Johnson waged a no-holds-barred primary campaign against Stevenson, traversing the state in a helicopter, a technological novelty that drew curiosity seekers, and countering his rival's charges that he was soft on communism with accusations of his own. A runoff election came down to a mere 87 votes of 988,295 cast, which gave a paltry win to Johnson. Once again, voter fraud was alleged against Johnson when voting irregularities turned up in three counties in the southern part of the state, though it was never proven. Johnson would go on to win the seat in a walk in the Democratically lopsided general election, easily defeating the Republican candidate, Jack Porter. But in January 1949 he entered the Senate derided as "Landslide Lyndon," under a cloud of suspicion that would hover over him for years to come.

It didn't much matter to his career. Senator Johnson thrived in his new surroundings, mastering the Senate's arcane procedures and rules of debate as he had in the House, and showing a deal-making prowess uncommon even among most tempered veterans in the chamber. He simply had a knack for making things go his way, knowing instinctively when to twist arms, trade horses, or inflate egos to hold sway with his colleagues. In the course of just six years, he would rise to Democratic minority whip, minority leader, and, at age forty-six in 1955, majority leader, by many accounts the century's most powerful.

LARRY TEMPLE, special counsel to the president, 1967–69: I heard [President Johnson] say a time or two, maybe more than that, that his happiest time was when he was Senate majority leader. Pretty interesting. [He] didn't say that he felt it was the most fulfilling time, didn't say that or use any term comparable to that. Just talking about the happiest time. My guess is that was a time when he could accomplish some things he wanted to get done, and he wasn't in a spotlight, with people backbiting and criticizing him, because nobody was paying that much attention, and they were once he was president. And yet he was able to get a lot of things done and accomplished because, from his standpoint, accomplishment meant legislation.

■ ■ ■

While ambition and events had swept Johnson into the corridors of power in the Capitol and momentously into the White House, making him a consummate Washington insider, the Hill Country was never far from his mind. Though the Johnson family eventually moved to a gated ten-bedroom mansion in northwest Washington—"Every time somebody calls it a chateau, I lose 50,000 votes back in Texas," Johnson once quipped—home was the LBJ Ranch along the Pedernales River in Stonewall, fifteen miles from Johnson City. The investment of Mrs. Johnson's family inheritance in an Austin radio station and other ventures added up substantially over time, allowing for the acquisition of the 250-acre property and ranch house from Johnson's widowed aunt Frank Martin in 1951. Johnson had grown up going to family gatherings there and helping his uncle Clarence as a ranch hand, with hopes of someday being a cattle rancher himself.

The 400 head of Hereford cattle roaming the ranch's expanded 2,700 acres testified to the fruition of Johnson's boyhood dream, as the modest ranch house grew to a rambling eight bedrooms and nine bathrooms. Johnson would retreat there often during his Washington years, including a stay of more than three months to convalesce after a nearly fatal heart attack sidelined him for almost half of 1955, the result of sixteen-hour working days and the three packs of Winston cigarettes he smoked daily. (When his doctor later insisted that he quit smoking, he replied, "I'd rather cut my pecker off.") It may have been fitting, then, that Mrs. Johnson called the ranch "our heart's home."

LADY BIRD JOHNSON: The sun is indomitable. You know if it is cloudy now the sun will come out in the next day or two. I fell in love with Texas Hill Country before I met Lyndon. It was a good courting country—a lot of wonderful places for picnics. I like the long twilight. I like the long horizon. You are part of the sky. There are lovely sunsets and at night you seem closer . . . the stars are so clear and bright.

LBJ: Here the sun seems to be a little brighter and the climate a little warmer, the air a little fresher and the people a little kinder and more interesting. It's dry country but there's always a breeze blowing and there is always sun here. We don't have dreariness. We don't have those dull gray skies when you look up. Here we have birds singing, flowers growing, girls smiling. And I guess it's a good deal in what you're accustomed to, and I still like to eat the food my mother cooked when I was a little boy, the types of food she cooked, and I still like to visit the scenes of my childhood.

■ ■ ■

Though fortune had smiled on Johnson as bright as the Texas sun, the Hill Country imbued in him reminders of life's fragility and hardship. It was a place where the capriciousness of the land meant a single rainfall could spell the difference between want and plenty; where the women, bent from struggle, "aged before their time"; and where word spread like a prairie wind when townsfolk died. He never forgot what it was to be poor, to want things. "Poverty was so common," he said later of the Hill Country, "we didn't even know it had a name." The rural populism he had learned at the knee of his father stuck, and he failed to understand the politicians from humble beginnings who met grand ambitions only to forget where they came from.

Johnson's proudest accomplishment in the House was bringing electrical power to the Pedernales Valley in 1939, a feat that required all of his political skill. The advent of electricity immeasurably eased lives throughout the Hill Country, particularly those of women, who, like his mother, endured daily rituals such as pumping water and stoking fires, often in oppressive heat, to cook and wash.

Even in Washington—or perhaps, especially in Washington—the Texas pride endemic in Johnson's character bubbled over even to the most casual observer. His speech was peppered with phrases that could have been plucked from a John Ford western:

"Best get there right quick."

"Much obliged."

"My daddy always said . . ."

He often addressed women as "ma'am," and was likely to treat them with a gentleman's deference, keeping in check the earthy profanity he was wont to use in the company of men. A gifted storyteller, he was seldom at a loss for one of the yarns that are as much a part of small-town Texas life as Main Street and Sunday school, liberally using them to underscore the points he was trying to make, or just to offer a thick helping of southern charm.

LBJ's toast at a White House state dinner for Maurice Yaméogo, president of Upper Volta (now Burkina Faso), March 29, 1965, is one such example:

> *I was thinking about a story that occurred in my own hills of Texas when one of our elder statesmen found difficulty in his hearing. And he went to the doctor and the doctor examined him carefully and said, "Well, how much are you drinking these days?" And he said, well, he drank about a pint a day. And [the doctor] said, "Well, if you want to improve your hearing you're going to have to cut out your drinkin'."*
>
> *And about ninety days later, why, the fella went back to the doctor and the doctor examined him again and his hearing hadn't improved a bit, and he said, "Now, have you cut out your drinkin'?" And he said, "No." And [the doctor] said, "Now, I can't do anything for you unless you take my advice, follow my prescription. Didn't I tell you when you were here that you should cut out your drinkin' if you wanted to improve your hearing?" He said, "Yes." And [the doctor] said, "Why didn't you do it?" And he said, "Doctor, I got home and considered it, and I just decided I liked what I drank so much better'n what I heard."*

Though conscious that his humble background and drawl made him, at times, the object of derision among the eastern establishment that dominated the capital, the Georgetown crowd, Johnson never changed his stripes to suit his audience. Beyond the de rigueur "just folks" air worn by many southern politicians, Johnson wielded his Hill Country persona almost self-righteously. One could sense him thinking, *I'll show these rich Ivy League boys what this country boy can do.* His resentment toward them was as deep as his accent, and would intensify during his presidency. Despite braggadocio claims that his forefathers "were teachers and lawyers and college presidents and governors when the Kennedys of this country were still tending bar," and his rise in the world beyond the fictional bounds of Horatio Alger, his feelings of inferiority ran just as deep.

A 1965 article by Ed Lahey of Knight Newspapers pointed to this demon in Johnson's nature: "Lyndon Johnson has been fighting a certain something all his life: a sense of insecurity, the feeling of not being accepted. These are only a few expressions of this curse. Whatever you call this thing, Mr. Johnson has got it, period."

BOB HARDESTY: I think that there are times he suffered not from the thought that he was badly educated, but the thought that he came from a school whose degree wasn't honored very highly. I draw that distinction. I think that if he suffered as a southerner and suffered from [those] corn pone stories, he suffered it voluntarily. I can't believe that anybody who went to Washington, if he'd wanted to, couldn't have lost a good deal of his accent. A great many other people do. I think he had a great sense of place. He was a Texan. He was a man from the Hill Country.

DEAN RUSK, secretary of state, 1961–69: [T]he British Prime Minister was in Washington, Harold Wilson, and he had several people with him, and Lyndon Johnson had several people on his side and we sat down at a table. Lyndon Johnson looked around at the table and said, "Well, I see we have four Oxford men and three Cambridge men and four Harvard men and three Yale men and a man from San Marcos State Teachers College." Well, we all chuckled at that a bit, but I was never able to figure out whether this was real or whether he liked to put on a little bit of an act and tease people with it, a little bit like [Democratic senator] Sam Ervin saying, "I'm just a country lawyer from North Carolina." At that point, you better start sewing up your pockets.

HELEN THOMAS, White House correspondent, United Press International: [Johnson had] an inferiority complex about, not Texas per se, but he felt that southerners had not really made their mark in Washington, and that he hadn't gone to Harvard and Yale and that he wasn't Ivy League. He would say, "I've got all these Harvard boys in my cabinet." You always felt there was a strain. He did have a deep inferiority complex. He overcame everything in his achievements, but it was always there. And a certain paranoia.

■ ■ ■

Even if Johnson was paranoid, it didn't mean that his distrust wasn't rooted in some inherent truth. In fact, there were many among the eastern establishment who looked askance at Johnson, passing judgment that didn't go much beyond the superficial. Johnson had made his political career in reading those with whom he dealt, how they thought, what made them tick. It was a good bet that he picked up on their prejudice and that, given his natural sensitivity and need for approval, it stung.

DEAN RUSK: I gave a long interview to a young woman who was completing a Ph.D. thesis for one of the big Midwestern universities. Her thesis was on the politics of the southern accent, and she had come to the conclusion that in other parts of the country, particularly on the northeastern seaboard, they would gladly take any accent in the world, Oxford, Yiddish, German, Russian, whatever it is, except a southern accent. They were simply convinced that a man with a southern accent is stupid. . . . [S]he was convinced that Lyndon Johnson suffered from this syndrome.

HUBERT HUMPHREY: He had to have people around him. Very much so. And his whole demeanor was one great big long reach. If you weren't there, he'd just reach a little further to get you. And if he couldn't get you physically, he'd pick up the phone and get you. If he couldn't get you that way, he'd send an airplane to get you. He'd get you.

Except for the "Beautiful People"—these were the people who had no love for Johnson and no respect for him. And he knew it. He tried desperately on one hand to get it, and on the other hand he was angry. Georgetown to him was the center of a political conspiracy against him and his administration.

LBJ: The greatest bigots in the world are the Democrats on the East Side of New York. [James] Eastland [U.S. senator from Mississippi and vocal opponent of civil rights] is charitable compared to an eastern bigot. Anyone south of the Mason-Dixon Line has two strikes against him as far as the eastern liberals are concerned. The best man I know in New York can't help but feel that way.

■ ■ ■

Though lacking in academic pedigree and cultural enlightenment, Johnson was hardly at a disadvantage intellectually, at least within the realm of Washington.

LARRY TEMPLE: I think he tended to exacerbate the problem by saying such things as "I have never read a book in twenty years," and yet he read [extensively] every night. He'd take his night reading in with a myriad of things. He may not have read a work of fiction, and he may not have read a book that was on the *New York Times* best seller list, but he was a very well read individual on what was happening in the country and what was happening in the world on a more current basis than anybody either in or out of government.

GEORGE CHRISTIAN: I doubt that President Johnson ever took the time or maybe never had the time for intellectual pursuits that some other people enjoy. I don't think he really felt that that was his bag, so to speak. He was street smart; he was educated very thoroughly in contemporary affairs. He learned a great deal from personal experiences.

HARRY MCPHERSON, special counsel to the president, 1966–69: If he wasn't the wisest man I ever knew, he was the smartest. He could process and collate things in his mind as fast as anyone I knew. He always wanted something from the person he was talking to, and he was high-minded and focused when trying to get it.

■ ■ ■

But any judgment of Johnson as lacking in polish—Ivy League or otherwise—was not unfounded. Along with his accent and Stetsons came an uncouth earthiness that could make him, in essence, his own caricature. The imperious, earthy LBJ would think nothing of leveraging a distinct home court advantage by meeting aides or lawmakers in his White House bathroom, like a king summoning subjects to his throne, and berating or wheedling them while he sat on the commode. On August 9,

1964, an Oval Office phone call from Johnson to Joe Haggar, scion of the founder of the Haggar Clothing Company, inventor of men's "slacks," shows not only the president's singular attention to detail and penchant for micromanagement, but also a cartoonish coarseness that, for him, wasn't altogether uncommon:

LBJ: *Mr. Haggar?*

Joe Haggar: *Yes, this is Joe Haggar.*

LBJ: *Joe, is your father the one that makes clothes?*

Haggar: *Yes, sir. We're all together.*

LBJ: *Uh-huh. Y'all made me some real lightweight slacks that he just made up on his own, sent to me three or four months ago. It's a kind of a light brown and a light green, rather soft green and soft brown.*

Haggar: *Yes, sir.*

LBJ: *And they're real lightweight. Now, I need about six pairs for summer wear.*

Haggar: *Yes, sir.*

LBJ: *I want a couple, maybe three, of the light brown, kind of an almost powder color, like a powder on a lady's face.*

Haggar: *Yes, sir.*

LBJ: *Then there were some green and some other light pair. If you had a blue in that or a black, then I'd have one blue and one black. I need about six pairs to wear around in the evening when I come in from work.*

Haggar: *Yes, sir.*

LBJ: *I need . . . they're about a half a inch too tight in the waist.*

Haggar: *Do you recall the exact size? I just want to make sure we get them right for you.*

LBJ: *No, I don't know. Y'all just guessed at them, I think, and sent them, but wouldn't you have the measurement there?*

Haggar: *We'll find them for you.*

LBJ: *I can send you a pair. I want them half an inch larger in the waist than they were before, except I want two or three inches of stuff left back in there, so I can take them up. I vary 10 or 15 pounds a month.*

Haggar: *All right, sir.*

LBJ: *So leave me at least two-and-a-half [or] three inches in the back where I can let them out or take them up and put a—make these a half an inch bigger in the waist. Make the pockets at least an inch longer. My money and my knife and everything fall out.*

Wait just a minute.

[Johnson puts Haggar on hold for about a minute and a half.]

LBJ: *Now, the pockets, when you sit down in a chair, the knife and your money comes out. So I need at least another inch in the pockets.*

Haggar: *Be fine.*

LBJ: *Yeah. Now, another thing: the crotch, down where your nuts hang, is always a little too tight. So when you make them up, give me an inch that I can let out there, because they cut me. They're just like riding a wire fence. These are almost—these are the best I've had anywhere in the United States.*

Haggar: *Fine.*

LBJ: *But, uh, when I gain a little weight they cut me under there. So, leave me . . . You never do have much of margin there, but see if you can't leave me an inch from where the zipper [belches audibly] ends around under my—back to my bunghole.*

Haggar: *All right, sir.*

LBJ: *So I can let it out there if I need to.*

Haggar: *Be fine.*

LBJ: *Now, be sure you got the best zippers in them. These are good that I have. And if you get those to me, I would sure be grateful.*

Haggar: *Fine. Where would you like them sent, please?*

LBJ: *White House.*

Haggar: *Fine.*

The phone exchange, it must be stated, is an anomaly among the 643 hours of recorded conversations from Johnson's White House tenure. While it may be among Johnson's most famous, showing up for a while as a staple on morning "zoo" radio, none of the other recorded conversations come close to its level of crudity. At the same time, though an extreme reflection of Johnson, it doesn't surprise those who knew him well.

A creature of excess, Johnson would eventually have a sea of custom slacks awaiting him at the LBJ Ranch, along with twenty-eight rooms (with Muzak piped into each), seventy-two phone lines, three planes, a helicopter, and a fleet of cars, including one convertible model that a prankish Johnson would drive into the Pedernales River without informing passengers that it was amphibious. Johnson would spend nearly a quarter of his 1,887 days in the presidency at what would become known as the Texas White House. Official Washington often journeyed there to do business, as did heads of state—German chancellor Ludwig Erhard, made a state visit to the ranch the month after Johnson took office, and other heads of state followed—giving Johnson a chance to show them a little unpretentious Texas hospitality and the wonders of his home soil.

LBJ: I had no regrets about going to Washington and spending a good part of my life there, but I've always found it possible and almost necessary to return to Texas. This country has always been a place where I could come and refill my cup, so to speak, and recharge myself for the more difficult days ahead. Here's where we come to rest our bones and collect our thoughts and to lay out our plans.

I visit with my neighbors, talk to them and my friends. You would be surprised how much—how they can clear up a lot of the things that seem pretty foggy to you when you get here.

■ ■ ■

Regardless of what was happening in the world—in Washington or Guantánamo Bay, Selma or Prague, Watts or Vietnam—there was a nurturing parcel of Johnson's beloved Hill Country awaiting him in Stonewall. It was, he said later, "the one thing they can't take away from me."

LBJ: In Johnson City the old men sit out in front on the sidewalk and play dominoes all day long. And one of them, after I became president, said, "Old Lyndon sure has moved up in the world, hasn't he?" And the other one said, "Yeah, up the road about a half a mile."

SEEKING THE ULTIMATE TO DO THE POSSIBLE

In the messy aftermath of Dallas, lingering questions about the assassination represented Johnson's most pressing matter upon inheriting the presidency. As rumors of conspiracy began to swirl around the country and throughout the world—many implicating the Soviet Union and Cuba—Johnson feared that a nuclear attack could be triggered.

The assassination tainted Texas and, by extension, in the minds of some, clung to Johnson as a native of the state. No investigation by a Texas judicial authority, or certainly the Dallas Police, would get to the bottom of what actually happened on November 22. Nor would any congressional committee. Johnson quickly came to the conclusion that he would appoint "a high caliber, top flight, blue ribbon group that the whole world would have absolute confidence in" to investigate the assassination. He spent much of his first week in meetings and working the phones with his Cabinet, congressional leaders, and FBI chief J. Edgar Hoover, to ensure that he had buy-in on the idea of the commission and that the seven members he would appoint would serve on it. The move fit a long-held and often expressed philosophy—"If they're with you at takeoff, they'll be with you at landing"—that would serve him well in the Oval Office.

On the evening of November 29, 1963, Johnson announced the commission, named for its chairman, Earl Warren, chief justice of the Supreme Court. The commission would also include U.S. senators Richard Russell and John Sherman Cooper, U.S. representatives Hale Boggs and Gerald Ford, former CIA director Allen Dulles, and former World Bank president John McCloy—though Warren and Russell were initial holdouts.

LBJ: I had no question about the Warren Report. I'm no student of it. All I know is this: I was no intimate of [Chief] Justice Warren. I didn't spend ten minutes with him in my life. But I concluded that this was something that [J. Edgar] Hoover and the Massachusetts and Texas courts could not handle. It was so much deeper in [the] affairs of men for the next several centuries. We had to seek the ultimate to do the possible. And who is the ultimate in this country from the standpoint of judiciousness and fairness and the personification of justice? I thought it had to be Earl Warren, chief justice of the United States.

I know it was bad for the Court to get involved. And Warren knew it best of all and he was vigorously opposed to it.

I called him in.

Before he came I was told that Warren had said he wouldn't do it. He was constitutionally opposed. If I asked, he would say no. He thought the President should be informed of that.

Early in my life I was told that it was doing the impossible that makes you different. I was convinced this had to be done. I had to bring the nation through this thing.

EARL WARREN, chief justice, U.S. Supreme Court, 1953–69; chairman, Warren Commission, 1963–64: I had a call from the Solicitor General and the Deputy Attorney General. They said they wanted to see me, and I said, "Certainly, come right over." So they came over. They told me that the President was contemplating setting up a commission to investigate the assassination of President Kennedy, and they asked me if I would be a member of it. I think they asked me if I would be chairman of it, I'm not sure about that, but I know they asked me if I would be a member of it. And I told them I should not do that; that we had discussed many times in the Court some of the occurrences of the past—Justice Roberts when he went over on the Pearl Harbor affair; [Chief Justice] Bob Jackson when he went to Nuremburg; and some earlier ones too. And practically all of us had expressed the belief that it was not wise for members of the Supreme Court to accept positions on presidential commissions. I had personally expressed that view, and I still think as a general thing it's a sound rule. Because in the first place, we have enough work to do here [at the Court]; and in the second place, it does get you over into another department of government which is supposed to be separated.

And in about one hour I got a call from the White House and was asked if I could come up and see the President. And I said, "Certainly," so I went up there. And the President told me he was greatly disturbed by the rumors that were going around the world about conspiracy and so forth, and that he thought that it might—because it involved both [Nikita] Khrushchev and [Fidel] Castro—that it might even catapult us into a nuclear war if it got a head start, you know, kept growing. And he said that he had just been talking to McNamara, who was Secretary of Defense then, and that McNamara had told him that if we got into a nuclear war that at the first strike we would lose sixty million people. And he impressed upon me the great danger that was involved in having something develop from all of this talk. He said that he had talked to the leaders of both parties and that the members of Congress—Dick Russell and [Hale] Boggs on the Democratic side and [Gerald] Ford and [John Sherman] Cooper on the other side—and John McCloy from New York and Allen Dulles would be willing to serve on that commission if I was to head it up. And he said, "I think this thing is of such importance that the world is entitled to have the thing presided over by the highest judicial officer in the United States." And he said to me, "You've worn a uniform, you were in the Army in World War I," and he said, "this job is more important than anything you ever did in the uniform."

And I said, "Well, Mr. President, I've told you what my views are, and I also told the Solicitor General and the Attorney General, but," I said, "things can get to a place where your own personal views shouldn't count. And if you think it is this important that I should do it, why, I'll consider that my own personal views don't count, and I will do it."

So that's the way it came about.

■ ■ ■

Richard Russell, Democratic senator from Georgia, also approached his appointment to the committee with reluctance, though his related to his antipathy for Warren. As with Warren, Johnson appealed to his patriotism:

LBJ: I called every man on that commission. Senator [Richard] Russell said, "You mean I have to serve on that commission with Warren?"

I said, "Yes, and don't tell me you're less patriotic than Earl Warren because I don't believe that—and he feels more strongly about this than you do."

Everybody Bobby [Kennedy] wanted to have me appoint, I appointed to that commission.

Telephone conversation between LBJ and Richard Russell, November 29, 1963, 8:55 p.m.:

Richard Russell, U.S. Senator, Georgia (D), 1933–71: *Now, Mr. President, I don't have to tell you of my devotion to you, but I just can't serve on that commission. I'm highly honored that you'd think of me in connection with it. But I couldn't serve on it with Chief Justice Warren. I don't like that man. I don't have any confidence in him at all. . . . So you get John Stennis . . .*

LBJ: *You've never turned your country down. This is not me. This is your country. . . . You're my man on that commission and you're going to do it! And don't tell me what you can do and what you can't because I can't arrest you and I'm not going to put the FBI on you. But you're goddamned sure going to serve, I'll tell you that.*

In the end, Johnson got his commission, and its conclusion that Kennedy's assassin, Lee Harvey Oswald, deranged and determined, had acted alone. The seven men found no credible evidence that Oswald and Jack Ruby, who shot and killed Oswald as he was being transferred from a Dallas city jail to a county jail on November 24, 1963, "were part of any conspiracy, domestic or foreign to assassinate President Kennedy," a finding that has been widely disputed by conspiracy theorists since its publication but never credibly challenged. Though not articulated at the time, doubts remained with Johnson long after the 888-page report was drafted and submitted to him by Warren and the other commission members with little ceremony on September 24, 1964. In a segment that never made it into a three-part CBS interview with Walter Cronkite in early 1970, Johnson said, "I can't honestly say that I have ever been completely relieved of the fact that there might have been international connections [in the assassination of Kennedy]. I have not completely discounted it." While the statement was edited out of the interview when it aired in April of the same year, as Johnson invoked a long-held right among presidents to order the removal of material that might compromise national security, his sentiments later became known.

EARL WARREN: I've tried to figure why he said it. I know he was very devoted to Dick Russell, and I just sort of thought he said that somewhat to placate Dick Russell because Dick had previously made the same kind of statement, although he signed the report just like the rest of us, in which we said there was no evidence of anything of that kind.

I occasionally see someone who worked on it—either one of the lawyers or one of the members of the commission—and I ask them if they have ever heard of anything to discredit the report factually, and they say no, they've never heard anything. And I think that's true.

■ ■ ■

Whatever doubts Johnson may have harbored about the report's conclusion, he never disputed the importance of the commission itself.

LBJ: Can you imagine what would have happened if we had no inquest on Kennedy? If there had been no Warren Commission, we would have been as dead as slavery.

"AN AMERICAN BILL"

Conscious of asserting himself as president, Johnson pursued his legislative priorities with characteristic intensity. "We can pass the tax bill in a week," he told Senate minority leader Everett Dirksen, in a phone conversation on November 29, 1963, "but Civil Rights is gonna take so much longer." It would take him until the end of February 1964 to get his tax bill passed; but he was right that the Civil Rights Act would take longer to clear the hurdles posed by a reluctant Congress.

Given the intractability of racism in mid-twentieth-century America, it's a wonder that Johnson was optimistic that meaningful reform could come at all, let alone the legislation he was proposing, the most far-reaching since Reconstruction. Racism and bigotry blighted nearly every corner of the country, but was practiced most virulently and openly in the Deep South, where it was culturally ingrained. Second-class citizenry for people of color included separate and disparate schools and public facilities and discrimination in hiring and voting. Though Johnson's upbringing was as much southern as it was western, particularly as it related to attitudes toward race, he was never fully aware of the obstacles for American citizens of color until the 1950s. An exchange with Gene Williams, an African American man who, along with his wife, Helen, worked as domestic help for the Johnson family, gave Johnson clear perspective on how racism was an everyday fact of life.

LBJ: Well it might amaze you, but I think a black boy, who only finished elementary school [and] who drove my car back and forth from Texas after each session of Congress, had more to do with bringing about a semblance of equal justice in this country than any president from Lincoln to Johnson. We had to come back to Texas every year after the congressional session ended. And as plane schedules got better, Mrs. Johnson and I would fly back to Texas with the children. And it would be up to the black man that worked for us to drive our car and bring the cook and all the kitchen utensils and the baby's [necessities].

And he came in one evening after I finished a hectic session in the Senate and he said, "Senator, I's leaving in the morning about daylight. You got . . . anything else you want to send?" And I said, "Well, you going to take Beagle the dog?" And he said, "Yes, sir, yes, sir. Do I have to take Beagle?" And I said, "Why of course, Beagle's a member of the family. We can't leave him here all summer when we're in Texas. Why, why? Don't you want to take Beagle with you?" He said, "Yes, sir, I guess so."

Dejectedly he went back to the kitchen where he'd been washing dishes.

And I said, "Gene, come tell me why you don't want to take Beagle."

And he said—and these are his words, "A niggra has enough trouble getting through the South without a damn dog." And that for the first time really aroused in my consciousness the terrible injustice that we whites had perpetrated in a nation where men were supposed to be created equal for almost two centuries.

He elaborated some. He said: "We drive all day but when we want to go to the bathroom just like you all do, we have to go out a side road and our women have to get behind a tree because we can't go into a filling station like you do. We get hungry and we've got to eat just like you do, but we have to go across the tracks to a grocery store and get some cheese and crackers because we can't go in a café. Or if some hamburger stand would take a chance on being insulted and try to get by them, we have to go around to the back and wait till everybody else is served to get something to eat. We drive hard all day long and it comes to 10 or 11 o'clock and Helen and I want to go to sleep. We can't go in a motel or a hotel. We have to drive across the tracks and find some boarding house way down there where they'll take us in for the night because we're not allowed in the hotels or motels in the country." He said, "You're not allowed in any place almost even across the tracks if you've got a damn dog you got to take with you."

I was chagrined at my insensitivity to my fellow man. And out of that conversation, when I got to be President, I urged in my first statement that we start on a course of equal justice for our fellow man.

■ ■ ■

His conscience heavy, Johnson championed the Civil Rights Act of 1957 and the Civil Rights Act of 1960 as Senate majority leader, overcoming the sectional rivalries that divided his party. Though the bills were rendered largely toothless in committee, their symbolism—the first civil rights legislation in nearly a hundred years—made them significant even if their effects weren't.

Johnson faced similar challenges in getting meaningful civil rights legislation through Congress as president in 1964.

His first hurdle toward the bill's passage was in the House, where it was hung up in the House Rules Committee, presided over by the openly racist Howard Worth "Judge" Smith, from Virginia's Eighth District. It was Smith's heavy hand that had gutted the earlier civil rights legislation. In an effort to outflank Smith, Johnson implored *Washington Post* publisher Katharine Graham to feature front-page articles every day on those House members who, by virtue of their passivity in not signing a petition to have the bill discharged from Smith's committee, prevented the bill from progressing:

> *Now every person that doesn't sign that petition has got to be fairly regarded as being anti-civil rights. . . . But I don't think any American can say that he won't let 'em have a hearing either in the committee or on the floor. That is worse than Hitler did. So we've got to get ready for that and we've got to get ready every day. Front page. In and out. Individuals.*

"Why are you against a hearing?" Point 'em up, and have their pictures, and have editorials, and have everything else that is in a dignified way for a hearing on the [House] floor. We've only got 150 Democrats; the rest of them are Southerners. So we've got to make every Republican [sign]. We ought to say, "Here is the party of Lincoln. Here is the image of Lincoln, and whoever it is that is against a hearing and against a vote in the House of Representatives, is not a man who believes in giving humanity a fair shake. Vote against it if he wants to. Let him do it. But don't let him refuse to sign that petition! Now if we could get that signed, that would practically break their back in the Senate because they could see that [this movement] here is a steamroller.

As the *Post* began featuring articles throwing light on the efforts of Smith and others on the Rules Committee to thwart the bill, pressure began to mount. When Smith's position and standing as committee chairman became tenuous, he agreed to hearings on the bill, to be conducted in early January. After three weeks of debate, the committee voted 11 to 4 to clear the bill and send it to the House floor. There it passed by a vote of 290 to 130.

JAKE PICKLE, U.S. representative, Texas (D), 1963–95: I voted for the Civil Rights Act, and it was not an easy vote for someone from my [Texas] district. We took the vote late that night, and then I went out with some friends. When I came in, early in the morning, the lady at the White House switchboard rang and said, "The President has been calling for you."

I said, "Well, I'll call in the morning."

She said, "No, he wants you to call [now]."

I said, "I will get him first thing in the morning."

She said, "No, it's the President himself calling and he said that's what you would say, that you would call in the morning. You've got to return that call [now]."

So I did return the call. And when I got him, the President said, "I . . . made a pledge to myself I was not going to let this night go by until I could call you and tell you that your President was immensely proud of your vote tonight." He remembered loyalty above almost anything else.

■ ■ ■

Johnson's hurdle in the Senate hit a little closer to home. Among those sitting silently in the House chamber on the evening of November 27, 1963, as Johnson made clear his intention of passing civil rights legislation, was the powerful Democratic senator and mentor to Johnson, Richard Russell, who had served in the body since 1933. Russell had opposed Kennedy's civil rights efforts, vowing to "resist to the bitter end any measure or any movement which would have a tendency to bring about social equality and intermingling and amalgamation of the races in our [southern] states." He would do the same to Johnson's attempts.

But Russell also knew that his old friend and Senate colleague would not allow a "watered-down, ineffective" bill as in 1957 and 1960. Johnson would accept nothing less than laws that rendered illegal the racial discrimination common in much of the country, particularly the South—and he had the legislative wherewithal to get it passed. Accordingly, as the White House pushed for the passage of a civil rights bill in the summer of 1964, Russell closed ranks, lining up eighteen southern Democrats to filibuster the bill on the Senate floor, a tactic that had effectively diminished the Civil Rights Acts of 1957 and 1960.

ORVILLE FREEMAN, secretary of agriculture, 1961–69: I was visiting with Dick Russell. He was very reserved, very impressive, quiet, seldom spoke very strongly, and I hadn't any real intimacy with him. But suddenly he said to me, "Wait until that man Johnson learns what the power of the presidency can do. Things are going to happen around here."

And he said, "Why, the son of a bitch will tear your arm off at the shoulder and beat your head in with it."

I could hardly believe my ears. And then he said, "And he is going to pass the Civil Rights Bill. I am going to oppose it. I don't think Kennedy could have passed it. But mark my word, he is going to pass it."

WILLARD DEASON: Occasionally, when LBJ got lonesome, I got invited down to have breakfast with him. I went down one morning and he was putting on his shirt as he always did, tying his tie and talking and all at the same time, and he kind of looked down at the floor, sad, and he said, "You know, I've got to do a hell of a thing today."

"What's that Mr. President?"

He said, "I've got to run over Dick Russell."

JACK VALENTI: [H]e called to the White House the patriarch of the Senate, his friend, his mentor, the man who was the most responsible for making him majority leader: Richard Russell of Georgia. I sat with the two of them that day, Russell and the President almost knee-to-knee, these men with their long-held, loving friendship that bound them together. There on the second floor of the Executive Mansion, the living quarters of the President, they talked.

Johnson leaned toward Russell, as he was apt to do. He said, "Dick, I love you and I owe you. But I'm going to tell you something. I'm going to run over you if you challenge me on this civil-rights bill," which later became the Civil Rights Bill of 1964. "I aim to pass this bill, Dick, only this time there is going to be no caviling, no compromising, no holding back. This bill is going to pass. And no one is going to stand in my way. I just want you to know that."

Russell listened. He was quiet for a minute. Then he said in those familiar, softly rolling tones, "Well, Mr. President, you may do just that. But I'm here today to tell you it's going to cost you the election, and it's going to cost you the South."

Johnson was silent for a moment, listening intently. Then he spoke very, very quietly. "Dick, if that's the price for this bill, I will gladly pay it."

■ ■ ■

The Senate's filibuster began on March 26, 1964, and would last through fifty-seven days of debate. In its midst, Johnson cultivated Illinois Republican senator and minority leader Everett Dirksen, who was key to delivering what members of Johnson's own party were determined to scotch. As Senate minority leader, Dirksen could rally enough Republican support to invoke cloture, a Senate rule that would limit debate and call for an immediate vote on the bill, putting an end to Russell's filibuster.

Telephone conversation between LBJ and Everett Dirksen, May 13, 1964, 4:30 p.m.:

Everett Dirksen, Senate minority leader, Illinois (R), 1959–69: *I talked to Dick [Russell] this morning and he gave me no comfort. I said, "Now, I thought that we vote on the Wednesday," meaning yesterday. But I said, "What are you going to do?" And he said, "Well, you're not going to vote this week, because we're going to keep the show going." I said, "Well, what about next week?" [He said,] "I can give you no commitment, because we'll have a caucus of our members Monday morning." Well, I said, "Dick, you're going to have to fish or cut bait, because I think that we've now gone far enough. And I think that we've been fair."*

LBJ: *Well, you've got—*

Dirksen: *So that's about where it stands.*

LBJ: *You've got . . . that's exactly right. That's what you've got to do; you've got to take care of your own people, and you're doing that. And I saw the other day . . . we don't want this to be a Democrat bill, we want it to be an American bill. And if these schools are out, they're coming out the end of this month, and if they're out and we haven't got a bill, we're in a hell of a shape. We're going to be in trouble, anyway.*

Dirksen: *Well, we're going to try.*

LBJ: *I saw your exhibit at the World's Fair, and it said, "The Land of Lincoln," so you're worthy of the "Land of Lincoln." And the man from Illinois is going to pass the bill, and see that you get proper attention and credit.*

Sensing the inevitability of defeat, Russell reluctantly put an end to his filibuster. As he had predicted, Johnson prevailed. The Civil Rights Act of 1964 passed on June 19, by almost three-quarters of the Senate vote, 73 votes to 27.

LUCI JOHNSON, younger daughter of Lyndon and Lady Bird Johnson: After that piece of legislation was passed, he went and took the first pen and gave it to Everett Dirksen. And we got back into the car and I said, "Daddy, there were all those civil rights leaders up there! Why, why didn't you give that first pen, that most important pen, to, to one of these greater civil rights heroes?"

He looked at me again, shook his head, and said, "You, you don't get it, do you?" And I [said], "No, I don't!" And he said, "Because all those civil rights leaders were already for that legislation. I didn't have to do anything to convince them. It was Everett Dirksen, making the courageous stand that he did, stepping up to the plate like he did, and bringing the people he brought with him that made the difference, and made the civil rights leaders' dream, and my dream, come true. That's why he got the first pen."

■ ■ ■

Yet, despite its historic nature, the passage of the bill was not an exultant moment for the president.

BILL MOYERS: The night that the Civil Rights Act of 1964 passed, I found [Johnson] in his bedroom, exceedingly depressed. The headline of the bulldog edition of *The Washington Post* said, "Johnson Signs Civil Rights

Act." The airwaves were full of the discussions about how unprecedented this was and historic, and yet he was depressed. I asked him why. He said, "I think we've just delivered the South to the Republican Party for the rest of my life, and yours."

That thought hasn't been lost on me. . . . We won that election but we lost the war, in time, because we lost the South.

JAMES DAVIS, employee of the Johnson family: The president told me, he said, "Look, I'm gonna get this Civil Rights Bill passed, but I'm going to lose a lot of friends." And he said, "[T]he country might go Republican, the South might go Republican," he told me that.

And I know one of his best friends, the senator from Georgia—What was his name? Russell—he used to come to the Ranch all the time [around] hunting season.

Well, after that Civil Rights Bill passed, I never saw Senator Russell from that day to this. [Russell did come to the ranch on November 23, 1964.]

JOHN GARDNER, secretary of health, education, and welfare, 1965–68: No one understood better than Lyndon Johnson that inertia of the political system and the deep resistance to cultural change. And no one was better equipped by temperament and experience to supply the enormous drive that was needed to deal with it. It was not the kind of effort designed to win popularity contests. He pushed and he shoved; he hammered away, he left bruises, he lost friends, he angered many, and he never rested; he never rested. And the system was set in motion.

JOSEPH CALIFANO: To me no greater example of presidential courage exists than Lyndon Johnson's commitment in the area of civil rights. He fought for racial equality even when it hurt him and clobbered his party in the South.

THE KENNEDYS

Throughout his career as vice president and president and on into history, Lyndon Johnson would be inextricably tethered to the Kennedy family. It was John Kennedy's pragmatic political decision to put Johnson on the Democratic ticket as his running mate in 1960—over the protestations of his brother and campaign chief Bobby Kennedy—that ultimately propelled Johnson into the White House after Dallas, and it was Bobby Kennedy's resistance to Johnson's Vietnam policy as a high-profile New York senator that accelerated Johnson's already considerable woes in the latter years of his presidency.

Like all of his relationships, and reflecting his own nature, Johnson's relationships with the Kennedys were complicated—only more so. It was marked by a resentment that ate away at him in his weakest moments. Fiercely competitive, Johnson was one-upped by the Kennedys from the start. Their Ivy League polish, megawatt smiles, and acceptance by the eastern establishment were advantages to be sure, but nowhere more so than in Johnson's own mind. His resentment long predated either man's attainment of the Oval Office. "Kennedy was pathetic as a congressman and as a senator," Johnson reflected later. "He didn't know how to address the chair." Yet that winning image and those connections helped John Kennedy, a Senate backbencher, leapfrog over him, the all-powerful Senate majority leader, to capture the 1960 presidential nomination.

After Kennedy's assassination, as the history of his administration was being written, much of it through a gauzy Camelot veil, none of its glory reflected back on his vice president. This was particularly evident in accounts of Kennedy's crowning moment, his cool leadership in outmaneuvering the Soviet Union in the Cuban Missile Crisis, preventing what might have resulted in nuclear winter.

DEAN RUSK: One curious thing reflecting LBJ is the way those who have tried to re-create the Cuban Missile Crisis have ignored LBJ's role in it. He spent long periods of time with Kennedy alone in the Oval Office during that week of the crisis. He played a much stronger role in that crisis than has been noticed. Now, part of that [1974 ABC special] program "The Missiles of October" was clearly based on Bobby Kennedy's little book *Thirteen Days*, and for all sorts of reasons that little book does not highlight in any way LBJ's role.

LBJ: Bobby's story on the missile crisis was another [William] Manchester deal. He said, "Also on occasion Johnson came in." They had thirty-seven meetings and I was in thirty-six of them. I missed one. I was in Honolulu at Kennedy's request. When he was out in Chicago and got that cold [that brought him back to Washington], we both agreed we had to show folks things were not so tense.

He called me back. I went swimming with him. He had Mac [McGeorge] Bundy brief me.

■ ■ ■

Most significantly, John and Bobby Kennedy were embraced by the media and the American public for the ideals that captured the best hopes of their era—civil rights and social justice—an impression deepened by their martyrdom and adding to their luster. Despite his remarkable political fortitude in putting those shared ideals into law, the same resplendent acknowledgment and esteem never found its way to Lyndon Johnson. For a man who craved approbation, that may have hurt most of all.

It may well have been, as many suspected, that President Kennedy would have fallen short in getting the Civil Rights Act passed. Martin Luther King Jr., among others, doubted that Kennedy could have gotten it through Congress. Though passage of the act owed much to Johnson's legislative prowess and political courage, most of the credit nevertheless went to Kennedy. If so, it was largely due to Johnson himself, who used Kennedy's martyrdom to impress upon reluctant congressmen that it was what Kennedy would have wanted—just as Johnson would have employed any effective tactic to get controversial legislation passed. Johnson also did the honorable thing by giving Kennedy credit for its passage, but paradoxically resented it when the achievement became more Kennedy's than his.

LBJ: On civil rights, I recommended to the President [Kennedy] that no savings and loan association [or] FDIC bank could continue if they did not make loans [to people of color] for open housing. Bobby called and said, "What are you trying to do, defeat the President?" We didn't get any executive order [on civil rights] from Kennedy, but we [the Johnson administration] got it in a bill later. I would try to get Congress to pass it in a bill, and we passed that bill before the year [1964] was out.

But the media was so charmed [by Kennedy]. It was like a rattlesnake charming a rabbit. But I believe men will look back on this era, fifteen years or so from now, they will look back and say, "Okay, how did we do it?"

NICHOLAS KATZENBACH, attorney general, 1965–66; undersecretary of state, 1966–69: [Johnson] made a point of associating the 1964 [Civil Rights] Act with Kennedy, a very generous, very human thing to do. But he did believe in civil rights strongly and firmly and unequivocally, and wanted to be identified with that. That's why we got the 1965 Voting Rights Act.

■ ■ ■

Despite sentiments that were at times tainted by pettiness, Johnson also respected the Kennedy brothers for their intelligence and political savvy. In particular, it seemed that Johnson appreciated the role John Kennedy had grown into as a "great public hero." By some accounts, their relationship evolved throughout Kennedy's presidency—as Kennedy evolved as president—into one of greater admiration, even affection, though others didn't see it that way.

LBJ: [President Kennedy and I] were not like brothers, we were not constant companions. I don't recall that we ever had an element of bitterness or deep feeling enter into any of our discussions. . . . I don't think of any—even in the tenseness of the [1960] campaign that we, even in the periods when we were aligned on different sides of a question, which was very rare—that I ever saw any indication of anything but friendship and respect.

BARRY GOLDWATER: I think in the first two and a half years in his presidency he was awed by the Kennedys. I don't think he ever liked the Kennedys. I don't think he ever respected the Kennedys. . . . I know we could get under his skin by saying, "You know, Lyndon, you said that just like Jack would have said it," and then, God, he'd get red! I think there was sort of a natural resentment from a poor-born Texan toward a rich-born Massachusetts boy.

WARREN ROGERS: [Johnson] had a difficulty with the Kennedy image, as far as projecting himself on television or any other way. He was not treated too well as vice president under Kennedy, if you'll remember—not by Kennedy so much as by the Kennedy supporters, the Kennedy followers. There were jokes about Lyndon Johnson being uncouth and not quite as smooth as some of the Harvard people thought he should be. I don't think he got over that. I think he resented that at all times.

TED KENNEDY, U.S. senator, Massachusetts (D), 1962–2009: I always was under the understanding that the relationship between President Kennedy and Johnson was . . . easy and cordial . . . based on a good deal of mutual respect and understanding.

■ ■ ■

Johnson's relationship with Bobby Kennedy was anything but easy and cordial. At best, Bobby Kennedy regarded Johnson warily, and no love was lost between the two men. Whatever contempt Kennedy had for Johnson, Johnson returned in kind.

LBJ: I thought I was dealing with a child. I never did understand Bobby. I never did understand how the press built him into the great figure he was. He came into public life as [Joseph] McCarthy's counsel and he was [John] McClellan's counsel and then tapped Martin Luther King's telephone wire.

It's hard for me to reconcile a man who had been McCarthy's counsel and McClellan's counsel when he investigated the labor situation—there's bound to be a little ambition there somewhere.

Martin Luther King's activity was financed by Kennedy. He tapped the phone with his right hand and gave him hundred dollar bills with his left.

TED KENNEDY: I think there were some obvious, strong personality differences between President Johnson and Senator Robert Kennedy. I think there was a strong belief, certainly on my part, that President Johnson had carried through the legacy of President Kennedy in terms of domestic policy. There was broad disagreement on Southeast Asia, which led to increasing kinds of personal antagonism between Senator Robert Kennedy and the President. I think there was a good deal of mutual respect for each other in terms of ability and concern and commitment.

GEORGE MCGOVERN, U.S. senator, South Dakota (D), 1963–81: Bobby had too much power to suit Lyndon and, you know, he hadn't earned it. He [had] earned it [only] because he was a brother to the president, and I think he also knew that Bobby played a key role in Jack winning the nomination in 1960 and defeating Lyndon Johnson. Bobby was given the role of being the tough guy, the guy to say no, and the guy to make the final decisions. I think that Johnson kind of liked Jack Kennedy but didn't like this little brat [who] was throwing his weight around.

BARRY GOLDWATER: It would have been difficult, if not impossible, for [Johnson] to have hidden [his feelings]. Any casual conversation that Bobby's name came up [in], you could see in his face right away that he just didn't like him.

HARRY MIDDLETON: [Johnson] would have liked a closer relationship with Kennedy, but he knew it couldn't have happened. He said, "We could have spent a lifetime trying to become close but there was too much separating us."

Johnson was like Will Rogers: He never met a man he didn't like. It was difficult for him to accept people who didn't like him. The animosity between Johnson and Kennedy sprang from Kennedy's point of view; Kennedy especially didn't like Johnson, and that was a thorn in [Johnson's] side.

■ ■ ■

Antagonisms between Johnson and Bobby Kennedy began brewing long before Johnson become president. After Johnson accepted John Kennedy's offer to join the ticket as his running mate at the 1960 Democratic National Convention in Los Angeles, the disapproving Bobby Kennedy tried to get Johnson to back out.

JOHN CONNALLY: At the 1960 convention, Jack Kennedy came down to see Mr. Johnson and offered him the vice presidency, and within fifteen minutes Bobby Kennedy came down to the Johnson suite.

Mr. Johnson did not see him. Speaker [Sam] Rayburn and I met Bobby Kennedy, who said in effect, "Lyndon has to get off this ticket. Lyndon cannot be on this ticket. This convention is going to go crazy. It's going crazy. He's got to withdraw." The Speaker listened to this for a while and finally he just said, "Ah," and spit, and walked out of the room.

Bobby left. He came back a second time. Nobody would see him but me. I went again into the bedroom and visited with him. He said that the convention was in an uproar, that Walter Reuther was leading a revolt, and that Johnson had to withdraw; that it was a terrible mistake that his brother had made in naming Johnson to the ticket.

I said, "Bobby, you're talking to the wrong man. Your brother offered him the vice presidency. If he doesn't want him to have it, he has to withdraw it. Johnson is not now going to withdraw from the offer. Jack Kennedy has to withdraw it if indeed he wants it withdrawn. And it has to come directly from him."

Bobby came in a third time; I won't repeat the conversation, but essentially with the same purpose. I said, "Look, let's don't kid ourselves. Jack Kennedy could control this convention, Walter Reuther notwithstanding.

Don't give me that. If there is some reason John Kennedy wants Lyndon Johnson off the ticket, he has to call him."

That call never came.

NICHOLAS KATZENBACH: [M]aybe President Kennedy and Lyndon Johnson understood politics at that point better than young Bobby.

LBJ: [Bobby] said Jack wanted me but he wanted me to know that the liberals will raise hell. He said Mennen Williams will raise hell.

I said, "Piss on Mennen Williams."

He said, "You know they'll embarrass you."

I said, "The only question is—is it good for the country and is it good for the Democratic Party?"

Prior to this, the President said, "Can I sell [it] to [Sam Rayburn]?"

Rayburn was against it because the Vice President is not as important as the Majority Leader. The vice president is generally like a Texas steer—he's lost his social standing in the society in which he resides. He's like a stuck pig in a screwing match.

Kennedy talked Rayburn into it. He said, "Mr. Rayburn, we can carry New York, Massachusetts, New England, but no Southern state unless we have something that will appeal to them." He asked, "Do you want Nixon to be President? He called you a traitor."

Rayburn always thought Nixon called him a traitor. Nixon brought me the speeches and they contained the phrase "treasonable to do that" or something like that. I thought Nixon's version was more just—but I lost the argument with Rayburn. Rayburn came in that morning and said, "You ought to do it [take the vice-presidential nomination]." I said, "How come you say this morning I ought to when last night you said I shouldn't?"

He said, "Because I'm a sadder and wiser and smarter man this morning than I was last night."

He said, "Nixon will ruin this country in eight years. And we're just as sure to have [Nixon] as God made little apples."

■ ■ ■

After Johnson took on the vice presidency, it was Bobby Kennedy, the president's attorney general and closest adviser, who often relegated Johnson to the sidelines.

LBJ: Bobby elbowed me out. Many times [John Kennedy] talked to me about the most intimate things one man can discuss. He asked me to do things [as vice president]. I'm sure Bobby didn't approve.

■ ■ ■

Bobby Kennedy's disapproval gave rise to Johnson's fear that one of the things Kennedy was trying to elbow him out of was the vice presidency itself, as rumors surfaced that Kennedy was working behind the scenes to remove Johnson from the 1964 ticket.

NICHOLAS KATZENBACH: I'm really quite confident that [Bobby] was not [working toward Johnson's removal from the ticket], that he regarded it as impossible. But I think Vice President Johnson was very concerned about that.

I think he took it more seriously than Bobby might have done. Sometimes Bobby made mistakes; we all do. But I think by that time, he wouldn't have made that big a mistake.

■ ■ ■

Bobby Kennedy hung on in the Johnson administration as attorney general, the post he had taken up under his brother, for almost ten months before resigning on September 3, 1964, after which Johnson gave the position over to Katzenbach.

NICHOLAS KATZENBACH: It must have given President Johnson pause when he named me attorney general, that I had worked as Bobby Kennedy's deputy. They did not get along well together. They were totally different kinds of people even though they shared many of the same objectives for society. They had such different personalities, such different ways of going about things.

I know Bobby Kennedy did not like LBJ. But he told me, "I cannot fault the President on his domestic programs. He has been magnificent." This was at the time he was criticizing him on Vietnam.

TED KENNEDY: [Robert Kennedy's] mood during that whole period throughout the latter part of 1963 and the early part of 1964—he wasn't really sort of thinking so much in terms of his own future or what plans he might have other than really spending time with Mrs. Kennedy and with the children, and really drawing within himself.

I remember—I think it was in the middle part of the winter of 1964—he mentioned to President Johnson his willingness to go to Saigon as an American ambassador over there. I know he had thought about this and made that offer, which President Johnson turned down. I heard afterwards it was primarily because he was concerned about the security of Robert Kennedy. So, in his mind he was thinking about—I'd say by early spring—alternatives.

DEAN RUSK: [Bobby] volunteered to LBJ to go to Saigon as our ambassador, and I vetoed it on the grounds that this country could not take another Kennedy tragedy and that Saigon was too dangerous a post for Bobby. Ironically, look what happened. If I had let him go to Saigon, maybe he'd still be alive. Who knows?

■ ■ ■

With the post in Saigon a closed door, Bobby Kennedy set his sights on the U.S. Senate, just as his brothers had done. Benefiting from Johnson's considerable help on the campaign trail, Kennedy secured a seat from New York in the fall—"This is ma boy," he told jubilant crowds as they appeared together, "I want you to elect ma boy!"—though it was not the fulfillment of Kennedy's ambitions. Throughout the bulk of Johnson's tenure in the White House, those ambitions and the inherent differences between Johnson and Kennedy would continue to create dissention between the two men—and problems for Johnson.

HARRY MCPHERSON: It must have been very difficult for [Johnson]. Here is this lightweight who hadn't done much of anything and this heavyweight who had been the all-powerful Senate majority leader and who had accomplished so much—Bobby Kennedy [had] worked for Joe McCarthy, and Johnson had brought McCarthy down. And the lightweight heaps contempt on the heavyweight, and Johnson regarded him in kind. Then Bobby crosses the finish line in the New York Senate race due to a gale force wind called LBJ.

■ ■ ■

Johnson's relationships with other members of the Kennedy family were strong. Kennedy patriarch Joe Kennedy held Johnson in the highest regard. As Ted Kennedy noted, had the presidential nomination gone to Johnson in 1956, Joe Kennedy supported the notion of JFK accepting a spot on the ticket as Johnson's running mate, a position he believed his son should otherwise have rejected.

TED KENNEDY: My first real direct contact with President Johnson was in an indirect way. It was at the time of the Democratic Convention [of 1956]. There was some speculation for two weeks prior to the nomination that President Kennedy might be interested in running for the vice presidential nomination. And there were conversations during the two or three days before the nomination itself with my father. My father was under a strong belief that President Kennedy should not make the effort to secure the vice presidential nomination. But the one exception to the rule in his conversations that I remember quite clearly was he felt that the only one that President Kennedy should serve as the vice president would be then-Senator Johnson. My father had a good deal of respect for Senator Johnson.

■ ■ ■

Not surprisingly, Joe Kennedy was supportive of Johnson as his son's running mate four years later, a factor that likely helped to override any objections by Bobby Kennedy.

TED KENNEDY: I remember [Johnson's] name being discussed by the President [Kennedy] and my father the day, or the evening, or two evenings, before the actual balloting, the nomination. Once again my father was sympathetic to that possibility. There were other names that were being considered: Senator [Henry] Jackson, Senator [Stuart] Symington, Senator [Hubert] Humphrey, and also Orville Freeman. And there was some consideration for one or two of the Midwestern governors. I've always believed the personal preference for [Johnson] had been my father's.

LBJ: With Joe and Rose, and Jackie and Ethel—and except for one incident with Teddy—our relations were always warm and friendly—non-political—they were all helpful to me. I have a feeling that Joe Kennedy felt his boy had no chance to be president except for what I did as majority leader.

■ ■ ■

Just as Johnson felt a responsibility as a "caretaker" of President Kennedy's people and policies, so he felt an obligation to his widow, Jacqueline

Kennedy. As the machine of government kept humming in the wake of Kennedy's assassination, the Johnson family remained at their home, The Elms, for eleven days to allow Mrs. Kennedy and her two children, seven-year-old Caroline and two-year-old John, who would turn three on November 25, to remain at the White House, as a means of easing the pain of their transition. (The children continued to go to school at the White House until shortly before Christmas.) On November 26, the day after her husband's state funeral services in Washington, Mrs. Kennedy penned Johnson an eight-page letter thanking him for the kindnesses he had extended, including marching behind Kennedy's casket during the funeral procession. "You did not have to do that," she wrote, "I am sure that many people forbid you to take such a risk—but you did it anyway."

> *[M]ost of all Mr. President, thank you for the way you have always treated me—the way you and Lady Bird have always treated me—before, when Jack was alive, and now as President.*
>
> *I think the relationship of the Presidential and Vice Presidential families could be a rather strained one. From the history I have been reading ever since I came to the White House, I gather it often was in the past.*
>
> *But you were Jack's right arm—and I always thought the greatest act of a gentleman that I had seen on this earth—was how you—the Majority Leader when he came to the Senate as just another little freshman who looked up to you and took orders from you, could then serve as Vice President to a man who had served under you and been taught by you.*
>
> *But more than that we were friends, all four of us.*

After Mrs. Kennedy and her children moved out of the White House and into nearby Georgetown, Johnson remained attentive. Even Mrs. Johnson recognized that he could get a little "mushy" when it came to Mrs. Kennedy.

Telephone conversation between LBJ and Jacqueline Kennedy, December 2, 1963, 2:42 p.m.:

Mrs. Kennedy: *Mr. President?*
LBJ: *I just wanted you to know you are loved and by so many and so much. . . .*
Mrs. Kennedy: *Oh Mr. President—*
LBJ: . . . *and I am one of them.*

Mrs. Kennedy: *I tried, I didn't dare bother you again, but I got Kenny O'Donnell over here to give you a message if he ever saw you. Did he give it to you yet?*

LBJ: *No . . .*

Mrs. Kennedy: *About my letter? That was waiting for me last night?*

LBJ: *No . . . Listen, sweetie, now first thing you gotta learn—and you've got some things to learn—and one of 'em is that you don't bother me. You give me strength.*

Mrs. Kennedy: *But I wasn't gonna send you in one more letter—and I was just scared you'd answer it!*

LBJ: *Don't send me anything, don't send me anything. You just come over and put your arm around me. That's all you do. And when you haven't got anything else to do, let's take a walk. Let's walk around the backyard and let me tell you how much you mean to all of us and how we can carry on if you give us a little strength.*

Mrs. Kennedy: *But you know what I want to say to you about that letter? I know how rare a letter is in a president's handwriting. Do you know that I've got more in your handwriting than I do in Jack's now?*

LBJ: *Oh, well . . .*

Mrs. Kennedy: *And for you to write it at this time, and then to send me that thing today of, you know, your tape announcement and everything . . .*

LBJ: *I want you to just know this, that I told my mama a long time ago, when everybody else gave up about my election in '48 . . .*

Mrs. Kennedy: *Yeah?*

LBJ: *My mother and my wife and my sisters—and you females—got a lot of courage that we men don't have. And so we have to rely on you and depend on you and you've got something to do. You've got the president relying on you—and this is not the first one you've had! So, there're not many women, you know, running around with a good many presidents. So, you just, you just bear that in mind that you've got the biggest job of your life!*

Mrs. Kennedy: *[Laughter] She ran around with two presidents. That's what they'll say about me. [Both laughing] Okay. Any time!*

LBJ: *[Kissing sounds] Goodbye, darlin'.*

Mrs. Kennedy: *Thank you for calling, Mr. President. Goodbye.*

LBJ: *Bye, sweetie. Do come by.*

Mrs. Kennedy: *I will.*

The chummy White House stroll Johnson proposed would not come to pass. Despite his effusive attempts to win her approval—hers would have been a big feather in his cap—Mrs. Kennedy politely withheld it. Undoubtedly influenced by Bobby Kennedy and pained by seeing Johnson in the role that had been so elegantly filled by her late husband, Mrs. Kennedy pulled away from Johnson soon after returning to private life. Conversations with historian and Kennedy White House aide, Arthur Schlesinger, recorded in March 1964, and released in August 2011, reflect her less-than-charitable private view of Johnson, whose legacy, she knew, would one day compete with Kennedy's. Far from Kennedy's "right arm," she characterized Johnson as an egotist and a do-nothing vice president, and held little hope for him as president.

JACQUELINE KENNEDY [Y]ou know what's going to happen. Lyndon can ride on some of the great things Jack did, and a lot of them will go forward because they can't be stopped—civil rights, the tax bill, the gold drain stuff. And maybe he'll do something with the Alliance and everything, but when something really crisis happens [*sic*], that's when they're really going to miss Jack. And I just want [the people] to know that it's because they don't have that kind of president, and not because it was inevitable.

■ ■ ■

That Mrs. Kennedy failed to recognize that Johnson had already laudably faced the first days of his presidency, precipitously steeped in crisis in the wake of her husband's assassination, was understandable. Regardless, as the seeds of Kennedy's legend began to be sown, there would be sufficient crises ahead that would test the mettle of Lyndon Johnson.

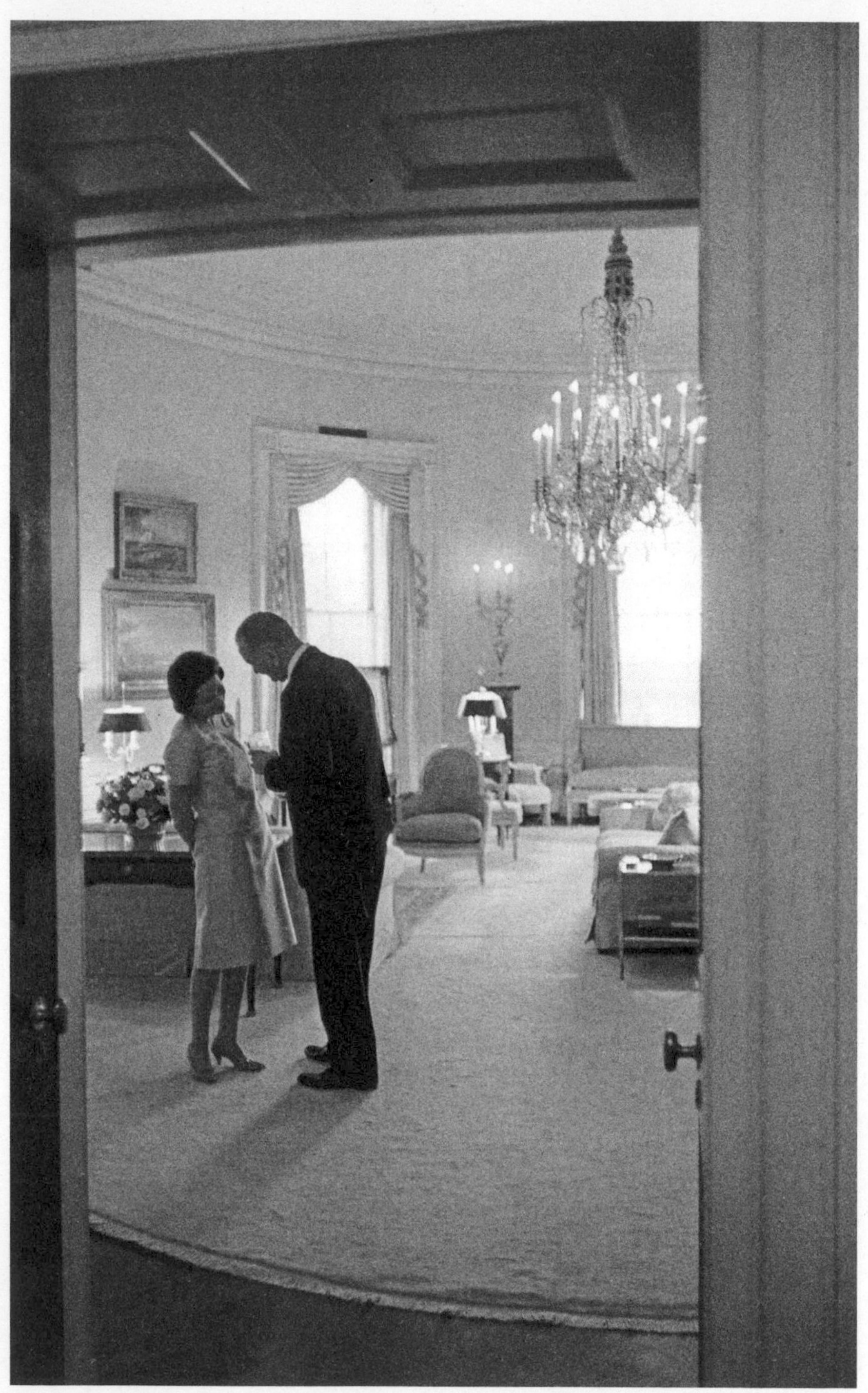

Lady Bird and Lyndon Johnson converse in the private residence of the White House, 1964

Chapter 4

THE JOHNSON TREATMENT

"BIRD"

LADY BIRD JOHNSON HAD FEW REGRETS IN HER LIFE, BUT ONE WAS her name—or nickname. She was born Claudia Alta Taylor in the small East Texas town of Karnack on December 22, 1912. When she was two, her African American nanny remarked of her, "She's as purty as a lady bird." The name stuck, much to young Claudia's chagrin. But like everything else in her life, anticipated or wholly unexpected, Lady Bird accepted it graciously and wore it with dignity.

Well born into the grandeur of the Old South, Lady Bird grew up in the biggest home in Karnack, "The Brick House," a two-story plantation mansion built by slaves. Her father, Thomas Jefferson Taylor Jr., a businessman and self-described "dealer in everything," was the wealthiest man in town. Her mother, Minnie Pattillo Taylor, a native Alabaman with progressive attitudes out of step with southern ideals of the time, died of complications after a fall when Lady Bird was five. Her death left Lady Bird and her two older brothers in the care of her doting father and a batch of adoring maternal relatives back in Alabama, where Lady Bird visited for long stretches.

Upon earning bachelor's degrees in the arts and journalism at the University of Texas in Austin, Lady Bird considered an adventurous career as a journalist, or becoming a teacher in Alaska or Hawaii, or just returning to her hometown.

LADY BIRD JOHNSON: I remember one time when I was about to graduate from college, I was just very casually talking [to my daddy], I wasn't meaning what I was saying. "I might do this, I might do that, or I might just come home to Karnack to stay." And my daddy just erupted, "Oh, no, you won't. You're going to get out of here. There will be better things for you to do," which sort of astonished me, because I knew how much he liked Karnack. He had spent his life in it. Also, he must have respected it a considerable amount or else he wouldn't have stayed there all his life. But I was very pleased that he could see that there might be a bigger world, and that maybe I better have a look at it.

■ ■ ■

The bigger world would soon find her. When she was twenty-one, Lyndon Johnson swept into her life with gale force. A date with the visiting congressional aide four years her senior led to a second the following day.

LADY BIRD JOHNSON: We wound up spending practically the entire next day together. We rode around and talked, and he was extremely direct. He told me all sorts of things about his job, what he liked about it, his family, his ambitions. I was just sort of listening wide-eyed and not really knowing what I felt.

My recollection is that he asked me to marry him on the first or second date. I just thought it was sheer lunacy. And I really didn't think he meant it. But after a while I realized that he really did mean it.

■ ■ ■

With no firm answer given on his proposal by the conflicted Lady Bird, Johnson returned to Washington, where he pressed his case through a series of letters, telegrams, and phone calls. Johnson, it seemed, was taken by more than just Lady Bird Taylor's poise and charm. An early present from Lyndon to the object of his affection hinted at his appreciation for her intellect, and at the broader worldview of the two young Texans: a book entitled *Nazism: An Assault on Civilization*, inscribed by Johnson inside the front cover, "To Bird—In the hope within these pages she may realize some little entertainment and find reiterated here some of the principles in which she believes and which she has been taught to revere and respect—LBJ," and dated "9/1/34," which was very likely the day of their first date.

Eventually, after Johnson's return visit to Texas and an ultimatum eleven weeks later, Lady Bird accepted his proposal of marriage out of concern that she would lose her dashing young suitor, and consoled by her father's advice: "Some of the best trades I've made, I've made in a hurry."

They married on November 17, 1934, as the groom slipped a $2.50 wedding ring from Sears, Roebuck on the finger of his new bride. Thereafter, Mrs. Johnson's life revolved firmly around that of her capricious husband, who often called her simply "Bird."

BILL MOYERS: [Mrs. Johnson] told me once that she didn't even understand everything about the man she married—nor did she want to, she said, as long as he needed her.

Oh, he needed her, alright. Once, trying to locate her in a crowded room, he growled aloud: "Where's Lady Bird?" And she replied: "Right behind you, darling, where I've always been."

"Whoever loves, believes the impossible," Elizabeth Browning wrote. Lady Bird truly loved this man she often found impossible. "I'm no more bewildered by Lyndon than he is bewildered by himself," she once told me.

■ ■ ■

Despite diametric differences in background, personality, and temperament, the marriage of the Johnsons stood the greatest test: it worked. Mrs. Johnson proved to be a complement to her husband, particularly as he began his political ascent. Her refined charm smoothed his rough edges; her equanimity calmed his frequent storms; her sound judgment compelled him to look beyond the heat of the moment. One wonders whether Johnson allowed his demons to graze, knowing that she would help run them off by quietly summoning his better angels. Jake Pickle, a family friend, called her Johnson's "North Star." He, in turn, challenged her to reach beyond her natural diffidence and, by her own account, to become more than she "would have been."

LADY BIRD JOHNSON: He was marvelous, contradictory, with a great natural intelligence . . . sometimes hurtful, but also sweet and caring and giving. . . . He valued my judgment and I think sometimes I might have been helpful. I know we were better together than apart.

■ ■ ■

As he devoted himself to his career, living and breathing politics with singular intensity, she minded everything else, including the raising of their daughters Lynda Bird and Luci Baines, running their home, and gently introducing as much balance into his life as he would allow. All the while she endured the pain in her marriage—her husband's frequent infidelities, domineering nature, and occasional withering criticism—with steel magnolia stoicism. "She never cried," recalled Lynda. "She'd say, 'If I ever started crying, I'd never stop.' "

JOHN CHANCELLOR, national affairs correspondent, NBC: I always thought that [Johnson] was quite lonely when Lady Bird wasn't around. He had a funny attitude. I could express it, I suppose, by saying that he never paid any attention to Lady Bird when she was around, and when she wasn't around, he seemed to miss her badly. I am a great, great admirer of Mrs. Johnson. I think she's a distinguished lady. I think, probably in the long run, she had a great effect on him in smoothing out some of the policies, smoothing out some of the attitudes he had, making him gentle when he ought to have been gentle.

[There was] a general pattern of her being protective about him, worrying about him, and being the kind of wife who believes that her husband is the most important thing in the world. This seems to me almost an old-fashioned attitude now, and Lady Bird had it, and she had it in an inspiring degree. She was *his* woman. You knew that. And sometimes it was terribly difficult to be *his* woman. He was not an easy man to be married to; he was not an easy man to associate with in many ways. But she did it, and I think she just did a marvelous job. I wish somebody would strike a medal for Lady Bird.

WILLIAM S. WHITE, syndicated columnist, United Feature Syndicate: He was, as the expression goes, quite a handful for a wife to deal with in the sense that he was always so preoccupied, of course, with his career.

Mrs. Johnson—Bird, as he always called her—was extremely skillful at handling him, particularly when he was upset or angry or tired or depressed. She never frontally challenged him on anything, but she had her very soft manner of getting around him. I remember on one occasion we were at the White House, just my wife and myself and the Johnsons, for supper, and she did everything, asked him to do something he didn't like. And he said to me with great indignation, "You see what I've had to put up with from that woman!" I said, "Yes, Mr. President. It's shameful the way that big bully has brutalized you all these years." And he laughed at that point.

[She] had the gentleness that he lacked and was very often through his life the agent for bringing him back together with people with whom he'd broken. She once said to me, "I will not take on Lyndon's animosities or quarrels because I don't want him to lose any friends." And whenever he seemed to lose a friend, a genuine friend, she would invariably come into the picture some way and bring him back together with that friend. It was a small sidelight on their purely domestic life, perhaps one that has some historical meaning.

■ ■ ■

Just as Johnson was an accidental president, Mrs. Johnson was an accidental first lady. "I feel like I am suddenly on stage for a part I never rehearsed," she told Nellie Connally in her first week as First Lady. Like her husband, she found herself thrust suddenly in a role she had inherited from a beloved, glamorous predecessor—she, an East Texas girl with an accent as thick as gravy on a chicken-fried steak, a stand-in for a woman who epitomized East Coast refinement and class. But Mrs. Johnson took it all in stride, did the best she could, and never complained.

BILL MOYERS: Early in the White House, a well-meaning editor up from Texas said, "You poor thing, having to follow Jackie Kennedy." Mrs. Johnson's mouth dropped wide open in amazed disbelief. And she said, "Oh, no, don't pity me. Weep for Mrs. Kennedy. She lost her husband. I still have my Lyndon."

■ ■ ■

As Mrs. Johnson shouldered her own burdens, her most vital role, as always, was as a support to her husband, acting as cheerleader or critic as appropriate to the moment. A telephone conversation from March 7, 1964, provides a glimpse of her forthrightness as she offered an unvarnished assessment of a press conference he gave earlier in the day:

Mrs. Johnson: *You want to listen for about one minute to my critique or would you rather wait until tonight?*

LBJ: *Yes ma'am. I'm willing now.*

Mrs. Johnson: *I thought that you looked strong, firm, and like a reliable guy. Your looks were splendid. The close-ups were much better than the distance ones.*

LBJ: *Well you can't get 'em to do it.*

Mrs. Johnson: *Well, I will say this, there were more close-ups than distance ones.*

During the statement you were a little breathless and there was too much looking down and I think it was a little too fast, not enough change of pace, a drop of voice at the end of sentence. There was a considerable pickup in drama and interest when the questioning began. Your voice was noticeably better and your facial expression was noticeably better. . . .

I think the outstanding things were that the close-ups were excellent. You need to learn, when you're going to have a prepared text you need to have the opportunity to study it a little bit more and read it with more conviction and interest and change of pace.

LBJ: *Well, the trouble is they criticize you for taking so much time. They want to use it all for questions, then their questions don't produce any news, and if you don't give them news you catch hell. So my problem was trying to get through before ten minutes and I still ran ten minutes today. I took a third of it for the questions and I could have taken, if I read it like I wanted to, fifteen minutes. But I didn't know what to cut out. . . .*

Mrs. Johnson: *In general I'd say it was a good B plus. How do you feel about it?*

LBJ: *I thought it was much better than last week.*

Mrs. Johnson: *Well, I heard last week, see, and didn't see it and didn't hear all of it. In any rate, I felt sort of on safe ground. I mean, like you had sort of gotten over a hump psychologically and in other ways. It'll be interesting to hear everybody else's reaction.*

TOM JOHNSON, special assistant to the president, 1965–69: LBJ trusted Lady Bird more than anybody. He knew she always would be candid with him. He knew any secret information—such as his private thoughts about not seeking a second term [in the presidency]—would be safe with her. He and she loved each other unconditionally, and he saw wisdom, judgment, and common sense in the advice he received from her.

■ ■ ■

Mrs. Johnson's southern heritage was brought to the fore in her first full year in the White House. After the Civil Rights Act was signed into law in June of 1964, in an attempt to heal the divide the legislation had caused throughout Dixie—and to help mitigate the political fallout it heaped on Johnson's election bid for the presidency—Mrs. Johnson, at her husband's behest, embarked on a whistle-stop tour on the nineteen-car *Lady Bird Express*, which took her 1,682 miles throughout the Southeast and Deep South. Lynda and Luci, aged twenty and seventeen, joined her. The four-day trip, which began on October 6, would include forty-seven stops in eight states from Washington to New Orleans, where Johnson would join them by plane at the trip's end. The journey was not for the faint of heart.

SCOOTER MILLER, political supporter of LBJ: The thing that I liked about Lyndon—now, this was a good while ago, when he was president and women hadn't gone as far as they have—was that he respected the ability of women, maybe because of the woman he had married and the kind of daughters that he had. [H]e trusted his wife and his children and us to go through the South, and we accomplished a lot.

He respected the ability of women. I know we did things we would never have done if, as Bird said, he hadn't stretched us.

■ ■ ■

"To me as to you," Mrs. Johnson told her fellow southerners of the trip, "the South is not a matter of geography, but a place of the heart. And so, it is with great joy that I undertake what is—for me—in every sense, a journey of the heart."

Her joy was not shared by the hostile crowds that spat invective at the white-gloved, soft spoken First Lady, particularly in the early part of her journey through South Carolina. She was met by boos, jeers, and placards on which sentiments such as "Johnson Is a Nigger Lover" were scrawled. A railroad car was sent on the tracks in advance of Mrs. Johnson's in the event that a bomb had been planted, as the FBI busily investigated threats from stop to stop. Even then, she was less worried about her own safety than that of the engineer and his crew in the car ahead of her, since it was they, not she, who would be in harm's way.

BESS ABELL, Lady Bird Johnson's White House social secretary, 1963–69: [In] one little town, one little stop, away in the back of the crowd there were two boys holding up a big sign that they had that was stretched out, I think it was on a sheet so that they had to hold it apart to keep it straight, and it said, "Black Bird, go home!" And Mrs. Johnson talked and her southern accent got deeper and she talked about all those summers she spent in Alabama, and she introduced some of her Alabama kinfolks, that sign kept getting lower and lower until finally those two boys put it down in the dust and walked away.

■ ■ ■

At a stop in Columbia, South Carolina, combating a flurry of vitriol, the five-foot-four-inch First Lady stood her ground. "This is a country of many viewpoints," she responded through the din. "I respect your right to express your own. Now is my turn to express my own." Afterward, Bill

Moyers received a phone call at the White House from an advance man at the Columbia train depot. Holding back tears, he told Moyers, "As long as I live, I will thank God I was here today, so that I can tell my children that I saw the difference courage makes."

Except for an allusion to "the most dramatic four days of my political life," Mrs. Johnson's recollection of the trip was devoid of any of the unpleasantness she encountered. Instead, she wrote:

> *Thinking back on that montage of depots, faces, signs—such delightful signs—my mind always turns to that little town in North Carolina—was it Ahoskie?—where a woman pushed through the crowd to grab my hand and said, "I got up at 3 o'clock this morning and milked twenty cows so I could get here by train time!"*
>
> *That may be as close as many people get to government—to the people connected with the government—and I am glad we touched.*

Lady Bird Johnson saw the good in things, a useful quality for life in the White House and in her long marriage to an often "impossible" man.

After their White House years were over, the Johnsons went on a vacation to Acapulco—the kind of holiday denied to Mrs. Johnson throughout her husband's intensive political career. While there, he asked his bride of nearly four decades why it had taken her so long—a year or two—to replace the $2.50 Sears, Roebuck ring he gave her on their wedding day. After all, he had told her repeatedly to go out and buy herself a new one. "Why darlin'," she replied before kissing him, "I wanted to make sure the marriage was going to last."

"THE SUMMERTIME OF OUR LIVES"

If being married to Lyndon Johnson was an all-consuming proposition, so was working for him. Aides endured workdays that took them from early morning to late night, often seven days a week, and were on call even in their few off hours. And they answered to a mercurial boss as demanding as he was driven. "I only think about politics eighteen hours a day," Johnson once said, perhaps without irony. He expected the same focus from those on his staff, and could be cruel when they didn't show it.

Still, as hard as they worked, few, if any, would dispute that Johnson worked even harder—Jack Valenti, only half-jokingly, claimed that Johnson was born with extra glands—and that Johnson's loyalty and magnanimity, along with his underlings' profound sense of purpose in what they were working toward, more than offset their daily hardship.

JACK VALENTI: Before I first went up [to Washington] . . . on that terrible trip back from Dallas, the President had called me over and said, "I want you on my staff, and you are going to fly back with me." Before we even took off, he said this.

I said two dumb things. The first was, "I don't have any clothes, Mr. President."

He said, "You can go buy some."

And the second thing was, "I don't have a place to live." That was really a mistake. He said, "You can live with me until Mary Margaret [Valenti's wife] gets there."

I thought it was very gracious of him and very loving and fine. Eleven days after he was president, he moved into the White House and put me up on the third floor. Being within arm's distance from Lyndon Johnson meant that you were with him every hour of the day, and the days were long and the nights were short. He would call me at about five thirty in the morning: "Well, what are you doing?" *What am I doing?* . . .

"Well," he said, "get out of bed. Come on. We have work to do." And I groggily would find my way down at six o'clock in the morning. And about one o'clock the next morning it would be over, and then it started again at five thirty in the morning.

I got down on my knees and thanked God for liberating me when my wife finally got up here and we went to an apartment to live in and I left that White House, away from the all-embracing impact of that man.

A reporter in Washington [once] asked me, "What about this [Robert] Caro book [depicting] this terrible man you worked for?"

The answer is that working with him was the summertime of our lives, when we were for a brief moment part of one of the greatest advances in history.

DOUG CATER, special assistant to the president, 1964–68: The notion that Lyndon Johnson was some new invention in having ego and vanity, in being able to bruise you—it never struck me as odd. I was not of a thin skin when I came [to work with him]. It didn't bother me to see him burst out sometimes. It was life with Big Daddy, and Big Daddy could beat you one moment and then hug you the next and invite you to eat. I read about other Presidents whose aides never had a meal with them. Hell, it was hard to avoid a meal with Lyndon Johnson.

But there was a spirit of family with him. The people who didn't observe that, if they had a one-shot experience, they could get an impression of a man who was overblown, that in this personality everything was too much by half.

We've got to get it written into history that it was a hell of a lot of fun working for this man. We did not cringe, although we took it and we didn't answer back. I never saw anybody successfully talk back to Lyndon Johnson. But we learned to live with him on satisfactory terms.

■ ■ ■

Many who worked in Johnson's White House came away with battle scars in the form of tales of being chewed out, humiliated, bullied, brutalized, or embarrassed. A memo to Johnson by Joe Califano, for instance, was returned to Califano with a handwritten note from the president that read, "Are you fucking crazy?" Thick skin was as requisite for staffers as a pristine suit and tie or stockings without runs, all of which were subject to Johnson's scrutinizing gaze. The president's acute insensitivity was evident in a January 25, 1964, phone conversation with his press secretary George Reedy, in which he berated Reedy for his slovenliness and suggested that he keep his obesity in check by donning a corset:

LBJ: *I'm going to try to build you up. Build you up gradually but where you're the—you've got some prestige and standing and not just Walter [Jenkins] or Bill Moyers—I want you . . . you're entitled to prestige . . . you've worked for it harder than anybody else . . . so I want to do it but you've got to help me yourself. You don't help yourself, you in those damned old wrinkled suits . . . and you come in with a dirty shirt . . . and you come in with your tie screwed up . . . I want you to look real nice . . . put on your corset if you have to . . .*

George Reedy: *Okay, sir.*

LBJ: *But look like a top-flight businessman. You look like a goddamned reporter and I want you to look better, so you work hard over the weekend and next week just work like hell on these reports and be sure that every briefing you've got plenty of things, and then come in and insist on 10 minutes with me before each briefing so you can get what I've been doing that day. . . .*

On another occasion, Johnson publicly embarrassed Reedy. When Pierre Salinger, a Kennedy holdover who served as Johnson's press secretary throughout much of the year after Kennedy's death, suggested that Johnson fly to the 1964 Democratic National Convention in Atlantic City to announce his choice as his running mate personally, Johnson embraced the idea. In the presence of the news media, he went on to ask Reedy, "Why don't you have good ideas like Pierre?" Only a rare private apology from Johnson prevented Reedy's resignation, which he had tendered shortly after Johnson's comment. Despite the bullying that seemed intrinsic in his job description, Reedy was of two minds about the boss.

GEORGE REEDY, White House press secretary, 1964–66: As a human being he was a miserable person . . . a bully, sadist, lout, and egotist. His lapses from civilized conduct were deliberately and usually intended to subordinate someone else to his will.

Were there nothing to look at save LBJ's personal relationships with other people, it would be merciful to forget him altogether. But there is much more to look at. He may have been a son of a bitch, but he was a colossal son of a bitch. . . . Nevertheless, he was capable of inspiring strong attachments even with people who knew him for what he was.

■ ■ ■

"That's just him," was how Liz Carpenter explained Johnson's shortcomings. "You have to face the fact that he was that way. You had to accept him warts and all." She was one of the few who did answer back. When Johnson once harangued her by demanding, "Why don't you use your head?" she responded in kind: "I'm too busy trying to get you to use yours!"

Then there was the matter of Johnson's gargantuan ego. Male aides invited to skinny-dip in the White House pool might be subjected to their genitalia being sized up unfavorably by the president, who nicknamed his own penis Jumbo. When one of Johnson's administrative assistants, Yolanda Boozer, gave her newborn son the middle name Lyndon in honor of her boss in 1963, Johnson, then vice president, offered her additional maternity leave if she made Lyndon his first name instead. (She did, though the number of extra maternity days she was given for her concession is forgotten to history.)

ERVIN DUGGAN, staff assistant to the president, 1965–69: He was very much like my mother's older brother, my uncle Ed. My uncle Ed was an irascible, difficult person who wanted to be irascible and difficult because when you're that way, people have to handle you, they have to placate you, they have to settle you down.

And it's kind of a wonderful thing for the ego to be irascible and to have everyone have to adjust to you. And I realized that this personality, this enormous—the cliché was that he was larger than life—that his irascibility was, in a way, a way of becoming the center of attention.

■ ■ ■

But there was no one-size-fits-all approach from Johnson toward his staff. He was more complex than that, more nuanced. While there are abundant accounts of his tyrannical behavior, there were many people who never experienced it at all.

DEAN RUSK: I never had an unkind word from LBJ. I had frank words, but there was never any blustering or intimidation or anything as far as I was concerned.

WILBUR COHEN: I certainly never felt that I was intimidated or brutalized in any way. I felt my contacts and relationships with President Johnson were always on the subject of the substantive issues, and while we had differences of opinion expressed, I consider that entirely normal and reasonable.

BOB HARDESTY: In all honesty, you have to say he treated different people in different ways. He was never impolite to me, but I would know when he was unhappy because he would give me the silent treatment. But I [did see] him blow up at people and be rather scorching.

WILBUR COHEN: I don't think you can characterize Johnson in any one dimension, because he had this very unusual ability to deal differently with different people and different problems.

I think he sized up every individual—this is the very conclusion I come to—I think he made a mental intellectual impression in his brain of every individual he dealt with. He related that to how he worked with the individual. I think he treated people differently, but I think that was based upon a very fundamental appreciation of human psychology.

■ ■ ■

For those subordinates who were subjected to Johnson's worst sides, though, the question is why were they willing to put up with it?

BETTY HICKMAN, secretary to Senator Johnson, aide to the president: I think there are several reasons. Possibly it was a sort of awesome job; everybody sort of stood in awe of you because you were on LBJ's staff. I know I could pick up the phone and order something from one of the [federal] departments, and they were knocking on the door before I hung up. [I]t was partially that, and I think [we] respected him. I think most people realized that the man was under a great deal of pressure and that he was really—he was married to the job. There was no such thing as making personal plans.

He didn't golf, he didn't socialize much. He did go to a lot of dinners and events, but it was not of his choosing. He worked in the car; he had a phone in the car. He would think nothing of calling you up at four and five o'clock in the morning to dictate something to you.

But you did feel, because he was so dedicated, that you were kind of responsible to be just as dedicated almost.

■ ■ ■

There was also Johnson's softer side. For all the accounts of his harshness and cruelty, there are at least as many stories of his generosity. "He never said, 'I'm sorry,'" recalled Bill Foster, a navy officer who filmed much of Johnson's public presidency as his official duty. "But he always made sure he made it up to you." That desire to make amends may have explained the brand-new Lincoln automobile Johnson gave to George Reedy out of the blue, one of many cars Johnson gave to friends, aides, and employees through the years. But his thoughtfulness went beyond the gifts he gave.

PHYLLIS BONANNO, personal assistant to LBJ, 1968–69: One day I came into the office and I'd had my hair done. The president said to me, "Today's a Wednesday. You don't have your hair done till Friday." Typical LBJ, right?

And I said, "Well, Mr. President, my parents are here, and they're in town for two or three days. And so I had my hair done."

And he said, "Your parents are here? Where are your parents?"

And I said, "Well, they're staying at the Washington Hilton."

[T]wo hours later, my mother calls me and she said, "Phyllis we just had a knock at the door and we have an invitation to the reception after the White House dinner tomorrow night for President Tubman of Liberia. What am I going to wear? Where's your father going to get a tuxedo?"

I said, "I don't know, Mom, but we'll figure that all out."

And unbeknownst to me, [President Johnson] had invited my parents to come, which of course was such an exciting moment for them because they really didn't know the President and First Lady.

And of course, when they went through the receiving line, Mrs. Johnson said all of those wonderful things you say to mothers about their children. And it was a very, very special night.

BOB HARDESTY: He was just so wonderful to work for. He treated you like family. If you were working at the Ranch, when you were down there you took breakfast, lunch, and dinner with the family. I don't think that had ever happened before. He took you out to look at deer at sunset, stop and have a scotch and soda, talk. He was wonderful to be around.

I had a major coronary when I first came to Austin [after Johnson had left the presidency] and I was in the hospital. It was touch-and-go for a few days, and we had just moved from Washington, and there was a knock at the door and my wife [Mary] went to the door and it was Mary Rather, who was Lyndon Johnson's secretary, and she said to my wife, "Mr. Johnson"—she always called him Mr. Johnson—"wanted you to have this." And she handed her an envelope. [I]n the envelope were ten hundred-dollar bills—that was a lot of money in those days. And she said, "What's this for, Mary?" She said, "Mr. Johnson didn't want you to have to worry about anything else while Bob is in recovery, and if there are any problems, he hopes this will take care of it."

You don't forget things like that.

■ ■ ■

Johnson's keen sense of humor also helped to make him bearable.

JACK VALENTI: [O]ne time John Kenneth Galbraith was in his office. And Ken was saying, "Now Mr. President, you haven't made an economic speech in quite a while. As a matter of fact, I haven't even heard one. You need to make economic speeches."

And the President [said], "Ken, let me tell you about economic speeches." He says, "[A] president making an economic speech is like a fellow peeing down his leg. It makes him feel warm but nobody else knows what the hell he's doing."

■ ■ ■

Another reason staffers may have been accepting of and affectionate toward Johnson was that he was part of a greater package that included the ever-gracious Mrs. Johnson, who made sure she "walked behind him and said 'thank you.'" The first couple came as a matched set. There was no dividing line between the East and West wings of the White House, as there would be in the Clinton White House, or of the downstairs formal mansion and upstairs family quarters, as there would be with the Nixon, Carter, and Reagan White Houses. Aides were as likely to see Johnson in his bedroom in boxer shorts as they would in the Oval Office immaculately clad in custom-tailored suits, which he changed after daily afternoon "naps" that often turned into horizontal work sessions. Even Richard Nixon recalled a 1966 meeting in the private quarters of the White House in which Johnson lounged in bed in his pajamas and Mrs. Johnson, entering late in her dressing gown, greeted Nixon warmly before climbing in bed with her husband for the remainder of their conversation. Johnson's was a personal presidency, with the "spirit of family" that Douglass Cater recalled being shared, by others, who were made to feel a part of the extended Johnson clan.

Loyalty, for the most part, was a reciprocal part of the bargain. Just as Johnson expected unconditional loyalty from his aides—"I want someone who will kiss my ass in Macy's window and say it smells like roses" was all he asked—he returned it.

LARRY TEMPLE: He always talked about loyalty. [O]ne time he told me that there were ten principles of politics, and that they were, in order of importance: loyalty, loyalty, loyalty, loyalty, loyalty, loyalty, loyalty, loyalty, loyalty and loyalty. And he believed that. And he said, "Some people have left me, but I've never left anybody."

BEN BARNES, speaker of the Texas House of Representatives, 1965–68: LBJ told me to think of the one hundred people who had helped me the most throughout my life, and make them your home base. He implored me to remember their birthdays, children's names, and attend their families' weddings and anniversaries, and to be there when they bury their dead. He went on to tell me that I was always to remember that there isn't anyone more important than those who brung you first. When you appreciate and value your friends you build trust. Trust that outlives your time as elected official. You learn real quick who your friends are when your political life ends.

■ ■ ■

In mid-October of 1964, Johnson's trusted aide and fellow Texan Walter Jenkins, a married father of six, was caught up in a sex scandal when arrested upon being caught with another man at a Washington YMCA after attending a party hosted by *Newsweek*. Mindful of protecting the presidency, Johnson, who was in the midst of campaigning for the 1964 election, was politically pragmatic about the situation. "The facts are that he's got to get out of the White House," he told confidant Clark Clifford after the scandal broke.

But an October 15 phone conversation between the president and First Lady, while Johnson was campaigning in New York, showed them rallying around Jenkins. Though Johnson resisted Mrs. Johnson's suggestion that they offer Jenkins a position as second in charge at KTBC, the family-owned radio and television stations, which Johnson knew would be rejected by the morally minded FCC, they agreed on offering him a position running the family's ranch holdings:

Mrs. Johnson: *I would like to do two things about Walter. I would like to offer him the number two job at KTBC. . . .*

LBJ: *I wouldn't do anything along that line now. I'd just let them know generally through Tom [Corcoran] that they'll have no problem in that connection. Go ahead—next!*

Mrs. Johnson: *I don't think that's right. Second, when questioned—and I will be questioned—I'm going to say that this is incredible for a man that I've known all these years, a devout Catholic, the father of six children, a happily married husband. It can only be a small period of nervous breakdown balanced against—*

LBJ: *I wouldn't say anything! I just wouldn't be available for anything because it's not something for you to get involved in now. . . . I feel it stronger than you do. But I don't want you to hurt him more than he's hurt, and when we move into it, we do that. We blow it up more. . . .*

Mrs. Johnson: *All right, I think if we don't express some support to him I think that we will lose the entire love and devotion of all the people who have been with us, or so drain them—*

LBJ: *Well, you get a hold of Clark and Abe [Fortas] and them and tell them how you feel about that. You'll see what advice I'm getting. I'm late now, and I'm going to make three speeches, and you can imagine what shape I'm in to do it. So don't create any more problems than I've got. Talk to them* *about it. Anything you can get them to approve, let me know. . . . I don't see any reason publicly, because then . . . you confirm it; you prove that you're a part of it. You just can't do that to the Presidency, honey! . . .*

I would try to get Abe and Clark to let me talk to Mrs. Jenkins. . . .

Mrs. Johnson: *All right, she's called me this morning, honey. . . . She is so hysterical and so bitter that . . . it's dreadful. She feels that her life is ruined, that their life is ruined, and it's all been laid on the altar of working for us.*

LBJ: *Well, is she angry at us?*

Mrs. Johnson: *Yes. You see, she doesn't believe any of this. She believes it's a framed, put-up job.*

LBJ: *Well, I think somebody better go talk to her and tell her the facts. And I think maybe he ought to . . .*

Mrs. Johnson: *I will try to be discreet, but it is my strong feeling that a gesture of support to Walter on our part is best.*

LBJ: *I'd make all the gestures I could, but I don't think that I would put myself in a position of defending what we say in the public in a situation like this because we just can't win it. The average farmer just can't understand your knowing it and approving it or condoning it. . . .*

Mrs. Johnson: *Are you unalterably opposed to the job offer?*

LBJ: *I am publicly. I am not unalterably opposed to giving him anything and everything we have. All of us. And letting him know it through Tom and through Abe and through you, but I see no reason why I ought to be tried again and blow it up and make the headlines that I gave him advancement because he did this! And I don't think that you'd have a license five minutes with a station being operated by someone like that. . . . I don't think the job is the important thing. . . . The finance is the minimum thing, honey.*

Mrs. Johnson: *I think a gesture of support on some of our part is necessary to hold our own forces together.*

LBJ: *Well, talk to Abe and Clark about it.*

Mrs. Johnson: *My poor darling, my heart breaks for you, too.*

LBJ: *I know it, honey, and—*

Mrs. Johnson: *And I suppose I will let you go now. But if I get questioned, what I'm going to say is that I cannot believe this picture that's put before me, this man whom I've known all these years. . . .*

LBJ: *Does she know that he walked in after he left the* Newsweek *party voluntarily in the YMCA?*

Mrs. Johnson: *I'm not sure that she does.*

LBJ: *Don't you think Tom ought to tell her, or Abe, right quick? . . . They were all afraid to tell her . . . and I think they ought to tell her what happened* *there. I think that's the first thing that's got to be done so she can understand. The second thing that's got to be done—they've got to tell her whatever we have, they have. Let's ride this thing out for two weeks. . . . Does she doubt that we are?*

Mrs. Johnson: *Yes. . . . She just said, "You ruined my life and you ruined my husband's life, and what am I going to tell my children?"*

LBJ: *Well, how did we ruin it?*

Mrs. Johnson: *Honey, she just sees her life being ruined around her, and she's got to reach out and lash at somebody. And she thinks it was overwork and overstrain, and that caused him to do whatever he did.*

LBJ: *Well, I think that's conceivable. I think that's likely. But I didn't take him to the cocktail party and I didn't get him tired and I didn't know it and I never asked him to work anytime that he didn't want to. Somebody's got to give her the other side. . . . That's why I said you ought to go out last night. They wouldn't allow that. . . . So Abe or Eddie Weisl or some of them better go see her this morning, because if we don't, she will be talking to the papers.*

Mrs. Johnson: *She will, darling. . . . If you don't mind me going to see her, if I can get the company of somebody like Ed Weisl or Tom Corcoran or anybody, I will. . . .*

LBJ: *I don't think you realize the First Lady can't be doing it. . . .*

Mrs. Johnson: *My love, my love. I pray for you, along with Walter. Goodbye. . . .*

LBJ: *Have Abe go see her, if he could. Or have a priest go talk to her.*

Mrs. Johnson: *All right. You are a brave, good guy, and if you read where I've said some things in Walter's support, they will be along the line that I have just said to you.*

LBJ: *You think I ought to call her?*

Mrs. Johnson: *Yes, I do. I do. I think we ought to offer support in any way we can.*

LBJ: *Well, why don't you talk to them and try to call her and tell her I'm in the plane, but I . . . asked you to call her . . . and tell her anything we have, they have. You can't put him with the station with the license. Do you understand that?*

Mrs. Johnson: *I hear you when you say it. But I'd just almost rather make an offer to do it, and then let the license go down the drain.*

LBJ: *Well, that doesn't do anybody any good, does it? Offer him something else—running the ranch.*

Mrs. Johnson: *All right, okay. . . . Goodbye, my beloved.*

Despite her husband's reservations, Mrs. Johnson would make her statement in support of Jenkins. And despite the story's scandalous overtones—particularly in 1964, five years before the gay rights movement was ignited with the Stonewall riots in Manhattan's Greenwich Village, and thirteen years before the election of San Francisco's Harvey Milk, the first openly gay man in America to win public office—the affair faded quickly, with no political ramifications for Johnson.

JACK VALENTI: The problem with Walter could have been a serious political blow [but for] the way the President handled it—[and] I think Mrs. Johnson's marvelous compassionate statement made on behalf of the family.

I really believe that Mrs. Johnson, and again I'm only speculating, had no desires about making political gains. Walter Jenkins was like her blood relative and she wanted to tell Walter that "we understand and we're with you even though by necessity, by hard political necessity, we have to do the things we have to do, such as accept your resignation."

■ ■ ■

Declining the Johnsons' employment offer, Jenkins left the glare and unrelenting pace of the White House and returned to Austin, Texas. He became a management consultant and construction company head, separating from his wife, Marjorie, in the early seventies but remaining married to her until his death in 1985. While his resignation was accepted gladly given the potential political fallout, Jenkins's relationship with the Johnsons, though mostly dormant for the balance of Johnson's presidency, would ultimately remain intact.

So, too, would the relationships between the Johnsons and most of their White House staff. Liz Carpenter, Marvin Watson, Harry McPherson, Tom Johnson, Larry Temple, Joe Califano, Jack Valenti, Bob Hardesty, Jim Jones, Harry Middleton—all, and many others, would say they loved him, and that he changed their lives.

LYNDA JOHNSON ROBB, elder daughter of Lyndon and Lady Bird Johnson: He knew he drove people, but he didn't drive anybody more than he drove himself. [L]ook at all the people who loved him—who considered themselves Lyndon's boys—and who would do anything for him. Having all that power heaped on your shoulders can be difficult; sometimes he had to ventilate. But he really loved [those] people.

■ ■ ■

In spite of the trials the relentless, hard-driving president put them through, they became wistful later when the summertime of their lives turned irrevocably to autumn.

JOSEPH CALIFANO: For all the tragedy and disappointment, for all the excitement of engagement and achievement, and, yes, for all the infernal frustration of working for a man who pushed you to the limit of your mental, emotional, and physical endurance from early every morning to late every night, and then had the balls to ask for more—for all that, to most of us the Johnson years were the most productive and exciting of our lives.

JACK VALENTI: [W]e were part of a brief but shining moment when we uncaged the better angels and set them loose to magnify hope in this free and loving land. It was a wonderful time; it was a difficult time. What we accomplished was glorious but what we accomplished came hard.

BILL MOYERS: [C]haracter is something that presidents transcend. And those of us who worked for him were willing to forgive his personal flaws, as he forgave ours, because in his best moments he had such a large and generous vision of America as a prosperous, caring, just society.

FINISHING FRANKLIN ROOSEVELT'S REVOLUTION

As Johnson pursued the legislative agenda unfinished by his immediate predecessor, pulling it "out of the ditch," he began laying the groundwork for his own agenda by picking up one unfinished by another president, one he would emulate more than any: Franklin Delano Roosevelt.

BILL MOYERS: It was February or March of 1964. I remember that particularly because we were approaching the thirty-first anniversary of the [first] inauguration of Franklin Roosevelt. It wasn't an anniversary most of us took special note of, except President Johnson, who seemed never to forget it. Franklin Roosevelt was the towering figure by whom he measured his own success.

He called me into the Yellow Room of the White House. . . . [H]e was working with a white-paper pad. . . .

[H]e had written "November 22, 1963," and then a column of months that went to January 19, 1965, and then another from January 20, 1965, to January 19, 1969, and from January 20, 1969, to January 19, 1973. He had added that up: nine years plus two months. Further down the page he had underlined "twelve years," and then there was "110 months" and "144 months." I subsequently realized that the 144 months referred to FDR's time in office, and 110 to the prospective or putative time Johnson would have in office.

He said, "Look, I've just been figuring out how much time we would have to do what we want to do. I really intend to finish Franklin Roosevelt's revolution." All of us [had] heard that at one time or another. "In an ideal world, that's how much time we would have; we would have 110 months to his 144 months. But of course he's laid the foundation down. I'll never make it that far, of course, so let's assume that we have to do it all in 1965 and 1966, and probably in 1966 we'll lose our big margin in the Congress. That means that in 1967 and 1968 there will be a hell of a fight."

But he was thinking of the future. He said, "I want you to start pulling together the best minds you can, in the government and in the universities, anywhere you can find them. I want you to pull in the best minds and we're going to start thinking about a program."

He said in this same conversation, "This is Kennedy's program and we're going to get it through, but if we're going to compete with Roosevelt's revolution, it's got to be Johnson's program and it's got to be bigger than anything that has been envisioned so far. But we're not smart enough to do it alone."

■ ■ ■

In April 1964, Johnson summoned Bill Moyers and Richard Goodwin, a Kennedy holdover and now a Johnson speechwriter, to the White House pool. As the three men skinny-dipped—bathing suits were an unnecessary formality, as they had been for JFK—the president, despite the ostensible frivolity of the moment, was all business. "We've got to use the Kennedy program as a springboard to take on Congress, summon the states to new heights, create a Johnson program, different in tone, fighting and aggressive," he barked at his young charges. "Now, boys, you let me finish the Kennedy program. You start to put together a Johnson program, and don't worry if it's too radical or if Congress is ready for it. That's my job."

The following month, before an audience of more than eighty thousand at the University of Michigan in Ann Arbor, the program would be packaged and proffered to the nation by Johnson as "The Great Society." The term was coined, or at least appropriated, by Goodwin, and had been used by Johnson in a few earlier speeches of less significance. After those soft launches, Johnson—riding an approval rating of 77 percent—rolled it out at the university's 120th commencement ceremony, said to be the world's largest. Bespectacled and clad in a black ceremonial robe, the president declared:

> *For a century we labored to settle and to subdue a continent. For half a century we called upon unbounded invention and untiring industry to create an order of plenty for all of our people.*
>
> *The challenge of the next half-century is whether we have the wisdom to use that wealth to enrich and elevate our national life, and to advance the quality of our American civilization.*
>
> *Your imagination, your initiative, and your indignation will determine whether we build a society where progress is the servant of our needs, or a society where old values and new visions are buried under unbridled growth. For in your time we have the opportunity to move not only toward the rich society and the powerful society, but upward to the Great Society.*
>
> *The Great Society rests on abundance and liberty for all. It demands an end to poverty and racial injustice, to which we are totally committed in our time. But that is just the beginning.*

Imploring the 4,943 graduates to enlist in the cause of the Great Society, Johnson concluded, "So let us from this moment begin our work so that in the future men will look back and say: It was then, after a long and weary way, that man turned the exploits of his genius to the full enrichment of his life."

It wasn't just Michigan's graduating class that Johnson needed to convince; it was lawmakers on Capitol Hill who would be needed to turn the Great Society into more than just the lofty words of a commencement address. There Johnson had a distinct advantage. "Knowledge of human nature is the beginning and end of political education," wrote Henry Adams in *The Education of Henry Adams*. If so, Lyndon Johnson, self-conscious of his Texas State Teachers College diploma, may have been the most educated man in Washington.

JOHN CONNALLY: He studied individuals with whom he was working. [H]e studied every member of the Senate; their strengths; their weaknesses; their needs.

He knew their wives; he knew their children; he knew their shortcomings. He knew what they were interested in, and he would figure out how he could provide what they needed. This was the way he operated.

LEE C. WHITE: LBJ's mastery in achieving legislative goals was an acknowledged fact of life during his career. There were numerous facets to his prodigious skill. While majority leader in the Senate, he learned every member's political situation at home, what issues were near and dear to his/her heart, what committee assignment was coveted, and what time of day was best to negotiate with the member. He knew the gritty details of key legislation. He knew the sense of accomplishment that the body would have collectively in a record of achievement; and he knew how to count. But, in my view, central to his technique was single-mindedness. He would establish a target and somehow every action and thought would be focused on that objective until it was accomplished, and then another issue would be elevated to the target position.

HUBERT HUMPHREY: Johnson was like a psychiatrist. Unbelievable man in terms of sizing people up: what they would do, how they would stand up under pressure, what their temperament was. This was his genius. He used to say to me many times, "You've got to study every member of this body to know how they're really going to ultimately act. Everything about them, their family, their background, their attitudes, even watch their moods before you even ask them to vote." He was a master of human relations when it came to that Senate.

JOHN BRADEMAS, U.S. representative, Indiana (D), 1959–81: I was invited to this [White House] reception. And I greeted the President, and the President said, "Good to see you," or something like that and he said, "I was glad to see you got that defense contract in your district this week." Pause. "And I'm sorry you couldn't be with me on the farm bill."

It's almost breathtaking to appreciate the degree to which he was informed on such matters.

■ ■ ■

Johnson's unrivaled ability to gain the support of reluctant lawmakers, or anyone else for that matter, was legendarily known around Washington as "the Johnson Treatment," or simply "the Treatment," since there was little doubt as to who was applying it. Using every inch of his long six-foot-three-inch frame to overcome his subject, Johnson plied his unique brand of persuasion with all the subtlety of a Mae West come-on. "Lyndon Johnson just towered over me and intimidated me terribly," said Robert Strauss, who gained renown for his own political persuasiveness. "He's the one person who had my number all his life. He was the best I ever saw. Tragic, but the best I ever saw."

In their 1966 book, *Lyndon B. Johnson: The Exercise of Power*, reporters Rowland Evans and Robert Novak described Johnson's technique in this way:

> *Its tone could be supplication, accusation, cajolery, exuberance, scorn, tears, complaint, the hint of threat. It was all these together. It ran the gamut of human emotions. Its velocity was breathtaking, and it was all in one direction. Interjections from the target were rare. Johnson anticipated them before they could be spoken. He moved in close, his face a scant millimeter from his target, his eyes widening and narrowing, his eyebrows rising and falling. From his pockets poured clippings, memos, statistics. Mimicry, humor, and the genius of analogy made The Treatment an almost hypnotic experience and rendered the target stunned and helpless.*

HUGH SIDEY: Way back when he was [Senate] majority leader, he took me down to the [LBJ] Ranch one time for a couple or three days. That was my first introduction to him and I remember it vividly. He pulled a book out of the bookshelf and all of a sudden turned to me and said, "Hugh, do you know the difference between a sheriff and a Texas Ranger?"

I said, "No, Mr. Leader, I don't."

He said, "Well, if you shoot a Texas Ranger, he just keeps coming on." And it struck me all those years that I covered him, that was kind of like Lyndon Johnson. He just kept coming on no matter what.

■ ■ ■

If there was a downside to Johnson's tenacity and persuasive powers, it was that he approached every situation with the same all-out, no-holds-barred sense of urgency, which made his appeals seem more about political power than principle. The Treatment itself often overshadowed the results that Johnson's leadership brought to key issues.

GEORGE REEDY: This mastery of debate technique actually hurt him in a very strange sort of way, because he'd throw himself into the most trivial arguments with all the same force that he would into the most important argument. He would argue just as hard to get a painter to reduce a bill for painting his house by forty dollars as he would to get a civil rights bill through. And the result was that after a while, people would begin to get the impression that he wasn't sincere about anything. That anybody putting all this force and all this vehemence into so many different aspects of life just couldn't mean it. I think the truth was that he really liked to argue, that it was a compulsion with him. Because this man, I'm convinced, was terribly sincere about certain things for which he was not given credit for sincerity.

THURGOOD MARSHALL, solicitor general, 1965–67; U.S. Supreme Court justice, 1967–91: That's the difference when you talk to him man-to-man; he's talking from his heart. When he does things, it doesn't seem so, but when you actually talk to him, the basic instincts of that come out, I mean, he has no reason to persuade me about it—no. I've got one solid vote. That's all I've got. I don't even control my wife's vote. But, of course, he had to use his political acumen to get these things through Congress. There is no other way to do it.

■ ■ ■

Just as he operated when working with his staff, Johnson observed few boundaries when dealing with Congress, aggressively challenging members on their views, berating them at times, and calling them at all hours for reasons large and small, but also extending unexpected kindnesses.

GERALD R. FORD, House minority leader, Michigan (R): Lyndon on a couple of occasions got quite irritated at my nitpicking [as opposition leader in the House]. And Lyndon had a thin skin on occasion, and I've forgotten the quote, but I think it was, "There's nothing wrong with Jerry Ford except he played football too long without a helmet." Well, you know, that was kind of a backroom comment but it got good publicity. [F]rom that [point] on, we had less than the best of relations.

JAKE PICKLE: [One] time he called [Democratic representative from Ohio] Wayne Hays, the notorious Wayne Hays, one morning about two-thirty or three o'clock. He said, "Wayne, I hope I'm not disturbing you."

Hayes says, "Why, no, Mr. President, I'm just lying here hoping you would call."

JOHN BRADEMAS: I was leaving home one night about seven o'clock. The phone rang and the operator said, "This is the White House. The President is on the line." I said, "Good evening, Mr. President."

He said, "Johnny, I see it's your birthday. If I had thought about it, I would have spent fifty cents on you. I know that young fellows like you could be out making a lot of money, but they prefer to serve their country. I appreciate it."

■ ■ ■

The word *ruthless* has often been applied to Johnson. Much of this has to do with accounts of his years in the House and Senate, as he plotted his ambitious ascent up the political ladder, always focused on the next rung. The legend of Johnson's stolen 1948 Senate seat—almost certainly true—adds to the impression of Johnson as the wheeler-dealer politician determined to win at all costs, especially after being burned himself by voter fraud perpetrated by the opposition in 1941. But while Johnson could be petty, he was hardly ruthless. Particularly when he was president, but going back to his Senate and House years, too, his prowess in getting legislation passed was based on fostering relationships with lawmakers through accommodation, compromise, and establishing common ground. Ruthlessness burns bridges; Johnson was smarter than that.

DOUGLASS CATER: He was guilty of a lot of things, but the one thing that escaped my ken—and I only knew him from 1950 on, after he became minority leader and then majority leader—I never saw him do a ruthless thing to somebody else. If somebody can name a specific act, I'm willing to listen.

BOBBY BAKER, secretary to the Senate majority leader, 1955–63: His favorite saying was, "Any idiot can kick the barn down, but it takes a pretty good carpenter to build one." Lyndon Johnson knew that you had to have fifty-one votes. He and Senator Dirksen were dear friends, yet Dirksen could never understand how he got so many votes. It was because Lyndon Johnson was always helping someone.

BARRY GOLDWATER: I never could quarrel much with the way he operated. He was heavy-handed; he was high-handed, he was a dealer. You could go to him in private and say, "I'd like to get this done. Now, how am I going to do it?" And he'd say, "Well, you do this for me and I'll do that for you." He was a great back scratcher. I don't think we've ever had a man in the Senate that so many people owed so much to in a personal way. And as a result, he had real power, and he used that power.

GEORGE MCGOVERN: Johnson was a doer. He wanted to get things done. I admired [him]. I thought he was a very capable, unusually capable, man. Very talented man in terms of understanding our political process. And from the very first, I was impressed by him. I didn't walk away thinking he was a blowhard politician. I saw a first-rate mind and somebody that loved government, loved politics.

■ ■ ■

Of course, it was a different day in Washington then. Party divisions weren't drawn like battle lines; congressional districts weren't gerrymandered to the point of being safe havens for one or the other party, breeding political extremism; the absence of cheap and abundant flights across the country meant that instead of commuting from their home states, congressmen made their homes in and around the district—their kids were classmates or teammates, their wives played bridge together. As a practice, partisan rancor was dropped after five o'clock, differences put aside, and cocktail glasses often hoisted.

GEORGE H. W. BUSH, U.S. representative, Texas (R), 1967–71: My view is that he was a good man—very good to me. My father served in the Senate with him and knew him, I'm sure, far better than I did, and he respected Lyndon. And I [asked him], "Why do you respect Lyndon?" And he said, "His word is good. He would tell us, 'There's going to be a vote at 3:30 p.m. for this bill, and here's the way it's going to work. It's going to come up, and there's going to be this amendment, and it's going to be voted on . . .' And dad said you could put it in the bank. You could make your plans, do what you needed to do, and know exactly [what would happen.] Just the fact that a guy like my dad, from the other side of the aisle, felt that way about him—I've never forgotten that.

TOM JOHNSON: He would be very unhappy that there is such extreme divisiveness [today] between the political parties and many other factions in our society. He genuinely believed in the biblical expression "Come, let us reason together." He was a master of bringing leaders of different sides together.

■ ■ ■

Johnson got 58 percent of his 217 requests passed by an obliging Congress in 1964, making it the most productive session since Eisenhower garnered a 65 percent success rate a decade earlier. A June 23, 1964, telephone conversation between Johnson and Everett Dirksen, the Republican senate majority leader, shows the ease with which business was conducted across the aisle, as Dirksen pressed the president for planning funds for a proposed dam project in his home state of Illinois:

Everett Dirksen: . . . *There is planning money in the bill for the Kaskaskia River Navigation Project. Now, all I want him to do is to have [General] Graham say to the Committee that the engineers do have construction capability for fiscal 1965 and it is only $25 or $50,000—that will be enough to nail things down. The total cost of the project is, I think, $30 some million. Now, it is in that area of Illinois that is distressed and already Kaiser Aluminum and a half dozen other plants have option sites in that area just waiting for the time when this thing can be finished so that they can barge coal out of there and raw material. And it is going to be the making of the southern thirty counties of the state.*

LBJ: *Let me get on that and I'll call you back.*

Dirksen: *All right. I just wanted to be sure that General Graham was apprised.*

LBJ: *Now, you're not going to beat me up on excise taxes and ruin my budget this year? I have Ways and Means holding hearings and we're going to come up with a recommendation one way or the other, but please don't beat me up on that. You can do it if you want to and you can ruin my budget, but you're hollering economy and trying to balance it. I cut the deficit 50% under what Kennedy had and if you screw me up on excise taxes, I'll have hell.*

Dirksen: *Well, look at the pressure I'm under.*

LBJ: *I know it but you're also for good fiscal prudence and you know the way to do this is through the Ways and Means House Committee—you know they're not going to let you write a bill over in the Senate on taxes. Please don't press me on that. Give me a few of your Republicans because I just don't have the votes to do it without you.*

Dirksen: *You never talked that way when you were sitting in that front seat [as Senate majority leader].*

LBJ: *Yes, I did when my country was involved. I voted for Ike one time when Knowland voted against him. I cast a vote on his foreign aid and brought it out of the committee.*

Dirksen: *You're a hard bargainer.*

LBJ: *No, I'm not. I'll look at this and see what I can do and call you right back.*

Dirksen got his funds, and Johnson got his excise tax cleared by the Senate Finance Committee.

A political pragmatist, Johnson didn't begrudge lawmakers a vote against him if voting in his favor would have hurt the lawmakers politically, because he had been there himself, conscious of the whims of voters. "You can't ask a man to cast a vote that'll beat him," he often said.

ROBERT STRAUSS, friend of LBJ: I remember once asking him, "Why did you cast that vote, Mr. President?" "Bob," he said, "one thing you'll learn someday is that you have to be a demagogue on a lot of little things if you want to be around to have your way on the big things." I'll never forget him saying that. A lesson in primer from the Master.

■ ■ ■

Having attained the highest political office, it was the big things that interested Johnson: a chance to make the country better—and to make his mark—through sweeping legislative reform. By the end of 1964, in addition to the Tax Bill and the Civil Rights Act of 1964, Johnson saw passage of the Food Stamp Bill, the War on Poverty, the Urban Mass Transit Act, the Housing Act, the Wilderness Act, the Fire Island National Seashore Act, and the Nurse Training Act. The Great Society had begun in earnest. But even as the groundwork for Johnson's domestic agenda was being laid, the jewels in his presidential crown, Vietnam began creeping cancerously into the White House.

NO MEN WITH UMBRELLAS

Long before Vietnam became a metaphor for a presidential quagmire it was an obscure former French colony in Southeast Asia, not much larger than New Mexico. Following the French defeat at Dien Bien Phu by Vietnamese forces seeking independence, the country was temporarily partitioned at the Seventeenth Parallel by the 1954 Geneva Peace Accords, with elections to reunify the country scheduled for 1956. These elections never happened, and the result was North Vietnam and South Vietnam. The former fell under the Communist rule of Ho Chi Minh. The latter became a noncommunist state, led in two years' time by Ngo Dinh Diem, a Catholic who would strive to consolidate power to the exclusion of the majority Buddhist population. Diem's weak regime was propped up by American economic and military aid, which was needed to ward off the Communist insurgency of the Viet Cong, a guerrilla force aided by Ho Chi Minh, who had designs to reunify Vietnam.

The political ambitions of Ho Chi Minh may have had little consequence to the United States but for the prevailing cold war doctrine of the time: the domino theory. It held that the fall of any nation to communism would lead inexorably toward increased regional instability and the swift capitulation of neighboring nations to the same influence. Accordingly, Eisenhower and Kennedy instituted policies to support the South Vietnamese government through financial subsidy and to provide military advisers who helped train South Vietnamese military forces, at a cost of $1 billion in seven years' time. Throughout Kennedy's administration, Vietnam remained a trouble spot that continued to fester. With the tacit backing of the Kennedy administration, a military coup occurred on November 1, 1963, resulting in Diem's assassination.

LBJ: They had just—with our encouragement—assassinated Diem before I went into office [as president]. They sent a cable to Kennedy who approved it. [Afterward] we found it difficult to put Humpty Dumpty together again. With all Diem's weaknesses, it was not easy to tear that government apart and put it together again.

I don't believe assassination is ever justified. They were ruthless people. Sure, Ho Chi Minh was. But I mean it was ruthless of the United States government, with our boasted list of freedoms, to condone assassination because you don't approve of a political philosophy. I don't believe the ends justify the means.

■ ■ ■

The new administration failed to bring stability to South Vietnam, which continued to lose ground to the Viet Cong. After Kennedy's assassination, Johnson immediately took on these problems. "Those first few days," he remembered, "Vietnam was on top of the agenda, before the visiting heads of state got home from the funeral."

Harry Truman once remarked, "The only thing new in the world is the history you don't know." Truman, a voracious reader who by age fourteen had read every book in the library of his hometown of Independence, Missouri, fortified his knowledge of history by devouring books on the subject. Never much taken by books, Johnson was not so much a student of history as he was of human nature. There he paid attention, picking up on the weaknesses and frailties of those around him in the corridors of power the way a dog senses fear, often exploiting them for political advantage.

Since coming to Washington in 1931, Johnson drew manifest lessons from the mistakes made by heads of state stemming from weakness that set the course of history. During Johnson's first term as a congressman, in 1938, British prime minister Neville Chamberlain appeased Adolf Hitler with the belief that he was offering his countrymen "peace for our time," while instead allowing for the German occupation of Czechoslovakia, the unchecked invasion of Poland, and the beginning of World War II. As the war wound down, Franklin Roosevelt, in not taking a firmer hand with Joseph Stalin at the Yalta Conference—where allied leaders met to discuss the fate of the postwar world—opened the door for the Soviet domination of Eastern Europe and the Soviets' attempts to spread their influence across the globe. Truman, FDR's successor, while keeping the Soviet wolf at bay by drawing bold lines in the cold war through a strict policy of containment, sent U.S. troops into battle in Korea without being fully prepared for what lay ahead as American support slipped. For the first time an American war ended in a draw.

During Eisenhower's eight White House years, while Johnson was Senate minority and then majority leader, the country was defined by its geopolitical position versus the Soviets. Any Soviet gain—a country falling to Communist rule, an American citizen yielding to Communist sympathies—was evidence that the Red Menace was knocking at America's door, giving rise to the domino theory and McCarthyism. Fear was the great motivator. In 1959, when Cuba's U.S.-backed military dictator, Fulgencio Batista, was overthrown by Fidel Castro's Communist guerrillas, bringing communism to the Western Hemisphere, Johnson believed the Eisenhower administration hadn't done enough to prevent the insurgency. "I think we ought to have stopped Castro in Cuba," he said later. "Ike sat on his fanny and let them take it by force."

In 1957, when the Soviets showed the world their superiority in space exploration through the orbital launch of Sputnik, a satellite no larger than a beach ball, Johnson was a catalyst for improving the country's shoddy space efforts. As he later asked rhetorically, "What American wants to go to bed by the light of a Communist moon?"

Kennedy also got into the act as a presidential candidate in 1960, exploiting American fears of a nuclear missile gap with the Soviets, less a reality than a campaign tactic effective enough to win him the White House in the thinnest of victories over Ike's vice president, bona fide cold warrior Richard Nixon. Kennedy's inaugural rhetoric—"We shall pay any price, bear any burden, meet any hardship, support any friend, oppose any foe, to assure the survival and success of liberty"—amounted to cold war bravado. But he would soon stumble with the U.S. support of a botched military incursion against Fidel Castro's Communist government in Cuba at the Bay of Pigs. Emboldened by Kennedy's humiliation, the Soviets led the United States to the brink of nuclear war a year and a half later as American ships blocked the Soviets from moving nuclear warheads into Cuba.

Throughout his years in Washington, Johnson saw that weakness was never rewarded. When he said of Vietnam, "We're not going to have any men with any umbrellas," a pointed reference to the hapless Chamberlain, the message was clear: America would stand up to the Viet Cong. But for the new commander in chief, Vietnam began less as a conflict he was determined to win than as one he couldn't afford to lose. Lyndon Johnson was not going to be the first U.S. president to lose a war—and to the Communists, no less. And what began as a reflexive response to support Kennedy's policy in the region, overwhelmingly supported by Congress, his Cabinet, and the nation, would over time become the central crisis of Johnson's presidency.

BILL MOYERS: [I]n February and March of 1964 the war in Vietnam was just a tiny shadow across the vast horizon, something that occasionally took his time in meetings to which the rest of us were not party, downstairs in the basement with McGeorge Bundy. The rest of the time we were planning what we never calculated would be interfered with by any distraction as bloody or as violent or as destructive as the war in Vietnam.

Then [Johnson] said, "It will be a fight in 1967 and 1968 because the Republicans will have Nelson Rockefeller, who will be a very strong candidate. Once we get rid of Barry Goldwater, it will be the Rockefeller Republicans. We don't have much time. So we've got to do it now. We've got to get ready for the next year." Mind you, just then we had been in office barely four months. We knew the President was preparing to run. We figured that his opponent would be Barry Goldwater. We were just beginning to gear up for the campaign of 1964, and he was thinking beyond the campaign.

It seems to me, as I look back on those years . . . in every respect except one he always had a better eye for the horizon than anyone else around, except on Vietnam. That's a gap, a blank, and enigma that I haven't figured out yet.

DEAN RUSK: Every President since President Truman had come to the conclusion that the security of Southeast Asia was vital to the security of the United States; that if Southeast Asia with its peoples and its vast resources were to be organized by elements hostile to the United States that would create an adverse and major change in the world balance of power; and that it was in the interest of the United States to maintain the independence of these Southeast Asian countries, particularly those covered by the Southeast Asia Treaty Organization.

So when President Johnson became President, he found seventeen or eighteen thousand Americans in Vietnam under a policy which was clearly aimed at maintaining the independence of South Vietnam and Laos and Cambodia and Thailand.

[But] there was no advice to President Johnson from any of his advisers that we cut and run in Southeast Asia. President Johnson took office determined to carry out the main policies of President Kennedy. He did that both in domestic and foreign affairs.

CLARK CLIFFORD, member and chairman, President's Foreign Intelligence Advisory Board, 1961–68; secretary of defense, 1968–69: There are a great many people who would blame President Johnson for the extent of the involvement in Vietnam. I think what they overlook is that President Johnson inherited a situation that almost inevitably dictated a continuation of the policy. First it had been set by President Eisenhower, and there are some statements by President Eisenhower that just go right down the line on the importance of Southeast Asia and the significance of Vietnam. At one point President Eisenhower said, "If Vietnam should become Communist, the Free World would have lost some twelve million souls, and then the spread of Communism throughout that part of the world would be almost inevitable," some such language as that.

President Kennedy came along, and he had similar comments to make on Vietnam, telling about how important it was, and he made a comment one time, I think in 1963, in which he said, "We are in Vietnam, and let me assure you we intend to stay in Vietnam." So the President inherited that and what was even more important, he inherited his senior advisers from President Kennedy. . . . And they all said, this is the issue that is important, the domino theory is unquestionably so. You will remember if we'd known then what we know now, we never would have permitted Hitler to get started when Hitler went into the Low Countries and into Czechoslovakia and Austria; if he'd been stopped then we might have prevented World War II and the death of practically millions of young men in the world, so all of this was very much in their minds. And I must say at that time I accepted the policy of assisting the South Vietnamese to defend themselves against the Communist aggression. As time went on and some years later, as you may now know, I've arrived at a rather different conclusion, but the President proceeded at that time on the basis of a solid phalanx of advice from the main advisers in that field, that this is what we had to do.

■ ■ ■

While continuing Kennedy's policy in Vietnam, Johnson sent mixed signals about the extent to which he wanted the United States to be involved in the war. In February of 1964 he maintained that Vietnam's strife was "first and foremost a contest to be won by the government and the people of that country for themselves." Later in 1964 he rejected the notion of "send[ing] American boys nine or ten thousand miles away from home to do what Asian boys ought to be doing for themselves." America doesn't want to "get tied down to a land war in Asia," he believed.

During the course of the year, another cold war crisis arose when the U.S. Coast Guard detained Cubans fishing in U.S. territorial waters. Fidel Castro demanded the return of the fishermen and turned off the water supplies to the U.S. Naval Base in Guantánamo Bay to make his point. In the spirit of Truman's Berlin Air Lift, Johnson adroitly circumvented the problem while averting military engagement; the navy created its own water supply; and eventually the truculent Castro, a burr in the sides of Eisenhower and Kennedy since seizing power in 1959, backed off.

By the summer of the same year, Vietnam would grow beyond the "tiny shadow across a vast horizon" that Moyers had seen in the initial days of Johnson's administration. Three torpedo boats in the little-known Gulf of Tonkin, just twenty miles from North Vietnam, would irrevocably change that.

On August 2, the U.S.S. *Maddox*, an American destroyer, was fired upon during a routine intelligence-gathering patrol of the area. Reports also indicated another attack on the ship two days later, on August 4. Later it would be revealed that the firing on August 2 came from three North Vietnamese vessels. None of the strike attempts made contact as the *Maddox* lumbered slowly southward unharmed. The president took action by asking Congress for a resolution supporting "the determination of the President . . . to take all necessary measures to repel any armed attack against the forces of the United States and to prevent further aggression" in Southeast Asia. The resolution passed unanimously in the House and captured 98 votes in the Senate, leaving only two senators—Wayne Morse of Oregon and Ernest Gruening of Alaska, both Democrats—to cast votes of dissent.

CLARK CLIFFORD: I guess those were the two who voted against it, they both had the reputation of being mavericks, so nobody paid too much attention. The rest of the Legislative Branch of the government was absolutely solid. They said, "We've got to face up to this." It wasn't until quite a long time later that some of them began to backtrack, and then when they backtracked an effort was made to break down the background of the facts that led to the Gulf of Tonkin Resolution. My own view is that those in Congress who attempted to do that were never successful at it, but they made a real effort to try to prove to the public that they had been misled in the facts regarding the attack on some of our naval vessels in the Gulf of Tonkin and that having been misled they passed the Tonkin Resolution, whereas if they had not been misled they wouldn't have passed it. But I don't believe they ever quite sold that. So that as you look at '64, the support for our involvement in Vietnam in the Executive Branch was solid and the support in the Legislative Branch was solid. It was rare to find a voice that counseled caution or advised that we not do it. The support for our involvement there was really overwhelming.

Telephone conversation between LBJ and John McCormack, Speaker of the House of Representatives, Friday, August 7, 1964, 3:01 p.m.:

LBJ: *That was a good vote you had today.*

John McCormack: *Yes, it was very good. Four hundred to nothing. What'd the Senate do?*

LBJ: *Eighty-eight to two—Morse and Gruening.*

John McCormack: *Can't understand Gruening.*

LBJ: *Oh, he's no good. He's worse than Morse. He's just no good. I've spent millions on him up in Alaska. . . . And Morse is just undependable and erratic as he can be.*

John McCormack: *A radical.*

LBJ: *I just wanted to point out this little shit-ass [Ed] Foreman [Republican representative from Texas] today got up and said that we acted impulsively by announcing that we had an answer on the way before the planes dropped their bombs. . . . It's just a pure lie and smoke screen.*

Would Kennedy have ultimately chosen another path in Vietnam? Would he have cut and run rather than face entrenched involvement in a war that looked increasingly bleak? During the early part of Johnson's administration those questions were hypothetical, just as they were for other policy matters. Then Kennedy loyalist Kenneth O'Donnell wrote an account in *Life* magazine's August 7, 1970, issue stating that Kennedy had planned to pull out of Vietnam if he had won reelection in 1964. If so, he would have had to brave inevitable political fallout at a time when Gallup polls showed that 66 percent of Americans believed the United States should press on in Vietnam while only 19 percent believed otherwise.

Others, too, including Kennedy aide Arthur Schlesinger and friend Mike Mansfield, Democratic senator from Montana, had similar recollections. As with other elements of the Camelot myth the notion stuck, given further credence by the strident antiwar stance taken later by Bobby Kennedy, which provided a rub-off effect on JFK's legacy. But as with the selection of Johnson as vice president, John Kennedy may have had another mind on the matter than his brother. Moreover, none among Kennedy's Cabinet, nor the chief advisers and administrators of Vietnam policy, saw any inkling from Kennedy of a departure from the course he had taken from the onset of his administration.

DEAN RUSK: Kennedy never said anything like that to me, and we had discussed Vietnam—oh, I'd say hundreds of times. He never said it, never suggested it, never hinted at it, and I simply do not believe it.

■ ■ ■

There would be no ambiguity, however, in the path that Johnson chose; he committed fatefully to Vietnam—and it would soon take its toll.

RAY SCHERER, White House correspondent, NBC: We have to remember that when [Johnson] first got into Vietnam with the Gulf of Tonkin Resolution the country was behind him. It was a patriotic war at that point. But as things got worse and we had to send more troops over there and the body bags began coming home, the tide started running out.

DOUGLASS CATER: In January of 1965, some of us were gathered working on a domestic message around nine-thirty in the evening, and the President came in. We all stood up and he looked forlorn and said, "Where are we sitting?" Apparently he wanted to sit where we weren't sitting, which is the first time that had ever happened. Usually he sat and then we re-sat. He sat down, and either Bill [Moyers] or Joe [Califano] attempted to brief him swiftly on what we were doing there. He didn't hear a word of it. He said, "I don't know what to do. If I send in more men, there will be killin'. If I take out more men, there will be killin'. Anything I do, there will be killin'."

Now here was a man who was capable of ambivalence before larger issues. Here was a man who did have self-doubts.

THE PUBLIC MAN

While those in Johnson's presence caught the true essence of the man—genuine and unguarded, compellingly persuasive—the American public saw someone very different. Johnson carefully tailored his public persona to fit an image he thought to be presidential, enigmatically, an imitation of the patrician eastern establishment he scorned in private. But the image had a contradictory effect: instead of presidential, he came off as artificially refined, stilted, and ultimately less effective. His public performances were often, as Hugh Sidey once put it, "a nervous bow to the Harvard faculty," and therefore very "un-Johnsonian."

After Johnson's presidency, Harry Middleton, one of his former speechwriters who helped Johnson write his presidential memoir, became frustrated when Johnson rejected passages that were crafted around his authentic voice instead of what he deemed to be presidential. "The prose had to be stately and boring and dull before he really was able to latch onto it," Middleton said. Johnson forged his own public image in the same way. "He was forcing himself into a posture that he was really not comfortable with," was the take of George Christian, Johnson's press secretary, in the latter part of his presidency. "And I think it told."

BOB HARDESTY: He used to say it's necessary to be presidential when you're talking to a big group. And I think we all felt that if he were himself, that would help to mold what the presidency is. If the country had gotten used to the Lyndon Johnson we knew, his style would become presidential.

■ ■ ■

Compounding the problem was the passive medium of television, which reined in Johnson's overwhelming bigness, the way a giant might be constrained to a wooden crate, limiting him to the parameters of the two-dimensional screen. When one was in Johnson's midst, in a private meeting or a small group, one could sense his intensity and depth of feeling, which didn't come through on television. Johnson often looked blankly into the camera, usually behind spectacles that became one more barrier to his connecting with the audience.

One of the marks of great leaders is their ability to master the media of their age to communicate their message, touch the people, and gain their support. Thomas Jefferson used party newspapers—often anonymously—to cut down his opponents and promote his own agenda. Lincoln attributed his presidential win in 1860 to his "House Divided" acceptance speech for the Republican nomination, circulated widely in newspapers, and to the portraits taken of him by Mathew Brady, who was pioneering the fledgling art of photography. During the depths of the Great Depression, Franklin Roosevelt used the new medium of radio to carry his booming message of hope and compassion to the struggling nation. More recently, Barack Obama engaged voters on the Internet, which, against all odds, helped spark an insurgent movement to defeat Democratic front-runner and presumptive nominee Hillary Clinton.

While Kennedy and Ronald Reagan became virtuosos of television, using their wit and natural charisma to beguile audiences, the medium evaded Johnson. "I just think the television camera was just too impersonal," surmised Hardesty. "He couldn't personalize it in the way Roosevelt personalized the mike and envisioned in his mind that it was the American people. I just don't think [Johnson] could do it."

LADY BIRD JOHNSON: Unfortunately, I don't think he really made friends with the instrument, because he couldn't see those people out there. He liked to look at the audience out in front of him. He used to always fuss at the advance men if, in setting up a speech for him, he was on the platform and the audience was way out across the street. He wanted them right up where he could look in the eyes of the front row.

DEAN RUSK: When he would meet with a group in the State Dining Room at dinner or in the East Room, meet with a group of congressmen that he had invited down to talk with him, he could be the most eloquent, persuasive, convincing kind of person you ever heard in your life.

Now, when he got on television, he seemed to freeze up. He wasn't himself. He seemed almost frightened by the camera. This extended even to toasts in the White House for distinguished foreign guests. He would often use a teleprompter for those toasts, which was a little awkward from a point of view just of plain style. I don't know whether it was partly because he knew that John F. Kennedy on television was a hard act to follow, whether he felt that he might inadvertently make a slip that would cause some problems in our foreign relations, for example, or just what it was. But he clearly seemed to lack the kind of confidence on television, which he clearly showed in his private discussions, when the camera was not present.

HARRY MCPHERSON: I don't know how many people I've heard, very distinguished people, say after leaving a small meeting with Johnson, "My God, if people could only see him that way." But if you look back over a transcript of what he said in a small meeting, you see that he used arguments and told stories and made analogies that simply would not do on thirty minutes of television. Sometimes, after touching first base, he goes to left field, climbs into the bleachers, sells hot dogs, runs back down on the field, and circles the bases and comes home. You think he's never going to get to the point. But it all comes back with tremendous force and with great comprehensive power when he ends his argument, and it's damned near irresistible when he's at his best. This can't be done on television.

■ ■ ■

Perhaps because he was uncomfortable with prepared speeches and wary of the television camera, Johnson wanted his speeches to be brief. "I want a Gettysburg Address," he would challenge his speechwriters. "I don't want a long-winded speech."

JACK MCNULTY, staff assistant, 1966–68: [He spoke to us] about the brevity of speeches. "Take the number four," he said. "Now you guys have all been to college. Can you count to four? One, two, three, four? Am I going too fast for you, Jack? Harry? No?"

Well, I thought of a few four [-letter] words I know.

And he said, "Take love, and home, and food, and peace!" he said. "I know peace is five letters but it should have four."

■ ■ ■

Johnson's level of comfort, however, also had to do with his audiences. While his presidential version of himself was his own incongruous imitation of a member of the eastern establishment, he became more genuine, more unleashed, when the eastern establishment wasn't among those he was addressing. He was particularly effective in communicating to people whose lives he could relate to and improve through legislative means. Unlike the eastern establishment, they, at least, would be more likely to accept him for who he was and give him the approbation he hungered for.

GEORGE CHRISTIAN: He had a rapport with black audiences that I have never seen another white politician have, and I've seen a lot of white politicians speaking to black audiences. I don't know what it was. And he ad-libbed, he talked freely. He talked about aspirations; he talked about what he had done. He always liked to tick off the laundry list of what he was doing. But in some groups he was very effective and in others he just flat didn't bring it off as well. I think it depended in large part on the feelings he shared with the group he was addressing.

WILBUR COHEN: I watched him particularly in connection with older people, senior citizens, blacks, poor people, Mexicans. . . . The thing that impressed me was the empathetic way he could relate to those particular audiences. Of course, it would be ad-libbed, it would be anecdotal, it would be responsive, but that's what seemed to me to be so striking in connection to the point that when he got before television he would seem so uptight. And yet when he'd talk to a group of older people about Medicare, or educators about education, he was so down to earth, so realistic, so empathetic, that it is obvious that he had a capacity for that that was unrivaled among most political people.

■ ■ ■

Another group Johnson labored to win over—largely unsuccessfully—was the White House press corps. Two custom pieces of furniture in

Johnson's otherwise august Oval Office pointed to his compulsion with the news media's coverage of his administration: a long console containing three separate television sets on which Johnson watched the three network newscasts simultaneously; and a soundproof cabinet that housed a news Teletype, the kind that could be found sputtering out the wire services in cacophonous city newsrooms across the country.

The media landscape was less cluttered then, before the advent of cable television and the Internet, and media diffusion and fragmentation. Only a few properties mattered nationally: ABC, CBS, and NBC were the sole proprietors of the television airwaves (PBS, along with NPR, would come later, through Johnson's Public Broadcasting Act of 1967), and the print world was dominated by newsmagazines *Time* and *Newsweek*; newspaper strongholds *The New York Times* and *The Washington Post*; and wire services the Associated Press and United Press International. (General-interest magazine icons *Life* and *Look*, still popular, were beginning to wane, victims of the redundancy of national television.) Johnson treated every news story aired or printed as a referendum on his presidency, monitoring all of them—plus those of lesser properties—with the same manic attention he paid to the legislative process.

RAY SCHERER: One of the things that impressed me about Lyndon Johnson, and mind you a lot of things did impress me, was his extraordinary obsession with the news. He kept those three television sets—ABC, CBS, NBC—going all the time in his office. He had them on in his bedroom; he had the tickers next to him; bang, bang, bang, all day long. And if you said something about him on television, you'd probably hear about it the next day.

DOUGLASS CATER: Sometimes in the midst of a meeting, he would walk over and read the latest thing coming out of the ticker. Then he would open the bottom of it—it was in a soundproof cabinet—and would disappear down into the bowels of the thing to read it as it was actually being typeset out on the spindle. He wanted to get even farther ahead of the news before it could surface. It was just part of his kind of obsessive communications system.

■ ■ ■

Instinctively, Johnson used "the Treatment" on members of the press, currying favor as he would to win over a senator or congressman, assuring them if they took care of him, he would take care of them. "He was certainly the most unorthodox president any of us ever covered," NBC's John Chancellor said. "He worked harder at press relations than any president I have seen." The problem was it didn't work.

CHUCK BAILEY, Washington correspondent, Cowles Publications: [H]e failed in press relations at the White House because he felt he could deal with the press as he had when he was majority leader of the Senate. The Senate was a chummy place and I covered him on both ends and—there's no judgment implied here, but it was a lot easier for the Leader in the Senate to control his press relations; it was a lot easier for him to play favorites and co-opt. He never understood that he could not co-opt the White House press corps. He took a run at all of us in those first few months [of his presidency], particularly on weekends in Texas, riding around the Ranch, talking about land and the springs and this place and that place and how the more little pieces of land you have, the better off you are—that's an A. W. Moursund quote, not a Johnson quote, but that's the flavor.

He would try to co-opt. He never quite understood the arms-length relationship and he never accepted it. And that, in the end, is why he failed, because he started his press relations from a premise that was faulty.

FRANK CORMIER, White House correspondent, Associated Press: I'm sure no president ever paid such close attention to what was said and written about him, or had a thinner skin about it. Even in this age of twenty-four-hour news, I'm sure the old rules would still apply: If you wrote something that pleased him, you'd probably never hear about it; if you displeased him you could get a call from himself [*sic*], or maybe somebody like Jack Valenti would bring you the word, or at Christmas time you might get a gift-wrapped empty box. All of those things happened to me. . . .

Several times to any number of us, I'm sure, he made these grand offers of, "I'll help make you a big man in your profession if you'll see things my way." It was that blunt, and that just doesn't work with reporters. Where he ever got the idea . . . Maybe it worked in the Senate!

GEORGE REEDY: Everything was overdeveloped in Johnson. And Johnson could simply not understand why it was he could buy a reporter a drink and take him out to the Ranch, show him a good time, and that a reporter would write a story he didn't like. He could not understand that. . . .

Johnson assumed that the whole world was in an adversary relationship. That people were either for him or against him. And if they weren't for him, then he defined them as being against him. And, of course, once he put them in that classification they quickly became against him.

■ ■ ■

Still, as Johnson began his presidency throughout much of 1964, he enjoyed a brief honeymoon with the press. But given the fourth estate's instinct to challenge him and his leadership, and Johnson's natural sensitivity, his attitude toward them began to sour.

GEORGE REEDY: [The White House press corps was] fascinated by him. Because he was a fascinating personality. There was a period when he had the press eating out of his hands. That was the first six months he was in the White House. He kicked that away himself. I think that if he had walked in and casually announced that he had just come back from a walk on the Pedernales [River], I believe they would have carried it with a straight face.

But then, he'd get mad at them for some reason, and they couldn't understand it. He, himself, didn't really know what a good story was. He thought a good story was something that began, "Lyndon Johnson is a calm, collected statesman who is the finest representative of the American dream."

■ ■ ■

Just as reporters would naturally scrutinize his presidency, Johnson would do likewise to their reporting. "Of course, he did not take kindly always to all reporting," Walter Cronkite recalled. "And when he didn't, he let me know about it almost instantly." If Cronkite was on the air, that meant a call from the White House before his broadcast was over, which Cronkite would hear about from his secretary during the commercial break. If Cronkite was in Johnson's presence, it meant a more physical response. "[W]hen Lyndon Baines Johnson wanted to make a point to you—he was a strong man, a big man, and strong—and he literally would grab you by the coat lapels and pick you up by the lapels . . . and he'd pull your nose next to his, and from that position, at great discomfort for the recipient, you would learn precisely how Lyndon Baines Johnson felt about that particular issue and even more importantly about your reaction to it."

CHUCK BAILEY: The press was a target of opportunity. We were always hanging him out to dry, so to speak. I mean, every evening, every day, we went to press, we went on the air. He paid obsessive attention to what was written about him, so he had this love-hate thing going with the press. He never gave up trying to seduce us, but he'd always get a good lick in when he wanted to.

■ ■ ■

Occasionally, Johnson's challenges over what was being written about him bordered on the absurd. Once, when a story appeared indicating that he had driven around the Ranch at ninety miles an hour while slurping Pearl Beer from a paper cup, he protested, "They warp everything I do, they lie about me and what I do, and they don't know the meaning of truth." But neither denying that he was driving ninety miles per hour or drinking beer, he added, "That wasn't Pearl Beer. I never had it on the ranch." When another piece was written accusing him of declaring an oil portrait by painter Peter Hurd "the ugliest thing I ever saw," he reacted just as strongly. When asked what he had actually said, Johnson replied, "It's hideous."

The relationship between the president and the press, while amusingly disputative by the end of 1964, would grow more strained over time as his presidency fell prey to the unexpected vicissitudes of events, some beyond Johnson's control.

BOB THOMPSON, White House correspondent, *The Los Angeles Times*; Washington bureau chief, Hearst Newspapers: As Johnson's presidency became more and more embattled, his behavior became more and more erratic. He did these arbitrary things like being at war with the press, almost like King Lear. He did exaggerate and he did lie, but he was also a very, very proud man, and a man in whom there was a lot of compassion. You can't talk about Lyndon Johnson as you would a normal human being. With a normal human being you would say there were two different streams running through his consciousness. In Lyndon Johnson there were rampaging rivers.

■ ■ ■

If rampaging rivers coursed through the thirty-sixth president's mind, the latter years of his next term in office would rage just as turbulently, weighing on it in ways both obvious and untold. In the fall of 1964 a couple of developments would make headlines as reminders of the uncertainty of an increasingly complicated and dangerous world: Nikita Khrushchev was ousted by the Politburo, leaving unclear who would assume party leadership in the Soviet Union; and the Chinese successfully tested a nuclear device, making the world's largest nation a nuclear threat.

But as Johnson's first full year in the presidency drew to a close, he was riding high. In the wake of tragedy he had seen the country through a dark night into a hopeful morning. From a disregarded presidential understudy to a beloved leader, Johnson had gracefully, triumphantly made the lead role his own. And before the year was out, he would be rewarded with what would be, to that point, the biggest electoral mandate in American history. As he prepared for the presidential election of 1964—his last election—the waters were navigable, belying the strong currents to come.

LBJ greets crowds during his presidential campaign, October 1964.

Chapter 5

"ALL THE WAY WITH LBJ"

FOREBODING

That Lyndon Johnson relished power is undeniable. He spent almost his whole adult life working toward its pursuit, retention, and consolidation, and he exercised it with reflexive ease. Indeed, he basked in the power of the presidency almost imperially, as reflected in two stories of Johnson lore:

HUGH ROBINSON, U.S. Army aide to the president, 1965–69: [O]ne time we were flying [helicopters] off the White House South Lawn. And we had three pads set up on the South Lawn so three helicopters could come in at once and go off. [W]e were getting ready to go on a major trip, and the passengers [who would be going on the trip on *Air Force One*] were gathered in the Diplomatic Reception Room on the south side of the White House.

[A]s time went on, we had assignments [for] all the people; we had them identified. When we called out the aircraft number coming in [we arranged it so] that they would come out and get in the helicopters and fly out to *Air Force One* out of Andrews Air Force Base. Well, the President had his assignment, of course; he was in Helo One. And I told the President that when his aircraft was on the ground I would come and get him. 'Cause he was having a good time, glad handing all the people that were going to go with him on this trip.

And we were about two thirds of the way through, and the President walks out of the Diplomatic Reception Room onto the South Lawn and starts heading for one of the helicopters. And I went over and tapped him on the shoulder and I said, "Mr. President, uh, this isn't your helicopter."

And he said, "Major, they're all my helicopters."

BOB HARDESTY: I had just started to work for the president and we were staying down at the Ranch. He called me one morning and asked me if I wanted to go for a ride. So I got in his car—a brand-new Lincoln Continental—and he begins driving around the grounds. As we were driving, the president became irritated at the Secret Service follow-up car tailgating him so closely. He suddenly turned off the road and took off across the rugged countryside, hitting stumps and branches along the way, dragging half of the Hill Country with him. I thought he was going to tear the car apart.

We got back on the road, and the car started making noise. "Do you hear that, Robert?" he asks. "Put your ear to the floor and see if you hear anything." I thought it might be brush or something under the car. And he's very irritated and he says, "Goddamn it, Robert, put your ear down there and tell me if you hear anything." I said I didn't know what it was.

Then he calls the operator and says, "Get me Roy Butler!" Roy Butler was the one who['d] sold LBJ the car. And the operator calls him back and says that Roy Butler is in Europe. And he says, "Get me Henry Ford!"

■ ■ ■

But adding to the paradox of LBJ is that he approached the office of the presidency, the ultimate political prize, with what appeared to be genuine ambivalence.

DOUGLASS CATER: [W]e need to remember the complexity of this man. I think I'm the only journalist in America that does not believe that Lyndon Johnson was born lusting, from his first day, to be president. In January of 1960, when I was a reporter for *The Reporter* magazine, which had a circulation of less than two-hundred thousand but was widely read among key politicians, I saw him on the opening day of the Senate. He took me into his office, and I asked the question that any journalist would, "When are you planning to throw your hat in the ring?"

For two hours he told me why he would be the worst candidate for president that could possibly be imagined. You can say, "Oh, that's all a farce," except that he ended by saying, "Doug, every afternoon about this time my heart is like lead. I had a heart attack, and I'm not sure I've ever gotten over it."

A guy who may have ambitions to be president, who is talking to a reporter who is getting ready to go out and write a story, doesn't talk about his heart attack.

BARRY GOLDWATER: I never got the feeling that Lyndon Johnson wanted to be president. I got the feeling from some of his friends like Sam Rayburn and others that they wanted him to be president, but he never showed any signs of it.

LBJ: In 1960, Mr. Rayburn called me a candidate for president and opened an office. I closed that office. There were several reasons. One, I've never known a man who I thought was completely qualified to be president. Two, I've never known a president who was paid more than he received. Three, my physical condition—I just couldn't be sure of it. [Though] I've never been afraid to die.

Every time I addressed the Chair in 1959 and 1960, I wondered if this would be the time when I'd fall over. I just never could be sure when I would be going out.

DOUGLASS CATER: We know that in 1964 he told Lady Bird he was thinking of withdrawing. This was only days before he was nominated [at the Democratic National Convention] in Atlantic City.

LADY BIRD JOHNSON: I did have reason to think that he didn't want to run previous to 1964. He was wrestling with that demon very hard. I think he always would have, in the end, gone along with the machine, which was already rolling. He would turn away from it, I think, simply because he knew how hard it was going to be and that it was going to get worse.

I can't describe his feelings or why, except that I think he had an extraordinary feeling of reverence for the job of president and a good conception of just how hard it would be and how some of those lowering clouds that were on the horizon might rise up to storm proportions.

■ ■ ■

Johnson wasn't the only president to express a sense of foreboding about the office. Even before the seat was occupied, just prior to being inaugurated as the first president in 1789, George Washington confided to a friend, "I fear I must bid adieu to happiness, for I see nothing but clouds and darkness before me." The difference was that Johnson had been in the job and knew firsthand the toll it took. Yoichi Okamoto, Johnson's personal photographer, who spent perhaps more time up close with the president than any one White House staffer, albeit mostly behind the lens of a camera, surmised that he was called on to make between two and three hundred decisions a day, almost all of considerable weight and bound to alienate some individual, group, or constituency. The burdens were awesome.

Johnson expressed his reservations to others, too, talking openly to members of his staff about withdrawing his name in 1964, including a conversation with George Reedy around the South Lawn of the White House the night before he was scheduled to arrive at the convention. His natural insecurity was part of it. Lack of support from the liberal wing of the party, he believed, would prevent him from bringing the country together, which was more and more defined by a North-South schism. "To [the liberals] my name is shit and always had been and always will be," he complained. "I got their goddamn legislation passed for them, but they gave me no credit."

But the bigger part of his misgivings was worries about his health. Acutely aware of his mortality after his heart attack in 1955, Johnson would often lament the fact that "the men in my family die young." His father, maternal grandfather, and paternal great-grandfather had all died in their sixty-first or sixty-second years; he didn't believe he would live much longer than that himself. And he was haunted by childhood memories of a grandmother who was confined to a wheelchair after a stroke.

LBJ: The best way I know to put this: My best judgment told me in 1964 in the spring—May or June—that if the good Lord was willing and the creeks didn't rise, if we had the best of everything, I could get the job done. I could get my ideals and wishes and dreams realized to the extent I would ever get them realized, by March of 1968. The odds were that I could survive that physically—but there was no assurance, and there were grave doubts.

No one can ever understand who was not in the valley of death how you were always conscious of that. I would see [Woodrow] Wilson's picture and I would think of him stretched out upstairs at the White House and I would think, what if I had a stroke like my Grandma did, and she couldn't move her hands. I would walk out in the Rose Garden and I would think about it. That was constant. With me all the time.

■ ■ ■

Once again, what could have been a moment of triumph for Johnson—the chance to seize the overwhelming support of his party and earn the presidency in his own right—became an occasion for gloom.

BILL MOYERS: The fact is that Lyndon Johnson knew life as a scale that somebody was always trying to tip. Perhaps it was because he had known poverty as a child or because his mother had greater ambitions for him than his own dreams. But he was often melancholy when he should have been triumphant. I never understood that.

■ ■ ■

One wonders if the melancholy that Moyers and others observed in Johnson was due to another factor entirely. Johnson's extreme sensitivity, irascibility, portents of bleakness, titanic mood swings, even his monthly fluctuations in weight—all were hallmarks of depression, however mild. Moyers and Richard Goodwin worried about Johnson's erratic mental state in his second term, independently consulting psychiatrists to explain his condition. Joshua Shenk's book *Lincoln's Melancholy* offers compelling speculation that Lincoln suffered from a melancholy that can be credibly identified as depression. It explains much about Lincoln, and makes his triumph of will in keeping the Union intact under the unimaginably dark days of the Civil War all the more remarkable. Depression may also explain both Johnson's often erratic behavior and, given the enormity of the burdens he carried in the presidency—almost as formidable as those carried by Lincoln, particularly in Johnson's last years in office—his ambivalence in carrying them forward.

As always, Mrs. Johnson—her husband's "strength"—buoyed him as much as she could, crafting a letter of reassurance that he received on August 25 that held up his bravery to that of any of his thirty-four predecessors:

Beloved—

You are as brave a man as Harry Truman—or FDR—or Lincoln. You can go on to find some peace, some achievement amidst all the pain. You have been so strong, patient, determined beyond any words of mine to express. I honor you for it. So does most of the country.

To step out now would be wrong for the country, and I can see nothing but a lonely wasteland for your future. Your friends would be frozen in embarrassed silence and your enemies jeering.

I am not afraid of Time [which had recently written an article critical of Mrs. Johnson] or lies of losing money or defeat.

In the final analysis I can't carry any of the burdens you talked of—so I know it's only your choice. But I know you are as brave as any of the thirty-five.

I love you always.

Bird

Perhaps bolstered by his wife's missive, Johnson overcame his uncertainty. On August 26, the eve of his fifty-sixth birthday, he arrived in Atlantic City's Convention Center prepared to accept his party's crown by announcing his choice as a running mate.

Throughout the early part of the summer, there had been speculation about whether Johnson would tap Bobby Kennedy, still serving as attorney general as a holdover from his brother's administration. The two were as wary as ever of each other, so the prospect gave both men pause. But while Kennedy overcame his reservations, deciding that he would be receptive to an overture from the president, Johnson's held firm. In order to preclude the possibility of choosing Kennedy but not to single him out specifically, Johnson announced that none of his Cabinet would be in the running, narrowing the field and making Hubert Humphrey the odds-on favorite for the nod. Humphrey, the liberal Minnesotan who began in the Senate with Johnson in 1949 and had served as the Democratic majority whip since 1961, offered the ticket regional balance and placation to the party's liberal wing.

If Johnson's announcement of Humphrey held little surprise, the convention still offered the prospect of unscripted drama, which the soon-to-be-named running mate helped to diffuse. Prior to the start of the convention, a group made up largely of blacks from Mississippi called the Mississippi Freedom Democratic Party (MFDP) arrived in Atlantic City demanding to be seated at the convention in place of their state's all-white official delegation. In a televised hearing in front of the convention's credentials committee, MFDP co-founder Fannie Lou Hamer, the youngest of the twenty children of a Mississippi sharecropper, movingly testified of being intimidated, beaten, and arrested for trying to vote, making Americans aware—many for the first time—of the brutal obstacles blacks routinely faced relating to suffrage. Just 6 percent of black voters in Mississippi were successful when attempting to tender their voter registration during Freedom Summer, an initiative supported by activists throughout the Deep South. In Alabama it wasn't much better, at 19 percent. After Hamer's testimony, the committee was split over whether to seat the delegates, a development that threatened to disrupt the convention.

While Johnson may have been sensitive to the plight of blacks attempting to vote—and a proponent of voting registration reform—he also wanted nothing to undermine his party's unity at the convention. In an implicit quid pro quo, Johnson called on Humphrey to soothe the party's liberals and strike a compromise before naming him as his VP choice.

Telephone conversation between LBJ and Humphrey, August 14, 1964, 11:05 a.m.:

LBJ: *What you better do is . . . we better just really try to see if the Negroes don't realize that they've got the president, they'll have the vice president, they've got the law, they'll have the government for four years, that we'll be fair with them and just with them, and why in the living hell do they want to hand-shovel Goldwater 15 states?*

Do you see any good that can come from it? Can it get us any votes anywhere?

Hubert Humphrey: *Not one damn bit of good. Not one bit. We're just not dealing with what I call emotionally stable people on this, Mr. President.*

LBJ: *Now if we, on the other hand, have a fight on this and win, and we support Mississippi, it seems to me that all the poor Negroes in Atlanta and in Harlem will say, "Well, Johnson and Humphrey, look at them. They stood up for Mississippi at the convention so we haven't got much choice between Goldwater and him and so we just won't vote."*

Humphrey: *Well, we've got to settle it before the Convention. I know that.*

LBJ: *Adam Clayton Powell called up yesterday and said he'd been looking at Goldwater's voting record and it wasn't too bad and he wants a little pay off. And that's already started talking. Martin Luther King said, "Well I'll tell you this, between Mississippi and these things, Johnson, well I don't know, maybe the Negroes won't vote."*

We can't let it get to that point. Because we're gonna have a hell of a time having unanimous for it.

Humphrey's friend, fellow Minnesotan Walter Mondale, the head of a subcommittee tasked with resolving the situation, came up with an answer: The MFDP would be given two seats and the promise that their entire delegation would be seated at the party's next national convention in 1968. And the entire Mississippi delegation would be seated as long as they signed an oath in support of the convention's ticket.

FANNIE LOU HAMER, civil rights activist, vice chair, Mississippi Freedom Democratic Party: You know [getting two seats for the MFDP] wasn't nothing, and that's the beginning of my learning of politics. Now I learned politics at its fullest—well, that's where politics was in 1964, in Atlantic City, New Jersey. I will never forget what they put us through. You see, by me being a Mississippi housewife and never exposed to politics, or nothing else too much, because I was just a housewife, a farmer, and they couldn't understand why we had to—we didn't feel like that we had to take other people's word. So, they first began to kind of drill us on this when they told us, you know, that Dr. King—now, Dr. King, this was funny, too, because at first he had said that what we were doing was right and he'd help us carry it out. But it began to be pressure brought about on different people, you know. Like President Johnson . . . I'll never forget him either. Because the time I was testifying, it was a man there, very close, that told me that he said to get—told them people with cameras to "Get that goddamn television camera off them niggers from Mississippi and put it back on the convention," because, you see, the world was hearing too much. . . .

President Lyndon Baines Johnson. I've got a book somewhere here on it. But it was somebody very close that knew what was going on that said he said, "Take them cameras off"—see because I found out after then women and men from all over the country wept when I was testifying—because when I testified, I was crying too. But anyway after that time I think the President became very angry, especially with the black delegation, and a lot of the stuff they covered up. But we've been victimized so much that we didn't watch what was going on.

■ ■ ■

Though no credible account has Johnson uttering the words as alleged by Hamer, it wouldn't have been entirely uncharacteristic; he had used the word *nigger* before and would again (though some would argue that the term Johnson used was *nigra*, a pronunciation of "negro" used by white southerners that was often misinterpreted in the North.) Harry McPherson, who worked closely with Johnson for thirteen years, for instance, said he heard Johnson use the word *nigra*, especially when speaking with southern senators, but never the word *nigger*. But the fact that Hamer believed it when she offered her recollection more than eight years after the convention reflected a skepticism African Americans held toward Johnson then and later, despite the fact that earlier in 1964 he had passed the Civil Rights Act, which was more than any president had done for civil rights since Lincoln, and would go on to do far more for the black cause.

Whites from the South held Johnson at a distance, too. The official Mississippi delegation walked out of the convention and did not return. Afterward, the remaining twenty-one members of the MFDP were seated but not officially recognized, but the other southern delegations stayed put. With things smoothed out, the convention continued unruffled, and Johnson was nominated by unanimous vote.

"IN YOUR HEART YOU KNOW HE MIGHT"

On the other side of the country, at the Cow Palace in San Francisco, the GOP nominated as their presidential candidate Arizona senator Barry Goldwater, and as his running mate, New York congressman William Miller. The conservative Goldwater staved off a challenge from moderate New York governor Nelson Rockefeller, bringing to the surface ideological fissures in the party that ran along regional lines, with old-guard moderates from the Northeast squaring off against a growing conservative contingent in the South and West. Upon his nomination, Goldwater did little to mend fences with moderates, squandering a chance to unite the party before delegates packed their bags. Goldwater's now-famous line in his acceptance speech—"Extremism in the defense of liberty is no vice"—contained the seeds of the conservative movement but also of his defeat, putting off not only swing voters but also much of his own party. Only a fifth of the party's voters believed that Goldwater should be the Republican standard-bearer.

Even the candidate himself was doubtful about his chances as the party's nominee:

BARRY GOLDWATER: When Kennedy was shot, I told my wife, "That's it. I would have enjoyed running against Kennedy, because he would have talked with me about the issues across the country. Lyndon would never do that. Lyndon is not going to expose himself. He's in. He doesn't want to take a chance of weakening himself. I can't beat Johnson; nobody's going to beat Johnson. Not that he's so good, but the country's not ready for three presidents in two and a half years." And this came out to be the truth.

The general feeling of Americans was, "Give the guy a chance."

■ ■ ■

Goldwater didn't do himself any favors by conducting an uninspired campaign, keeping himself at arm's length from the people. His campaign slogan, "In Your Heart, You Know He's Right," was acknowledgment that while Goldwater wasn't likable, he made sense, an appeal as enticing as asking voters to stomach unpalatable medicine because it was good for them.

Johnson, on the other hand, ran the kind of Texas-style campaign where every hand was shaken and every baby kissed, allowing his stiff presidential persona to drift away as he became the accessible, countrified politician of earlier days. Riding around in an armor-plated limousine he would call to the people through a bullhorn: "Come on down to the speakin'. Y'all don't need to dress up. It's not formal. Bring the kids and the dogs and come on down to the speakin'." His exuberance, while giving his Secret Service detail heart palpitations, particularly less than a year after Kennedy's assassination, worked in revving up crowds and generating enthusiastic support for his cause.

The candidates established one ground rule before hitting the campaign trail, agreeing that they wouldn't stir up racial tension in order to gain political advantage. Two weeks after the Civil Rights Act went into law, riots broke out in Harlem, creating national news and the threat of white backlash, which could have amounted to an opportunity for Goldwater. Johnson worried that if civil rights became a focal point in the campaign, Goldwater would gain ground. But, fearful of history's judgment, Goldwater's campaign looked to his own ethnicity to take race off the table.

BARRY GOLDWATER: [Johnson] asked me if I could see him right after the convention, and I told him that I wanted to discuss the racial problem, that I thought it would be wise in not pushing it. Those were hot days, you know. And he agreed with me. He said, "All right, I'll make the release." I said, "Fine." I forget what it said, but in effect it was that neither one of us was going to exploit the racial issue, and we didn't.

LBJ: [Goldwater] came in, just wanted to tell me . . . that he was a half-Jew, and that he didn't want to do anything that would contribute to any riots or disorders or bring about any violence; because of his ancestry he was aware of the problems that existed in that field and he didn't want to say anything that would make them any worse.

■ ■ ■

The Johnson camp did, however, exploit fears among much of the American electorate that Goldwater, as commander in chief, might have a hair trigger when it came to using nuclear warheads. "In your heart, you know he might," critics said of Goldwater, turning his campaign slogan on its ear. Johnson was among those who worried about the Republican candidate. "We can't let Goldwater and Red China get the bomb at the same time. Then it would really hit the fan," he said. In one of the most controversial, albeit effective, television campaign ads ever produced, a little girl in a bucolic meadow counts as she plucks the petals from a daisy, unknowingly leading up to the countdown to a nuclear explosion as the camera zooms to a close-up of her eye, which turns into an image of a mushroom cloud from a nuclear explosion. As the cloud rises, Johnson, quoted from a speech, says, "These are the stakes: to make a world in which all of God's children can live, or go into the dark. We must either love each other, or we must die." The ad ends with a voice-over: "Vote for President Johnson on November 3. The stakes are too high for you to stay home." Though it was shown only once, the commercial's message hit home, ushering in the era of negative television advertising that has flourished ever since.

Goldwater offered no effective counterattack, quashing attempts by his staff that might have caused further damage to his campaign.

BARRY GOLDWATER: I had a movie my staff made, and thank God I caught it. I'd heard how bad it was. I was making a speech in Philadelphia and I made them fly a copy to me. I got a projector and looked at it. It was well done, but it was just wrong. It showed a Lincoln Continental going down [like] a bat out of hell, with beer cans coming out both sides. I said, "You're going to stop that. That's not going to be shown anyplace. I want every film destroyed."

Then another one came out that was even worse. It was in color. It depicted the times we were in as being "Hitler times," and even went so far as to say, "Venereal disease is on the increase because Johnson is president." It was being done by a man in Hollywood, a brilliant producer but no idea of ethics. So I don't think it was any worse a campaign than most of them are.

■ ■ ■

It was hardly a contest on Election Day. Johnson took 61 percent of the popular vote, besting Goldwater by over fifteen million ballots—the widest margin in U.S. history to that point—and garnered 90 percent of the votes in the Electoral College. Any southern stigma he might have encountered earlier had clearly been overcome: he was the first true southerner to be elected to the office since Zachary Taylor's election in 1848. (Tennessean Andrew Johnson was never elected to the office; Woodrow Wilson left his home state of Virginia in his mid-twenties; and Eisenhower was born in Texas but raised in Kansas, which he considered home.) He also had coattails: Democratic majorities in Congress grew by thirty-six seats in the House, and two in the Senate. "Landslide Lyndon," Johnson's disparaging nickname from his anemic and controversial 1948 senatorial primary win, now stuck without irony.

LADY BIRD JOHNSON: I remember the nomination, and the election, with no high sense of elation. I felt pride, and great happiness for the thousands of people who had worked so hard, but I think my chief emotions were simply satisfaction in people's faith in Lyndon and the renewed determination to help him use the next four years to the best of his ability to make some steps forward.

BARRY GOLDWATER: I just never fooled myself for one minute into thinking the campaign could have been won. People say, "What would you do differently?" I said, "When you lose 60–40, you couldn't begin to count the things that went wrong. If you lose by less than 1 per cent, you remember it the rest of your life." As a result, I never have had any bitterness about that campaign; I've never felt unkindly toward Johnson or Humphrey or anybody else.

THE LOOPHOLE

The results of the election, while overwhelmingly in Johnson's favor, contained a portent: among the six states that Johnson lost, excluding Goldwater's home state of Arizona, were five in the Deep South—Alabama, Georgia, Louisiana, Mississippi, and South Carolina—states usually a lock for the Democratic win column. In time they would become just as predictably Republican, diminishing the strength of the party, as Johnson had anticipated with the passing of the Civil Rights Act earlier in the year. But after the electorate had made its choice, Johnson allowed himself a rare moment to revel in victory.

MARIANNE MEANS: When he won in 1964 in that big landslide, he had a bunch of us down to the [LBJ] Ranch . . . and the mood was really sky high. A nearby small town had given him its used fire engine. Why they thought the President of the United States would want a fire engine, I do not know. But it was the perfect gift for him, and he got in this thing and steered it around, and he clanged the bell and everything—and as he swiveled around past me he yelled out, "This is why Barry Goldwater wanted to be President!"

■ ■ ■

The celebration didn't last long. Johnson held that when a president is elected he's a giraffe, but after six months he becomes a worm. As long as he stood tall, he was going to make the most of it, which meant getting back to work. "Now, look," he told an aide. "I've just been re-elected by the overwhelming majority. And I just want to tell you that every day while I'm in office, I'm going to lose votes. I'm going to alienate somebody. We've got to get this legislation fast."

BOB HARDESTY: [Johnson] said, when he came back to Texas—after the presidency—recalling those days, "I never considered the 1964 election a mandate. I considered it a loophole, and I figured we had to get through it as fast as we could before it closed."

JACK VALENTI: He would say, "I want ideas; let's move." "We don't have time," he would roar. He stormed through that White House like an impatient lion chafing at delay, galled by bureaucracy, never sleeping, and daring any of his assistants to doze while the leader of the Free World was in motion.

He shouted, "I want people around me who care. I want people who work for me who will cry when they see a little old lady fall down in the street."

He cornered each of his aides, saying, "Now let me tell you something: I want you guys to get off your asses now. I want you to work. I want you to think, and I don't want you to leave this building tonight until you have answered the call of every congressman and senator who called you that day. And goddammit, you treat them with respect, because they got elected and none of you guys ever even ran for constable."

NICHOLAS KATZENBACH: President Johnson was very conscious that the Great Society program had to be gotten through in the first two years [after his election], and he kept emphasizing that. He would say, "We're not going to be able to do it if we don't do it in these two years; it's not going to get done." At every cabinet meeting he would go into that. He really didn't understand why a lot of the cabinet secretaries were not on top of pending legislation. They had legislative liaison people to work on that, and occasionally one or two of them in a cabinet meeting weren't that familiar with just where their legislation stood. LBJ knew exactly where their legislation stood, and it was embarrassing if they didn't.

LARRY TEMPLE: He referred to his popularity much akin to Green Stamps. He said, "You've got this popularity, and what value is it if you don't spend it? If you don't spend it for something worthwhile, you may lose it; it may just dissipate and go away." He always was talking about spending that to get the legislation through or to get some action taken that he wanted to get done.

LAWRENCE F. O'BRIEN, special assistant to the president for congressional relations, 1961–65: It was Johnson's landslide in November of 1964 that turned the tide. Suddenly the Democratic membership in the House went from 258 to 295. The President had a mandate. He had the votes, and we intended to maximize power. He would propose legislation in every area of challenge. We were accused of the arrogance of power and strong-arming the Congress. I prefer to recall the spirit of that period as the exuberance of power.

The President spearheaded every effort, giving his programs deep and passionate attention. Every day, every hour it was drive, drive, drive.

■ ■ ■

One of the initiatives Johnson would drive through the halls of Congress would be legislation to ensure that Fannie Lou Hamer—and all Americans of color—would be able to vote, free and unobstructed. Far more than any civil rights legislation to that point, it would offer the prospect of real social change.

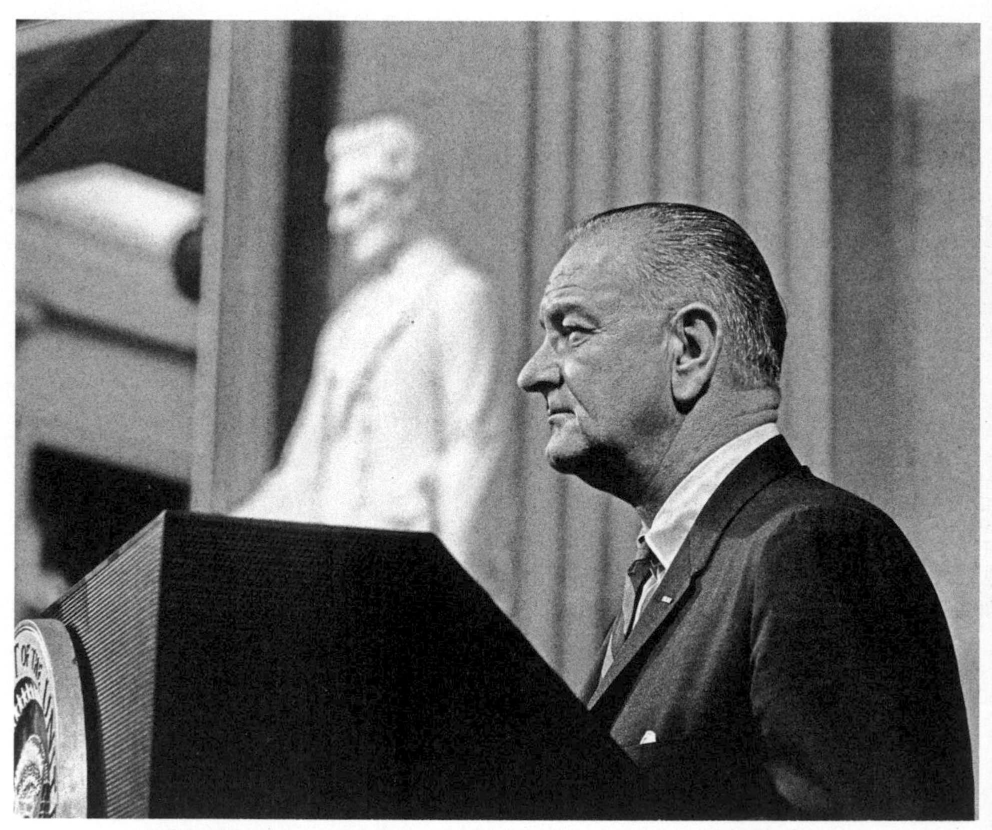

LBJ addresses a joint session of Congress on the Voting Rights Act in the shadow of Abraham Lincoln, March 15,1965.

Chapter 6

POWER AND GLORY

"WE SHALL OVERCOME"

The cover of *Time* magazine's first issue of 1965 would have been the envy of any politician: an artist's rendering of Lyndon Johnson standing strong and tall in a business suit, with his birthplace and beloved Texas Hill Country in the background, squinting unflinchingly toward the horizon—a man of vision. In the upper-left-hand corner, across the *T* in the magazine's iconic logo, appeared the words "Man of the Year." "There is a tide of affairs which, taken at the flood of 1964, led on to fame for Lyndon Baines Johnson," the feature story opened. "From that November afternoon when he made it clear that the torch of continuity was safe in his hands to that November night nearly a year later when he won by the biggest election triumph in history, it was his year—his to act in, his to mold, his to dominate."

Around the time that copies of the issue were being stuffed into mailboxes across America, the Eighty-ninth Congress was being sworn in at the Capitol, stronger in Democratic numbers than the Eighty-eighth and even more obliging of the president, as would soon be apparent. If Johnson had made his mark in 1964, the Eighty-ninth Congress would be virtually pliant to his vision for America, making 1965 among the most transformational years in American history. Medicare, the Arms Control and Disarmament Act Amendments, Arts and Humanities, the Immigration Act, the Poverty Act, Water Pollution Control, the Clean Air Act, Elementary and Secondary Education, Higher Education—all would be signed into law throughout the course of the year with sweeps of Johnson's official presidential pens, which turned from fountain nibs to ballpoint at midyear, a symbol of the changing times.

A record 1.2 million people turned up in Washington to be a part of Johnson's inauguration festivities on January 20, reflecting the nation's hope in him to lead the country forward. Johnson's attendance record would stand for forty-four years until Barack Obama's inauguration before an estimated crowd of 1.8 million people who witnessed a moment of jubilance that far transcended a republic's celebration of the peaceful transfer of executive power. One wonders if Johnson imagined that little more than a generation would pass until a person of color would take the same oath he had taken. Were his dreams for equal opportunity for a country rooted in racial injustice so audacious?

But Johnson knew that putting into law the right to vote among minorities would be the chief catalyst. Granting blacks equal access to public schools and public accommodations, as he had with the Civil Rights Act of 1964, was an important step in advancing the cause of blacks in America; giving them unrestricted access to the ballot, though, would give them real political power.

HUBERT HUMPHREY: Johnson used to tell me just simply this: "Let me tell you something, Hubert, [about] all this civil rights talk. The thing that we've got to do is get those blacks the right to vote. When they've got that vote power there will be no more of this segregation around here." He said, "That's what will shape up all these people in Congress, because they've got the swing vote." And he said, "Now you fellows are trying to get them public accommodations. You want them to ride in a bus"—and he'd go over all the little things—"but what they need is the vote. That's what I'm going to get them. I'm going to get them the vote power. When they get the vote power, they got the power. You wait and see. In any state where the blacks have got the vote power, you'll see their senators are much more willing to listen to their requests."

■ ■ ■

Still, much as he wanted it, Johnson the political pragmatist didn't think he could get voting rights through the Eighty-ninth Congress. In early January, before a joint session of the newly assembled body, he outlined his legislative priorities in his State of the Union address—poverty eradication, Medicare, and education—conscious that his call to knock down "every remaining obstacle to the right and opportunity to vote" would likely fall on scores of deaf ears. It had been just over six months since the Civil Rights Act of 1964 was passed by the Eighty-eighth Congress, and it was too much to ask, he believed, for another landmark civil rights bill to go through so soon.

The previous month, in a brief White House meeting, Johnson had stated his concern to Martin Luther King Jr., head of the Southern Christian Leadership Conference (SCLC), who had just returned triumphantly from Oslo where he had accepted the Nobel Peace Prize for the nonviolent movement for civil rights he had led since the Montgomery Bus Boycott of 1955. While King may have agreed with the president's read on Congress, he would not accept its complacency. If Congress was prepared to wait to guarantee blacks the right to vote, King would take the matter directly to the people, a strategy that Johnson advocated.

Soon afterward, King was plotting the next major campaign in the civil rights movement, targeting Selma, Alabama, as the battleground. Selma had a history of denying African Americans access to the ballot—less than 1 percent of possible black voters were registered—in large part due to Jim Clark, a villainous sheriff of almost cartoon-like proportions, who considered blacks "the lowest form of humanity" and wore a button that read simply, "Never." There, emblematically in the Alabama town where one of the last battles of the Civil War had been fought, King and the soldiers of the movement would "make it clear to the nation that we are determined to vote." In doing so, they would compel Congress to act.

On January 15, 1965, Johnson called King in Selma on the latter's thirty-sixth birthday. In a remarkable dialogue that leaves little doubt that Johnson and King were allies in the cause of civil rights, Johnson gave King counsel on how to structure his movement for voting rights to appeal to the fairness of the average American. King, in turn, offered Johnson political advice on how granting blacks an unrestricted right to vote would allow for a more moderate—more Democrat-friendly—electorate.

LBJ: *Just got down here to meet with the Prime Minister of Canada this morning and I thought maybe I better try to reply to your call.*

Martin Luther King Jr.: *I don't want to take but a minute of your time. First I want to thank you for that great State of the Union message. I think we are on the way now toward the Great Society.*

LBJ: *I'll tell you what our problem is. We've got to try with every force at our command—and I mean every force—to get these education bills that go to those people under two thousand dollars a year income. And this poverty [bill] is a billion and a half, and this health [bill is] going to be $900 million* *next year. We've got to get them passed before the vicious forces concentrate and get them a coalition that can block them. Your people ought to be very, very diligent in looking at those committee members that come from urban areas that are friendly to you to see that those bills get reported right out. Because you have no idea—it's shocking to you—how much benefits they will get. There's $8.5 billion this year for education, compared to $700 million when I started. Now, if we can get that, and we can get [a] Medicare [bill passed]—I ought to get that by February—and then we get our poverty [bill passed], that will be more than double what it was last year. Then we've got to come up with the qualification for voters [as voting registration reform]. That will answer seventy percent of your problems.*

King: *That's right.*

LBJ: *No tests on what Chaucer said or Browning's poetry or constitutions or memorizing anything else [as random tests to qualify black voters]. And then we may have to put [voter registrations] in the post office. Let the postmaster [do it]. That's a federal employee that I control. Who they can say is local . . . If he doesn't register everybody, I can put a new one in. They can all just go to the post office like they buy a stamp. I talked to the Attorney General, and I've got them working on it. I don't want to start off with that any more than I do with 14.B [of the Taft-Hartley Act], because we wouldn't get anything else [passed by Congress].*

King: *Yes, I well remember your message to me when we met at the White House, and I [was] very diligent in making this statement.*

LBJ: *Your statement was perfect about the votes. Very important. I just don't see how anybody can say that a man can fight in Vietnam but he can't vote in the post office.*

LBJ: *There's not going to be anything though, Doctor, as effective as all of them voting.*

King: *That's right.*

LBJ: *That'll get you a message that all of the eloquence in the world won't bring 'cause the fellow will be coming to you instead of you calling him.*

King: *It's very interesting, Mr. President, to notice that the only states you didn't carry in the South, those five southern states, have less than forty percent of the Negroes registered to vote. It's very interesting to notice. I think it's just so important to get Negroes registered to vote in large numbers in the South. It will be this coalition of the Negro vote and the moderate vote that will really make the New South.*

LBJ: *That's exactly right. I think you can contribute a great deal by getting your leaders, and you yourself, taking very simple examples of discrimination—where a man's got to memorize a Longfellow or whether he's got to quote the first ten Amendments or he's got to tell you what Amendment 15, 16, or 17 is and then ask them if they know, and show what happens. Some people don't have to do that, but when a Negro comes in he's got to do it. And we can just repeat and repeat and repeat.*

If you can find the worst condition that you run into in Alabama, Mississippi, Louisiana, or South Carolina—well, I think one of the worst I ever heard of was the president of a school at Tuskegee, or head of the Government department there or something, being denied the right to cast a vote. If you just take that one illustration and get it on radio, get it on television, get in the pulpits, get it in the meetings, get it every place you can; pretty soon, the fellow that didn't do anything but drive a tractor will say, "that's not right, that's not fair." And then, that'll help us in what we're going to shove through in the end.

King: *You're exactly right about that.*

LBJ: *And if we do that, we'll break through—it'll be the greatest breakthrough of anything, not even excepting the '64 Act. I think the greatest achievement of my Administration. I think the greatest achievement in foreign policy, I said to a group yesterday, was passage of the 1964 Civil Rights Act. But I think this'll be bigger. Because it'll do things even that '64 Act couldn't do.*

King: *That's right, that's right.*

LBJ: *That's exactly right. I think it's very important that we not say that we're doing this because it's Negroes or whites, but we can take the position that every person born in this country, when they reach a certain age, that he have the right to vote just like he has a right to fight—and that we just extend it whether it's a Negro, whether it's a Mexican or who[ever] it is.*

The campaign in Selma would expose Americans to far more than unfairness—it would expose them to insidious bigotry and violence that was impossible to ignore or accept. Beginning on January 2, demonstrations were orchestrated there over a period of weeks, the response to which would draw the nation into the story. National television coverage showed disturbing images of demonstrators being roughed up and arrested by Clark and his men, who were armed with cattle prods. Among those taken to jail for demonstrating, which had been outlawed for groups of more than three people, were hundreds of schoolchildren. The movement's momentum grew, along with America's awareness of the problem.

ANDREW YOUNG, executive director, Southern Christian Leadership Conference, 1964–70: We saw ourselves on the side of the Constitution, and we [thought the press saw itself] on the side of the Constitution, and we were sure that President Johnson and the Justice Department [were] on the side of the Constitution.

■ ■ ■

As outrage began to fester, Johnson publicly denounced the actions of Clark and his men and proclaimed his intention to use the Civil Rights Act of 1964 and the federal courts as a means of ensuring the enfranchisement of blacks—but stopped short of introducing voting rights legislation. It wasn't enough for King, who wanted nothing less than a law guaranteeing blacks the right to vote. As the demonstrations and violence in Selma continued unabated, Johnson was forced to reconsider, voicing his intention to press for a voting rights law. But with no specific plan from the president, King kept pushing, orchestrating a protest march from Selma to Montgomery, Alabama's capital.

Despite a ban imposed by Alabama's governor, George Wallace, six hundred demonstrators—excluding King, who had returned to Atlanta in the face of death threats—lined up in Selma on Sunday, March 7, and began their march. They didn't get far before state law enforcement officials repelled them in a horrific confrontation that would severely injure seventeen. Among them was John Lewis, the chairman of the Student Nonviolent Coordinating Committee (SNCC), whose skull was fractured. Dozens more sustained lesser injuries. The attack was picked up by national television, including ABC, which interrupted an airing of *Judgment at Nuremberg*, watched by forty-eight million viewers, to show for twenty uninterrupted minutes the scenes that had unfolded. Bloody Sunday, as the day would become infamously known, proved to be a turning point.

ROY WILKINS, executive secretary, 1955–64, executive director, NAACP, 1964–77: [T]he campaigners marched over the Edmund Pettus Bridge and were met by the Alabama State Police and the Dallas–Alabama County Sheriff's Department. Some of the law enforcement officers were mounted on horses. I don't recall whether the marchers were told to stop, but my recollection is that they were not. My recollection is that the law enforcement officers simply formed up a line and shot tear gas into the crowd, rode horses into the crowd, wrung their sticks, and generally stopped the march with an overwhelming display of force that was captured by television cameras and [that] shocked and stunned the consciousness of the United States. Suddenly a campaign which had threatened to be a disaster for the civil rights movement had caught fire.

RICHARD VALERIANI, NBC news correspondent: Television news came of age during that period. One of the things it did was, in the South, if there had been a demonstration—I remember somebody telling me, the wire service bureau would call the local people and say, "What happened?" And the Sheriff would say, "Well, there were these bunch of nigras who insisted on throwing their heads against my boy's—deputy's—clubs." And when we went down [to Selma] with our film crews, it forced the newspapers of the area to cover [the events] because they couldn't fake it anymore. [I]t was on the national screen and they had to do the same.

HAYNES JOHNSON, reporter and editor, *Washington Evening Star*: This was a piece of history we were watching. It had all the characters—it was biblical almost in its terms, and people instantly reacted to [the violence] as an American tragedy. And no writer could ever capture what you see in those films.

JOHN LEWIS, chairman, Student Nonviolent Coordinating Committe: People wanted action. There was a sense of righteous indignation. And [afterward] Dr. King made an appeal for religious leaders to come to Selma. And more than 1,000 people came in less than two days.

■ ■ ■

As the dust settled in Selma, Johnson called for a voting rights bill, while King committed to finishing the march from Selma to Montgomery later in the month. It fell to Johnson to determine how to protect the demonstrators, a task that Alabama governor George Wallace, who had made his name by upholding the Jim Crow policies of the Old South, would unwittingly help to ensure.

RICHARD GOODWIN, speechwriter for John F. Kennedy, 1959—63; special assistant to the president, 1964–66: Wallace sent a telegram to the White House saying he'd like to meet with the President to discuss the situation. Johnson said, "Well, you just come right ahead." [Wallace came to the Oval Office and he's] about 5'4", and Johnson is about 6'4". So, he leads Wallace in and he sits him down on the couch. Wallace sits down so he's now about 3' tall, and Johnson sits at the edge of [his] rocking chair leaning over him. And [Johnson's] Southern voice always deepened when he spoke to other Southerners. And he says, "Now, you agree that the Negro's got the right to vote, don't you?"

He says, "Oh, yes, Mr. President, there's no point about that."

He says, "Then why don't you let them vote?"

And he says, "Well, you know, now, I don't have that power. That belongs to the county registrars in the state of Alabama." And Wallace insists that, no, he didn't have the legal authority.

"Well, why don't you persuade them, George?"

He said, "Well, I don't think I can do that."

He said, "Now, don't you shit me about your persuasive powers, George. You know, I sit down in the morning when I get up, and I've got three TV sets lining up right after the other . . . and I had it on this morning, and I saw you when I pressed the button. And you was attacking me, George."

He says, "Well, I wasn't attacking you, Mr. President. I was attacking the whole principle of states' rights."

And he says, "You was attacking me, George. And you were so damn persuasive, I almost changed my mind."

Well, this goes on for a half hour or more and he finally turns to Wallace and says, "George, you and I shouldn't be talking about 1964, we should be talking about 1984. We'll both be dead and gone then. Now, you got a lot of poor people down there in Alabama, a lot of ignorant people. A lot of people need jobs, a lot of people need a future. You could do a lot for them, George. Your president will help you. Now, in 1984, George, what do you want left behind? Do you want a great big marble monument that says, 'George Wallace—He Built.' Or do you want a little piece of scrawny pine board lying across that harsh, caliche soil that reads, 'George Wallace—He Hated'?"

NICHOLAS KATZENBACH: That was the most amazing conversation I've ever been present at. Because here was Lyndon Johnson, the consummate politician, and George Wallace just didn't know what was going on at that meeting.

■ ■ ■

After their three-hour meeting, Johnson spoke to the press and discussed his meeting with Wallace. LBJ said, "I told the Governor that the brutality in Selma last Sunday just must not be repeated," and furthermore that Wallace "agreed that he abhorred brutality and regretted any incidence in which any American met with violence." Painted into a corner to protect the demonstrators in their planned march from Selma to Montgomery, Wallace, citing lack of funds, would later cede the responsibility to Johnson, who would mobilize 1,800 Alabama national guardsmen for the purpose.

Johnson then went to work on lawmakers. Seizing the moral high ground and changing the public mood to achieve his legislative ends, he addressed a joint session of Congress on March 15, eight days after Bloody Sunday, to press for passage of his Voting Rights Bill. His speech would take him to rhetorical heights he would not see again, and would become among the most important and effective in American history. Written by Richard Goodwin with Johnson's inevitable micromanagement, it captures Johnson's best self in a voice as authentic and personal as in any speech he would deliver. For many African Americans who heard it, Johnson's pointed use of the phrase "We shall overcome," a borrowed reference to the Negro spiritual and now sung as a tonic by soldiers of the civil rights movement, was the most poignant and hopeful sign that their struggle was not in vain.

"I speak tonight for the dignity of man and the destiny of democracy," he began. "I urge every member of both parties, Americans of all religions and of all colors, from every section of this country, to join me in that cause." He continued:

> *At times history and fate meet at a single time in a single place to shape a turning point in man's unending search for freedom. So it was at Lexington and Concord. So it was a century ago at Appomattox. So it was last week in Selma, Alabama. There, long-suffering men and women peacefully protested the denial of their rights as Americans. Many were brutally assaulted. One good man, a man of God, was killed.*
>
> *There is no cause for pride in what has happened in Selma. There is no cause for self-satisfaction in the long denial of equal rights of millions of Americans. But there is cause for hope and for faith in our democracy in what is happening here tonight. For the cries of pain and the hymns*

and protests of oppressed people have summoned into convocation all the majesty of this great government—the government of the greatest nation on earth. Our mission is at once the oldest and the most basic of this country: to right wrong, to do justice, to serve man. . . .

We cannot, we must not, refuse to protect the right of every American to vote in every election that he may desire to participate in. And we ought not, and we cannot, and we must not wait another eight months before we get a bill. We have already waited a hundred years and more, and the time for waiting is gone.

So I ask you to join me in working long hours—nights and weekends, if necessary—to pass this bill. And I don't make that request lightly. For from the window where I sit with the problems of our country, I recognize that from outside this chamber is the outraged conscience of a nation, the grave concern of many nations, and the harsh judgment of history on our acts.

But even if we pass this bill, the battle will not be over. What happened in Selma is part of a far larger movement which reaches into every section and State of America. It is the effort of American Negroes to secure for themselves the full blessings of American life. Their cause must be our cause too. Because it's not just Negroes, but really it's all of us, who must overcome the crippling legacy of bigotry and injustice.

And we shall overcome. . . .

The real hero of this struggle is the American Negro. His actions and protests, his courage to risk safety and even to risk his life, have awakened the conscience of this nation. His demonstrations have been designed to call attention to injustice, designed to provoke change, designed to stir reform. He has called upon us to make good the promise of America. And who among us can say that we would have made the same progress were it not for his persistent bravery, and his faith in American democracy. . . .

Above the pyramid on the great seal of the United States it says in Latin: "God has favored our undertaking." God will not favor everything that we do. It is rather our duty to divine His will.

But I cannot help believing that He truly understands and that He really favors the undertaking that we begin here tonight.

LBJ: I never was suspected of being very dramatic or colorful or a charismatic individual, but when I looked the Congress in the eye and said, "We shall overcome," it was very significant to me that some of my dearest friends, with whom I had associated through the years, who thought I was just another crooked Confederate, sat on their hands and wouldn't applaud. But I'm very proud to say that it was a matter of weeks until I signed the [Voting Rights Act].

LEE C. WHITE: [Johnson] wasn't a good orator, but he did a wonderful job on the Voting Rights Bill at the joint session of Congress. Everybody was feeling so good that night; we were back at the White House, and happily the Eisenhower notion of [having] no hard alcohol [present] had been scrapped. So we were walking around and enjoying ourselves, having a drink. The President says to [Larry] O'Brien, "Have you talked to Manny Celler"—the chairman of the House Judiciary Committee—"about hearings?" The message wasn't two hours old, and he already wanted to know if we've got hearings set up. And he said to me, "Have you called Ben Bradlee from the *Washington Post* to get a good editorial yet?"

I felt like a slackard. Here it was eleven o'clock at night and I hadn't called Ben Bradlee to get a good editorial for that wonderful speech, and we didn't have hearings set up yet. He had that way of always pushing and pushing and pushing. But those of us who were involved in it had the great benefit of seeing how it worked, and now we look back and see the accomplishments of the President in the civil rights field.

JOHN LEWIS: I was in the home of Dr. [Joseph H.] Jackson in Selma [where] we watched and listened to Lyndon Johnson. And there were two or three of us with [Dr. King], and when [President Johnson] said, "We shall overcome," I looked at Dr. King and tears came down his face, and we all cried a little to have the President of the United States say, "We shall overcome." And Dr. King said, "We will march from Selma to Montgomery. The Voting Rights Act will be passed."

■ ■ ■

King was right on both counts. His march culminated on March 25, ten days after Johnson's speech, as an army of twenty-five thousand, led by King himself, made the journey unharmed and unimpeded from Selma to Montgomery. Just over four months later, on August 6, the Voting Rights Act would be signed by Johnson in the Capitol Rotunda in the shadow of a statue of Abraham Lincoln. Like the Civil Rights Act, it had taken all the legislative skill Johnson could muster, but in the end the Senate rallied to the cause with a vote of 77 to 19, and the House 333 to 85.

MARTIN LUTHER KING JR., president, Southern Christian Leadership Conference, 1957–68: A president born in the South had the sensitivity to feel the will of the country and in an address that will live in history, one of the most passionate pleas for human rights ever made by the president of our nation, he pledged the might of the federal government to cast off the century's old blight. President Johnson rightly praised the courage of the Negro for awakening the conscience of the nation.

■ ■ ■

It was Johnson and King who brought the Voting Rights Act to fruition: Johnson, in King's words, "pledged the might of the federal government to cast off the century's old blight," as King "awakened the conscience of the nation." Just as both anticipated, the power of the ballot among African Americans would change the balance of power throughout the South and within the nation as a whole. Just two years after the Voting Rights Act went into effect, the eleven states of the old Confederate South saw voter registration among possible African American voters exceed 50 percent, except in Georgia, Louisiana, and Virginia, all at 47 percent, and in Mississippi at 35 percent. By 1968, African American registration in all southern states would far exceed the 50 percent mark, with the laggard, Mississippi, reaching 59 percent. While it would take longer for meaningful progress, the number of elected black officials would also increase dramatically. In 1964 there were only 79 elected officials in the South and 300 across America, a number that climbed to 6,170 and 9,040 respectively by 2000. By 2010 the total number of black elected officials in the United States reached approximately 10,500. Among them was Barack Obama, the fulfillment, to be sure, of the distant dreams of Lyndon Baines Johnson and Martin Luther King Jr.

A WAR FOR THE POOR

During the course of the "We shall overcome" speech, Johnson related one of his life's experiences that reflected far more than his passion for civil rights. His stint as a teacher of Mexican American children in Cotulla, Texas, at the age of twenty, gave him a sobering look not only at the ravages of racial injustice, but also at poverty, the fight against which would become the central pillar of the Great Society. Memories of his students "going through a garbage pile shaking the coffee grounds from grapefruit rinds and sucking the rinds for juice" stayed with him long after he had left and moved up in the world. "Remember those children in Cotulla," he would demand of his staff when working toward reform that would help those like those same children. It was them he invoked in his March 15 speech:

> *My students were poor and often came to class without breakfast and hungry. And they knew even in their youth the pain of prejudice. They never seemed to know why people disliked them, but they knew it was so because I saw it in their eyes.*
>
> *I often walked home late in the afternoon after the classes were finished wishing there was more that I could do. But all I knew was to teach them the little that I knew, hoping that I might help them against the hardships that lay ahead. And somehow you never forget what poverty and hatred can do when you see its scars on the hopeful face of a child.*
>
> *I never thought then, in 1928, that I would be standing here in 1965. It never occurred to me in my fondest dreams that I might have the chance to help the sons and daughters of those students, and to help people like them all over the country. But I do have that chance.*
>
> *And I'll let you in on a little secret—I mean to use it.*

ANDREW YOUNG: The biggest mistake that we have made, I think, is we have tried to make [Lyndon Johnson's contributions to civil rights] more of a black issue than it was. For Lyndon Johnson this was [part of being raised in] the South out of poverty. The poverty program wasn't about helping black people primarily. It gets linked up with the Civil Rights movement, but the Great Society was out of Lyndon Johnson's growing up as a schoolteacher in Texas and understanding what it was to be poor.

ROY WILKINS: In the first place, he was a poor man. He started poor. He understands poverty. He understands the limitations of people. His understanding of racial restrictions came largely with his contact with the Mexicans—Spanish-speaking people and how wrong people were treating them. And he looked around and found these conditions existing with respect to Negroes in his own country.

■ ■ ■

During the depths of the Depression, Franklin Roosevelt, in his second Inaugural Address, added the line "I see one third of a nation ill-housed, ill-clad, ill-nourished." Creatively using the instrument of government through his New Deal as no president had before, Roosevelt designed an arsenal of programs to address the issues affecting Americans head-on. Many of the New Deal's programs worked, including the National Youth Administration (NYA), in which Johnson served as Texas director for two years. Others failed. Part of the New Deal's centerpiece, the National Industrial Recovery Act, was struck down as unconstitutional by the U.S. Supreme Court. Still, Roosevelt's efforts, whether successful or in vain, gave the dispossessed comfort that they weren't being ignored; the president was aware of their plight and was doing what he could.

Since the Depression, no president had set his sights on poverty until it found its way onto Kennedy's agenda, sparked by his time in impoverished West Virginia during the election of 1960, where he won an all-important primary in the state in the face of long odds. In 1961 he pushed the Area Redevelopment Act through Congress, providing much-needed infrastructure throughout Appalachia. More broadly, he put into effect an experimental food stamp program, and the Manpower Development and Training Act, and the President's Committee on Juvenile Delinquency and Youth Crime, which provided a template for community action strategies. Other plans were on the drawing board, which Kennedy intended to carry out after his reelection in 1964. When Johnson took over in 1963, antipoverty carried over naturally to his agenda, a cause far more personal, drawn from the experiences of his youth and early adulthood. After learning of Kennedy's future antipoverty plan on his first full day in office, Johnson called it "my kind of undertaking" and ordered his aides to pursue it "full tilt."

LAWRENCE F. O'BRIEN: [Johnson] embraced the concept when it was proposed. Even the designation of it as a war on poverty underscored his often-mentioned concern about the poor, his often-repeated stories about his childhood and his youth. It was his nature to become almost emotionally involved in this subject. I think the whole concept of federal involvement in a program to reduce and hopefully eliminate poverty, which would be your blue-sky objective, [was] something that involved a strong personal commitment on his part. . . .

I think with Jack Kennedy there was an element of repayment. He felt that what West Virginians had put on the record regarding him, and their attitude toward him, deserved repayment. But the repayment went toward the heart of the problem in West Virginia: poverty and widespread unemployment. And Kennedy became totally caught up in it. Johnson was obviously caught up in it, similarly, but he approached it from a different background and experience. Both came out at the same place.

■ ■ ■

The difference was that Kennedy's program was a limited plan that stood on safe political ground. Johnson's plan would be far bolder and more immediate. He wanted to be nothing less than the president who put an end to poverty in America, and would combat it no less pressingly, comprehensively, and creatively than FDR had—even if the plight of poverty wasn't top of mind for the average American caught up in the halcyon haze of postwar prosperity.

LBJ: I realized that a program as massive as the one we were contemplating might shake up many existing institutions, but I decided some shaking up might be needed to get a bold new program moving. I thought that local governments had to be challenged and awakened.

JACK VALENTI: During the Christmas holidays at the Ranch in 1963, [President Johnson] closeted Kermit Gordon, Walter Heller, Bill Moyers and myself in his little guest house right off the main house, and he said, "We're going to abolish poverty in this country, and I'm going to lock this door and you guys can't come out until you bring me a plan to do just that."

So we labored and we labored and we came out. We didn't have the details but we had a cause, and we had a plan, and we had a name, "The War on Poverty."

■ ■ ■

Johnson declared "an unconditional war on poverty" in his first State of the Union speech, in 1964. "It will not be a short or easy struggle," he said. "No single weapon or strategy will suffice. But we shall not rest until that war is won." He made the lifting of the poor central to his vision for the Great Society, determined that the nation's population of 192 million would know of the poverty experienced by the 22 percent of Americans who earned less than $3,000 per year—and would resolve to fight back.

JOSEPH CALIFANO: He thought of the War on Poverty as an extension of the New Deal as helping people get in positions where they could be on their own and where they could pull off their own share of the economic pie. That was the reason for all the vocational education, health, but especially manpower training. It was a "hand up" rather than a "handout."

RAMSEY CLARK, assistant attorney general, 1961–65; deputy attorney general, 1965–67; attorney general, 1967–69: As far as I can see, he is the first president to be consumed with a desire and to communicate his consumption with the desire to eliminate poverty. Now, this was a matter of real vision, because he was far from the first, but he was the first major political leader to come out strongly and clearly for the elimination of poverty, which I think many can now see is essential in urban mass society.

■ ■ ■

Broadly defined, the War on Poverty would encompass nearly every aspect of the Great Society. A rash of laws would provide a more level playing field in education, health care, and employment opportunities, not only for those who were victims of racial bias, but for any American left behind unjustly. Other legislation would change the fabric and complexion of America through immigration reform, take steps toward protecting the environment, and make culture more accessible to the masses.

At its heart was the Economic Opportunity Act of 1964, which would bring just under $1 billion to battle poverty through various means. (By comparison, the New Deal's work appropriations would be funded at over $4 billion.) The multifaceted act included a community action plan designed to "give every American community the opportunity to develop a comprehensive plan to fight its own poverty—and help them to carry out their plans." It also created the Job Corps and Neighborhood Youth Corps, allowing for work study and training opportunities and a modest stipend for underprivileged youth. It secured funding for the Volunteers in Service to America (VISTA), which recruited young people to live and work in underserved communities in the same way that the Peace Corps had gotten youth involved in working in developing nations. It offered financial incentives to those hiring unemployed workers. And it provided for a new federal agency—the Office of Economic Opportunity (OEO)—to create and administer antipoverty programs, sometimes in conjunction with other agencies. On August 7, 1964, the night before the act was voted on in the House, Johnson outlined his vision for the Economic Opportunity Act in a phone call with Bill Moyers:

LBJ: *I'm going to rewrite your poverty program. You boys got together and wrote this stuff. I thought we were just going to have NYA [the National Youth Administration under which Johnson had served as Texas director under FDR's New Deal], as I understood it. You know what I think of the poverty program? What I thought we were going to do? I thought we were going to have CCC [Civil Conservation Corps] camps [like the New Deal].*

Bill Moyers: *We got that.*

LBJ: *I thought we were going to have community action, where a city or a country or a school district or some governmental agency could sponsor a project. The state highway department could sponsor it, and we'd pay the labor and a very limited amount of materials on it, but make them put up most of the materials and a good deal of supervision, and so forth, just like—*

Moyers: *We got that.*

LBJ: *I thought you'd let a college boy do the same thing, and a college girl.*

Moyers: *We got that.*

LBJ: *Now I never heard of any liberal outfits where you could subsidize anybody. I think I'm against that. If you all want to do it in the Peace Corps, then that's your private thing. That's Kennedy. But [in] my Johnson program I'm against subsidizing any private organization. Now if we had a hundred billion, we might need to. But with all the governmental agencies in this country, I'd a whole lot rather [Chicago mayor] Dick Daley do it than the Urban League. He's got heads of departments, and he's got experienced people at handling hundreds of millions of dollars. And every one of these places, I'd made them come in and sponsor these projects. I just think it makes us wide open, and I don't want anybody to get any grants. Now you got the grants [taken] out for farmers, didn't you?*

Moyers: *Altogether and got that thing out on handicapped that I mentioned to you last night. Everybody has to work.*

The field general whom Johnson chose in his war was Sargent Shriver, who had been tapped by President Kennedy, Shriver's brother-in-law, to run the Peace Corps. Shriver had taken the reins of the Peace Corps with the program's creation in 1961, and had little desire to leave. As with Johnson's recruitment of Earl Warren and Richard Russell as members of the Warren Commission, Johnson didn't so much ask Shriver to take the job as tell him, compelling Shriver to accept with virtually no advance warning or preparation. Shriver would find that improvisation would be a job requirement. He was given a broad charter—find out as much as you can about poverty and wipe it out—and little direction.

SARGENT SHRIVER: I think he gave me the job, or forced the job on me, because he thought it was going to be difficult to get it through Congress and he thought I could help get it through. He as much as told me that when I suggested men like Sol Linowitz or LeRoy Collins. He said to me, "Sarge, look, those men are excellent. But let me tell you something. It will take them a year to get their feet on the ground in Washington. It isn't a question of them being competent, but it's a question of just getting accustomed to what's going on down here and how to operate in Washington. We don't have a year. This thing has got to work. And it has to (a) get through Congress, and then (b) it has to work right away. It's going to get a lot of opposition; people are going to attack it. And we cannot afford to have it run by somebody who's inexperienced in Washington. You can get it through, and you can succeed in this very initial stage with it."

■ ■ ■

It also helped that the competent, charismatic Shriver came with the bright halo of Camelot around him, a great political advantage in 1964. An added benefit for Johnson was undoubtedly the great satisfaction of knowing that the Kennedy family would look dimly on Shriver's service to him. In a phone conversation with Johnson in December 1966, Shriver's wife, Eunice Kennedy Shriver, said, "[T]here have been situations—and you can imagine that there are, of course, with Bobby and Teddy, in which there have been questions in the past which Sarge could have decided one way in which he would never have been accused of disloyalty to you. . . . I've lived through this, so I know it. In every single case he's always said, 'I'm part of the Johnson Administration and this is the way it's going to be, and if your family doesn't like it, that doesn't matter to me.'"

With Shriver tapped to lead the charge in the War on Poverty, the Employment Opportunity Act of 1964 made its way to Congress. The act was not without its share of opponents. Many members of the GOP believed it would dilute the authority of states to combat the problem, and would result in the creation of a bureaucracy lacking in both efficiency and effectiveness. Racism was another factor, with many southern Democrats resisting the measure as another civil rights bill. A White House aide recalled presenting the bill to Wilbur Mills, Arkansas congressman and chairman of the Ways and Means Committee, who threw it across the room while offering "a few choice words about how he was not going to be involved in a program to help a bunch of niggers."

Johnson made two trips to Appalachia in the first half of 1964, to generate awareness about the depth of poverty in America and to show that it had a white face as well as a black one. As he told a reporter earlier that same year, "I don't know if I'll pass a single law or get a single dollar appropriated, but before I'm through, no community in America will be able to ignore the poverty in its midst." Turning up the volume on the problem worked. By summer, the country became attuned to the issue, which gained traction as a blight that needed to be removed. In July, two-thirds of the Senate approved the Economic Opportunity Act, which was then passed in the House by a vote of 226 to 185, and signed into law by Johnson on August 20. However, the controversy over the War on Poverty would not end with the act's passage. Before the Senate vote, in a debate on the Senate floor an impassioned Barry Goldwater wrote off the act as a "Madison Avenue publicity stunt," which portended further backlash from conservatives well after the bill became law.

JAMES C. GAITHER, staff assistant to the president in the War on Poverty, 1966–69: OEO was set up really without a program, [but with] a very ambitious goal, and a charter to go out and innovate and experiment and see if somehow we could provide an opportunity and give people a chance to escape poverty. None of these programs—Head Start, Upward Bound, Legal Services, Neighborhood Youth Corps—were in the original bill. They were all invented administratively by the administration. And we launched them nationwide. Now, it's rather phenomenal that many of them worked, and have worked extremely well. But we didn't know where we were going. We didn't have very precise goals other than eliminating poverty and understanding poverty.

■ ■ ■

Like FDR's New Deal, most of Johnson's War on Poverty programs would succeed, while others would fail. The latter would be used by conservatives to paint the War on Poverty as wretched government excess. To be sure, some of its failed policy gave them plenty of red meat to sink their teeth into. Community action, in particular, gave voice to angry African Americans liberated to some degree by civil rights legislation but still subject to oppressive urban conditions. In the wake of riots in Watts, a largely black section of Los Angeles—which occurred just six days after the Voting Rights Act was signed and caused the deaths of more than thirty bystanders and between $50 million and $100 million in damages—those voices seemed radical and ominous. Racial unrest in other American cities would follow, compounding those fears. To an even larger extent, the War on Poverty was hampered from the beginning by inflated rhetoric that was doomed never to match the magnitude of its promise. Could poverty in America ever be eradicated entirely?

Johnson's stirring call in the State of the Union address to end poverty was rebutted by Ronald Reagan nearly a quarter of a century later. In his own State of the Union address, Reagan, in 1988, contended that in the War on Poverty, "poverty won." The comment elicited snickers, and it was clear that Congress's—and the public's—appetite for ambitious social programs had diminished. If the Great Society was a grand experiment using federal government action to address social ills during a time of relative prosperity, the Reagan Revolution was its antidote. (Though, perhaps unaware of its origins, Nancy Reagan would make the Foster Grandparents program, a product of the OEO, one of her pet causes as First Lady.)

The OEO would come and go in ten years, dismantled by the Nixon administration in 1974. But almost all of its components—Head Start, the Legal Services Corporation, Job Corps, Foster Grandparents, Community Health Services, Upward Bound, Indian Opportunities, Green Thumb, and Migrant Opportunities—continue to survive in some form (with the last two now called Senior Community Service Employment and Seasonal Worker Training and Migrant Education respectively). The only program to be terminated outright has been the Neighborhood Youth Corps, which saw its last days with the OEO in 1974 after enlisting more than five million young Americans. It was as though the OEO had been a car that went to the scrap heap but was salvaged for nearly all of its parts.

Though the War on Poverty did not—could not—result in total victory, more battles were won than lost as statistics pointed indisputably toward poverty's weakened hold across the nation. According to U.S. Census Bureau data, the poverty rate stood at 21.9 percent when Kennedy took office and dropped slightly to 19.5 percent as Johnson assumed the presidency. By the time Johnson left the White House in 1969, the rate would fall to 12.1 percent, representing the greatest one-time reduction in U.S. history. Not since then has the rate of poverty come close to afflicting over a fifth of the American population as it did before Kennedy added it to his agenda and Johnson vowed to annihilate it. Poverty levels would hit their lowest number since the War on Poverty began when they fell to 11.1 percent in 1973, just before OEO folded its tent, and before peaking at 15.2 percent ten years later, during the Reagan administration. In 2008 the poverty rate stood somewhere in between, at 13.2 percent.

The African American population would see the greatest drop in poverty rates among demographic groups. The same census data shows that 55.1 percent of blacks lived below the poverty line in 1959, a number that would plunge to 32.2 by 1969.

JOSEPH CALIFANO: Johnson's relationship with his pet project—the Office of Economic Opportunities [*sic*]—was that of a proud father often irritated by an obstreperous child. For years conservatives have ranted about the OEO programs. Yet Johnson's War on Poverty was founded on the most conservative principle: put the power in the local communities, not in Washington; give people at the grassroots level the ability to walk off the public dole.

Reagan quipped that Lyndon Johnson declared war on poverty and poverty won. He was wrong.

JOHN GARDNER: I see a society learning new ways as a baby learns to walk. He stands up, falls, stands again, falls and bumps his nose, cries, and tries again—and eventually walks. Some of the critics now sounding off about the Great Society would stop the baby after his first fall and say, "That'll teach you. Stick to crawling."

"ALL THE EDUCATION THEY CAN TAKE"

In the Great Society's official unveiling, Johnson's speech at the University of Michigan in the spring of 1964, the president asserted that "our society will not be great until every young mind is set free to scan the farthest reaches of thought and imagination. We are still far from that goal." He then outlined the crisis in education that was brewing in America: the baby boomer population—babies born from 1946 through 1964—had markedly increased the number of students in schools and universities, by 43 percent, in the past decade; classrooms were overcrowded; curricula and teaching methodology were outdated; and teachers were overwhelmed, underpaid, and, in some cases, underqualified. As he pointed out, a quarter of Americans—54 million—hadn't graduated from high school, and 100,000 high school graduates every year lacked sufficient funds to go on to college.

JOHN GARDNER: [His speech] was an impressive example of how an effective leader can determine which problems receive national attention. No president before him had ever said anything remotely like that, and the statement released tremendous energies.

■ ■ ■

The reason that no president had made education a legislative priority to that point was that the notion of using federal aid to bolster American education had been met with predictable resistance in the halls of Congress, which had leaned toward funding at the state and local levels. Consequently, American schools as a whole were lacking. Johnson often invoked a saying that characterized the situation: "The kids is where the money ain't."

It boiled down to the three issues: Race had been among them. But the controversial issue of offering federal aid to states with segregated schools was neutralized by the Supreme Court's 1954 *Brown v. Board of Education* ruling striking down school segregation, and Title VI of the Civil Rights Act of 1964, which granted federal authority to enforce it. Religion was another stumbling block. Lawmakers disagreed on the level of support that should be allocated to parochial schools; Catholics from predominantly urban areas wanted inclusion in federal funding, while opponents, Protestants, pointed to the separation of church and state. Finally, there was the general wariness of federal government intervention in the lives of citizens, particularly by southern Democrats and conservative Republicans, who favored regional control of education and funding through local school boards.

The issue of education had personal resonance for Johnson. Education had rescued him from poverty, or at least a mundane and uncertain blue-collar future, and he wanted to use it to save others by giving kids in America "all the education they can take."

HUBERT HUMPHREY: He was a nut on education. He felt that education was the greatest thing he could give people; he just believed in it, just like some people believe in miracle cures.

■ ■ ■

Aware of the formidable challenges before him, Johnson sent Congress the Elementary and Secondary Education Act (ESEA) on January 12, 1965, as a means of bridging the inequities in American schools. It was composed of six titles, Title I being its most significant, providing federal aid for "educationally deprived children," and allocated to school districts with the highest composition of students from families earning $2,000 or less a year or those who were on public assistance. Sensitive to fears of government control, the bill granted districts the authority to direct the federal funds to schools themselves and for schools to offer funds to those students most in need. Other titles in the bill allowed for the funding of library resources, textbooks, and teaching materials to public and parochial schools (pacifying the wary Catholics); supplemental educational services and programs; educational research and teacher training; and grants to enhance state departments of education. The cost of putting the bill into effect would come to approximately $3 billion in the first two years; more than $4.5 billion would be set aside for fiscal years 1968 and 1969.

Putting the "entire power and prestige of the presidency behind it," Johnson spent the next six weeks micromanaging the legislative process. A little luck was with him. When Bill Moyers took a call from a prominent Baptist leader who called Johnson one afternoon to register concern over the unfair advantage ESEA would give Catholics, Moyers informed him that Johnson was swimming in the White House pool with Billy Graham, who was visiting the White House. "Is that with *our* Billy?" the caller asked. When Moyers, a former Baptist preacher, insisted that it was, assuring the caller that, regardless, Johnson would gladly be interrupted to take his call, he replied, "Oh no, no, no. Just give the President my very warm regards."

The bill's overwhelming support by Congress—263 to 153 in the House, and 73 to 18 in the Senate—gave Johnson as much pleasure as any that would pass throughout his presidency. "Since 1870, almost a hundred years ago," he stated, "we have been trying to do what we have just done for all the children of America. . . . We did it, by all that's good we did it and it's a wonderful proud thing. . . . This is the most important bill I will ever sign." He also called ESEA "the most significant education bill" in the history of the U.S. Congress. While he was given to hyperbole—Bill Moyers remarked that "hyperbole was to Lyndon Johnson what oxygen is to life"—there is little doubt that he meant every word of it. Returning to the tin-roofed one-room schoolhouse he attended as a child, just a mile and a half east of his ranch house, Johnson signed ESEA into law on

April 11 with his first-grade teacher, Kate Deadrich—"Miss Kate" to her young charges—by his side.

Nearly three years later upon signing amendments to ESEA, Johnson the former teacher boasted of providing special educational and health services to nine million of the country's poorest children, the creation of 3,600 new school libraries and 20 new regional laboratories for educational research, and opportunities for 17 million students to gain experiences outside the classroom in 2,200 new education projects. Moreover, by 1969, American high school graduation rates climbed to 32.5 percent, from 24.6 percent in 1964, an increase of 32 percent. In the same period, African Americans saw graduation rates jump 50 percent, from 13.8 percent to 20.7 percent.

LAWRENCE O'BRIEN: This guy's committed to quality education, and that was very impressive to me. We were all committed to civil rights [and] all committed to Medicare. But in education, particularly at the elementary-secondary level, that was conceived by many as an impossibility, and there was no way you could overcome the barriers. From my personal observations of the man, my feeling is that historians haven't noted how deep his commitment was in that field.

■ ■ ■

Higher education was Johnson's next concern. In mid-twentieth-century America, a college education was a luxury few could afford, this despite the G.I. Bill passed by Franklin Roosevelt in 1944, allowing returning veterans from World War II—many of whom would otherwise never have pursued higher education—to draw on federal funds to enroll in college or receive vocational training. In 1940, before the bill went into effect, 4.6 percent of Americans attended four years of college or more, a number that grew to 6.2 percent by 1950.

As with other Great Society measures, the bill Johnson handed to Congress, the Higher Education Act (HEA), was a scaled-up version of one Kennedy had drafted. The key title of the bill—one of six—was Title IV, which put college within greater reach for those with limited means by offering student grants, low-interest loans, and work-study options. (The student grants, limited to and initially awarded by a specific college, would later become Pell Grants, which are transferable among institutions.) Other provisions in the HEA allowed for additional library resources and personnel; improvement in the quality of teachers; and financial aid to "developing institutions," fledgling schools for black students that fell short of minimum standards of accreditation. Getting HEA through Congress required less heavy lifting for Johnson than had been necessary for ESEA. None of the issues getting in the way of federal funding for elementary and secondary education came to bear, and the bill passed with relative ease. Johnson went back to his alma mater to make it official on November 8, signing HEA into law in a gymnasium on the campus of what had become Southwest Texas State College, the last legislation he would sign publically in 1965. Mulling over the two dozen education bills the Eighty-ninth Congress had approved, including HEA, he bragged that it had done more for the cause of education than all previous sessions of Congress together.

HEA's modest $785 million annual price tag proved a worthy investment. From 1960 to 1970, the number of Americans attending four or more years of college grew by 39 percent, constituting 10.7 percent of the population, up from 7.7 percent.

RAMSEY CLARK: It's hard to remember that our expenditures at the federal level for education were only three billion dollars a year when he came in '64, and had risen four-fold to $12 billion dollars in four years. [I] think education was his real love—I think he sees it as the salvation of mankind.

LAWRENCE O'BRIEN: These laws [passed by Johnson] not only removed from our political debate sterile arguments over church-state relationships, they also ended the old repetitive and largely empty rhetoric of States Rights versus Federal Control. These laws, and others like them, signaled the birth of a new and more creative Federalism.

LBJ: My creed was simple: I thought if you could educate the people—all the people, that every boy and girl in this country [had] a basic right, just like the Bill of Rights, and was entitled to all the education that he or she could take, or would take—that would preserve this democracy. I thought that good health was essential to a good education. I thought that their environment was a very important asset. I thought an absolutely rigid requisite was equal justice to all men. And there were many other things like consumer problems, space, defense, our relations with other nations. But those things were [part of a] relatively simple creed that I tried to promulgate in the form of statutes, the laws of the land.

MAKING HARRY TRUMAN'S DREAM COME TRUE

At the top of Johnson's legislative agenda in 1965 was Medicare, a federally funded insurance program to provide low-cost medical and hospital care for America's elderly under Social Security. Half of the country's population over age sixty-five had no medical insurance, and a third of the aged lived in poverty, unable to afford proper medical care; Johnson believed it was high time to do something about it. Shortly after his November election win, he told Health, Education, and Welfare's assistant secretary, Wilbur Cohen, to make Medicare the administration's "number one priority." On January 4, Johnson put the issue front and center in his State of the Union message; three days later he pressed for passage of Medicare, issuing a statement to Congress demanding that America's senior citizens "be spared the darkness of sickness without hope."

Franklin Roosevelt was the first president to seriously consider a federal health insurance program. As Congress churned out New Deal legislation, Roosevelt advocated inclusion of a federal health insurance component in his Social Security Act of 1935, before dropping it to avoid jeopardizing the bill's passage. Fourteen years later, Harry Truman sent the House a bill that would offer health insurance to those age sixty-five and older, but it was blocked by an intractable Ways and Means Committee. Kennedy tried, too, sending a comparable bill to Capitol Hill in 1962, where it missed passage in the Senate by a few votes. In each case, the American Medical Association (AMA) was the chief culprit in killing the legislation, spending millions to brand the concept as "socialized medicine," an ambiguous characterization that nonetheless made it intrinsically un-American. Conservatives also cast a wary eye. Actor Ronald Reagan, a darling of the growing conservative movement and soon-to-be California gubernatorial candidate, warned that such a program would "invade every area of freedom in this country" and would, in years to come, have Americans waxing wistful to future generations about "what it was like in America when men were free."

But sixteen years after Truman's efforts were derailed by an unwilling Congress, Johnson believed "the times had caught up with the idea," though it didn't hurt that his electoral mandate and increased majorities in the House and Senate gave him the tools. The AMA would prove to be as big and powerful an obstacle as it had in earlier years, but unlike

Truman, Johnson would find some leeway with the House Ways and Means Committee.

Along with most members of the committee, its Democratic chairman, Arkansas congressman Wilbur Mills, had been a fierce opponent of Medicare when Kennedy proposed it, professing it to be fiscally irresponsible. He felt no differently in 1965. Principle, however, would give way to pragmatism; Johnson, he knew, could find the votes to bring Medicare to fruition. Shortly after Johnson's 1964 election victory, in which Johnson improbably added Arkansas to his win column, Mills stated publicly that he was willing to "work something out" on Medicare and would work closely with Cohen to help shape the bill to ensure its passage and effectiveness.

Telephone conversation with LBJ, Wilbur Mills, U.S. representative, Arkansas 1939–77, and Wilbur Cohen, March 23, 1965, 4:54 p.m.

LBJ: *When are you going to take it up?*

Wilbur Mills: *I've got to go to the Rules Committee next week.*

LBJ: *You always get your rules pretty quickly though, don't you?*

Mills: *Yeah, that's right.*

LBJ: . . . *For God's sake, let's get it before Easter!* . . . *They make a poll every Easter.* . . . *You know it. On what has Congress accomplished up till then. Then the rest of the year they use that record to write editorials about. So anything that we can grind through before Easter will be twice as important as after Easter.*

[Mills gets off the line as Johnson continues the conversation with Cohen.]

LBJ: *Now, remember this. Nine out of ten things that I get in trouble on is because they lay around. And tell the Speaker and Wilbur [Mills] to please get a rule just the moment they can.*

Wilbur Cohen: *They want to bring it up next week, Mr. President.*

LBJ: *Yeah, but you just tell them not to let it lay around. Do that! They want to but they might not. That gets the doctors organized. Then they get the others organized. And I damn near killed my education bill, letting it lay around.*

Cohen: *Yeah.*

LBJ: *It stinks. It's just like a dead cat on the door. When a committee reports it, you better either bury that cat or get some life in it.* . . . *[To Mills as he gets back on the line:] For God's sakes! "Don't let dead cats stand on your porch," Mr. Rayburn used to say. They stunk and they stunk and they* *stunk. When you get one out of that committee, you call that son of a bitch up before [our opponents] can get their letters written.*

The plan Mills came up with was described by Cohen as a "three-layer cake." In addition to including the administration's original bill to provide hospital care for the elderly as part of Social Security, Mill's legislation would include Medicaid, a supplemental medical welfare program to offer federal matching funds to states for the indigent, and an opt-in federally subsidized insurance program for doctors' bills. Much to Cohen's surprise, Mills had approved a $500 million government subsidy for the latter program after Cohen persuaded him that it would eliminate 80 percent of the doctors' bills if the patient paid the first $50.

When Cohen asked the president what he thought of the $500 million subsidy, Johnson responded by telling him not to worry about the $500 million before relating a Hill Country yarn:

LBJ: I told [Wilbur] about the test that had been given to a man in Texas who wanted to become a railroad switchman. One of the questions he was asked was: "What would you do if a train from the east was coming at sixty miles an hour, and a train from the west was coming at sixty miles an hour on the same track, and they were just a mile apart, headed for each other?"

The prospective switchman replied: "I'd run get my brother."

"Now why," he was asked, "would you get your brother?"

"Because," the fellow answered, "my brother has never seen a train wreck before."

I told Wilbur I thought I would run and get *my* brother if the Ways and Means Committee reported out this extended Medicare bill he had described to me. I approved the proposal at once.

■ ■ ■

Suddenly, Mills, "the villain of [Medicare]," in Johnson's words, was "now a hero to old folks" as Medicare sailed through the House and was approved by the Senate on July 9.

But another villain would rear its head: the AMA threatened a national boycott of Medicare, holding out the possibility that as many as 95 percent of American doctors would follow suit. Johnson, who had sent Cohen away with instructions to "watch out for trains," would shrewdly railroad the AMA into compliance in a meeting at the Ranch with eleven of its officers on July 11. After reminding the group that John Byrnes, the ranking Republican member of the House Ways and Means Committee and former opponent of Medicare, had urged that "all do their utmost to make the program work as well as possible," Johnson switched gears, asking that the AMA support a program of rotating doctors in and out of Vietnam to serve the civilian population. When they agreed to the latter, Johnson ordered an impromptu press conference, in which he praised the AMA for its commitment to the Vietnamese. When asked inevitably about whether the AMA would support Medicare, Johnson declared, "These men are going to get doctors to go to Vietnam where they may be killed. Medicare is the law of the land. Of course, they'll support the law of the land." He then turned to the AMA president, "You tell him." Put firmly on the spot, he replied, "Of course, we will. We are law abiding citizens, and we have every intention of obeying the new law." Within a matter of weeks, the AMA would formally endorse Medicare, with 95 percent of doctors not resisting it but following suit.

On July 30, 1965, Johnson traveled to the Harry S. Truman Library and Museum in Independence, Missouri, where the eighty-one-year-old Truman, lean and bent with age, his wife, Bess, in tow, watched Johnson sign Medicare into law. Proclaiming the thirty-third president the "real daddy" of Medicare, Johnson awarded President and Mrs. Truman the first two Medicare cards, numbers one and two. "He had started it all, so many years before," Johnson wrote of Truman later. "I wanted him to know that America remembered."

JACK VALENTI: [Johnson] said, "I'm going to make Harry Truman's dream come true. Old folks are not going to be barred from a doctor's office or a hospital because they don't have any money for medical attention. They are never again going to have to be sick and hurt and cry alone. It's a goddamned crime," he said, "and we're never going to have that happen again in this country. When this bill is passed, I'm going to Independence, and I'm going to sign it in Harry Truman's presence." He did exactly that.

JOHN GARDNER: Medicare made an enormous difference in the lives of older Americans. It has had its problems, as every great social program inevitably must have. But it stands as a towering achievement. That's not really debatable. You'll encounter, occasionally, financially secure people who scorn Medicare—and Social Security, too—and cry for the good old days when each family looked after its own aging members. I'm . . . old enough to remember those good old days. So was Lyndon Johnson. In that time old age and poverty were firmly linked, and a good many old folks went "over the hill to the poorhouse." That was the phrase of the day, "over the hill to the poorhouse." . . . Don't talk to me about the good old days.

NATURE WAS MY COMPANION

Shortly before Minnie Taylor died in 1917 from injuries sustained from a fall down a flight of stairs, she had a bedside visit from her five-year-old daughter, Lady Bird. "My poor baby, you're so dirty," she said, in what were to become the last words Lady Bird would hear from her. "Who's going to take care of you?" With her two older brothers in boarding schools, and her industrious father consumed by his businesses, the answer was that she would more or less raise herself, at least while she was at home in Karnack, far from her mother's nurturing family in Alabama with whom she spent summers. Left alone, Lady Bird took to the woods of East Texas like Huck Finn had to the Mississippi; they became her escape and refuge, and their wonders her muse. Wildflowers reaching blithely from the earth were a particular inspiration. "Nature was my first and most reliable companion," she said, and one that stuck with her for the rest of her life.

She shared her love of the land with her husband, whose mind was never far from the Texas Hill Country of his youth. As he wrote later, "My deepest attitudes and beliefs were shaped by a closeness to the land, and it was only natural for me to think about preserving it." Had the urgent issues of civil rights, poverty, health care, education, and immigration not dominated his domestic agenda, he "would have been content to be simply a conservation president." Here Johnson looked not to Franklin Roosevelt but to Roosevelt's distant cousin, Theodore, the twenty-sixth president, who increased the protected land throughout the country fourfold, from 42 to 172 million acres, while creating 150 national forests and 5 national parks. Less than a year into his presidency, Johnson took action, protecting over 9 million acres in federal land through the Wilderness Act, which he signed into law in September 1964. It was one of a number of landmark laws Johnson would see enacted throughout his administration, making him the most environmentally progressive president short of TR.

Mrs. Johnson was her husband's partner in the cause—and a catalyst. "Beautification" became her crusade, consuming much of her time and passion, though she was never completely satisfied with the "unimaginative name," which, she confessed, sounded "purely cosmetic."

LADY BIRD JOHNSON: In sum, beautification means our total concern for the physical and human quality we pass on to our children and the future.

Tackling the subject of beautification is like picking up a tangled skein of wool—all the threads are interwoven: public plantings, clean air, clean water, highway beautification, the protection of our parklands and seashores. It is hard to hitch the conversation into one straight line because everything leads to something else.

■ ■ ■

What it amounted to was environmentalism at a time when little thought was given to the ravages the earth, air, and water sustained as an outgrowth of population expansion, rampant consumerism, and unchecked industrialism. Author Rachel Carson had awakened environmental consciousness with her 1962 book, *Silent Spring*, which sounded alarms about pollutants and pesticides, but it did little to cause immediate changes in the habits of Americans. Mrs. Johnson helped further bring the issue to the minds of Americans, raising awareness about the importance of conservation, the "beauties of their country," and the "shore-to-shore varied splendors" available to them by traveling to the nation's least-used national parks with Secretary of the Interior Stewart Udall, an assignment she relished.

STEWART UDALL, secretary of the interior, 1961–69: We started at an Indian reservation, we went to the Grand Tetons National Park, we dedicated a dam at the Utah-Wyoming boundary, we went on the Salt Lake and looked at some of the things that were happening under government programs—the restoration of an old mining town, for example. And the press went along with us and it resounded in the country. So since we had done one good one, we began doing about two a year from then on.

LIZ CARPENTER: When we were going down the Snake River (by raft), Art Buchwald, dressed in a Scottish golf outfit, threw his arms toward the Grand Tetons and said, "Look, Mrs. Johnson, what a great place for billboards."

GEORGE HARTZOG, director, National Park Service, 1964–72: She was the greatest salesman we had. She was not in the least reticent about picking up the phone on behalf of the parks. But it didn't have to be a telephone call from her. A little tea at the White House could improve a lot of attitudes about legislation on the Hill. We added more acres to the National Park system in that period of time than had been added in the previous 30 years.

STEWART UDALL: She was one of the more influential first ladies. When she ran up her flag, the other people in the Cabinet noticed. She had influence with the President. And in subtle ways and not so subtle ways, this influenced his agenda.

■ ■ ■

One of the "not so subtle" ways Mrs. Johnson influenced her husband's agenda was on highway beautification. The First Lady saw billboards and junkyards as blight on the nation's interstate highway system, which she had seen firsthand in her frequent drives back and forth between Washington and Texas during Johnson's House and Senate years. Upon her urging, Johnson proposed legislation toward the end of 1965 that would lead to controls on outdoor advertising, the removal or aesthetic improvement of unsightly junkyards and scrap heaps, and scenic enhancements. The lobbying efforts of the Outdoor Advertising Association of America, however, made the bill a hard sell in Congress. Taking no chances on a defeat, Johnson took to the phones to enlist support for the bill inside and outside the Washington Beltway, as he did on August 6, 1965, with Phil Potter, editor of the *Baltimore Sun*, who was hard pressed to get a word in edgewise:

LBJ: *I never see you around anymore. Damn, if I don't believe you just loaf all the time.*

Phil Potter: *I don't. I was over there today.*

LBJ: *Ah, I wanted to ask you if there is any chance of getting a little campaign started in the* Baltimore Sun. *A little propaganda. Do you all do any of that ever?*

Potter: *No, sir.*

LBJ: *You against it, huh?*

Potter: *Uh huh.*

LBJ: *Well, I thought maybe that you could get old Jerry Griffin and Price Day to give a little thought to whether we might analyze—at least find one or two of these four or five bills we got on beautification—*

Potter: *On beautification?*

LBJ: *—desirable. Now, I don't know of a city in the world that needs it more than Baltimore.*

Potter: *I think we can do that. It seems to be news rather than propaganda.*

LBJ: *Well, I'm kidding you. What I mean is a little editorial coverage. I see some good editorials in [the* Sun*] and I think that I rarely find one I disagree with. I think that if you would make a little note to them sometimes, I would appreciate it. Fallon is the chairman of the committee. The billboard people are awfully active. The highway engineers are awful active. I am losing two billion this year in balance of payments. People going to see de Gaulle. And if our highways were a little prettier and our parks were a little more attractive, and a few other things, why, it would be helpful to us.*

And we are doing a good job over the country. Most of the governors are doing it. A good many of the mayors are doing it. And we need some of this legislation and Fallon has just put it off now until the end of the month and then August and it looks like that maybe the billboard boys are kinda going to stop everything if we don't look into it. I thought you might—I might get some of our boys [to] give you some of the bills and let you look at them, and let you look at some of the testimony, and maybe Bill Moyers would sit down at lunch with you and tell you what our hope is. We had a very moderate billboard provision. We weren't vicious at all.

You do that?

Potter: *Yes, sir.*

LBJ: *Call you next week. (LBJ hangs up.)*

Potter: *Yes, sir, fine. Now, Mr. President . . .*

The Eighty-ninth Congress had been receptive to environmental reform earlier in the fall when it approved the Water Quality Act, a landmark water pollution deterrent that set mandatory federal standards for interstate waterways, which Johnson signed into law on October 2. Just over a week later, on October 10, he signed the Clean Air Act, the first legislation to regulate automobile exhaust emissions as a means of reducing air pollution. The same month, as it prepared to recess from its first session, the Senate was far less amenable to the passage of the Highway Beautification Act. Here again, Johnson mounted an offensive, making no bones about why he wanted the bill passed.

BOB HARDESTY: Just before the first session of the 89th Congress ended, the President announced a meeting in the Cabinet Room at 3:30—don't be late! He didn't say why. So, I went over there and I was stunned, the place was just jam-packed. The entire Cabinet was there, the top staff of the Democratic National Committee was there, the whole top staff of the

White House was there; I thought, what in the world is going on? And he said, "The Congress is about ready to adjourn, and they haven't passed Lady Bird's Highway Beautification Act. And at the moment we don't have the votes. Now, she wants that bill. And if she wants it, I want it, and by God, we're going to pass it!"

So, then he gets out thc tally sheet for the Senate. He went through every member. Every member. "Who knows this person? How close are you? Who can make a call? Who's got chips to call in?" He said, "Alright, do it! This weekend, not Monday. Do it, call them—all of them." [H]e didn't have his votes, but he had the whole Senate covered. And everybody had their assignments, and they knew what they were supposed to do. And he had most people double-covered.

■ ■ ■

Mrs. Johnson's influence on the legislation did not go unnoticed. During an acrimonious late-night debate in the Senate on October 7, Bob Dole, of Kansas, suggested sarcastically an amendment to the bill to replace the title "Secretary of Commerce" with "Lady Bird." After compromises were made to the bill, including "just compensation" for outdoor advertisers who lost billboards and allowances for advertising signage in certain areas, the bill passed by a vote of 245 to 138, just before 1:00 on the morning of October 8.

Mrs. Johnson didn't confine her interest in beautification to the highways of America, turning her attention to the sprucing up and regaining the luster of the nation's capital, which, like other U.S. cities, had suffered from aesthetic neglect.

LIZ CARPENTER: Our goal was the city of Washington, which was her hometown at the moment and had been for 30 years. The purpose was to say in deeds to the rest of the country: "I have decided I'll roll up my sleeves and go to work in the town that's mine to make it look better. You can do the same back home."

Waves of things began to happen that made us know we had really hit a dormant nerve in the American public. Suddenly we had a host of telegrams, letters, phone calls, requests for meetings, from what I would call the "true believers." The garden clubs of the United States, the town planning councils, the conservationists, the ones who had been hard at work at it but had no national podium. It was like a great awakening and suddenly their voices were louder in their hometowns than they had ever been.

■ ■ ■

As she traveled through the country to beat the drum of her growing crusade, the First Lady learned to pack "tree-planting dresses," those with A-line designs allowing her better to get her foot on a shovel. By 1966 she was receiving two hundred letters a week at the White House relating to beautification. Would she be willing to intervene to ensure cosmetic improvements would be made to a certain stretch of highway? Could she help save an aged tree in a local park? Some letters were simply to extend thanks for the focus she had brought to the issue.

"Where flowers bloom, so does hope," Mrs. Johnson once said. It may have explained their ubiquity in the times, which were to grow increasingly turbulent: "Flower Power" and flower stickers affixed to car bumpers and plastered on VW buses; flowers painted on the faces of children; flowers placed by antiwar protesters in the barrels of rifles pointed at them by National Guardsmen. The flower became a symbol of hope. So, in her own quiet way, did Lady Bird Johnson.

"WHAT CAN YOU DO FOR OUR COUNTRY?"

When Johnson assumed the presidency, an impediment to the American Dream, bigotry, stood not only within America's borders but also at its gates. The National Origins Act of 1924, the country's abiding immigration law, had been put in place during the Calvin Coolidge administration to stem the tide of immigrants to America's shores, eventually setting the total number of immigrants for any given year at about 150,000, and establishing quotas based on national origin. (The limit of 150,000 was postponed and eventually changed to around 154,000 in 1929. By 1965, the quota had increased to roughly 158,000.) In essence, the law favored immigrants from northern Europe and the British Isles, while discriminating against those from southern and eastern Europe, deemed as less desirable by U.S. officials. It also prevented Asians and other nonwhites from entering the country. Additionally, the act also upheld the Naturalization Act of 1790, which allowed only white people of good moral character to become naturalized Americans.

LAWRENCE O'BRIEN: The national origins quota system had been in place without a change for a long time. And historically, of course, it favored northern Europe, back to the founding of the country. It was established in the climate of northern European presence in the development of this country. It had neglected to reflect the dramatic changes that had taken place as this country progressed. The southern European and others had been limited. You had a quota system that oftentimes was not fully utilized. It was based on an old concept that no longer existed or should exist. And so it was massive in the sense that you were to completely restructure immigration procedure, severely limiting some countries that had pretty much an open door historically. [We] were trying to establish an equitable immigration policy. It was a heavily debated, controversial and prolonged struggle. And the outcome brought about a revolution in immigration policy.

■ ■ ■

John Kennedy, whose Irish ancestors had been the target of prejudice in Boston in the middle and latter part of the eighteenth century, had added the abolishment of the National Origins Act to his legislative agenda in 1963, a goal that remained unrealized upon his death. Like civil rights and antipoverty measures, the issue flowed naturally to Johnson's agenda. He had seen the ugliness of bigotry through the eyes of his students in Cotulla, and had encouraged them to look beyond it. Later, as a congressman in the thirties, Johnson had helped Jewish refugees in Europe by seeing to the immigration of family members of constituents or advising them on how to obtain visas at a time when other lawmakers—and the U.S. government as a whole—were turning a blind eye to Nazi tyranny. (The total number of Jews Johnson helped immigrate remains in question. None of the case files in his congressional office were saved from 1937 through 1942; nor were they saved at the State Department, leaving the total extent of Johnson's involvement in the cause a mystery. There has been some speculation, found abundantly on the Internet, that Johnson was an unheralded hero to the Jews, helping hundreds to find refuge in the United States. But, though Johnson's efforts were admirable, had he been involved far beyond serving his constituents' interests it is likely he would have disclosed this in later years as a point of pride or political leverage.)

Johnson used his 1964 State of the Union address to condemn the National Origins Act as being out of step with American principles. "In establishing preferences," he said, "a nation that was built by immigrants of all lands can ask those who now seek admission: 'What can you do for our country?' But we should not be asking: 'In what country were you born?' " Immigration reform, he said later in the year, was "a matter of common sense and common decency." He pursued the issue the following year, tapping congressman Emanuel "Manny" Celler of New York, and Ted Kennedy, who had assumed his brother's Massachusetts Senate seat in 1963, to steer the bill through the House and Senate respectively. Johnson took the occasion as an opportunity to strengthen his working relationship with the collegial Kennedy, which would remain on solid ground, and to quash rumors about the growing strain between him and the Kennedy clan.

Telephone conversation between LBJ and Ted Kennedy on March 8, 1965, 9:10 p.m.

LBJ: *I know this, there's not a member of the Senate I'll go as far to meet as I will you, 'cause I think you've been fair and decent and fine as anybody. And I think your area has and you can count me in. And if you quote me a little too far, I'll just stand up . . .*

This business about me being crossways with the Kennedys is just a pure lot of crap. Uh, I started out here to keep faith and I'm gonna do it, and I think if New England's next in line, I want to do anything I can for it. And I think you know something about how I feel about you. And I have no antagonisms, no antipathy, no wars to settle with anybody else. I just don't want you to let the damn press do that.

And there's nothing else I want. I've got more than I can take care of right now. And all I want to do is what's right. . . . I want to be true to the trust that's been placed in me.

Ted Kennedy: *We've had some good hearings on immigration. They're going—*

LBJ: *Yes, you have. And I heard Bobby made a helluva good statement the other day. And it looks like it might be a possibility to get it out of both houses. Do you think so?*

Kennedy: *Well, I think in the Senate we're in better shape than over in the House. . . .*

LBJ: *Well, you've got to work on [Celler] a bit.*

Kennedy: *He's a tough cookie. . . . it's coming along. . . .*

Overcoming predictable opposition by southern Democrats, and with much prodding by Johnson, Kennedy and Celler delivered both the upper and lower houses: 76 yeas versus 18 nays in the Senate, and 320 versus 69 in the House. Emblematically, on October 3, Johnson signed the Immigration Act on Liberty Island, at the foot of the Statue of Liberty, with the island of Manhattan gleaming in the distance as a dramatic backdrop. The law put an immediate end to the national origin quotas that had been in effect for more than forty years, capping the annual total of Eastern Hemisphere immigration at 170,000, and Latin America at 120,000, while allowing for the preference of relatives of American citizens and, more important, favoring those with advanced education, skills, and professional credentials. In effect, it would become the nation's most sweeping immigration reform, forever changing America's cultural fabric and broadening its promise.

CARL ALBERT, U.S. representative, Oklahoma (D), 1947–77: The first speech John McCormack made as a freshman member of Congress, before Lyndon Johnson was old enough to be in Congress, was a bill to abolish the National Origins Quotas on immigration statutes. They had been fooling with this through the years. Johnson got over it. Of course, he had a good Congress to do it with.

"THE FABULOUS EIGHTY-NINTH CONGRESS"

Johnson affectionately referred to the Capitol Hill lawmakers of 1965 and 1966 as "the fabulous Eighty-ninth Congress"—and for good reason. Sixty-nine percent of the 469 proposals the Johnson White House sent to Congress were approved, compared to Kennedy's high of 48 percent in 1961. Of the 115 bills Johnson sent to the Hill, 89 would make it into law, a prodigious record for its sheer volume and success ratio, but more for the magnitude of change the laws delivered.

In addition to the Voting Rights Act, Elementary and Secondary Education Act, Higher Education Act, Medicare, Medicaid, Clean Air Act, Highway Beautification Act, and the Immigration Act, 1965 would see the enactment of other key laws. The Arts and Humanities Act created the National Endowment for the Arts and the National Endowment for the Humanities, making the federal government, for the first time, a patron of American culture. Gregory Peck, Ansel Adams, and Ralph Ellison were among the luminaries crowded into a Rose Garden signing ceremony in late September that would result in the creation and development of arts programs across the nation and the support of the study of the humanities. Additionally, the Department of Housing and Urban

Development Act created HUD as a new cabinet-level agency, and the Federal Cigarette Labeling and Advertising Act, in response to cautionary reports from the Surgeon General, mandated health warning labels on cigarette packaging by the following year, and similar warnings in television advertising by 1969.

The budget Johnson would submit for fiscal year 1966, which included most of the legislation passed in 1965, included a relatively modest deficit of $3.7 billion, or .5 percent of gross domestic product, marking a time when fluid party compromises between tax surcharges and domestic spending cuts characterized the budget process. Throughout his tenure in office, Johnson's budgets would range from a deficit high of $25.2 billion for fiscal year 1968 to a surplus of $3.2 billion for fiscal year 1969, the last time a federal budget surplus was delivered until the latter years of the Clinton administration. (Johnson's 1968 budget deficit constituted 2.9 percent of gross domestic product versus George W. Bush's high of 18.5 percent in 2007, and Barack Obama's 14.9 percent in 2010.)

Just as Johnson had predicted, the Eighty-ninth's second session, in 1966, would not bear the fruit of its first. As the *Congressional Quarterly* wrote, "The monumental record of the first session of the 89th Congress stands as a lesson in Presidential power and leadership," but as the second session progressed, "the rosy glow of the Johnson Administration waned." Many on Capitol Hill who had been allied with Johnson would step back from radical legislative reform as Americans adjusted to the pace of change, and Johnson's opponents would close ranks as the commander in chief slowed in the mire of Vietnam. But the mark the Eighty-ninth would make on the country was indelible. Only the Seventy-third Congress, which convened as the Franklin Roosevelt administration took the White House during the depths of the Great Depression, enacting much of Roosevelt's New Deal, would produce a record of greater significance in the twentieth century; not because the Seventy-third's accomplishments were more transformational in the long term—many New Deal programs were temporary fixes—but because it set a precedent and standard for what the federal government could do to enhance American life.

Still, whatever accomplishments were racked up between the executive and legislative branches, they were never enough for the restless Johnson, who always wanted more. A phone conversation between him and House speaker John McCormack in the early evening of August 6, 1965, just after the Voting Rights Act was signed at the Capitol—perhaps Johnson's proudest moment—shows Johnson not dwelling on a momentous stride in history but looking beyond it, toward the next pressing items on his agenda.

LBJ: *I thought [the signing ceremony at the Capitol] went off good. Television—been watching it here for a few minutes and it's got some real good stuff on it. I believe it will get out all over the country.*

John McCormack, Speaker of the House of Representatives, Massachusetts (D), 1962–71: *There couldn't be a better place than signing it in that historic room. It's all a part of the history of the act. Your [unclear] . . . is not only effective but structurally dramatic.*

LBJ: *Wonderful.*

Well, I told Larry [O'Brien] to call you and Carl [Albert] and Hale [Boggs] if you want to bring him. We ought to meet Friday and just look over the House's problems for the next three weeks so we can be sure we got our schedule and we're going. I'm worried about Wayne Morse holding me up on one or two things. I don't think the House and Senate need to get together Tuesday—I'll have y'all on Monday and have them Tuesday. And then next week we can get together jointly and see what we got to work out.

Now the things I'm primarily interested in, in y'all, is what you ought to be able to get a rule on. Our big problem, as I see it in the House, is gonna be the Farm Bill—it's going to be number one.

McCormack: *The big problem there is going to be that [unclear] . . .*

LBJ: *Yes that's right. The Farm Bill.*

I think we ought to be able to get a rule on Immigration; we ought to be able to pass the Public Works. We ought to be able to—

McCormack: *Public Works?*

LBJ: *ARA [Area Redevelopment Administration]. Then we ought to be—*

McCormack: *We've got a meeting today on it—*

LBJ: *Yeah. We ought to be able to get Higher Education. I've got to get that because Morse handles it and he's got $700 million in it. And I've got all my college kids. And we've just raised hell—*

CARL ALBERT: [Johnson] would never rest on his laurels, or let us rest on ours. He would insist and urge us to go on with the next bill just as fast as we could. He had his staff, himself personally, working with not only the leadership, but with committees—everybody that had something to do with them. I'm sure that in all the history of Congress there has never been so much presidential activity in pushing legislation as we were able to do with his leadership in the 89th Congress. I'm sure it stands out as the greatest in history, because more landmark bills were passed than had been passed at any other time. Bills which presidents had been recommending for years were passed.

I've never seen a time when so many people were trying so hard to get so much done. And they were inspired by the great leadership which the President was giving.

JAKE PICKLE: I came in at the time that President Johnson became president, and I take great pride in the fact that I was an active member of the Eighty-eighth and Eighty-ninth Congresses. We were the most productive sessions of Congress in the last thirty years, and that's because of the drive and push and the vision of our leader.

TED KENNEDY: The achievements of President Johnson, in the domestic field, were truly historic and outstanding. I'd like to believe and I feel it's true that these programs, to a great extent, had been outlined and presented during the early 1960s, but President Johnson added an enormous amount of resourcefulness, energy and knowledge of the ways of Congress and the Senate in bringing them about and executing them. I think this is particularly true in that 1964 and 1965 period. I think really the record that was achieved during that period of time will go down in history as one of the most productive in history.

GEORGE MCGOVERN: It was a very creative time in the life of the country. It was a very transformative time in the country. I remember being very proud that I was a senator during that period. It was very satisfying to see those victories rolled up. [Johnson] had a hand in all of that—very definitely.

LAWRENCE O'BRIEN: History will be the final judge. But the record is clearly inscribed. Equal rights for all Americans; better education for the young at all levels; hope for older people who face ill health—Medicare, after three decades of struggle—jobs for the unemployed; families helped out of the slums; massive housing programs and health research.

President Johnson fulfilled the Democratic Party's commitments to the people, and his record with the Eighty-ninth Congress will live on as a monument to his energy, his vision, and his compassion. Yet there will always be unfinished agendas. There are no final victories.

"NEARLY EVERY PERSON IN THE WORLD IS GOOD"

It is difficult to reconcile Lyndon Johnson, the profoundly imperfect man, with the estimable purity of the change he drove through Washington and swept into the nation with singular devotion. The beauty of his intention almost inevitably gets marred by the blemishes in his nature. Bill Moyers once posed the question of his former boss, "Why did a man as flawed as any human vessel that was ever made rouse a nation to reach beyond itself in such a time?" This is at the core of the riddle that was LBJ.

GEORGE REEDY: When he argued [his position on issues] it was to achieve a positive purpose. Now maybe the positive purpose was to get people to beg him to do it. That's entirely possible, but if you don't grasp that basic concept you'll never understand Lyndon Johnson. . . .

The man, I'm convinced, was terribly sincere about certain things for which he was not given credit for sincerity. I think he was very sincere about civil rights. I think he was very sincere about the war on poverty. I think he was very sincere about the education legislation. That really was what he would have regarded as his finest achievement, because he was obsessed with this concept of giving every child—how did he put it?—"as much education as the child can take." I don't know that all of it was precisely an intelligent sincerity, but nevertheless it was sincerity. And yet, people didn't give him credit for it. Now, he thought it was because he was a Westerner, and a Texan, and a Southerner, sort of thing. That wasn't it. It was just because they saw him constantly arguing this way over things that were of little account.

JAKE PICKLE: The devil with a pitchfork forged in Johnson City didn't pass Head Start and Civil Rights and Voting Rights and Open Housing, Medicare and Upward Bound and Higher Education and Elementary and Secondary Education. These were no lucky Sunday punches of legislative achievements.

They weren't programmed, waiting for him to act. They were conceived originally by JFK, many of them, and put into force by Lyndon Johnson. But they weren't something that just happened out of the sky.

They are programs that help people, they are lasting, and they're on the books today because of President Johnson.

JOHN GARDNER: I have read a great deal about Lyndon Johnson's arm-twisting and domineering and manipulating. I haven't read much about his convictions. I had many private talks with him about education, health, civil rights, and similar subjects. He wanted racial justice. He wanted every child to have a chance. He wanted the sick to be healed and the elderly to be cared for. He had faith in human possibilities. That was the generative element that kept the whole enterprise moving.

A political town such as Washington is superbly equipped to appraise the degree of sincerity in a leader. Every leader expresses high ideals. The task is to figure out the degree of hypocrisy, and Washington makes the calculation swiftly and precisely. It took the town no time at all to figure out that with respect to health, education, poverty, and the like, President Johnson meant exactly what he said, and the impact was great.

Washington is a city that lives by signals, and the most powerful signals emanate from the White House. If a president is known to be negative or indifferent respecting some course of action, or if he advocates it publicly without really believing in it, a great many people in Congress and the executive branch will strike the subject off their lists.

BILLY GRAHAM, evangelist and friend of LBJ: I think that [there] was a very deep conviction that he had, that he wanted to do something for the underprivileged and the people that were oppressed in our society, especially black people. I remember after he left office I visited the Ranch a number of times. Just to see him with little children, little black children, and how he loved them and would take them for rides and take them up in his arms. This had no political motivation whatsoever.

I think that he did have a very deep conviction at this point. I'm not sure where it originated. I do not know what influences. But I know that he had it even when I first knew him. He might have gotten it from Mr. [Franklin] Roosevelt, the Roosevelt era. I don't know.

■ ■ ■

It was, of course, Roosevelt's legacy to which Johnson aspired. But Johnson also saw himself as having more heart than FDR in advancing the cause of civil rights where Roosevelt, afraid of politically alienating the South, had fallen short.

LBJ: Roosevelt didn't have any southern molasses compassion. He didn't get wrapped up in going to anyone's funeral. Roosevelt never submitted one civil rights bill in twelve years. He sent Mrs. Roosevelt to their meetings in their parks and she'd do it up good. But President Roosevelt never faced up to the problem.

ERNIE GOLDSTEIN, special assistant to the president, 1967–69: There were times when Lyndon Johnson also operated for a principle which was against politics. I got this from Grace Tully, one of Roosevelt's secretaries.

It is the story of the young Congressman [Johnson] from the Tenth District [of Texas] on his first trip to Washington. After about six weeks of calling the White House and saying he had an urgent problem that he wanted to discuss with the President, finally "Pa" Watson, the appointments secretary to Franklin Roosevelt, agreed to humor the young congressman who insisted on taking the time of the most important president in the history of the United States.

So in comes Congressman Johnson and he says, "Mr. President, I have a problem in the Tenth District. Milo Perkins, the great darling of the New Deal and the AAA, is not giving loans to Negro farmers in the Tenth District."

Roosevelt's first reaction was, "Boy, this is a politician. He's going to get all the Negro votes." But then his second thought was, "My God, they have lily white primaries in Texas, and here is this young congressman hardly six weeks into his first term, and he's willing to put his entire career on the line by taking a stand on behalf of Negro farmers."

LADY BIRD JOHNSON: I remember one incident in Somerville, Texas, when he went to make an outdoor speech [as a congressman]. It was customary in outdoor speeches for blacks to come and listen, standing at the edge of the crowd. When he would issue his usual invitation to come up and shake hands, meet the congressman and tell him their problems and their views, they always melted away—I don't mean [just] in our district, I mean everywhere throughout the South, except for a very few cultured, educated, perhaps preachers or schoolteachers. That was a very limited number. I would say in our district I can't name any.

But I remember at this time some blacks in this Somerville meeting came up and shook hands with him, and he was just as friendly with them as with anybody else. I remember murmurs and ripples of disapproval

early forty years after his death, Lyndon Baines Johnson remains enigmatic. "Allowing for shades subtlety," wrote Johnson aide Bob Hardesty, "there were as many LBJs as there were people who ew him."

Texas Governor John Connally, Vice President Johnson, and President John F. Kennedy on a rainy but auspicious morning in Fort Worth, Texas, on November 22, 1963, before their fateful trip to Dallas.

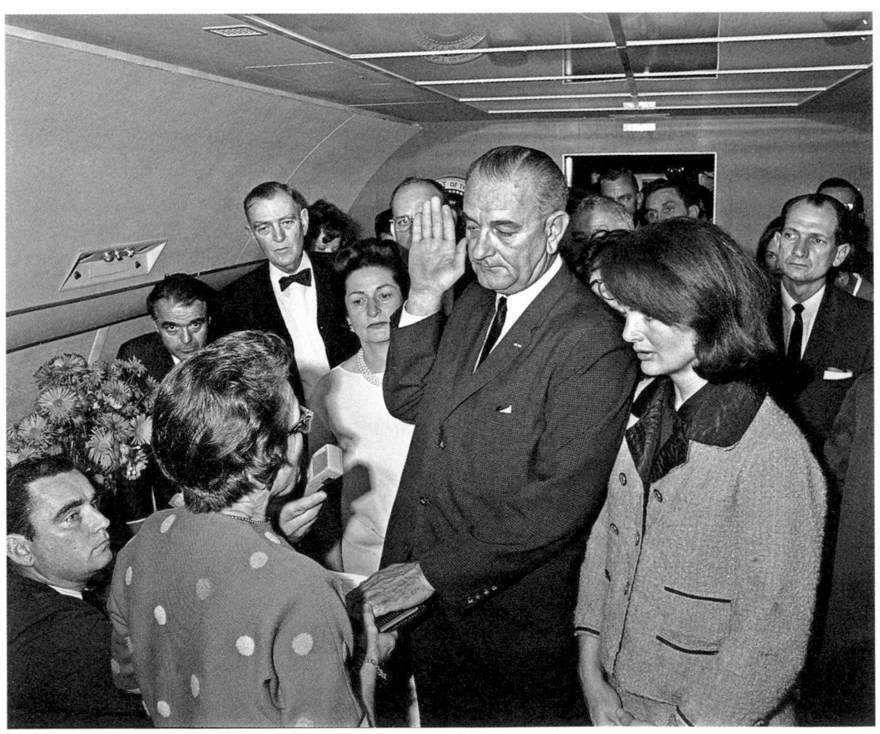

At Dallas's Love Field, Johnson takes the presidential oath of office in the sweltering cabin of Air Force One *at 2:38 p.m. CST, flanked by Lady Bird Johnson and Jacqueline Kennedy. In the wake of Kennedy's assassination, "People looked at the living and wished for the dead," Mrs. Johnson said.*

Upon arrival at Andrews Air Force Base from Dallas, Johnson addresses the nation for the first time as president. "I will do my best. That is all I can do," he said in his fifty-eight–word statement. "I ask for your help—and God's."

At the White House on July 2, 1964, Johnson signs the Civil Rights Act of 1964, which brought the first meaningful civil rights reform since Reconstruction. But it came at a price. Though Johnson would take the cause much further, he lamented presciently to an aide, "I think we've just delivered the South to the Republican Party for the rest of my life, and yours."

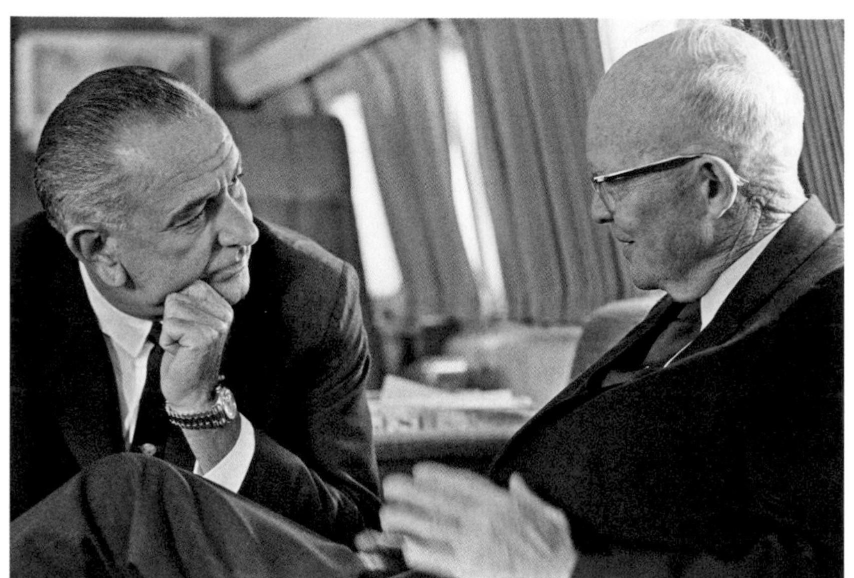

Johnson confers with Dwight Eisenhower on the war in Vietnam, October 5, 1965.

Johnson visiting impoverished Appalachia, May 7, 1964, after declaring a "War on Poverty" earlier in the year. The poverty rate fell from 19.5 percent when he took office to 12.1 percent by the end of his tenure, the greatest one-time reduction in U.S. history.

The First Family—(left to right) Lynda (19), Luci (16), Lyndon and Lady Bird Johnson—on November 30, 1963. Johnson's singular devotion to his political career came at the expense of nearly everything else. It fell largely to Mrs. Johnson to raise their daughters.

Johnson talks with Bobby Kennedy in the Oval Office, September 3, 1964. Though Johnson would help Kennedy win a U.S. Senate seat in New York the same year, bad blood divided them. "We could have spent a lifetime trying to become close but there was too much separating us," Johnson said.

Inauguration Day, January 20, 1965. In just under a year as president, Johnson had triumphantly made the role his own. The previous November, he won the presidential election by over 15 million votes, securing the biggest electoral mandate in American history to that point.

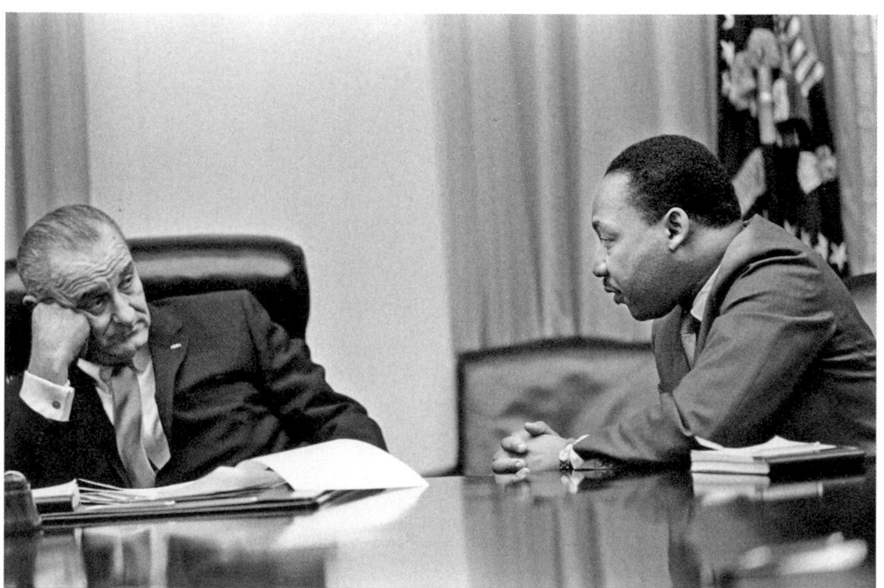

LBJ and Martin Luther King Jr., White House, March 18, 1966. In 1965, as LBJ's Great Society hit its stride, the nation saw the most sweeping social reform since FDR's New Deal began in 1933. Among the laws included were the landmark Voting Rights Act of 1965, on which Johnson had worked closely with King.

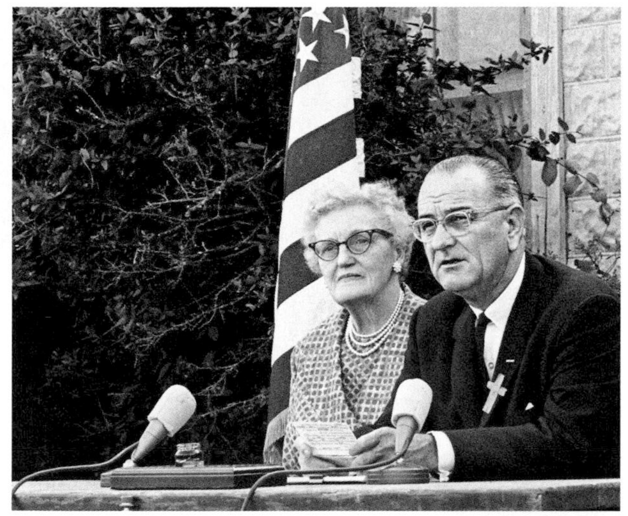

With Kate Deadrich Loney, his first-grade teacher, at his side, on April 11, 1965, Johnson signs the Elementary and Secondary Education Act before the one-room schoolhouse he attended in Stonewall, Texas. The law put general federal aid into education for the first time. From 1964 to 1969, U.S. high school graduation rates rose by 32 percent.

Harry Truman, Lady Bird Johnson, Hubert Humphrey, and Bess Truman watch Johnson sign Medicare into law at the Truman Library, Independence, Missouri, July 30, 1965.

On October 3, 1965, Johnson speaks before the Statue of Liberty prior to signing the Immigration Act, which abolished quotas favoring immigrants from the UK and northern Europe. "[W]e should not be asking, 'In what country were you born,' " he reasoned, but " 'What can you do for our country?' "

Johnson applying the legendary "Johnson Treatment" to U.S. Supreme Court Justice Abe Fortas, July 29, 1965.

The Johnsons at the LBJ Ranch among the wildflowers Mrs. Johnson loved (July 15, 1968). Gracious and strong, Lady Bird was a stabilizing force for her mercurial husband.

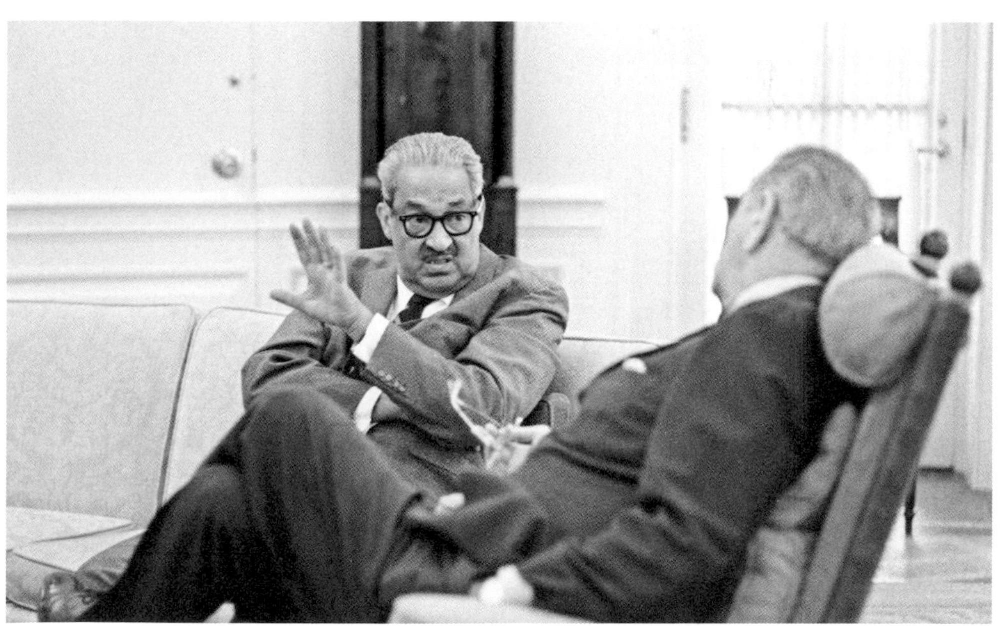

With Thurgood Marshall in the Oval Office, September 26, 1968. Marshall became the first African American justice to serve on the U.S. Supreme Court when Johnson appointed him the previous year.

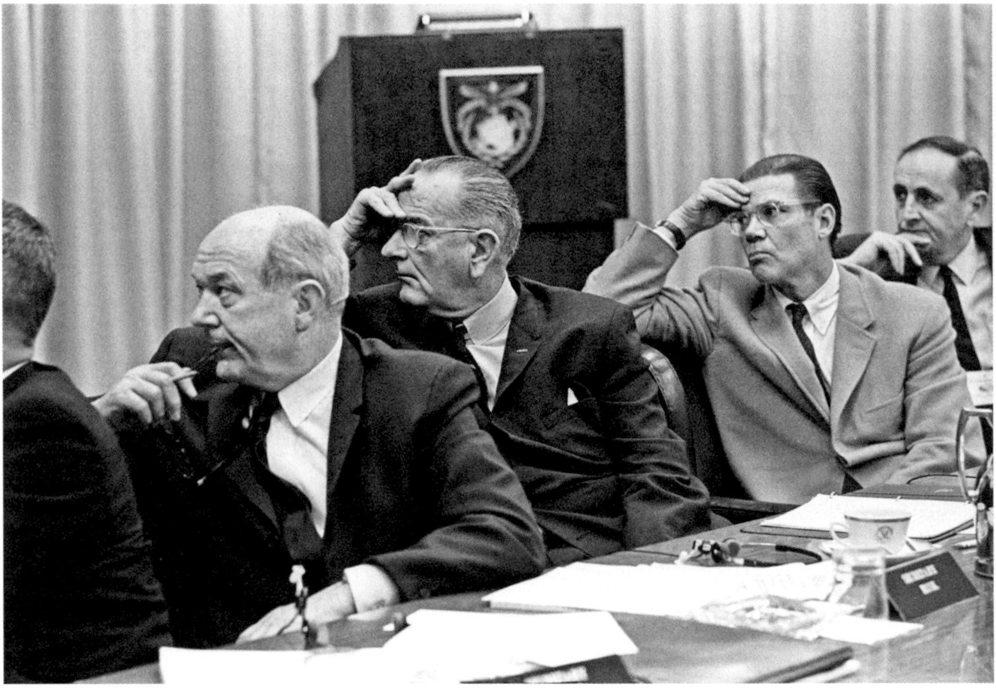

By 1966, as Johnson escalated troop levels, Vietnam began to consume his presidency. Above, he attends a conference on Vietnam with Secretary of State Dean Rusk and Secretary of Defense Robert McNamara (Honolulu, February 7, 1966). Below, he attends a national security meeting with Vice President Hubert Humphrey (White House, March 27, 1968).

Johnson visits troops in Cam Ranh Bay, South Vietnam, October 26, 1966.

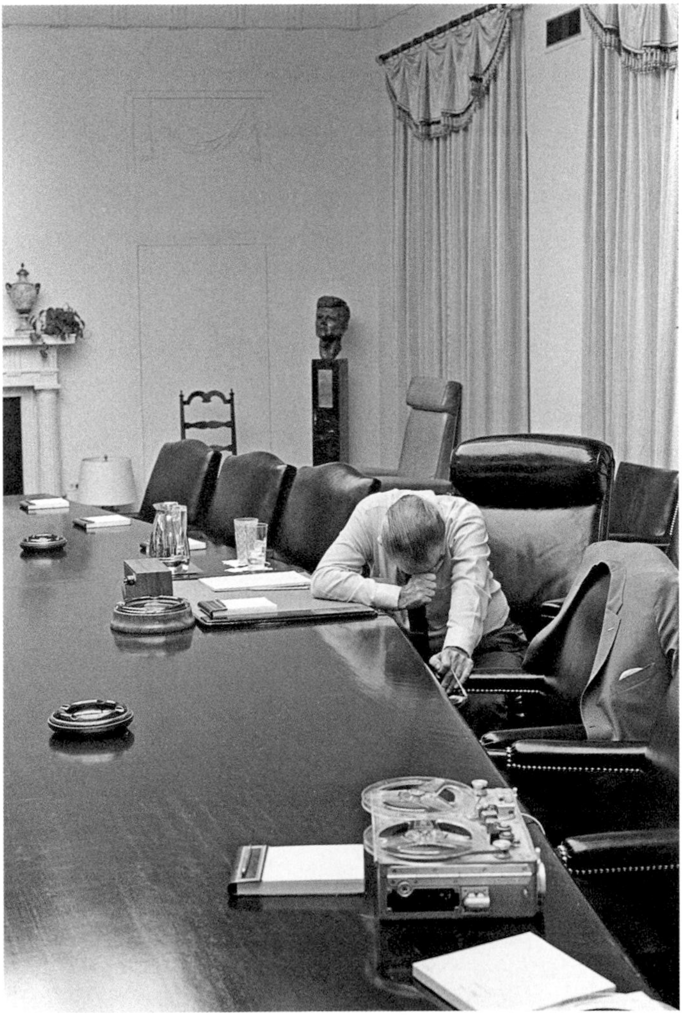

Johnson listens in anguish to a tape recording from his son-in-law, Captain Chuck Robb, in Vietnam, July 31, 1968. Both of Johnson's sons-in-laws served in Vietnam, adding to his heartache over the war.

C
VETERANS
BRING
OUR GI's
HOME
NOW!

Left: Coretta Scott King and famed pediatrician Benjamin Spock (both center) join in an antiwar protest outside the gates of the White House on May 17, 1967. At a rally during the March on the Pentagon later in the year, Spock declared, "The enemy is Lyndon Johnson; the war is disastrous in every way."

Bottom left: Vietnam War protesters Veterans for Peace at the March on the Pentagon, October 21, 1967.

Below: U.S. troops of the Twenty-fifth Infantry Division conduct a search-and-destroy mission northeast of Cu Chi, Vietnam, May 16, 1966. (Courtesy of the National Archives)

Johnson addresses the nation from the Oval Office, March 31, 1968, announcing a bombing halt in Vietnam and his intention not to seek reelection.

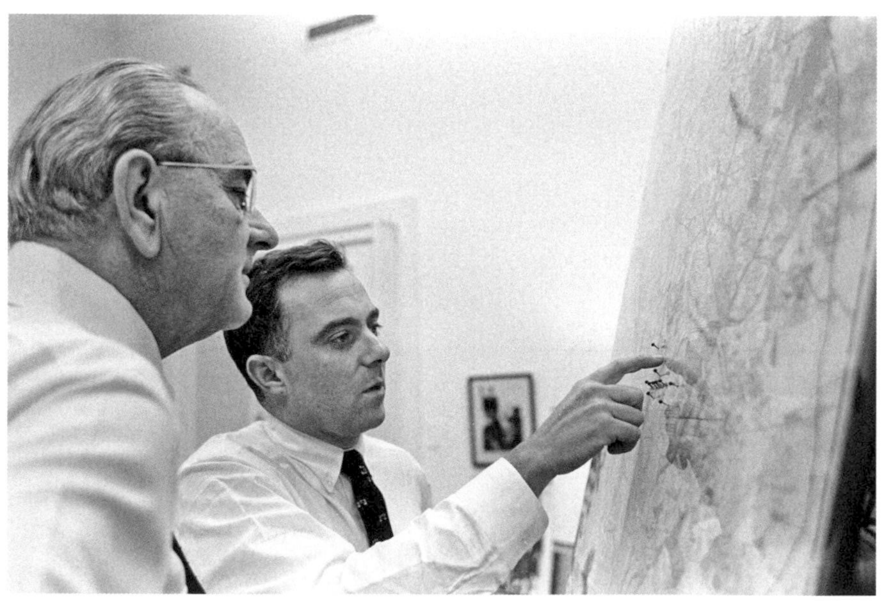

After the assassination of Martin Luther King Jr. on March 4, 1968, riots broke out in 125 American cities. Johnson, with aide Joe Califano, charts outbreaks in Washington, where martial law was instituted for the first time in the United States since the Civil War (White House, April 5, 1968).

Johnson used King's assassination to compel Congress to pass the Civil Rights Act of 1968, commonly known as the Fair Housing Act, which he signed on April 11, 1968 (Walter Mondale and Thurgood Marshall at right). "[T]he proudest moments of my presidency have been times such as this when I have signed into law the promises of a century," he said.

Johnson, meeting with the crew of Apollo 8, is presented a photograph, Earth Rising, *by astronaut Jim Lovell, January 9, 1969. Apollo 8's circumlunar flight the previous month marked the first time human beings had journeyed beyond Earth's atmosphere and would lead to Apollo 11's lunar landing on July 20, 1969.*

Johnson at the LBJ Ranch with his first grandchild, Lyndon, and dog, Yuki, January 6, 1968. Th Ranch, in the Texas Hill Country where LBJ was born and raised, gave him solace. He spent nearl a fifth of his presidency there, and it was there that he died at age sixty-four on January 22, 1973.

through the crowd, and some of his friends saying to him later, "You better not do that. You're just going to lose by doing that." And him saying, well, he didn't agree and he thought their opinions needed listening to. I don't think he lost any friends over it. "Well, that's just old Lyndon. You have to put up with a few things."

I think one factor, oddly enough, [was] his size. They thought he looked like a Texan, and they were kind of proud that he did look like a Texan, and they knew one thing for sure: he loved Texas and fought as he envisioned Texas ought to be, and they could forgive him for that.

■ ■ ■

Johnson's commitment to the advancement of civil rights—of human rights—seems most to have been shaped by another big Texan, and an even greater influence on him than FDR: his daddy. Sam Johnson had his own flaws. Rough-hewn and overbearing at times, he was fond of drink and took to it often, which led to turmoil in his marriage and failure that may not otherwise have come. Young Lyndon, egged on by his mother, held his father in judgment for his intemperance (though he himself would go on to drink liberally, favoring Cutty Sark scotch whisky, which he consumed in large doses), but Sam provided a role model for his son in the political arena. During his political career in the Texas legislature—confined to two chapters: one before his marriage and into its first years and the second after his five children were born a decade afterward—he showed himself to be a man of conviction and independent mind.

WRIGHT PATMAN, U.S. representative, Texas (D), 1929–76: I'll tell you this: As a member of the legislature, when Sam Ealy Johnson said something, it was that way. No mealymouth business, no ifs, ands, or buts.

I never did know him to vote the way anybody told him to or wanted him to. He voted the way he felt. He was a contrary man, and he was an honest man, and you can take my word for that.

■ ■ ■

Moreover, Sam Johnson was a man of unusual political courage and compassion. At a time when nearly three-quarters of the Texas legislature was sympathetic to the KKK, if not members themselves, Sam Johnson, who had always made his contempt of the organization plain, gave a speech in front of the Texas House of Representatives denouncing them and their actions.

LBJ: The Ku Klux Klan was at its height when my father was in the Texas legislature. They'd elected a couple of senators and they had power and position around. They threatened him. Those campaigns could get pretty hot. Men were called upon and told they'd be tarred and feathered, and a good many of them, friends of ours, were. I was only a fifteen-year-old boy in the middle of all this, and I was fearful that my daddy would be taken out and tarred and feathered.

■ ■ ■

Or shot. Sam's life was threatened on a number of occasions. His son Sam Houston, Lyndon's younger brother, recalled a phone call in which his father was told he would be gunned down for his position on the KKK. "Now, listen here, you KuKluxsonofabitch," he remembered his father replying. "If you and your goddamned gang think you're man enough to shoot me, you come on ahead. My brothers and I will be waiting for you out on our front porch. Just come on ahead, you yellow bastards." The threats never went further, and his father's stand made a lasting impression on Lyndon.

LBJ: My father fought the Ku Klux Klan many long years ago in Texas and I've fought them all my life because I believe them to threaten every community where they exist. I shall continue to fight them because I know their loyalty is not to the United States of America, but instead to a hooded society of bigots.

■ ■ ■

One can speculate, too, that he heard his mother's voice admonishing him to do better—to *be* better—and felt the cold shoulder that she would have turned on him if he hadn't given his best, driving his sometimes desperate need for approval.

There were also the experiences of Johnson's childhood and young adult life that made their mark on him: the effects of growing up poor, without basics such as electricity or indoor plumbing, in Johnson City, a place, as his father described it, "where folks care when you're sick, and go to your funeral when you die." Neighbors feel a certain responsibility toward each other and help out when they can, and Johnson took to heart the struggles they endured as a daily fact of life. And, of course, there were those poor Mexican American schoolchildren of Cotulla, who were seared into Johnson's consciousness, plus the experiences he had in the National Youth Administration, where he first came into close contact with African Americans.

LADY BIRD JOHNSON: Lyndon had the most extraordinary streak, sort of like he was born yesterday. I can hardly think of any prejudices that he had. And also there was the fact that he grew up in a community that did not have blacks. He often told how the first black came there working on a highway contract when he was a young man. So he did not grow up absorbing the attitudes of his parents and neighbors toward blacks. I really think that one of his first acquaintances with this was during the NYA, which was a very formative period in his life when he worked closely and with more success than most of his [colleagues] in trying to get jobs or education for black youngsters.

■ ■ ■

That didn't mean that Johnson was entirely free of the racial insensitivity that was reflexive for some members of his generation, particularly those from the South. The word *nigger* crept repugnantly into his vernacular on occasion, even after he became president. During the summer of 1967, in the wake of riots that ravaged downtown Detroit, Johnson sent in a White House task force to accompany army paratroopers. Roger Wilkins, a member of the task force, recalled the direction Johnson provided the group before their departure:

ROGER WILKINS, assistant attorney general, 1965–69: [H]e started in a low key. "I don't want any bullets in those guns. You hear me? I don't want any bullets in those guns! You hear me, gentlemen? I don't want any bullets in those guns. I don't want it known that any one of my men shot a pregnant nig—" And he looked at me and his face got red. I was the only black man in the room. "Well, I don't—I just—no bullets in those guns." But he was clearly embarrassed, and everyone in the room was embarrassed. So he told us to go home and pack and get on an Air Force plane to go to Detroit.

And as we're leaving, he called me and he said, "Come over here, Roger," and I went into his office with him. And he didn't say anything. I mean, I know what he wanted to say. "I didn't mean to say 'nigger.'" But he meant to say "nigger." And I knew he wanted to say, "I apologize." He didn't know how to say it.

And so he walked me over to the French doors that went out to the Rose Garden, and it's the area where Eisenhower had his putting green. And he looked out, and he looked at me, and he looked down, looked out, looked down. There were pockmarks on the floor where Eisenhower's golf shoes had hit the floor. And finally, he looked at me, looked at the floor, and he said, "Look at what that son of a bitch did to my floor!" And he patted me on the back and said, "Have a nice trip." And that was his way of apologizing. It was very human, I thought.

■ ■ ■

Whatever epithets were endemic to his vocabulary, Johnson related to the downtrodden, the forgotten, the disenfranchised, and the victims of bigotry, sexism, and hate. It was in Johnson's outsize nature to feel deeply. Whatever it was—the sting of feeling judged by the eastern establishment, or the outrage of being mischaracterized or misrepresented by the media, or compassion over the oppression of the impoverished and people of color—Johnson felt it to his core. He wasn't one to let things roll off his back; he internalized things, and they became him. "He felt too much," Marie Fehmer, one of his secretaries, believed. It was a product of his natural tendency toward excess. Mrs. Johnson recalled with some embarrassment seeing a Broadway production of *The Grapes of Wrath* prior to becoming First Lady, and hearing open sobbing from a member of the audience as the play depicted the Joad family facing their Depression-era travails, only to discover that it was coming from her husband seated next to her.

LAWRENCE O'BRIEN: If you're President of the United States, it must give you a warm feeling to find yourself in a position where you can do something about a matter that's of overriding significance. I don't know how to describe Lyndon Johnson in one word in that regard, but in that and similar areas, he was constantly articulating his interest and concern for people. It's not an exaggeration to say that, and I ran into it often.

THURGOOD MARSHALL: He intended to be to this century what Abraham Lincoln was to the last century, and he was going to do it. I frankly believe if he had had four more years, he just about would have done it. I mean, he rebelled at the discrimination against women—women judges. He always did. He said he wanted to leave the presidency in a position that there was no government job with a race tag on it—none! That's what he was driving at. He would constantly say, "If you've got any ideas, let me have them. If you don't want to bother with me, give them to Ramsey [Clark] or Nick [Katzenbach] or somebody like that. But if there's any way we can break through, let me know."

I just think Lyndon Johnson, insofar as minorities, civil rights, people in general, the inherent dignity of the individual human being—I don't believe there has ever been a president equal to Lyndon Johnson—bar none!

■ ■ ■

Like many of those who had held the office before him, Johnson grew by being president. It made him bigger and more empathetic; he was conscious of his responsibilities to all Americans "from the biggest corporation president to the poorest sharecropper." "They have babylike faith in me," he said in his first year in office, "and I want to be worthy of that faith."

At the same time, the job made him aware of his own limitations under its weight, and more open to God's hand. Not one to wear religion on his sleeve, Johnson spoke more often of God after taking office but was not bound to one denomination. The Johnson family was spread throughout the Christian church. At age eleven, the young Lyndon, without warning, had broken his scripture-quoting mother's Southern Baptist heart when he joined Disciples of Christ, a local Christian church. Later, Luci Johnson gave up her mother's Episcopalian church to embrace Catholicism. After becoming president, Johnson often attended multiple Sunday services of different Christian demoninations.

LUCI JOHNSON: My father would go to a nine o'clock Christian service, then turn around and go to an eleven o'clock service with [my mother], then try to go to mass with me at one. I would say to him, "Daddy, go watch *Meet the Press* or whatever you have to do. You've been to church twice, you don't need to do this for me." He said, "You don't understand, Luci. I'm not doing this for you. When you're in this position, you need all the help you can get."

LYNDA JOHNSON ROBB: [Daddy] was religious [but] not parochial. He found the responsibilities of being president overwhelming and felt the need for God's guidance. But God was in a very big tent for him. He respected all religions. God was an important part of his being, and he spoke of it more as he got older.

He used to say, "I know how much I need the Lord." [Going to] church made him feel closer to God.

■ ■ ■

It also made him feel closer to the people; being among them gave him comfort. Just as he had faith in a greater being, he had faith in his fellow man. Throughout a lifetime of considerable study of human nature, particularly in Washington, where motives are often tainted by personal gain, Johnson came out believing in people, and he wanted to do something for them. Even after he left the presidency, when, in his darkest hours, he bemoaned being wronged by many he thought had had a hand in his political demise, his belief never wavered. "If you really trust people," he said to Harry Middleton less than a year after leaving the White House, "there are few who don't reciprocate. Nearly every person in the world is good. Those who are not were messed up by someone."

Moreover, Johnson believed in the *American* people. In effect, he bet much of his presidency on the notion that the ideals that united Americans—belief in democracy and egalitarian liberty, the rule of law, and basic fairness—were more powerful and transcendent than the intrinsic flaws that divided them, even those as deep-seated as racism and xenophobia. When he implored Martin Luther King Jr. to expose the measures that bigoted southern officials were taking to prevent blacks from registering to vote, he was confident that "the fellow that [doesn't] do anything but drive a tractor will say, 'That's not right, that's not fair.'"

RAMSEY CLARK: For all his realism, which he never abandoned for all his practicality, he was an idealist. I mean, he—this was a man who believed you could end poverty—you know, how, how glorious—who believed you could end racism.

You can't get more idealistic than that, more wonderfully idealistic. But he always worked at it in a very practical, hardheaded, realistic way.

■ ■ ■

"Doing right isn't the problem," Johnson often said. "It's *knowing* what's right." Civil rights for all citizens, eradicating poverty, health care for the elderly, fostering education, further opening the promise of America to immigrants from across the world, protecting the environment for future generations. All were moral imperatives that Johnson knew were right.

Things weren't as clear with Vietnam.

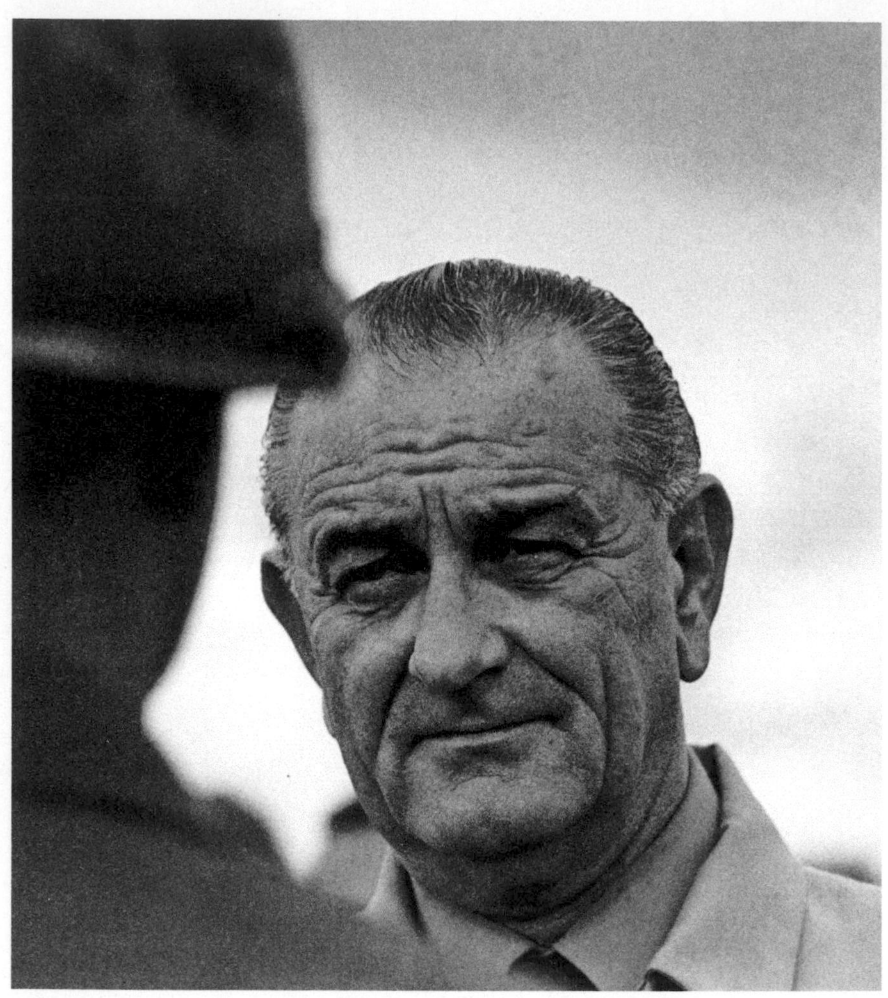

LBJ visits U.S. troops in Vietnam, October 26, 1966.

Chapter 7

COMMANDER IN CHIEF

"WHAT THE HELL IS VIETNAM WORTH TO ME?"

On the morning of May 27, 1964, a little more than two months before the Gulf of Tonkin Resolution passed easily through the House and Senate, allowing the White House the military authority to do what was needed in the region, Johnson had two telling phone conversations expressing his doubts about Vietnam. The first was with Georgia senator Richard Russell. Johnson called his soft-spoken friend and mentor to get his take on the war, before Johnson squared off against him for passage of the Civil Rights Act a few weeks later.

LBJ: *What do you think about this Vietnam thing? What—I'd like to hear you talk a little bit.*

Richard Russell: *Frankly, Mr. President, if you were to tell me that I was authorized to settle it as I saw fit, I would respectfully decline to undertake it. (Johnson chuckles) It's the damned worse mess I ever saw, and I don't like to brag, and I never have been right many times in my life, but I knew we were going to get into this sort of mess when we went in there. And I don't see how we're going [to] ever get out of it without fighting a major war with the Chinese and all of them down there in those rice paddies and jungles. I just don't see it. I just don't know what to do.*

LBJ: *Well, that's the way I've been feeling for six months.*

Shortly afterward, Johnson placed a call to McGeorge Bundy, the president's special assistant for national security affairs, in which he expressed in clear terms the dilemma Vietnam threw squarely on his lap.

LBJ: *I'll tell you, the more—I just stayed awake last night thinking about this thing—the more I think of it, I don't know what in the hell . . . it looks like to me we're getting into another Korea. It just worries the hell out of me. I don't see what we can ever hope to get out of there with once we're committed. I believe the Chinese Communists are coming into it. I don't think that we can fight them 10,000 miles away from home and ever get anywhere in that area. I don't think it's worth fighting for and I don't think we can get out. And it's just the biggest damn mess I ever saw.*

McGeorge Bundy, National Security Advisor, 1961–66: *It is, it's an awful mess.*

LBJ: *And we just got to think about [it]. I look at this sergeant of mine this morning, got six little ol' kids over there, and he's getting out my things and bringing me in my night reading and all that kind of stuff, and I just thought about ordering those kids in there, and what in the hell am I ordering him out there for?*

Bundy: *Ordering him out there . . . One thing that has occurred to me—*

LBJ: *What the hell is Vietnam worth to me? What is Laos worth to me? What is it worth to this country?*

Bundy: *Now we have to get into the [unclear] to explain this.*

LBJ: *Now . . . we've got a treaty, but hell, everybody else got a treaty out there and they're not doing a thing about it.*

Bundy: *Yup . . . yup . . . yup.*

LBJ: *Now, of course if you start running [from] the Communists, they may just chase you right into your own kitchen.*

Bundy: *Yup. That's the trouble. And that is what the rest of that half of the world is going to think if this thing comes apart on us. That's the dilemma. That's exactly the dilemma.*

LBJ: *What action do we take, though?*

Bundy: *Well, I think that we really need to do you some target-folder work, Mr. President, that shows precisely what we do and don't mean here. And the main object is to kill as few people as possible while creating an environment in which the incentive to react is as low as possible. But I can't say to you this is a small matter. There's one other thing that I've thought about, that I've only just thought about overnight. And it's on this same matter of saying to a guy, "You go to Korea, or you go to Vietnam, and you fight in the rice paddies." I would love to know what would happen if we were to say in this same speech, "And from now on, nobody goes to this task who doesn't volunteer." I think that we might turn around the atmosphere of our own people out there* *if it were a volunteers' enterprise. I suspect the Joint Chiefs won't agree to that, but I'd like to know what would happen. If we really dramatize this as Americans against terror, and Americans keeping their commitment, and Americans who have only peace as their object, and only Americans who want to go have to go, you might change the temper on its own.*

LBJ: *You wouldn't have a corporal's guard, would you?*

Bundy: *I just don't know. I just don't know. If that's true, then I'm not sure we're the country to do this job.*

LBJ: *I don't think it's just [Wayne] Morse and [Richard] Russell and [Ernest] Gruening. I think it . . . I think it's . . . did you see—*

Bundy: *I know it isn't, Mr. President. It's 90 percent of the people who don't want any part of it.*

LBJ: *Did you see the poll this morning? Sixty-five percent of them don't know anything about it, and of those that do, the majority think we're mishandling it, but they don't know what to do. That's Gallup.*

Bundy: *I'm sure that's right, yup . . . yup.*

LBJ: *It's damned easy to get in a war, but it's going to be awfully hard to ever extricate yourself if you get in.*

On the one hand, Vietnam was worth nothing to Johnson; he was wracked with the anxiety stemming from how to get out of the war once he was in it. On the other was his underlying fear that if the Communist insurgency went unchecked, the Soviet Union or China might threaten countries that were of greater consequence and the dominoes would start to fall. As he explained after leaving the presidency:

LBJ: They want what we've got and they're going to try to get it. If we let them take Asia, they're going to try to take us. I think aggression must be deterred. That's just sound policy. I believe big nations have to help the little nations. . . . I believe you've got to keep your guard up and your hand out. I want to be friendly with the Soviets and with the Chinese. But if you let a bully come in and chase you out of your front yard, tomorrow he'll be on your porch and the next day he'll rape your wife in your own bed.

■ ■ ■

While much of Johnson's reasoning for taking a stand in Vietnam reflected the accepted Domino Theory that prevailed in American geopolitical thinking during the cold war, his interest went beyond convention. Just as he had reformed U.S. immigration policy, which had previously favored Western Europe, he also resisted the traditional U.S. foreign policy paradigm—perpetuated by the eastern establishment—that had been geared toward the same region. His worldview was more inclusive. By taking a greater interest in Asia, he would challenge the Western orientation that had dominated America's approach to the world up to that point. At the same time, he was fearful of incurring the kind of criticism for losing Vietnam that had been directed at Truman after Communist revolutionaries, led by Mao Zedong, seized China in the late 1940s. The "Who Lost China?" debate, led in the media by *Time* and *Life* and its founder, Henry Luce, who was born in China, was less a question than an accusation that implicated Truman and the Democratic Party at large. Besides all that, Johnson and his predecessors had made a commitment to the people of South Vietnam, and he believed in seeing it through.

DEAN RUSK: Lyndon Johnson quoted [Arkansas senator William] Fulbright as having said about Vietnam that "They're not our kind of people." Lyndon Johnson was very derisive of that kind of approach to problems of that sort.

GEORGE CHRISTIAN: I don't know whether he read this or ascertained it or where it came from, but he sometimes referred to the fact that the East Coast academic, liberal establishment always looked to Europe, that they had a European connection that was very close, and it frustrated him that they didn't give a fig about the rest of the world. And he put Fulbright into this category. He said, "All Fulbright thinks about is going to England or being connected with the Marshall Plan or something European." He said, "He doesn't care about the Asians."

I think [Johnson] deliberately involved himself in Pacific affairs because so few of his predecessors had been in that area. I think this was unplowed ground through his eyes. It was their turn. That's where the action was. That's where the future was, and he wanted to be involved in it.

■ ■ ■

Ultimately, despite his consternation, which proved prescient, Vietnam *did* mean something to Johnson. It became evident with the escalation of U.S. military involvement in the war beginning in 1965. If Johnson had bet much of his presidency on the programs of the Great Society, he stacked the balance of his chips behind Vietnam.

At the beginning of 1965, 23,000 U.S. troops were stationed in South Vietnam as military advisers, providing logistical support and military strategy to South Vietnamese forces. That would change with a North Vietnamese attack on a U.S. military base in Pleiku, in South Vietnam's Central Highlands, in the small hours of the morning, on Sunday, February 7. As servicemen slept, their barracks fell under a hail of mortar fire that left eight dead and more than a hundred wounded. The news came as the South Vietnamese government was on the brink of collapse with the continued advancement of Viet Cong insurgents, aided by the North Vietnamese army. Just four hours after the attack, Johnson met with advisers to plot a strategy for going forward. Of those in attendance—Defense Secretary Robert McNamara; Undersecretary of State George Ball; chairman of the Joint Chiefs of Staff Earle Wheeler; deputy director of the CIA Marshall Cater; and Senate Majority Leader Mike Mansfield—all except Mansfield agreed that U.S. forces needed to strike back. McGeorge Bundy, who was in Vietnam at the time of the attack, had come to the same conclusion.

Johnson agreed, ordering a retaliatory air strike against the North Vietnamese army just over the country's southern border. "They are killing our men while they sleep in the night," he reasoned. "I can't ask our American soldiers out there to continue to fight with one hand tied behind their backs." For the first time since the Gulf of Tonkin incident, American forces engaged directly with the North Vietnamese through a sustained air campaign that would eventually be known as Operation Rolling Thunder. The strategy Johnson took was to tread a delicate balance between deterring the North Vietnamese through the strikes while taking care not to draw the Chinese or the Soviet Union into the fight. That meant refraining from bombing targets of strategic importance, Hanoi, North Vietnam's capital, and Hai Phong, its major seaport, while exerting enough force through the buildup of troops to bring the enemy to the peace table. On March 8 two Marine battalions constituting 3,500 soldiers landed at Danang to protect U.S. airfields, with orders to engage with the enemy if fired upon, marking the first time combat forces had been sent to the Asian mainland since the Korean War over a decade earlier. With the dispatch of two additional Marine battalions the following month, the United States had embarked on a full-scale ground war. "If I don't go in now and they show me later I should have gone," Johnson said of the escalation, "then they'll be all over me in Congress. They won't be talking about my Civil Rights bill, or education, or beautification. No, sir.

They'll be pushing Vietnam up my ass every time—Vietnam, Vietnam, Vietnam."

By the summer, the number of troops had increased to seventy-five thousand, more than threefold what it had been before the attack at Pleiku in February. Each request for additional servicemen was accompanied by assurances from Johnson's advisers and military leaders that it would be enough to push the war effort in America's favor—only to be followed by requests for more troops.

Johnson and Kennedy had shared a mutual distrust of the military. Their impressions had been shaped by two crises that unfolded under Kennedy's watch: the botched Bay of Pigs invasion and the Cuban Missile Crisis, during which the Joint Chiefs seemed intent on military engagement with the Soviets, provocative action that could have resulted in a hot war. "[Johnson] once said very bitterly that he and Kennedy agreed that the generals always wanted, 'More, more, more,'" recalled Helen Thomas. In a conversation with Mike Mansfield, Johnson predicted the Pentagon's consistent requests for more troops, saying, "If they get 150, they will have to get another 150, and then they will have to get another 150."

SID DAVIS: [Johnson] did have what would seem to be a congenital dislike and distrust of the military. Even when he was vice president, down in Florida at Palm Beach, when they were going over the budget he made those derisive comments about General LeMay, whom he held up as typical of everybody in the military. And yet there was something about [William] Westmoreland [commander of military operations in Vietnam] that impressed him. He called him Westy; there seemed to be a relationship there. He trusted Westmoreland up to a certain point and then it was all over. He did have a distrust.

WARREN ROGERS: Westmoreland was a protégé of Omar Bradley, and Johnson had the greatest admiration for Omar Bradley.

But he had nobody to turn to. The only experts he had were in the military. I remember Valenti saying to me when I'd come back from Vietnam, "Go see the President." He'd get excited and say, "Come back. Come back. We need somebody to provide some antidotes for the stuff he's getting from the generals."

HUGH ROBINSON: I didn't see [Johnson] as having a real option because there were already American boys in Vietnam as advisers. He didn't send the first ones to Vietnam. What he could have done was to [keep U.S. troops] in the advisory role, but he would not have been successful [in the war], as he was told constantly by the Joint Chiefs of Staff.

He agonized every time he sent anyone to Vietnam, whether it was one or one hundred thousand. He kept trying to put a brake on it. And he was always being told, "Just a hundred thousand more, Mr. President."

■ ■ ■

To a greater extent, Johnson heeded the counsel of the men who would become the chief architects in the war, Secretary of Defense Robert McNamara, National Security Advisor McGeorge Bundy, and Secretary of State Dean Rusk. All advised Johnson that Vietnam was a conflict that the United States could ill afford to turn its back on.

DOUGLAS KIKER, White House correspondent, *The New York Herald Tribune;* NBC news correspondent: Lest we forget, [Robert] McNamara, McGeorge Bundy, and Dean Rusk were all telling this man, "We can win there if we put in just a few more troops." They waited until after Lyndon had won on his own in 1964 and then they went down to the Ranch and said, "Here's how we're going to win in Vietnam." Johnson thought, "I can put this thing over. I can give them guns and butter or make them think they're getting guns and butter. It won't take that many troops. I'll get myself a negotiated settlement." He didn't trust them but he thought he could pull it off, and he couldn't.

■ ■ ■

As Kennedy observed after the Bay of Pigs, "Success has many fathers, but failure is an orphan." Though revisionist history was offered up by some administration officials and military leaders after the war in Vietnam began to founder, only George Ball, Johnson's undersecretary of state, and Kennedy's before him, sounded a voice of dissent among principal Johnson advisers. Dispensing with the Domino Theory, Ball came to believe that Southeast Asia was inconsequential in the cold war, and that the key to U.S. strength against the threat of Communist infiltration lay in a unified Western Europe.

GEORGE BALL, undersecretary of state, 1961–66; U.S. representative to the UN, 1968: [I] thought that the balloon was going up much too fast, so I spent a few nights preparing a memorandum which was 75 pages or so, which is now in the public domain, in which I challenged every assumption of our war in Vietnam and came to the conclusion that it wasn't a war we could win. And the next morning, I got a call [from President Johnson]. He said, "Damn you, George, you've kept me awake all night. I read that thing three times. Why didn't you get to me before? Get over here in the morning and we'll discuss it if it takes all day."

■ ■ ■

The problem was that Ball offered Johnson no plausible reasoning for how pulling out of Vietnam wouldn't embolden the Communist world and lead to a greater conflict as nations of strategic significance fell to the same influences.

DEAN RUSK: George Ball was the only officer in the Department of State who walked into my room and dug his heels in the rug and said, "I don't like it." Yet some of these characters in Department of State, when they left the department, turned out to be the pluperfect doves. Why didn't they say that to me when they were in [the department]?

HARRY MCPHERSON: We had a series of meetings between February and April, and Johnson kept saying [to Ball], "Tell us, tell us, what else can we do?" And Ball couldn't come up with a better alternative.

WALT ROSTOW, special assistant for national security affairs (national security advisor), 1966–69: The problem for President Johnson was that neither George Ball nor anyone else was able to give him a picture of what would happen if he did get out. No one assured him that he wouldn't be moving into a greater disaster and a larger war. That was the question that none of the people who objected to his policy was ever able to answer.

■ ■ ■

Regardless, well into 1965, there was little reason to think that Ball was on to something. The war seemed a winnable campaign. All it would take was a little more.

CHET COOPER, senior member, National Security Council staff, 1964–66; special assistant to Ambassador Averell Harriman, 1966–67: [M]any of us felt quite optimistic about what was going on; the bombing raids had started. There were now about 75,000 troops there, and who are we dealing with? We were dealing with a bunch of guys with sharp sticks, the Viet Minh. Unless I was alone in this, I think there was a sense that we're not going to lose; we're going to win this one.

■ ■ ■

Still, Johnson harbored doubts.

SID DAVIS, White House correspondent, Westinghouse Broadcasting Company: It was April 6, 1965. Mrs. Johnson and the girls were out of town. The President had been invited over to the Smithsonian to dedicate a new fish—something they'd hung on the wall—and he went over and made a little speech. There were several of us reporters—myself, Charlie Mohr of *The New York Times*, and a couple of other people. It was a beautiful April night and we were walking back to the White House, and a car pulled up alongside of us; it was the presidential limousine. The window rolled down, the President stuck his head out the window and said, "How would y'all like a ride?" So we said, "Sure," and we got in the car.

Jack Valenti was in the jump seat. All four of us piled in the car, with Jack Valenti and the President in the back. He said, "Jack, when's my next appointment?"

Valenti says, "It's right now."

He said, "Well, I think I've got time to buy these fellows a drink."

So we went over to the White House . . . up to the family quarters—incidentally, I don't think many reporters through history traipsed through the family quarters of the White House the way we did during Lyndon Johnson's time. I don't know how Mrs. Johnson ever put up with it. I've known vice presidents who have never been up to the family quarters, yet we'd been up there a lot. But anyway, we went to the family quarters; we went to the Yellow Sitting Room, had a scotch and soda.

He talked about the war. We could tell it was a great burden for him. This went on for about an hour, and then he took us to the Lincoln Bedroom, and we stood there with him and he said, "Sit down on the bed." And none of us wanted to sit on Lincoln's bed. He said, "No, I want you to sit on the bed. Everybody else does. We have visitors who come here and sleep on the bed." So we sat down on the bed, and he said, "I come down here virtually every morning about two o'clock, and I pick up that phone and I call the Situation Room. And I say, 'How many of my boys are out there?' And I may stay here through the night, and I keep calling to find out how many didn't come back."

It was a side of Lyndon Johnson many of us had never seen. And then he walked over—I believe there's a picture of Lincoln in the room—and he walked over to the picture of Lincoln and he said, "You know, doing what is right is easy. The problem is knowing what is right." And then he said, looking at Lincoln, "I sure hope I have better generals than he did."

"ANOTHER CUBA"?

Vietnam wasn't the only foreign policy matter to keep Johnson awake during the month of April—and not the only one that would eventually stir controversy. On April 24 he got word of civil unrest in the Dominican Republic, where an uprising propelled by the PRD (Dominican Revolutionary Party) was underfoot to unseat the nation's unpopular civilian dictator, the pro-American Donald Reid Cabral, and restore his predecessor, Juan Bosch, to power. Bosch had been deposed by a military coup in 1963, after holding office for just seven months, during which time he ruled as a liberal anticommunist, though still thought by Washington to be a "dangerous demagogue" who could open the door to Communist influences. As the insurgency festered, word in Santo Domingo and Washington was that it had been co-opted by Fidel Castro. Never mind that the situation was cloudy as to who stood where, the rumors were enough to arouse fear that the Dominican situation would turn into "another Cuba," and Johnson would not sit idly by and allow the United States to suffer a second Communist sucker punch in the Western Hemisphere.

Monitoring events closely, Johnson concluded, along with his advisers, that American troops were needed in the Caribbean nation to help restore order and prevent a Communist takeover—only initially he didn't position it that way to the American people. Already sensitive to criticism regarding Vietnam that he was a reflexive anticommunist who saw military action as the only way to keep communism at bay, Johnson justified his decision by saying in a statement on April 28 that "hundreds" of American lives were "in danger."

On April 28, as the situation intensified, he ordered four hundred marines to the island before dispatching the Eighty-second Airborne. Two days later he called Senate Majority Leader Mike Mansfield to ask for support of his actions in anticipation of pressure to respond forcefully from "the Dirksens," the hawkish members of the GOP in Congress:

LBJ: *The Castro forces are really gaining control. . . . They're marching [nine hundred police] down the streets as hostages. . . . They're going to set up a Castro government. . . . We begged the OAS [Organization of American States] to send somebody in last night. They won't move. They're just phantoms. They're just the damnedest fraud I ever saw, Mike. They won't move. . . . They just talk. These international organizations ain't worth a damn, except [as] window dressing. . . . The big question is, Do we let Castro take over and us move out? . . . The OAS called for a cease-fire last night, but they went home and went to sleep. . . . I'm trying to get them back today. And I suppose they don't [meet] today? Do I let them take over? It looks to me like I'm in a hell of a shape either way. . . . I'm putting heat on, but how would you respond to this call for help of the nine hundred police? If I let them fall, you know what the Dirksens are going to do to us.*

Mike Mansfield, U.S. senator, Montana (D), 1953–77: *That's right.*

LBJ: *They're going to eat us up if I let another Cuba come in there. They'll say, "Why did you sit on your big fat tail?" I'm afraid to talk to them, Mike, because they go out and talk. . . . I'm really afraid to talk to anybody. I'm afraid if I talk to Fulbright . . . he'll tell* The New York Times *. . . you just can't talk to Fulbright or Dirksen. They just talk.*

Afterward Johnson took to the airwaves offering a statement indicating that there were "signs that people trained outside the Dominican Republic are seeking to gain control," and announcing his support of the OAS peacekeeping delegation in helping to find a democratic solution to the problem.

As the conflict escalated, along with troop levels, so did Johnson's rhetoric. Two days later he reinforced the gravity of the situation, stressing in a public statement that "at stake are the lives of thousands, the liberty of a nation, and the principles and the values of all the American Republics." He further explained that what had begun as "a popular democratic revolution" had been "seized and placed into the hands of a band of Communist conspirators." By mid-May some twenty thousand American troops would be drawn into the conflict.

John Bartlow Martin, the U.S. ambassador to the Dominican Republic under Kennedy, was summoned to the White House from his home in Connecticut to weigh in on the crisis with Johnson and his advisers. During the course of their meeting, Martin was asked by Johnson to go to the Dominican Republic to try to establish contact with the insurgents and get a read on the situation.

JOHN BARTLOW MARTIN, U.S. ambassador to the Dominican Republic, 1962–64: The President ran the Dominican intervention like a desk officer in the State Department. I mean, I talked to him at least once a day, and sometimes I talked to him three times a day. . . . [T]he President ordinarily withholds himself a little bit. But this President did not. He was in that Dominican thing. He told me to call him any time of the day or night. I believe once I called him about three in the morning, after I talked to Bosch in San Juan, Puerto Rico.

He ran it the way he runs everything, I gather: in an intensely personal way, with total attention to detail, and he doesn't stand back. I think that might account for his intemperate utterances on television.

Nobody was really sure what the hell they were going to do when they got there. That was what the meeting was about, you see. At one point, Secretary Rusk reminded the President that it was a serious matter to start shooting up a capital city with American troops. And I said, "That's the last thing we want to happen, Mr. President." And he said, "No, it isn't. The last thing we want to have happen is a Communist takeover in that country."

■ ■ ■

Johnson's storyteller's penchant for exaggeration did not serve him well in the crisis. Among his "intemperate utterances" was one in which he claimed that "some 1,500 innocent people were murdered and shot, and their heads cut off, and six Latin American embassies were violated and fired upon over a period of four days before we went in. As we talked to our ambassador to confirm the horrors and the tragedy and the unbelievable fact that they were firing on Americans and the American embassy, he was talking to us from under a desk while bullets were going through his windows." According to independent reports, his statement bore little resemblance to the facts.

MAX FRANKEL, Washington bureau chief, *The New York Times:* Johnson was fundamentally dishonest in presenting the facts about what was happening in the Dominican Republic to the American people—pouring troops in there and telling ridiculous stories about fifteen hundred heads rolling around the streets and so on. Whatever the credibility gap ultimately became, the combination of opposition to the policy and the horror at the government's handling and explanation of the event is probably where it was born.

J. WILLIAM FULBRIGHT, U.S. senator from Arkansas (D), 1945–74: What astounded me about the Dominican Republic was that the first excuse given was that we were there to save American lives. The next was to prevent another Cuba. But when they asked [director of the CIA] Admiral Raborn how many Communists they had identified as participating in the revolt, I think he said three.

That made us look kind of silly, the whole idea that we were stopping a Communist takeover. Later they tried to identify more.

JOHN BARTLOW MARTIN: Our policy seemed more erratic than it was. During the first few days, in a situation so chaotic and confused, it would be surprising if we had been able to lay out a policy neatly. But in fact, on two fundamental points, our policy did settle early and went unchanged: to protect United States lives and to prevent a Castro/Communist takeover.

I have no doubt whatsoever that there was a real danger of a Communist takeover in the Dominican Republic.

■ ■ ■

The time Johnson spent dealing with the crisis during the course of April and May suggests that he felt the same threat acutely. Of the fifty-one hours he spent in phone conversations throughout the same period—the phone being a virtual appendage to LBJ, who used it constantly and had lines installed ubiquitously—roughly thirty-five were spent attending to the Dominican situation. Despite his overblown public rhetoric during the crisis, his concerns, based on all he was hearing at the time, were justified.

Unlike with Vietnam, Johnson would find a way out of the Dominican Republic. The OAS peacekeeping delegation, headed by OAS secretary-general José A. Mora, made headway in negotiations that resulted in a cease-fire agreement on April 30. Later in August, in addition to John Bartlow Martin, Johnson would send a string of advisers to the Dominican Republic in the coming weeks, including McGeorge Bundy, Undersecretary of State Thomas Mann, Deputy Secretary of Defense Cyrus Vance, his personal friend Abe Fortas, and Ellsworth Bunker, who would later become U.S. ambassador to South Vietnam. Bunker, as part of the special OAS Committee, would finally succeed in resolving the crisis. In late August, the OAS Committee's continued negotiations led to the formation of a provisional government and eventually to a national election, on June 1, 1966, deemed by the OAS to be "an outstanding act of democratic purity."

The outcome of the election saw Juan Bosch defeated by another former president, Joaquín Balaguer, who had held office from 1960 to 1962, prior to Bosch's tenure. The OAS's successful resolution to the conflict allowed for the withdrawal of U.S. troops.

Johnson's relief was manifest in another intemperate statement: Praising the job Mora had done in negotiating a settlement, he told reporters, "He can have anything I've got. He can have my little daughter Luci. Why, I'd even tongue him myself."

LYNDON JOHNSON'S WAR

During the late spring and summer of 1965, as the crisis in the Dominican Republic simmered down, the war in Vietnam heated up. Word from U.S. military intelligence in Saigon indicated that the situation was worsening. A report on June 7 stated that the Army of the Republic of South Vietnam (ARVN) was in shambles, and the South Vietnamese government had little chance of standing on its own. On June 12, the South Vietnamese government changed again, bringing to power Nguyen Cao Ky as prime minister, and Nguyen Van Thieu as commander of the armed forces. The thirty-five-year-old Ky, dubbed "the Cowboy," flamboyantly wore a pearl-handled revolver by his side and a silk scarf wrapped around his neck, and openly admired Adolf Hitler. Not surprisingly, he had a reputation for ruthlessness. So did the forty-two-year-old Thieu. Neither inspired great confidence as the leaders of a wobbly nation. Without the military intervention of outside forces, South Vietnam faced certain collapse.

Concurrent with the June 7 report came a request from Westmoreland, backed by McNamara, to boost U.S. troop levels to 175,000. Once again, as the stakes got higher, Johnson was left to wrestle with the question of whether to pull forces from the region or commit to the war in far greater numbers, putting U.S. prestige further on the line—fold or double-down? The difference this time was that a presidential go-ahead would make Vietnam not only America's war but Lyndon Johnson's.

It was not a decision he took lightly. "What I would like to know," he challenged his advisers in a series of intensive meetings over the next several weeks, "is what has happened in recent months that requires this kind of decision on my part? What are the alternatives? I want this discussed in full detail from everyone around the table." With the exception of George Ball, his advisers maintained their belief that fighting the war was a national security imperative. Johnson also sought outside counsel. On July 2, he consulted with Dwight Eisenhower by telephone:

LBJ: *I'm having a meeting this morning with my top people. . . . McNamara recommends really what Westmoreland and Wheeler do—a quite expanded operation, and one that's really going to kick up some folks like [Gerald] Ford. He says that he doesn't want to use ground troops. He thinks we ought to do it by bombing. We can't even protect our bases without the ground troops, according to Westmoreland. And we've got all the Bobby Kennedys and the Mansfields and the Morses against it. But [Westmoreland] recommends an all-out operation. We don't know whether we can beat them with that or not. The State Department comes in and recommends a rather modified one through the monsoon season, to see how effective we are with our B-52 strikes and with our other strikes. . . . Westmoreland has urged . . . about double what we've got there now. But if we do that, we've got to call up the Reserves and get authority from Congress. . . . That will really serve notice that we're in a land operation over there. Now, I guess it's your view that we ought to do that. You don't think that we can just have a holding operation, from a military standpoint, do you?*

Dwight Eisenhower, U.S. president, 1953–61: *You've got to go along with your military advisers, because otherwise you are just going to continue to have these casualties indefinitely. . . . My advice is, do what you have to do. I'm sorry that you have to go to the Congress . . . but I guess you would be calling up the Reserves.*

LBJ: *Yes, sir. We're out of them, you see. . . . And if they move on other fronts, we'll have to increase our strength, too. . . . [The State Department says] we ought to avoid bombing Hanoi until we can see through the monsoon season whether, with these forces there, we can make any progress . . . before going out and executing everything. Of course, McNamara's people recommend taking all the harbors . . . mining and blowing the hell out of it . . . They go all out. State Department people say they're taking too much chance on bringing China in and Russia in. . . . They [want] to try . . . during the monsoon season to hold what [we've] got, and to really try to convince Russia that if she doesn't bring about some kind of understanding, we're going to have to give them the works. But they believe that she doesn't really want an all-out war.*

Eisenhower: *. . . [For them to] agree to some kind of negotiation . . . [you must say,] "Hell, we're going to end this and win this thing. . . . We don't intend to fail." . . .*

LBJ: *You think that we can really beat the Vietcong out there?*

Eisenhower: . . . *This is the hardest thing [to decide,] because we can't finally find out how many of these Vietcong have been imported down there and how many of them are just rebels.*

LBJ: *We killed twenty-six thousand [enemy forces] this year. . . . Three hundred yesterday . . . Two hundred and fifty of them the day before. But they just keep coming in from North Vietnam. . . . How many they're going to pour in from China, I don't know. . . .*

Eisenhower: . . . *I would go ahead and . . . do it as quickly as I could.*

LBJ: *You're the best chief of staff I've got. . . . I've got to rely on you on this one.*

On July 8, Johnson met with a group of foreign policy sages who would become known as the Wise Men. All were former high-ranking government and military officials who had helped to contain the Communist threat at the dawn of the cold war after World War II. The august group, which Johnson would convene throughout the war, included men such as Dean Acheson, who had served as Truman's secretary of state, and five-star general Omar Bradley. All reached the same conclusion: to yield to the Communists might only lead to a greater conflict down the line.

Outside of the White House, voices opposed to the war were beginning to murmur, and a movement was burgeoning. In the halls of Congress, Wayne Morse and Ernest Gruening, who had been alone in their votes against the Gulf of Tonkin Resolution, were joined in their opposition to war by William Fulbright, George McGovern, and Frank Church, despite the war's overwhelming support among their colleagues. Mansfield had also been consistently critical of the war, but mainly in private. McGovern had been the first vocal critic of Vietnam, expressing doubts as early as September 1963, as Kennedy made his stand, that the United States could prevail there. But he held back his criticism of Johnson, giving the new president the benefit of the doubt on the war.

GEORGE MCGOVERN: When Jack was killed and Lyndon took over, I felt this new administration is entitled to be free of criticism on any point until they get their feet on the ground. So I quit talking against Vietnam in late '63 and early '64. And I thought, were Johnson reelected in '64 he would get us out of there overnight. I remember telling people, "I tell you this, when Lyndon Johnson—once he's elected—he'll terminate that thing overnight." I really believed that: that Johnson was too shrewd to continue [our involvement]. He didn't want to go into the '64 campaign by repudiating a military involvement that his predecessor had thought was important.

So I didn't say anything during the Johnson administration [against the war] until after he was [elected]. Frank Church took the same course. He said, "Lyndon will pull us out of there." [T]hen, after the election, when [Johnson] started to escalate the war, that's when Frank Church and I both opened up. Up until then the ball on dissent was carried by Morse and Gruening, 'cause they *did* think we were going to get in deeper. I don't know why. What I was told was that Morse had a former staff member in the administration at the State Department who they never would identify—or would never admit that he was leaking them information. But I'm sure that was true. Now, neither one of them ever told me that, but it was a strong belief in the Senate that they had a pipeline. And those speeches they made were brilliant. And they liked Lyndon, so they talked about "McNamara's war! McNamara's war!" They never mentioned Lyndon.

They kept a drumbeat almost daily. They led the dissent movement in '63 and '64. Then I think it's fair to say that beginning in early '65, Frank Church, Bill Fulbright, and myself, maybe, were the big three in going after the war. And we did it feeling we'd almost been betrayed by Johnson. He assured the country we're not putting additional forces in there. So we felt somewhat betrayed.

■ ■ ■

An April 17 antiwar demonstration in Washington staged by Students for a Democratic Society brought together as many as sixteen thousand protesters showing up at the White House, many of them dressed in suits and ties, carrying signs with sentiments such as "No More War" and "We Want Peace Now." Renowned journalist Walter Lippmann, whom Johnson had awarded the Presidential Medal of Freedom a year earlier, was openly questioning Johnson's actions in Vietnam in his newspaper column.

Among the most prominent critics of the war was Martin Luther King Jr., who had been quoted by *The New York Times* on July 3 as saying the war in Vietnam "must be stopped," advocating its end even if it meant negotiating a settlement with the Viet Cong. As the White House prepared the bill that would become the Voting Rights Act, Johnson called King on July 7 to discuss potential obstacles on Capitol Hill. Toward the end of their conversation, the talk turned to Vietnam:

Martin Luther King Jr.: *Now there's one other point that I wanted to mention to you, because it has begun to concern me a great deal. . . . In the last few days . . . I made a statement concerning the Vietnam situation. . . . This in no way is an attempt to engage in a criticism of [your] policies. . . . The Press, unfortunately, lifted it out of context. . . . I know the terrible burden and awesome responsibilities and decisions that you have to make are very complicated, and I don't want to add to the burdens because I know they're very difficult.*

LBJ: *Well, you, you, you're very . . . helpful, and I appreciate it. I did see it. I was distressed. . . . I'd welcome the chance to review with you my problems and alternatives there. I not only know you have a right, I think you have a duty, as a minister and as a leader of millions of people, to give them a sense of purpose and direction. . . . I've lost about 264 lives up to now. And I could lose 265,000 mighty easy. I'm trying to keep those zeroes down, and at the same time not trigger a conflagration that would be worse than if we pulled out.*

I can't stay there and do nothing. Unless I bomb, they'll run me out right quick . . . by taking their bridges out . . . [and] their radar stations. . . . A good many people, including the military, think that's not near enough. . . . I've tried to keep it to that so I won't escalate it and get into trouble with China and Russia, and I don't want to be a warmonger. . . . If I pulled out, I think our commitments would be no good anywhere. I think we'd immediately trigger a situation in Thailand that would be just as bad as Vietnam. . . . And I'm trying. . . . I didn't get us into this. We got into it in '54. Eisenhower and Kennedy were in it deep. There were 33,000 men out there when I came into the presidency. I don't want to pull down the flag and come home running with my tail between my legs. . . . On the other hand, I don't want to get us in a war with China and Russia. So, I've got a pretty tough problem. And I'm not all wise. I pray every night to get direction and judgment and leadership that permit me to do what's right. . . .

What was right, Johnson decided, was to stay the course in Vietnam. He signaled as much in a Rose Garden meeting with the press on July 14, stating, "[O]ur national honor is at stake in Southeast Asia, and we are going to protect it, and you might just as well be prepared for it." At the same time, he portended the "dark days" that would follow.

Two weeks later he made it official. While he had used overstatement to justify his actions in the Dominican Republic, he pursued a markedly different communications strategy in conveying the escalation, underplaying the matter and forgoing any attempt to rally the nation to the cause of war. The president's announcement that he had "ordered to Vietnam the air mobile division and certain other forces which will raise our fighting strength from 75,000 to 125,000 men almost immediately" with additional forces to "be sent as requested" came not in an evening prime-time address, but in an afternoon press conference, during which Vietnam was one in a list of items he discussed. He insisted that his decision did "not imply any change in policy whatever" nor "any change of objective."

There were two reasons for understatement. First, Johnson was conscious of Vietnam becoming a speed bump that would slow the advancement of his Great Society. With pivotal legislation on the line, he added that he would "not allow" his domestic goals to be "drowned in the wasteful ravages of cruel wars." Second, and more important, he didn't want the din of drumbeats for war to compel the Soviets and Chinese to sound their own.

WILLIAM BUNDY, assistant secretary of state for East Asian and Pacific affairs, 1964–69: [M]ost certainly [Johnson] did low-key it. In dealing [with] the Soviet Union, you did not want to raise the decibel level, because it would interfere with other ongoing relationships, some of them quite constructive and important, like the non-proliferation treaty. He did not want to get into a confrontation with the Soviet Union. He did not want to get into a confrontation with China, for an even more direct and immediate reason: Any possible chance, whatever the percentage you want to assign it, of a repeat of the crossing of the Yalu [River in the Korean War], the Chinese really coming in hard.

There were a great many foreign policy arguments advanced to him, forcefully by George Ball in the case of the China danger, certainly as to the overall relationship with the Soviet Union by both Dean Rusk and [U.S. Ambassador Llewellyn] "Tommy" Thompson. He had enormous respect for Tommy and his judgment in that field. And these people were not thinking Great Society. They were thinking the overall foreign policy context and the merits of a low-keyed as opposed to a high-keyed policy.

LBJ: From November 23[, 1963,] until July 1965, I tried to keep from going into Vietnam. Nearly 85 percent of the people in Congress said, "We're not for your poverty program, but we're sure behind you in Vietnam." If I'm the only man left standing in this country to say aggression must not succeed anywhere in the world, I'll say it.

■ ■ ■

Along with Johnson's announcement to boost troop levels came a commander in chief's directive to double the draft call. Structured as it was, the draft was not an equitable lottery but a registration system that allowed for the relatively easy deferment of young men who were college or graduate students or married, or who had opted to serve instead in the Reserves or National Guard (neither of which was called into battle). Though the system gave Johnson some political cover in the escalation of the war, offering those of financial means or personal connections a way around Vietnam, he was troubled by its basic unfairness. It would have been a conflict for a man whose Great Society meant further paving the way toward America's inherent promise of equality. But despite whatever reservations he had, and the recommendation to end college deferments by an independent commission he appointed, Johnson chose the path of least resistance, and the draft remained unchanged.

LBJ: A great part of our student population became professional students—they dodged the draft for four or five years.

I had to make a basic decision on the draft. I had two fellows [from my staff] argue the merits of both sides. Larry Levinson argued that students should be further deferred. DeVier Pierson argued the other way. And I made up my mind.

■ ■ ■

The draft was one of an endless stream of decisions over the war served up to Johnson by staff members. Every Tuesday in particular there was a rash of them. Whenever possible throughout his White House tenure, Johnson convened a weekly "Tuesday Lunch" with his senior foreign policy advisers, to review the progress of the war and plot strategy. True to form, Johnson micromanaged certain aspects of the war. While granting leeway to military leaders in conducting the ground war, he kept an active hand in determining where bombing campaigns would be concentrated.

WALT ROSTOW: The procedure as far as the President was concerned was the following: McNamara, later with Wheeler, jointly came in with a list, which had been forwarded from CINCPAC [Commander in chief, U.S. Pacific Command]. The President would ask the following questions: What is the strategic importance of the target? How many planes will we lose? What will be the civilian casualties? There would be a discussion around those three points and the President would make a calculus, and I would say that nine out of ten lists that ever came up were approved. It was not a big part in the Tuesday lunch, but it was a part. The other restrictions—the question of bombs, for example—never came up in my experience, certainly not at the White House level. It might have been debated in the Pentagon. But those were the three questions and the rationale was quite clearly that the President wanted to make sure that the American lives lost were being lost for worthy targets, and he was anxious that we not kill an excessive number of civilians for a trivial target.

His other questions were about ships. He had a "Remember the Maine" anxiety about the Russians and Chinese, that bombing might trigger something if you hit them. So that was the fourth element: What chance is there of hitting a ship and engaging the Chinese or Russians?

■ ■ ■

Part of Johnson's low-key approach in not antagonizing China or the Soviet Union meant pursuing a strategy of "gradualism" advocated by McNamara and Rusk, which would steadily build up U.S. troop presence over time. But by July there was no illusion about the war being over quickly or easily. The greatest hope was to end the campaign by flexing enough military muscle to bring the North Vietnamese to the peace table.

ROBERT MCNAMARA, secretary of defense, 1961–68: We recommended an increase in troops not, I emphasize, to win the war by military means, but to prepare a foundation for a political settlement. We recommended a specific number of troops be approved for an addition at that time, but stated specifically that it was likely that additional troops would be required. The specific numbers are referred to in the memorandum of 20 July, 1965, to the President. We emphasized then that several hundred thousand troops above and beyond the numbers recommended for immediate deployment might be required. So it was very clear by mid-1965 that we believed that if we pursued the course of action that was being considered at that time, a very large number of troops would be in Vietnam at the end of 1965 and in later years as well.

I think the policy of gradualism will be debated for decades to come with hindsight. At the time I was a major proponent of it—perhaps *the* major proponent of it. But I proposed it for several reasons: One, because I wished to avoid—to minimize the risk of a military confrontation—confrontation with the Soviet Union and the People's Republic [of China]. Two, because I wished to minimize the damage—the loss of lives and the other damage—to both the U.S. and its allies and to the people of Indochina. And three, because I never did believe that a military victory in the narrow sense of the word was possible, with a gradual application or non-gradual application of military power. So, for all these reasons I favored gradualism.

■ ■ ■

By November, troop levels stood at 184,000, with nearly 200,000 more to be shipped out by the end of 1966, but by all indications far more would be needed to turn the war's tide. McNamara, who had visited Vietnam the same month, prepared Johnson for the worst, informing him that as many as 600,000 troops would be required by 1968. Even then, McNamara maintained it wouldn't be enough to guarantee success.

The following month, Johnson ended the year on a hopeful note. At McNamara's suggestion, and despite the advice of the Joint Chiefs of Staff, he dangled an olive branch before the North Vietnamese, ordering the cessation of the bombing of North Vietnam as a goodwill gesture to entice Ho Chi Minh into peace negotiations. On Christmas Eve, Operation Rolling Thunder was temporarily suspended as Johnson sent Hubert Humphrey, American UN ambassador Arthur Goldberg, U.S. ambassador-at-large Averell Harriman, and others on a diplomatic foray to the capital cities of forty nations to ask their help in getting the North Vietnamese to the bargaining table. "The Paul Reveres are riding all over the world," Mrs. Johnson wrote in her diary of their efforts. "Hubert has just returned from a five-day trip to four countries; Goldberg has been to see the Pope, [French president Charles] De Gaulle and [British prime minister Harold] Wilson; Harriman is traveling on and on, country after country. There are no real flashes of hope. But there is, I believe, a feeling in the country that we are doing all we can, sort of a tour-de-force peace offensive that leaves no door unknocked." In his State of the Union address on January 12 of the new year, Johnson said, "There are no arbitrary limits to our search for peace. . . . We will meet at any conference table, we will discuss any proposals—four points, or 14, or 40—and we will work . . . for a cease-fire now or once discussions have begun. We'll respond if others reduce their use of force."

Thirty-seven days after Johnson ordered a halt to the bombing, after his diplomatic overtures were written off by Hanoi as "deceptive" and "a trick," Operation Rolling Thunder resumed with no end to the war in sight.

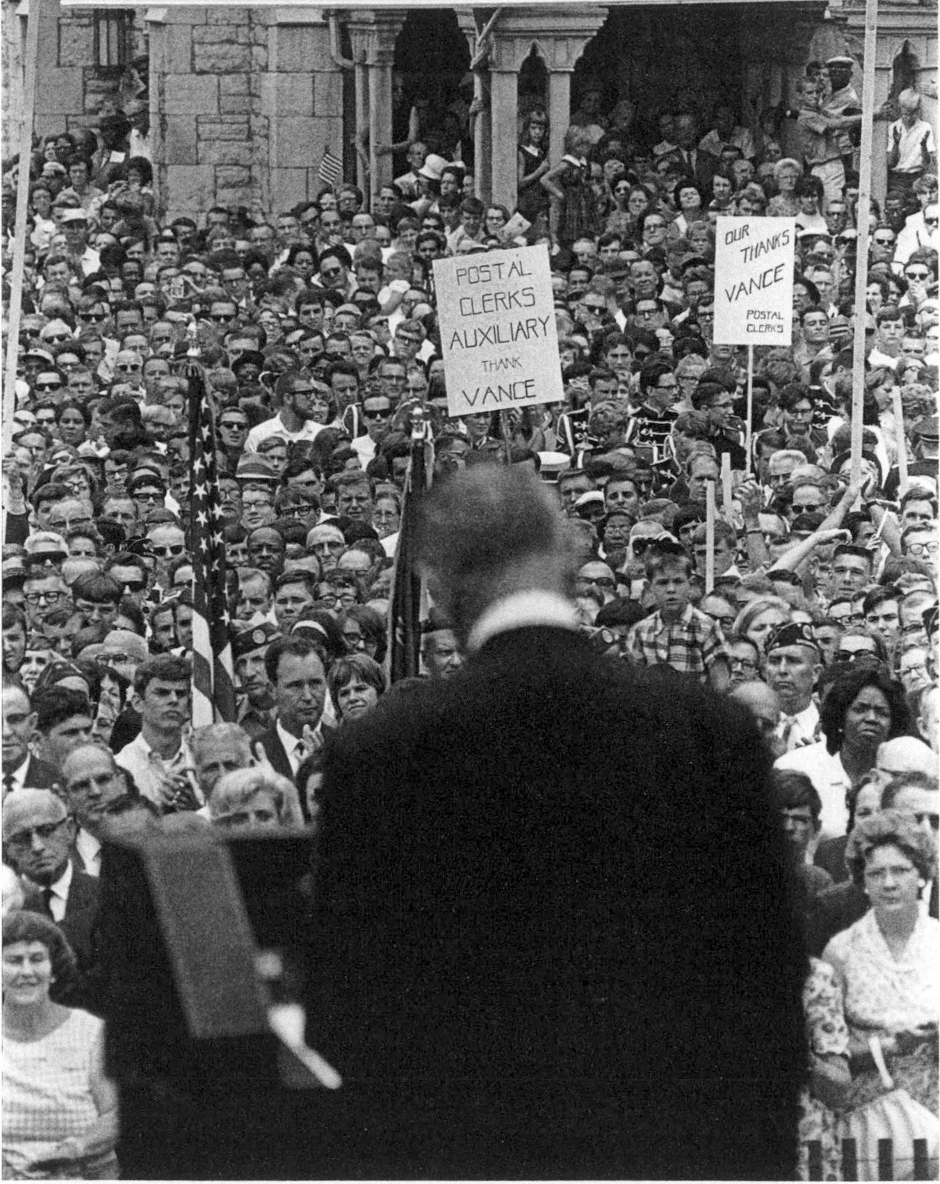

LBJ addresses a crowd in Indianapolis, July 23, 1966.

Chapter 8

HAWKS AND DOVES

FISSURES

Despite any troubles Johnson may have had overseas, 1966 began nearly as auspiciously for him as 1965 had. For the third year in a row, he was named the "most admired man in America," according to an annual Gallup poll. Other polls by Gallup, released in early January and February respectively, reflected an overall public job approval rating of 57 percent, and 50 percent approval of his handling of Vietnam, while another, by Harris, showed that 71 percent of the public approved of the job Congress was doing—more than twice what it had been during Kennedy's tenure. And it seemed that Congress, nearly to a man, approved of Johnson's handling of the war. A letter from Bobby Kennedy, sent to the White House shortly after the Eighty-ninth Congress convened at the beginning of the year, read in part:

> *Reading the newspapers and their columnists and listening to my colleagues in Congress (including myself) on what to do and what not to do in Vietnam must become somewhat discouraging at times.*
>
> *I was thinking of you and your responsibilities while I was reading Bruce Catton's book* Never Call Retreat.
>
> *I thought it might give you some comfort to look again at another president, Abraham Lincoln, and some of the identical problems and situations that he faced that you are now meeting. . . .You see on page 381 that he became so discouraged in the late spring of 1864 that he wrote a memorandum saying he was expecting to lose the election.*
>
> *Of course the situation improved a few months later but it does show how terribly distressed even he must have been at times. . . .*

> *In closing let me say how impressed I have been with the most recent efforts to find a peaceful solution to Vietnam. Our position within the United States and around the world has improved immeasurably as we face the difficult decisions of this year.*

Kennedy was one of ninety-two senators to vote against a repeal of the Gulf of Tonkin Resolution after Wayne Morse proposed it in early March. The only other "doves" to support Morse in the Senate were Ernest Gruening, Eugene McCarthy, William Fulbright, and Stephen Young. Johnson was willing to excuse Morse and Gruening, who had voted against the resolution in August 1964—at least they had been consistent. He wasn't as forgiving of the other senators who had deserted him on Vietnam.

CHUCK BAILEY: When you think of enemies, I think of hearing him speak so contemptuously of people like Fulbright and Church. On the war, he regarded politicians who opposed him as enemies and it stuck.

HELEN THOMAS: There was a reception. It was at a critical point in the Vietnam War. Johnson beckoned to Senator Frank Church who had been criticizing our policy in Vietnam. LBJ said, "Where do you get your ideas on Vietnam?"

Church said, "From Walter Lippmann."

Johnson replied, "Well, the next time you need a dam in Idaho, you just ask Walter Lippmann."

■ ■ ■

But he reserved particular scorn for Fulbright, his one-time Senate colleague and friend of twenty years, who had actually sponsored the Gulf of Tonkin Resolution. In February 1966, Fulbright began nationally televised Senate hearings on Vietnam, in the Caucus Room of the Old Senate Office Building, and became Congress's leading voice against the war. In the days when three television networks reigned supreme, the fact that the hearings were televised—often in their entirety—was a statement in itself. For the first time, the nation bore witness as a chairman of the Foreign Relations Committee openly condemned a president's war policy, a position Fulbright further clarified in his book *The Arrogance of Power*, published later in the year. Many of the questions he raised related to whether Johnson had deliberately misled Congress about the attacks on the U.S.S. *Maddox* in the summer of 1964, when the administration reported that unprovoked strikes on the ship were attempted on August 2, and two days later, on August 4, resulting in the swift passage of the resolution.

J. WILLIAM FULBRIGHT: Well, as I recall it, he had me and a number of the [Senate Foreign Relations C]ommittee down at the White House and told us about this terribly unprovoked attack. We were very peaceably going about our business and all without provocation, they attack us, sent out these gunboats, you know, and surrounded us and shelling. They even had a little shell. This is evidence. It had fallen on the deck of one of our ships. It didn't occur to me to think he was lying about it or misrepresenting. I swallowed it. I mean, it was a year or two before I discovered I had been taken in.

■ ■ ■

In fact, the administration's telling of events *was* inaccurate, though Fulbright hadn't been intentionally misled. While there was little doubt that the attack on August 2 occurred, unprovoked, as claimed, the second attack, on August 4, simply didn't happen—only Johnson couldn't have known this. His belief that the August 4 attack had taken place was based on highly classified North Vietnamese communications intercepted by the National Security Agency (NSA). Given the sensitive nature of the intelligence, Johnson believed those reports should remain sealed.

There was, however, no reason for Johnson to question the accuracy of the intelligence on which he asked Congress to pass the Gulf of Tonkin Resolution. It wasn't until December 2005 that NSA reports about the attacks were scrutinized internally, showing that they contained translation errors by intelligence officers reflecting an August 4 attack, when actually it was additional intelligence on the August 2 attack. (The report was declassified in 2008.) After discovering their mistakes, the intelligence officers altered documents to cover their tracks, though their cover-up wouldn't be known for forty-one years.

As Fulbright continued to cast doubts on the administration's account of the Gulf of Tonkin incident in his ongoing hearings, a phone conversation between Johnson and McNamara on February 19, 1968, indicates that neither Johnson, McNamara, nor anyone else in the administration questioned the accuracy of the intelligence they had received:

Robert McNamara: . . . *PT Boat personnel in the intelligence reports of the interrogation, one of which reports Fulbright has, state that the PT boat* *commander, who gave a very detailed account of what happened on the 2nd of August, states categorically that no PT boats could have participated in an attack on the 4th. The second attack. Now, he admits that Swatow boats might have participated although the way the intelligence report came in it indicates that if they had he probably would have known that, too. So we've got a bit of a problem there. But I'm going to try to meet it head on and just say we didn't know anything about Swatow and we knew Swatows were in and we had some other evidence of PT boats.*

I've included in my statement the information we got from communications intelligence reports and I simply identified it as "highly classified intelligence from an unimpeachable source." We've just got to say it because it's the best evidence that we have that an attack took place on the 4th.

LBJ: *[Mm, hm] What is it? We heard them say it?*

McNamara: *No we had several messages. Yes, we actually received the message and decoded it at the time. We had three messages. One said that an attack was planned. We got that before the attack was placed and I informed you of that at nine o'clock in the morning the day of the attack. The second message said that the attack was taking place. And the third message said that two boats were destroyed. Their boats.*

LBJ: *What time was this? Now the other two messages . . . End of the day?*

McNamara: *Yeah. They came in before the execute order went out.*

LBJ: *When did it go out? That night?*

McNamara: *Yeah. The execute order. Well it went out sort of over a period of time from 5 o'clock p.m. to about 7 o'clock p.m.*

LBJ: *But weren't they urging us to move faster really than we did move?*

McNamara: *No I don't think so. But there was a lot of doubt in the afternoon as to whether it took place and we went back and forth and did they have evidence or didn't they have evidence. And the record was pretty clear that by the time that the execute order was finally released everybody signed on that an attack had taken place.*

LBJ: *Well, as I remembered it—I haven't looked at my diary—but as I remember it, they gave us a statement and asked us to make it from out there and we held it back for some time—*

McNamara: *No, I don't think so, Mr. President. I went over it all yesterday and I don't see any evidence of that.*

LBJ: *What day is this?*

McNamara: *The day is August 4th. Which was a Tuesday, August 4th.*

LBJ: *Okay. Alright.*

Fulbright would continue to be a burr in Johnson's side throughout the remainder of his administration. Johnson retaliated by putting him under FBI surveillance and quoting Truman when he referred to Fulbright as "half-bright."

LBJ: I remember Mr. Rayburn saying about Fulbright when someone asked him what is your judgment of Mr. Fulbright. Mr. Rayburn said, "Well, I'll tell you. My evaluation of Fulbright is: He's just about as big as Arkansas."

Fulbright voted against the twenty-five-cent minimum wage—and he voted against the $1.60 minimum wage in my administration. He voted against civil rights. He never cast a vote for a human being in his life.

I honestly think he believes that he is the only man qualified to be secretary of state.

GEORGE CHRISTIAN: [H]e called Senator Fulbright a revolving son of a bitch, didn't call it to his face but he said it in front of two or three other people. And then he said, "You know what a revolving son of a bitch is, don't you?" Somebody said, "No, I've never heard that expression." And he said, "That's a son of a bitch any way you look at him."

GUNS AND BUTTER

In spite of Congress's backing of Johnson on Vietnam, which would recede over time, its appetite for being spoon-fed legislation from his White House agenda had diminished—just as Johnson had predicted. Resistance to him, regardless of his redoubtable powers of persuasion, was building. At the end of 1965, at the urging of *Washington Post* publisher Katharine Graham, Johnson tried to push a bill through Congress granting district home rule to Washington, D.C. The measure proved to be a bridge too far, becoming his first major legislative defeat. Johnson considered it a portent. So, too, did *The Washington Post*, which, in an ironic twist of fate, wrote about Johnson's waning influence in an editorial.

HARRY MCPHERSON: [Toward the end of 1965,] *The Washington Post* had the temerity to write an editorial saying that the President had overworked Congress and had made one too many demands. Imagine how he felt about that. I said, "I imagine you'd like to take somebody's head off."

He said, "No, they're right. I pushed too hard. These people are tired.

But you know, you only have one year. No matter what your mandate is you have one year, and you've got to get everything done in that year. The second year a lot of the people who were elected, many of them don't belong in those seats—and a lot of our boys beat some old-time Republicans. We'll lose a lot of those seats. Then in the third year you'll lose a lot of seats. In the mid-term election everybody always does. If this war goes on another year, we'll lose a lot of them."

■ ■ ■

Though Johnson was right about the ephemeral nature of political capital, his ability to move forward with his Great Society programs was also imperiled by Vietnam. Inevitably, the war's mounting cost meant that a choice between guns and butter needed to be made—no matter what Johnson had said in his State of the Union address in January, in which he asserted that the country was "mighty enough, its society healthy enough, its people strong enough to pursue our goals in the rest of the world while building a Great Society here at home." Around the same time (around 1966), LBJ appealed to Congress for $12.8 billion for the war. While the country had enjoyed the longest period of sustained growth in its history, the war was beginning to get in the way. Its cost, which stood at $103 million in 1965, rose to $6 billion in 1966, and would grow to $20 billion the following year. As with many in Congress, Everett Dirksen's mood toward ambitious social programs had soured, particularly if it meant raising taxes. "You ask for a billion here, a billion there," he carped to administration officials at the war's escalating cost, "pretty soon that adds up to real money."

Johnson came to the same realization just prior to the midterm elections, during an October White House meeting with African Americans seeking political office, acknowledging that guns were beginning to win out over butter. After recounting the success of the Voting Rights Act—the reason that many of those attending the meeting were viable candidates in the first place—he talked about the increases he had seen in the budget for his fight against poverty, from the $800 million he had gotten in 1964 to the $1.75 billion he was requesting for the following year. "Now, I would have liked to have doubled it or tripled it or quadrupled it," he explained, "but I just can't honestly say that I am going to hold back anything from the boys in the rice paddies in order to do it here, and I'm trying to do both at the same time. If you try and put two kids through college at the same time, you've got a man-sized job. Now when you're trying to fight in Vietnam and take everything they need and then do everything we need here at home, you've got a problem."

Moreover, as the economy slowed in the face of the war, the opportunity for blacks to gain greater financial standing and improve their lives was compromised, leading to unrest, in spite of the gains they had made under federal law. The summer of 1966 saw riots in black sections of Chicago's West Side and Cleveland's East Side, and racial agitation in Brooklyn. The rioting in Chicago was touched off in mid-July when police turned off a fire hydrant that had been opened illegally by local residents to relieve the summer heat. After three days of looting and violence, two African Americans were dead and nearly four hundred arrested. Chicago remained a powder keg for the remainder of the summer, a disquieting reminder that racial tensions were stirring. The uprisings made it doubly difficult for Johnson to go back to the well with Congress on civil rights actions as the goodwill of formerly supportive members began to dry up. "[R]iots in the street will never bring about lasting reform," he told a group of businessmen in Indianapolis on July 23, but rather made reform "more difficult by turning away the very people who can and who must support their reforms."

One bill that Johnson failed to bring forward was a measure that would have outlawed discriminatory practices common in the sale, rental, and financing of housing across America. The act he had hoped to propose would have been the last in a triumvirate of civil rights laws—alongside the crown jewels of his legislative triumphs, the Civil Rights Act of 1964 and the Voting Rights Act of 1965—designed to make all Americans equal under the law. "I want a fair housing bill," he told Joe Califano a year earlier, jabbing Califano's shoulder for emphasis. "We've got to end this Goddamn discrimination against Negroes. Until people—whether they're purple, brown, black, yellow, red, green, or whatever—live together, they'll never have the same hopes for their children, the same fears, troubles, woes, ambitions. I want a bill that makes it possible for anybody to buy a house anywhere they can afford to." But it was not to be in 1966. His hold on Congress now weakened, Johnson refrained from sending fair housing legislation to the Hill, where it would have faced almost certain defeat.

Nonetheless, he saw 42 major laws get passed through Congress throughout the year. Two hundred and seven—or 56 percent—of the 371 proposals he submitted to Congress were approved. Although it was a slump for Johnson, his average for the year bettered all of Kennedy's years and all but one of Eisenhower's, and was far greater by volume.

Among the bills he passed was the Freedom of Information Act (FOIA), which compelled federal agencies to respond to the public's request for information either by allowing for its release or by justifying its being withheld due to any of nine provisions under the law. While Johnson was supportive of FOIA, he resented the GOP's demand for its immediate passage. Donald Rumsfeld, a young Illinois congressman elected in 1964, who co-sponsored the bill in the House, invoked as one of its justifications the Johnson administration's "continuing tendency toward managed news and suppression of public information that the people are entitled to have." Johnson neglected to sign FOIA publicly, doing so instead privately at the Ranch on July 4.

He also racked up major environmental victories with the passage of the Clean Water Restoration Act, which created water treatment plants and provided research on water pollution, advanced waste treatment, and water purification methods, while putting in place quality standards for intrastate waters. Additionally he saw to the creation of five national recreation areas across the country, which he hoped would more than offset sprawling development. Nodding to his wife's influence on the bills at the signing ceremony in October, Johnson joked that "if we don't stop Mrs. Johnson from going out there, we'll be increasing [the number of recreational areas] some more."

In the fall, he won approval to hike the minimum wage from $1.25 an hour to $1.60. This would not only benefit the thirty million Americans already making minimum wage, affecting a 28 percent increase, but would compel employers to pay at least a portion of the minimum wage to the ten million who worked for tips, primarily in retail stores, restaurants, and hotels. The fight was still in the impassioned Johnson as he told a group of White House visitors that the law was "for that little charwoman who scrubs the floor of that motel" and "the waitress that's got three kids at home, that goes in there in the morning before daylight to be ready to serve coffee when they drop in at six o'clock, and usually stays until dark."

After Joe Califano's son accidentally ingested a bottled of aspirin, requiring his stomach to be pumped, Johnson demanded a Child Safety Act, which included mandatory child safety caps, while incorporating other measures, including warning labels.

■ ■ ■

Johnson did what he could in other areas, too. On January 13, he nominated Robert Weaver, described as a "quiet man" by *Ebony* magazine, as secretary of housing and urban development, a newly created post, making Weaver the first African American member of a presidential Cabinet. The appointment made a loud statement. After Weaver's swearing-in on January 18, Mrs. Johnson wrote in her diary of the occasion, "It was one of those moments when a sense of history hung in the air. The acceptance of Congress and the country has been good; our hopes are high."

■ ■ ■

The Johnsons' hopes were not high on Vietnam—nor increasingly were the country's. The war "is about two-thirds of what we talk about these days," Mrs. Johnson wrote of her conversations with her husband, and it accounted for countless hours of sleeplessness for the president even after his briefing books had been put aside for the night. The war was also creeping further into the consciousness of the American public. Though Fulbright's televised Senate hearings hadn't led to a repeal of the Gulf of Tonkin Resolution, they did take their toll on the public's support of Johnson, with Fulbright and others openly questioning his foreign policy at large and some critics advocating his impeachment. According to Gallup, Johnson's approval rating on Vietnam fell from 59 percent in January to 50 percent in March, and would stand at 43 percent by September. In the interim, almost a third of the Senate was now opposed to the war. A chasm was developing across the nation over U.S. policy in Vietnam. "Hawks" supported the war, though many hard-liners believed that efforts should be stepped up, and condemned Johnson for not doing more to vanquish the enemy. "Doves," in disproportionately loud choruses, opposed it, and wrote off Johnson as a warmonger for his dogged determination to prevail where America had no business. Johnson's support was waning except among the members of his administration.

JACK VALENTI: Down to June of 1966, not a single member of the White House staff, not a single member of the administration, with the exception of George Ball, in any meeting or by written memorandum, ever urged the President to get the hell out of there. Not one. I want to make that clear because I saw it all.

In every meeting, the notes will clearly show that. They're almost verbatim notes of what everybody said. I say this because as Edmund Burke said, retrospective wisdom does not make us all quite intelligent.

Given the information that I had at the time and given the accumulated wisdom that was provisioning the President's decision, I would have done exactly what he did, exactly. I never saw anybody at a meeting say, "Now, Mr. President, let me tell you the reason why I disagree," and that includes the "Wise Men" outside the administration who would come into those meetings and offer their opinions.

I want history to record that during the time I was there, zero voices were raised in a way to tell the President his policy was not only unpleasant and untidy but would soil the future of the country.

DEAN RUSK: At every Cabinet meeting, Lyndon Johnson would have McNamara and me report on Vietnam. Then he'd go around the table asking each cabinet member, "Do you have any comments? Do you have any questions?" and they sat silent. George Ball was the only senior member of that administration who earned the respect and affection of his two presidents and his secretary of state by the courage and ability with which he put the other point of view on Vietnam. But Ramsey Clark, as soon as he quit being attorney general, could go all the way to Hanoi [to express his opposition to the war]. But while he was attorney general he couldn't lean eight inches to the left and say to the secretary of state, "I don't like what you're doing in Vietnam."

Now how did that come about? Why was that?

■ ■ ■

Did Johnson invite dissent among his advisers? Or did he intimidate them so that they kept their opposing views to themselves, or gave him the answers he wanted to hear?

DEAN RUSK: I think he sort of sensed that with 35 people in the room at a Cabinet meeting, people lined up around the walls and all that sort of thing, that if there was any real quarreling in those circumstances that he'd read about it in *The Washington Post* or *The New York Times*. But at those Tuesday luncheon sessions, where each of us knew that we were not going to read what we were saying in *The Washington Post* or *The New York Times*, there were times when we would argue with him like the dickens, fight like hell.

GEORGE CHRISTIAN: I think it is absolutely true that President Johnson wanted to portray unity in his administration. I think any president does. I don't think that means necessarily that he wasn't listening to somebody privately if they had some difference of opinion, or if there was difference of opinion at a Tuesday luncheon. But I really believe that he didn't want that cabinet to be out speaking or doing things that were contrary to administration policy in any area.

LARRY TEMPLE: I think he used to see if he could intimidate people from their positions just to see how strong their positions were. He would say such things as, "That is the dumbest thing I ever heard. Any sixth grader would know better than so-and-so."

The President, I think, frequently would do that just to try to test people. I think all of us had the experience where somebody would tell him something and he'd say, "Oh, everybody knows better than that," and then within 24 hours he'd be repeating that same position as his own.

■ ■ ■

As attitudes throughout the nation began shifting with regard to Vietnam, Johnson proved ineffective in drawing on his persuasive abilities to better define U.S. objectives and articulate the war's long-term strategic importance. "It is unbearably hard to fight a limited war," noted Mrs. Johnson, and Johnson contended that "it would have been easier to break out the flag for an all-out military effort." Saddled with the difficulties of waging a limited war, Johnson was further hampered by his failure to stir the kind of patriotic fervor that had united the nation over earlier military causes.

BARRY GOLDWATER: Now [in] World War II, hell, they were knocking down the walls to get in the army. But here was a war that nobody understood.

I spent literally three years of my life talking to some hundred and fifty colleges a year on this subject, explaining Vietnam, why we were there. I [had] asked President Johnson to go on national television and explain it. He didn't. . . . I feel that the American people gradually grew to have a feeling of distrust of Lyndon. Gradually may not be the word, because actually I think the average American distrusts anybody in political life, and if you give them a little more reason, that distrust gets pretty heavy. . . .

[T]here was no Pearl Harbor. There was no killing of American boys when they were not in war. Or there were no "Remember the Maine" type of incidents. The war in Vietnam is a nameless thing, where our big wars have all been understood, even Korea. Truman told the people about this. They didn't like that war, but they didn't tear Truman apart because of it.

■ ■ ■

In addition to his ongoing fear of drawing China or the Soviet Union into the fight, Johnson's reluctance to fan the flames of hatred toward North Vietnam may have been due to his faint hope that Ho Chi Minh would yield to the peace process. Johnson went so far as to promise to pour billions in economic aid into not only South Vietnam but North Vietnam, too—as long as a settlement in the war was reached at the bargaining table. Even the most obstinate opponent, after all, could be turned around with pork barrel promises. Wasn't that the way the world worked? Bill Moyers recalled Johnson saying, "My God, I've offered Ho Chi Minh $100 million to build the Mekong Valley. If that'd been George Meany, he'd have snapped at it!" But the gesture went unheeded by Ho, who remained elusive and inscrutable. Johnson could not exact his treatment on him—couldn't look him in the eye, measure his handshake, or size up his intentions; flatter him, squeeze his arm, or talk about their mutual hopes for their children.

Would it have mattered anyway? There is a mixed view on whether the treatment would have worked on Ho, or whether Johnson's lack of appreciation for cultural nuance prevented him from understanding Ho and what drove him.

ROBERT KOMER, National Security Council, 1961–66: LBJ had no particular grasp of foreign cultures. He felt no particular need to delve into what made Vietnamese Vietnamese—as opposed to Americans or Greeks or Chinese. He was a people man, and he thought people everywhere were the same.

He saw the Vietnamese farmer as being like the Texas farmer or the Oklahoma farmer. "We're going to provide them with rural electricity. We're going to provide them with roads and water, and we're going to improve the rice crop."

NICHOLAS KATZENBACH: President Johnson was marvelous with people, particularly when it was one-on-one. Yet everybody in the State Department absolutely panicked when he would take a foreign head of state and sit him down in the backroom. It never worried me a bit. He was terrific. That was what he was best at. He had learned that in the Senate and he knew how to do it. He was remarkable that way, and he often got concessions on things that the State Department, in its wisdom, had said we shouldn't even mention.

HUGH SIDEY: His weakness was that he did not know the world, because he was not a creature of it in any way. Dwight Eisenhower had spent his adult life in contact with Churchill and Roosevelt and Marshall and people like that. John Kennedy read ten books a week while he was in the White House. He read about foreign affairs; he liked it. Lyndon Johnson was probably the best president we've ever had: as a legislator; as a man who understood Washington, who could persuade people, who could understand the workings of men. But he missed a lot of the world outside the United States. He was never interested in it. He never studied it that much. He wasn't exposed to it as much.

I'll always remember, on *Air Force One*, flying back from one of those Asian trips after meeting with Thieu and Ky, and he turned to us and said, "Boys, I don't understand foreigners. They're different from us."

■ ■ ■

Despite their differences, Johnson had decided he could do business with Thieu and Ky. Their government had brought some semblance of stability to South Vietnam. It had been in place longer than any regime since the coup that resulted in Diem's assassination in 1963, and Johnson considered them courageous. Even after he left office, he had "no reluctance about those two men." At a meeting with the two young leaders in Honolulu, Hawaii, in early February, he pressed them for Democratic reform and human rights in South Vietnam in exchange for his continued support in the war effort. But neither the meeting nor reports from Saigon reassured Johnson or his advisers that the corner would be turned in Vietnam anytime soon.

A QUESTION OF CREDIBILITY

Compounding Johnson's mounting woes throughout 1966 were questions relating to his credibility, which began eroding along with his approval ratings. Here again, he could often be his own worst enemy. Speaking to a group of servicemen in South Korea in a swing through Asia in late October and early November, Johnson, caught up in the moment, bragged about his martyred great-great-grandfather, who had died in the Alamo. It was a false boast (though he had a great-uncle who had fought in the Texas battle of San Jacinto), giving peaceniks and pundits reason to believe that Johnson's commitment to Vietnam was nothing more than the jingoist instincts of a Hill Country boy who used the Texas legend on which he was reared as a measure of his courage.

His credibility took another hit around the same time, when he failed to campaign for struggling Democratic candidates in the midterm elections, as he had earlier implied he would. Instead, upon returning home from his trip to Asia, where he had spent time with U.S. troops in Vietnam, he went to the hospital to have a polyp removed from his throat and to repair a ventral hernia that was a defect in the scar from the gall bladder surgery the year before; then he retreated to the Ranch to recover. As accusations of broken promises surfaced along with resentment among Democratic hopefuls, Johnson denied that he had pledged to campaign, blaming the story on "the imagination of people who phrase sentences and write columns and have to report what they hope or what they imagine." He later claimed that his not taking to the hustings was due to his refusal to politicize the war. "I never wanted to get mixed up in the campaign in the first place. I felt bad about it because of some of the people I loved, who had been with me all the way. But I didn't want to get the war mixed up in it."

Johnson's optimistic public pronouncements on the war were also brought into question. While they might be more accepted as standard media spin today, there was heightened sensitivity to them at the time, given the war's increasingly controversial nature and the belief among a growing number of people that Johnson had been deceptive on the war since the Gulf of Tonkin incident. Many felt that Johnson had led them astray on fiscal matters relating to the war, too. A 1968 *Fortune* magazine editorial implicating the Johnson administration pointed out that "the public was deceived on the true costs of the Vietnam War for more than a year following the 1965 decision to mount a major U.S. military effort." Over time the inside-the-Beltway perceptions of Johnson as being less than honest gained ground. A joke began making the rounds: "How do you know when Lyndon Johnson is telling the truth? When he pulls his ear lobe, scratches his chin, he's telling the truth. When he begins to move his lips, you know he's lying."

MARIANNE MEANS: Of course Johnson was so complex he was very hard for us to understand. Almost immediately he had a credibility problem. He was a wonderful storyteller, but he did love to embellish, and sometimes the facts would get a little confused or exaggerated.

WARREN ROGERS: The Vietnam War obviously was something he could never get over, and even if he had not had the Vietnam War, he still would have had a credibility problem because he did like to tell tales. I remember in particular one time sitting with him in the little office off to the side of the Oval Office. He was watching TV while he was conducting the interview. There were three screens going, and he'd click them on from one station to another, and Bill Lawrence came on ABC to say that Abe Fortas would be nominated to the Supreme Court. I'm sitting with the president of the United States, who was going to make the appointment, and I said, "What about that?"

And he said, "Do you believe that?"

I said, "Well, I believe Bill Lawrence is a great reporter. Is he telling the facts, Mr. President?"

He said, "No!"

Of course, two days later Mr. Fortas was nominated. Lyndon Johnson was a walking credibility problem—no question about that.

HARRY MCPHERSON: [One question] is to ask how much Lyndon Johnson mirrored his hero, Franklin Roosevelt, who in 1939, 1940, and 1941, lied like a rug to the American people, to Congress and everyone else, concealed what he was doing, literally on a number of occasions, and became a great hero because we got in and fought a war that we won. And Lyndon Johnson behaved in much the same way and didn't win.

■ ■ ■

The president's widening credibility gap didn't help the Democratic Party in the midterm elections. Two years after he helped to build handsome Democratic majorities into both chambers of Congress through his massive electoral mandate in 1964, the midterms saw the party lose three seats in the Senate and forty-seven in the House as eight statehouses fell to the GOP. An added blow was the departure of three key members of his staff: McGeorge Bundy, Jack Valenti, and Bill Moyers.

Other numbers around the time of the election were more ominous. Johnson's approval rating had fallen to 43 percent, as his disapproval rating rose to 37 percent; the number of troops in Vietnam climbed steadily to around 400,000—and, at that point, 6,664 of them would not be coming home.

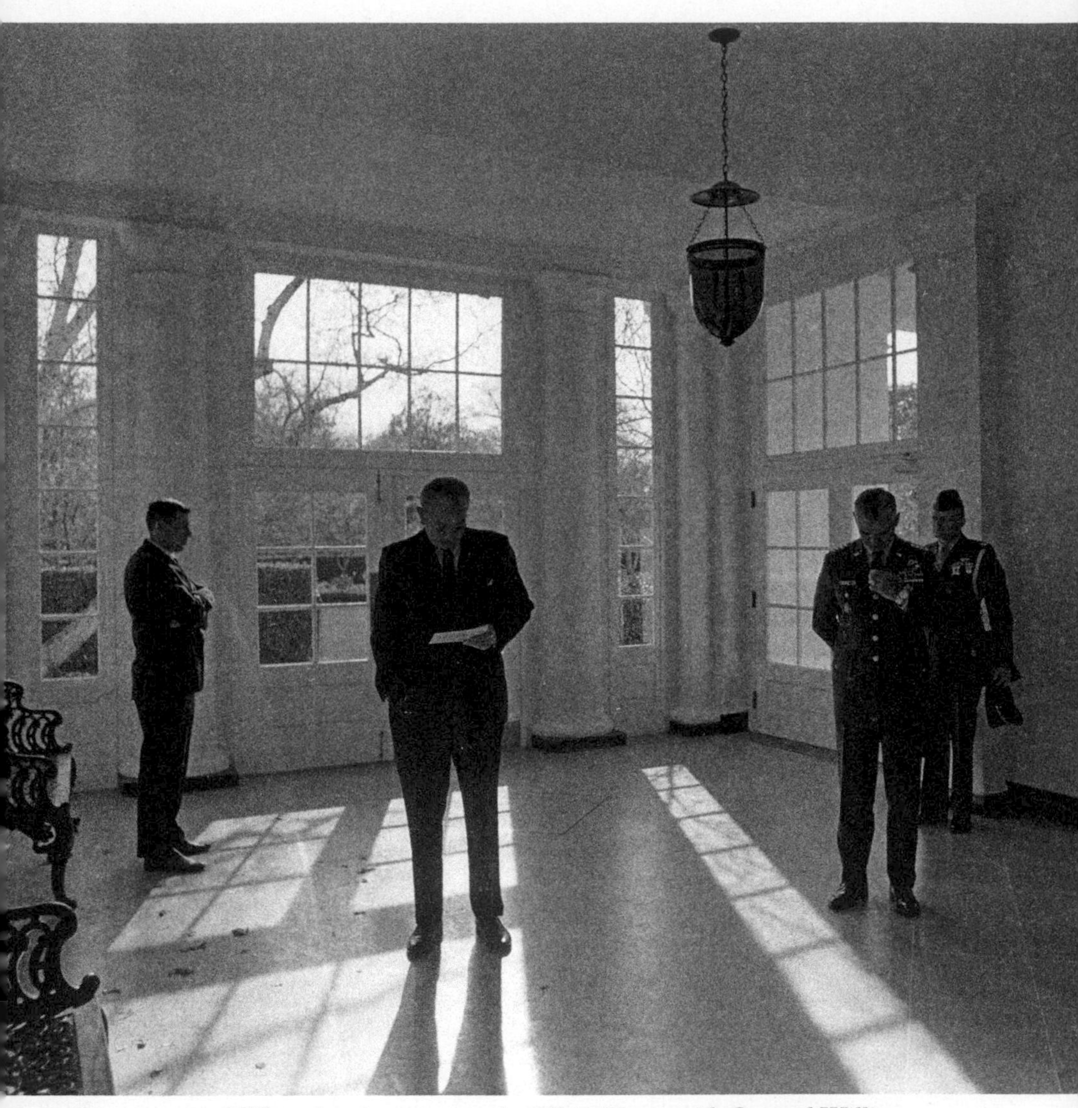

LBJ reads a document at the White House with General William Westmoreland on his immediate left, November 16, 1967.

Chapter 9

UNDER FIRE

"WE'RE BURNING UP!"

It was, as Johnson later put it, "an assembly of hope," and an increasingly rare moment of triumph as he passed the midpoint in his elected presidential term. Late in the afternoon of January 27, 1967, senior administration officials and the representatives of fifty-seven nations, including the ambassador of the Soviet Union, gathered together at the White House to witness Johnson signing a treaty that would prohibit weapons of mass destruction in outer space. "This is an inspiring moment in the history of the human race," he said in brief remarks to the group afterward. "We are taking the first firm step toward keeping outer space free forever from the implements of war. . . . This treaty means that the moon and our sister planets will serve only the purposes of peace and not war. . . . astronauts and cosmonauts will meet someday on the surface of the moon as brothers and not as warriors."

Though the treaty aided in easing tensions with the Soviet Union at a time when "duck and cover" drills were standard practice in American schools, the exploration of space still achieved an important cold war end. Just over six years after John Kennedy announced to the nation and the world that the United States would "commit itself to achieving the goal, before this decade is out, of landing a man on the moon, and returning him safely to the earth," the space race between the United States and the Soviet Union continued in earnest. The stakes were technological superiority and superpower bragging rights. The rewards were adventure on par with any quest on which humankind had embarked and a chance to show the world true greatness by touching ground on a new world.

As Johnson signed his name to what the administration called the Outer Space Treaty, the crew of Apollo 1—Gus Grissom, Ed White, and Roger Chaffee—prepared at the Kennedy Space Center, in Cape Canaveral (later Cape Kennedy) Florida, for Apollo's maiden manned voyage, which would take them on an orbital flight the following month. Subsequent Apollo missions would journey past Earth's orbit a quarter of a million miles to the moon, where Americans would be the first to set foot on a celestial body. There were nearly as many Americans employed on Project Apollo to that end—four hundred thousand—as there were troops in Vietnam.

Few achievements meant more to Johnson than the American dominance of space; he had championed the nation's space efforts from the beginning. It was Johnson who sponsored the National Aeronautics and Space Act (NASA) in 1958 as Senate majority leader and acted as a catalyst to take on the Soviets in the space race, as he himself would readily point out.

MARIANNE MEANS: I remember once riding in the limousine to Camp David with him and Senator Dick Russell. Russell was an old friend, and Johnson got to talking about the space program that they'd worked together on, and had really created. As majority leader Johnson was very instrumental in persuading Eisenhower to establish NASA and our own space program after Sputnik went up. But Johnson went on and on, and as the story went on his role got bigger, and pretty soon he had done everything and Eisenhower wouldn't have done anything without him. And Russell, who knew all the facts of the case, of course, after listening to him for a long time finally looked at him and said, "That's the joy of being president; you get to rewrite history."

■ ■ ■

It was also Johnson who, as Kennedy's vice president, chaired the National Space Council at Kennedy's behest, and hired James Webb as NASA's administrator. And it was Johnson who urged Kennedy to take aim at the moon. After the Soviets put the first man in space when cosmonaut Yuri Gagarin thrice orbited the Earth in an April 1961 flight that took Americans by surprise (just as the launch of Sputnik had in 1957), Kennedy asked Johnson by memo if the United States could manage a moon shot. After receiving Johnson's response—"The U.S. can, if it will firm up its objectives and employ its resources with a reasonable chance of attaining world leadership in space during this decade"—Kennedy went forward with his bold challenge.

SARGENT SHRIVER: Kennedy said that in this very decade of the sixties, we shall put a man on the moon. Well, like many Americans, I thought he had gone crazy. But Kennedy said it; he said it was going to happen, and in the decade, now, right now. Who would believe it or even dream it? Kennedy could dream it, believe it, say it, and Johnson could make it happen. The can-do presidents put that man on the moon.

■ ■ ■

Despite an early and embarrassing lag in the space race, it looked in 1967 as though the United States had finally overtaken the Russians. Six inaugural manned space flights from Project Mercury, four of them orbital, were followed successfully by project Gemini, in which American astronauts walked in space and perfected rendezvous with spacecraft, setting the stage for the lunar missions of Apollo. The moon was within reach—and comfortably before the decade was out, in keeping with the deadline Kennedy had set. Or so it seemed as astronauts Grissom, White, and Chaffee went through their routine training on the afternoon of January 27.

After signing the Treaty on Outer Space, Johnson attended a small gathering of staff members in the White House family quarters for outgoing commerce secretary John T. Connor, when his appointments secretary, Jim Jones, slipped him a folded note. "Mr. President:" it read, "James Webb just reported that the first Apollo crew was under test at Cape Kennedy and a fire broke out in the capsule and all three were killed. He does not know whether it was the primary or backup crew, but believes it was the primary crew of Grissom, White and Chaffee." "I watched him as he read it," Mrs. Johnson recalled later of that moment. "My face sagged and my heart lurched. I knew the news was something bad and something close."

An update would quickly confirm that it was, in fact, the primary crew. After the fire broke out at 6:31 p.m., its origins unknown, the capsule's hatch failed to open as Grissom, White, and Chaffee struggled helplessly to break free from an inferno that reached 2,500 degrees Fahrenheit. "We've got a fire in the cockpit!" yelled Chaffee, as it spread precipitately in the capsule's pure-oxygen environment. "We've got a bad fire. . . . We're burning up!"

As the astronauts were buried on January 31—Grissom and Chaffee at Arlington National Cemetery, White at West Point—NASA's outlook was uncertain. Mistakes had been made. Engineers on Project Apollo arrogantly dismissed the experience and best practices of those on Project Gemini. Projects had been mismanaged. Shortcuts had been taken to meet deadlines, and work unintentionally compromised. The upshot was that there was no certainty that American astronauts could reach the moon by 1970. More work needed to be done.

The tragedy of Apollo 1 presaged the grave setbacks Johnson would face in the coming months. So did the fire. There would be more fire in the balance of Johnson's White House term—student protesters burning draft cards and American flags, and lighting Molotov cocktails; U.S. aircraft dropping napalm copiously on the dense, verdant jungles of Vietnam; black rioters in wretched urban conditions, who had simply had enough, setting cities ablaze—much more.

"THE HOT LINE IS UP"

"When the phone rings in the White House, it's always bad news," Johnson reflected on the presidency after he had left it. "They don't let the good news get through to you." On Monday, June 5, 1967, at 4:30 a.m., Johnson was awakened by a phone call from Walt Rostow, and the news was not good: War had broken out between Israel and Egypt.

Johnson had seen it coming, and had worked to prevent it. Tensions in the Middle East were nothing new; Israel was surrounded by hostile nations, and had been since its creation in 1948. Skirmishes occurred often around its borders, many of them initiated by Syria. But the situation heated up further in May of 1967. Two days after a Radio Cairo broadcast stated, "[T]he battle has come in which we shall destroy Israel," Egypt's president, Gamal Abdel Nasser, successfully lobbied UN secretary-general U Thant to remove UN troops from the Egyptian-Israeli border, freeing up the possibility of direct military aggression. Exacerbating things for the United States was the fact that Nasser had established an alliance with the Soviet Union, which supplied Egypt and other Arab nations with aid and military arms. Johnson viewed the possibility of a war in the Middle East as being far more ominous than the one in Southeast Asia. "The danger implicit in every border incident in the Middle East was not merely war between the Israelis and Arabs but an ultimate confrontation between the Soviet Union and its NATO allies," he wrote in his memoirs. "This was the danger that concerned me, as well as the tragedy of the war itself, in those hours before dawn on June 5, 1967."

Shortly after the UN troops had left the Egypt-Israeli border and Nasser had threatened a "holy war" against Israel, Egypt stirred the pot by blocking the Straits of Tiran, and access to the Red Sea, to Israeli ships, a provocative action in violation of an agreement that had been struck ten years earlier. Johnson moved quickly to defuse the threat of war by stating, "[T]he United States strongly opposes aggression by anyone in the area, in any form, overt or clandestine." He also called for UN intervention to resolve the conflict, while extracting promises from the Israelis that they would abstain from attacking Egypt preemptively. Despite their assurances to the contrary, and convinced that Egypt, with the aid of the Soviet Union, was poised for an attack against them, Israel launched an attack by air, land, and sea. Within hours, Egypt waged a counterattack, with Arab nations joining in the hours and days ahead.

DEAN RUSK: In 1967 we became disturbed because we found that the Soviets were circulating rumors of Israeli mobilization against Syria, which did not check out as being factually true when we looked at the situation on the ground. But those rumors excited the Arabs and probably had something to do with the formation of the alliance between Syria and Egypt, and later Jordan and Egypt. The Soviets played a considerable role in stirring up the sense of hostility and crisis in the Middle East just prior to the June war.

Then when President Nasser closed the Strait of Tiran and insisted on the departure of the UN forces, I think the Soviets became concerned that the situation was moving too far and too fast. So they then tried to work with the United States to cool off the situation. We and they were in touch with each other, and we tried to get commitments from both sides that hostilities would not begin. They got such commitments from the Egyptians, for example; we got such a commitment from the Israelis. And when the Israelis then launched their attack in June 1967, it was in the face of a commitment to us that they would not do so, so we were very disappointed. The views in the Israeli Cabinet were closely divided—there was almost a tie-vote on most of these issues. But the so-called hawks in the Israeli Cabinet carried the day and precipitated the hostilities there, which caused the crisis of '67.

ROBERT MCNAMARA: The facts were, I think, very clear then and are clear in my mind today. Number one, the Egyptians were planning an attack on Israel. Number two, we knew it; the Israelis knew it, the British knew it.

Number three, we were convinced that the Israelis could repel the attack. Number four, [British prime minister Harold] Wilson came over here for a meeting with Johnson, totally unrelated to that initially, but by the time he got here that was the only subject on the agenda. The only difference between the British and us was as to how long it would take the Israelis to beat the Egyptians. I have forgotten whether we thought it could be done in seven days and they in ten, or vice versa. Wilson left.

Johnson was trying to prevent this from happening and in any event he didn't want the Israelis to preempt, which we were beginning to feel they might. [Abba] Eban was in the city at the time and Johnson asked Rusk and me to join him on the second floor of the White House, in the family quarters, with Eban. And Johnson really worked him over to try to persuade him to persuade his government not to preempt. Well, of course, they went ahead and preempted.

■ ■ ■

At 7:57 a.m., after talking by phone to Rostow, Rusk, and George Christian, and approving a message for Soviet foreign minister Andrei Gromyko urging a UN Security Council resolution to the conflict, Johnson received another call in his bedroom. This time it was McNamara. "Mr. President," the secretary of defense informed him, "the hot line is up." It marked the first time that the hot line connecting the Kremlin and the White House, installed in August 1963 so that the leaders of the superpowers could communicate directly in the event of a crisis, had been used outside of tests and cordial New Year's greetings.

Phone conversation between Johnson and Robert McNamara, June 5, 1967, 7:57 a.m.:

LBJ: *Yeah?*

Robert McNamara: *Mr. President, the Moscow hot line is operating and allegedly Kosygin is at the end and wants to know if you are in the room in which the receiving apparatus is located. Now we have a receiving station over here in the Pentagon and you also have a hookup over in the Situation Room in the White House. My inclination is to say that—to reply that you can be in the room if he wishes you there in a few minutes. Here is what has come in: "Dear Mr. President, having received information concerning the military action between Israel and UAR, the Soviet government is* *convinced the responsibility of all the great powers is to attempt to end the military conflict immediately."*

LBJ: *Yes.*

McNamara: *Then the question. Are you in the room?*

LBJ: *Yes, I'd say that we could be there soon. I'd say ten minutes.*

McNamara: *All right.*

LBJ: *What do you think they will want to do then?*

McNamara: *I don't know. I don't know. From this I think they would want you to indicate that you agree the responsibility of all the great powers—*

LBJ: *We have done that in our message to them, haven't we?*

McNamara: *We did before it started.*

LBJ: *No, no, we sent a message to Gromyko this morning.*

When the two leaders connected, they exchanged assurances that they would both exert whatever influence they had to bring the war to a swift end. The hot line would be employed often in the days ahead as the war played out and the Israelis routed their Arab enemies, opening up the Straits of Tiran and gobbling up munitions, tanks, and land. The crisis heightened for Johnson on June 8, when the U.S.S. *Liberty*, a U.S. Navy communications ship, was targeted by Israeli planes and gunboats in international waters off the Sinai coast. The attack, which the Israelis claimed was accidental, left 34 Americans dead and 171 wounded. Johnson took the Israelis at their word, accepting their deep regret over the incident and declining to retaliate against the urging of several of his advisers.

On June 9, Egypt and Israel indicated a willingness to abide by the cease-fire that the UN Security Council called for. Syria did not. Israeli forces pressed into Syria's Golan Heights like a steak knife through butter as Jordan, which had entered into the war in support of Egypt, suffered similar humiliation. The following day, Soviet premier Alexei Kosygin sent word to Johnson through the hot line calling for Israel to suspend military action "unconditionally."

■ ■ ■

Much to the world's relief, the Israelis accepted the cease-fire on June 11, ending what would become known as the Six-Day War with a spectacularly lopsided military victory. When the smoke cleared, Israel had captured the Sinai Peninsula from Egypt; Jerusalem, Hebron, and the West

Bank from Jordan; and the Golan Heights from Syria, with no intention of giving up the occupied territory. (An added bonus was that as tensions defused in the Middle East, they also eased slightly for Johnson at home. Liberal Jews, who formed a vocal and influential bloc in the antiwar movement, quieted for a time as they basked in Israel's military triumph.)

LBJ: My last message to Chairman Kosygin went over the hot line just before noon. I pointed out that military action in the Middle East was apparently ending. I expressed my hope that both of our countries in the time ahead would be devoted to achieving a lasting peace throughout the world.

■ ■ ■

Later in the month, Johnson seized the chance to work to make good on the sentiment of "achieving a lasting peace throughout the world"—and relieve the strains of the cold war—in a hastily arranged summit between the superpowers in the unlikely burg of Glassboro, New Jersey. After learning that Kosygin would address the UN General Assembly in late June, the White House reached out to the Kremlin to unite Johnson and Kosygin. Glassboro, a nondescript Garden State suburb and point on the map directly between New York and Washington, was chosen as a compromise site. The two leaders convened in the dowdy environs of Glassboro State College president Dr. Thomas E. Robinson's living room, on worn furniture that wouldn't have been out of place in any modest middle-class home in America. (LBJ asked his staffers to secure the two chairs he and Kosygin had used, and the table between them, claiming that they were now historical artifacts that belonged in his presidential library. Reluctant to part with a rocking chair that had been in her family for generations, Mrs. Robinson eventually acquiesced to the urgent requests of the president's staffers after arm-twisting by New Jersey's governor, Richard Hughes, who had been enlisted in the cause.) Johnson used the birth of his first grandchild, Patrick Lyndon Nugent—born to Luci and her husband, Pat, on June 21, and whom he would meet for the first time midway through the summit—to bond with Kosygin over grandpaternity and talk about the peaceful world in which they wanted their grandchildren to grow up.

After the summit concluded, Johnson called Dwight Eisenhower to summarize what had transpired.

Telephone conversation between LBJ and Dwight Eisenhower, U.S. president, 1953–61, June 25, 1967, 9:44 p.m.:

LBJ: *I wanted to call you, but I waited until [Kosygin] got through with his Press Conference. He played about the same old broken record in private that he did in public. We tried to get agreement on four or five points. We may have made a little progress on non-proliferation. We are going to have Rusk and Gromyko work on it some more tomorrow.*

We may be able to table an agreement, but we are not positive. It looked like there was some movement on arms limitation and on arms shipment and on disclosure and on reducing military expenditures, cutting our budget down for nuclear weapons or for offensive or defensive missile systems, etc.

We both agreed in general principle, but he never would set a time, and never would set a place, never would get down to really executing it. It was just largely conversation. Pleasant. No vitriolic stuff. No antagonistic stuff. No bitter stuff. Two or three little low blows below the belt every now and then; when you would meet him the same way why he would get back to a normal level.

He made clear they didn't want any confrontation with the United States; didn't want to fight us; didn't want to go to war; but on the Middle East just one simple instruction—looked like he couldn't move one inch away from it on anything: there must be complete, absolute, immediate withdrawal of troops. Period. Nothing else with it. That was going to be their resolution. They could pass that in the General Assembly. They wanted us to support it there, and in Security Council, and nothing else, and that unless and until that was done, there was going to be a great war and those people would be fighting for ten years. That they would have to support the Arab Nations; that he couldn't understand why we would want to support the Jews—3,000,000 people when there are 100,000,000 Arabs. I told him that numbers did not determine what was right, and we tried to do what was right regardless of the numbers, and we felt like we would have to take in maritime passage, that we would have to consider where they were before they closed the Gulf, and if they were going to go back where the Armistice line [was], why they were going to have to go back to the Gulf of Aqaba as it was.

LBJ: *He said well that would have to be done later. It would take two or three years to work out all these other things. Wouldn't give an inch on that.*

On Vietnam he said we have got to stop our bombing. We have got to pull out. That is what he said on television. Got to get all our troops out. That we are the aggressor there. We are an invader there. We are a perpetrator of aggression, and not anything else will do; no substitute.

We exchanged some views, and I asked some questions of him in that connection. Asked him what would happen if we stopped our bombing; would they talk and if so how long; would it just be another Korea talk to delay it; or would it be serious; or what would come from it; and what could he guarantee or underwrite or assure, or what did he think?

The net of it was just another line. Stop your bombing. Send your troops home. Then things will work out.

Dwight Eisenhower: *And then after that we will start talking?*

LBJ: *Yes. Then—but I submitted him some questions and things to think about, and his folks. I asked him to let McNamara sit down and talk to them about disarmament and give me the name and the date and the time and place. He would always dodge it. He claimed to be for it in principle but specifically he wouldn't. He claimed that there should be other elements taken into the Middle East settlement, but he wouldn't do any of them until withdrawal was effected.*

The New York Times wrote later of the summit, "Nothing really concrete came out of the Glassboro talks, but they produced what came to be known as 'the spirit of Glassboro,' a subtle easing of tensions between the Soviet Union and the United States that Mr. Johnson said made the world, 'a little less dangerous.'" The "spirit of Glassboro" aside, the meeting didn't result in the arms control agreements—and the concrete steps toward peace—Johnson had hoped for.

JUSTICE AND LAWLESSNESS

Johnson's efforts on arms control stymied, he used June to take another leap at home in the area of civil rights. After the resignation of U.S. Supreme Court justice Tom Clark, Johnson, on June 13, nominated Thurgood Marshall as his successor, making Marshall the first African American to be named to the high court. The grandson of slaves, Marshall had served for twenty-five years as a lawyer for the NAACP, winning twenty-nine of the thirty-two cases that he argued before the high court while escaping a near lynching at least once while pursuing legal justice in the Deep South. In 1961 he left the NAACP to accept an appointment by Kennedy as a federal appellate judge. Four years later, in 1965, Johnson called on him to become U.S. solicitor general, which marked another first for African Americans.

THURGOOD MARSHALL: He called one day, around [July of 1965] I think, and I was up in the judges' dining room at the courthouse. My bailiff came up and tapped me on the shoulder. I said, "Fred, what in the world is wrong?" I mean, he's not supposed to bother us at lunch. He was as red as a beet. I said, "What's wrong, Fred?" He said, "The President wants to speak to you. He's on the phone!" I said, "The President of what?" "The President of the United States!" So he had held an elevator and I went down. Sure enough he was on [the phone]. We chatted for about two or three minutes, and he said, "I want you to be my Solicitor General." I said, "Sir?" We chatted about it, and I said, "Well, Mr. President, I'll have to think this over." He said, "Well, go ahead, but don't tell a living soul." I said, "I assume that means nobody but my wife?" He said, "Yes, that's what I mean by nobody." He said, "Take all the time you want." I said, "Very well, sir." He hung up and I hung up.

I went home and talked to my wife and we discussed the problems, because one was a lifetime job to trade in for a job at the beckoning of one person. Secondly, it was a $4,500 cut in salary. Third, the living expenses in Washington would be twice what I was paying in New York. We kept thinking about it, and the next day the phone rang. He was on the phone again. I said, "Well, Mr. President, you said I had all the time I needed." He said, "You had it." I said, "Okay."

I started telling him these things. He said, "You don't have to tell me. I can tell you everything including what you've got in your bank account. I'm still asking you to make the sacrifice."

He said what he wanted. Number one: He wanted me in his Administration. Number two: He wanted me in that spot for two reasons. One, he thought I could handle it. Secondly, he wanted people—you people—of both races to come into the Supreme Court Room, as they all do by the hundreds and thousands, and [for] somebody to say, "Who is that man up there with that swallow tail coat on arguing," and somebody to say, "He's the Solicitor General of the United States." Somebody will say, "But he's a Negro!" He wanted that image, number one.

Number two: He thought that he would like to have me as his representative before the Court. The other thing which goes through every conversation we had from then on—he would say at least three or four times, "You know this has nothing to do with any Supreme Court appointment. I want that distinctly understood. There's no quid pro here at all. You do your job. If you don't do it, you go out. If you do it, you stay here. And that's all there is to it."

■ ■ ■

Johnson was bluffing. When Clark resigned from the Supreme Court, Johnson had every intention of naming an African American to replace him, and his man was Marshall. He made his choice apparent in an interview meeting with Larry Temple, who would soon become his White House counsel, before his nomination of Marshall.

LARRY TEMPLE: [H]e asked me who I thought he ought to appoint to the Supreme Court. Well, I wasn't so naïve to think he really wanted my opinion. I knew that he wasn't going to ask some young lawyer his opinion. He had all kinds of assistance on that, but I don't remember now specifically the names we talked about. And he said to me, "Well, I've given some thought to appointing Thurgood Marshall. What do you think about that?" and I said something along the lines of, "Well, he certainly is a stellar lawyer with a great reputation, and would be a great justice." [B]ut then he said, "Well, you know there are some other really outstanding African American lawyers and judges." And I believe the name was William Hastie, who was a judge on the Court of Appeals, I believe the Seventh Circuit, covering Chicago—I said, "And you may want to consider William Hastie." And the president leaned over, as he was wont to do, kinda get in your face, and he said, "William Hastie! William Hastie! There ain't nobody ever heard of William Hastie but you and his mamma. If I'm going to appoint a black man to the Supreme Court, I'm going to appoint a black man everybody *knows* is a black man." And that was on Saturday, and he nominated Thurgood Marshall on Monday.

■ ■ ■

After a debate in Congress that often grew heated, Marshall was appointed on August 30. His confirmation in the Senate passed by 69 votes to 11, though the vote would have been closer if some of the senators opposed to Marshall on the basis of his color hadn't refrained from voting at Johnson's urging. "I don't know how he got my nomination through,"

Marshall said later. "I don't know [to] this day. It took some doing, I'm sure."

In December of the previous year, Johnson had met at the White House with Democratic governors from the southern and border states during which they harangued the president for civil rights policy they believed was causing irreparable damage to the party, just as they resisted the desegregation that had been put into law. "Nigger, nigger, nigger," Johnson fumed to Joe Califano the following day, recalling the meeting. "That's all they said to me all day. Hell, there's one thing they better know. If I don't achieve anything else while I'm president, I intend to wipe that word out of the English language and make it impossible for people to come here and shout 'nigger, nigger, nigger' to me and the American people." Marshall's historic appointment to the high court—Johnson's proudest—would represent one more achievement to that end, though as Johnson later stated, "[T]he American struggle for justice was just beginning."

But while southern politicians thought Johnson had given away too much on civil rights, urban blacks in the northern states believed Johnson had done too little; despite any strides he may have made to alleviate racism and offer opportunity to people of color, the summer of 1967 saw rioting and chaos in 125 American cities. In Newark, New Jersey, the arrest and brutal treatment of a black cab driver touched off four days of violence that saw twenty-six people dead, including a ten-year-old boy, as rampant looting and arson brought over $10 million in property damage. It was worse in Detroit, where racial tensions, economic frustration, and repeated incidents of brutality among the predominantly white police force gave way to uprisings the same month. Five anarchic days in late July resulted in more than seven thousand arrests and $50 million in property damages, and left more than forty people dead and hundreds more injured. Army paratroopers and National Guardsmen were brought in to reinforce the city, which looked like a police state.

Like the cities themselves, Johnson was devastated. "How is it possible that all these people could be so ungrateful to me after I had given them so much?" he lamented to Doris Kearns after leaving office. "Take the Negroes. I fought for them from the first day I came into office. I tried to make it possible for every child of every color to grow up in a nice house, to eat a solid breakfast, to attend a decent school, and to get a good and lasting job. I asked so little in return. Just a little thanks. Just a little appreciation. But look what I got instead. Riots . . . Looting. Burning. Shooting. It ruined everything."

ROGER WILKINS: He reacted badly. How would you react? You're sitting there in the White House, you're in charge of the country and people think you have all this power, and the country starts burning up. Johnson had a good heart, but he wasn't a civil rights expert. He knew Texas, but he didn't know big city guys. He wanted black people to be grateful. "I did this," and he'd pull out a bill and he would tell what he did on it, "and I did this," and he'd pull another bill and tell, "I did this, I'm doing this. How can they do this to me?" And people would try to tell him, and it was hard to tell him.

JAMES FARMER, civil rights activist, national director, Congress of Racial Equality, 1961–65: Lyndon Johnson could not understand that the civil rights movement had changed its class content. Johnson felt particularly uncomfortable with this new group of poorer blacks from the inner cities of the North. They were not like the poor blacks and Mexican-Americans that he had contact with down in Texas. These were different. They were raucous people, they were angry people, they were belligerent folk. They did not see Lyndon Johnson as a friend. They saw Lyndon Johnson as a white man.

■ ■ ■

Southern whites and northern blacks added to the cacophony of voices opposed to Johnson in the latter days of his presidency. Those voices, growing in numbers by the day, included protesters lined up against the war, which by 1967 could be seen every night on the evening news in scenes of blood and chaos that seemed increasingly hopeless. By August, Johnson would see the nadir of his popularity as support for his handling of Vietnam plunged to 27 percent while disapproval surged to 60 percent.

"HEY, HEY, LBJ . . ."

To those who lived in the White House, the din was constant. At least once or twice a week, student antiwar protesters in groups of various sizes would march back and forth in front of the mansion's black iron gates—some with picket signs, others without—all shouting the same chorus: "Hey, hey, LBJ, how many kids did you kill today?" or "Hell no, we won't go!" Even after they left, only to come back later, their voices echoed all day against the hum of activity that continued around the White House, and in the stillness of the night.

LUCI JOHNSON: One of the things that people don't realize, at least when we were living in the White House, is that my sister and I [had bedrooms] on the north side of the White House, right next to Pennsylvania Avenue, and the walls of the White House are very thin. Back then you could protest on Pennsylvania Avenue, and so the last words I often heard when I went to bed were "Hey, hey LBJ, how many kids did you kill today," and in the morning they were my wake-up call.

■ ■ ■

The demonstrations looked like those going on all around the country. Protesters and their antiwar cries became fixtures on college campuses, in front of county courthouses, and in city parks, sparked by growing outrage over the war and fear among many young men that their draft number would be picked. The nation's changing mood could be heard on transistor radios and stereo turntables. When the Beatles came to America from England in February 1964, a quartet of cute mop tops in matching ties and collarless suits, they had been light relief to a nation still reeling over the assassination of John Kennedy. The music they played on *The Ed Sullivan Show*— "All My Loving," "She Loves You," "I Want to Hold Your Hand"—was little different from the frothy, halcyon pop fare of the 1950s. By 1967 the love they were singing about in their song "All You Need Is Love" was a broader love, a simple answer to the ravages of war, and a staple in the sound track of what would be called the "Summer of Love" the same year. Their 1968 release "Revolution," featuring a shrieking vocal track by John Lennon, was a plea for reason against a backdrop of civil unrest. The youth movement, reflected in the evolving music of the Beatles, was shaking establishment foundations.

In mid-April, more than 250,000 people came together in New York to protest the war and listen to antiwar speeches by Martin Luther King Jr., Stokely Carmichael, and renowned pediatrician Benjamin Spock, making it the nation's largest public demonstration to that point. Across the country, in San Francisco, a concurrent demonstration brought together 100,000 protesters. But the most potent demonstration, at least symbolically, came later in the year, on October 21, with the concerted, uproarious March on the Pentagon. Thirty-five thousand protesters flocked to the capital, many representing more than a hundred organizations with little or nothing in common save a growing antipathy toward a war that seemed increasingly futile and meaningless. Mothers, fathers, hippies, neo-Nazis, Leninists, Maoists, pacifists, Hells Angels, and clergymen all united together amid Viet Cong flags and signs that read "Dump Johnson" or "Where Is Oswald When You Need Him?" Among the vast minority under age thirty was the sage Dr. Spock, who had written child-rearing manuals that had become required reading for mothers of the 1950s, many of whose sons had been added to the draft pool for Vietnam. At a rally at the Lincoln Memorial held before the crowd marched northwest across the Potomac River and toward the redoubtable Pentagon, just under three miles in the distance, Spock proclaimed, "The enemy is Lyndon Johnson; the war is disastrous in every way." The president, meanwhile, was hunkered down at the White House, conspicuously conducting business-as-usual while careful to ensure that the demonstrators' freedom of expression was preserved short of breaking the law.

Among the more than two hundred protesters arrested during the March on the Pentagon was Pulitzer Prize–winning novelist Norman Mailer, fueled by equal parts alcohol and rage, who chronicled the episode in his book *Armies of the Night*, published the following year. In it, Mailer wrote, "There is no greater importance in all the world like knowing you are right and that the wave of the world is wrong, yet the wave crashes upon you." Johnson believed in his heart that *he* was right on Vietnam, but by 1967, the waves of dissent were beginning to crash in on his presidency.

Johnson's has been called a "personal presidency"; much of what he did was connected to something that related to personal experience: growing up poor in small-town Texas, teaching impoverished Mexican American school kids, securing a college degree despite financial hardship, finding young people jobs through the NYA during the Great Depression. Johnson's presidential policy, more than that of any other president who has held the office, was as much a reflection of him as a man as of him as president. He wanted to make things better, and to right wrongs he had seen in more than five decades of twentieth-century American life; he was a revolutionary within the system. Yet none of the policies of his administration were more closely associated with him by the public than the war—and the antiwar protests were personal indeed. The "Hey, hey, LBJ . . ." chants were an assault on a man who had striven to give so much to those crying out. How could they not understand how much he had done for them—how much he was *like* them?

GEORGE REEDY: I think [Johnson's] downfall was basically a kind of separation from reality. He'd reached a point where he didn't know what was real and what wasn't. I know he was terribly bewildered by the student demonstrators . . . [b]ecause nobody, nobody, had done more financially for college students [and for civil rights] than Lyndon Johnson. . . . And he didn't realize a number of things. When he was a young man, a college education was a tremendous prize. Just tremendous. It meant the keys to the kingdom. Well, it doesn't mean the keys to the kingdom today. Today, a lot of college is a babysitting proposition. And I doubt whether students value it that much. And it didn't mean anything to them that this was the man who'd gotten all those scholarships and educational funds. What do they care? They were more interested in Vietnam.

Second, their life style was totally different from his life style as a young man. When he was a young man, as soon as you graduated from college you were very careful to comb your hair right and tie your tie right, get a pressed shirt, pressed suit, and you'd start making the rounds looking for a job which you'd get pretty quick. The long hair bothered him, the careless, sloppy clothing, the blue jeans, and he'd look around in the White House and he'd see a lot of young people that looked exactly like his ideal—what a young person should look like. And so to him that was the real American youth. I don't know where he thought those people outside came from, probably Mars or Neptune, or something like that. But he did, he got separated from reality.

■ ■ ■

But it's also possible that Johnson understood the protesters better than he let on, and that, in some ways, paradoxically, they strengthened his resolve on the war. In October 1966, as the antiwar demonstrations outside the White House intensified, Johnson met with Henry Fairlie, a White House correspondent, in the Oval Office. "You saw those protesters outside carrying the Vietcong flag," he said. "They'll never bring me down. But as long as I'm President of the United States, they'll be allowed to parade the Vietcong flag out there." He didn't blame them, and believed that in the long view of history, he would be vindicated. "The young people I've dealt with are the finest I've known in any generation," he observed after leaving the presidency. "I've never come into contact with a cleaner or finer bunch than those I see. . . . I don't think the country is going to hell. But you can't do everything in the name of freedom and still preserve freedom."

LYNDA JOHNSON ROBB: He was [not concerned] so much about the young people who were protesting. He could understand their sympathies. It didn't make him happy; he was angry and hurt and sometimes he exclaimed, "I have tried to do so much for those people. Why don't they appreciate me? Why don't they understand?" And yet, he understood why.

LBJ: My heart was with the students, although they would never know that, and I don't suppose they would ever believe it. I'd hear those chants—"Hey, hey LBJ, how many kids did you kill today?"—and I knew there was a long gulf between them and me, which neither one of us could do much about. I was doing what was right, right for them, and right for their future and their children. But they couldn't see that. What we were doing was based on decisions that were made and actions that were taken before some of them were born, and that's a hard thing to understand. I didn't blame them. They didn't want to get killed in a war, and that's easy to understand. It would be wonderful if there were a way each generation could start off fresh, just wipe the slate clean all around the world and say, "OK, the new world begins today." But nobody's ever found a way to do that. There's a continuity in history that's one of our greatest strengths, and maybe it's one of our weaknesses, too.

If a young man says, "You're sending me to Vietnam because of the [Southeast Asia Treaty Organization (SEATO)] treaty, but I wasn't around when you passed the SEATO treaty, and I don't believe in it and I don't think it's right to put my life on the line for decisions that were made by men when I was in the cradle"—well, there's something there to listen to. But it's possible for us to say to young men and women: "You're free, you can vote, you can deny the state the right to enter your house, you can speak your mind without fear of prison." And we can say all these things to them because of the decisions made and actions taken by men before any of us were born, before our parents and grandparents were born.

■ ■ ■

The war would become personal for Johnson in another way. In August 1966, in a Washington wedding that captured the country, Luci, at nineteen, married Pat Nugent, a twenty-three-year-old airman first class in the Texas National Guard. The following year, in 1967, she gave birth to Patrick Lyndon, the president's first grandchild, as Nugent requested a transfer to the 113th Tactical Fighter Wing in Washington. The same year, twenty-three-year-old Lynda married Marine captain Chuck Robb, four years her senior, in a shimmering White House wedding that seized the public's imagination as much as her sister's had. Their first child, Lucinda Desha, would be born on October 25, 1968. By March of 1968 both of Johnson's young sons-in-law would leave their wives to be among the more than half a million troops serving in Vietnam.

LYNDA JOHNSON ROBB: [The protesting] was very difficult, knowing how hard Daddy was trying—and to have people outside your window . . . on Lafayette Square, screaming "baby killer," and "how many kids did you kill today" and all that. And it was personally hurtful. Here I thought, "My husband is over there trying to do what he thinks is right, and you're screaming about my father and my husband." [I]t was terrible the way we treated our men and women over there and, you know, it certainly made me bitter.

But I was one of the lucky ones, because I had a healthy baby and her father came back at her six-month birthday. He had never seen her, and he came back—and he came back healthy. And we had friends who didn't [come back]. And sometimes you never [knew] how are the parents or the spouses—how are they going to feel toward you? Are they going to hate you because they think your father made them go?

LUCI JOHNSON: [Daddy] would be watching [coverage of the war on] the 11:00 o'clock news and he looked like somebody had taken a lance and just thrust it into his gut. And I knew that he so desperately wanted resolution to what seemed to be impossible to resolve. And it was all very personal. Every one of those men and women who were in that theater mattered to [D]addy, and two of them were the husbands of his children and the fathers of his grandchildren. It was very, very personal, and he wanted with all that was in him to find a way out.

"EYES ONLY—FOR THE PRESIDENT"

As protests were staged and riots festered incongruously throughout the "Summer of Love," the Johnson administration slogged on with the war.

McNamara visited Vietnam in July, and returned sanguine. When asked by Johnson, "Are we going to be able to win this Goddamned war?" he replied, "I am convinced we can achieve our goals and end the fighting if we follow the course we have set for ourselves." It was welcome news to Johnson, who, in addition to the antiwar protests, faced daily criticism from hawks that the conflict was hopelessly deadlocked. The results of the South Vietnamese national election on September 3 were encouraging, too. Conducted hastily after a constitution had been put into place with the considerable help of the United States, the election, to the surprise of very few, installed General Thieu as president and Marshal Ky as vice president.

Walt Rostow was confident about the U.S. situation in Vietnam, too—always had been. The national security advisor "almost never brought bad news to Lyndon," wrote Johnson's biographer Merle Miller. "[O]n the subject of Vietnam, for instance, he was eternally optimistic. The light he saw at the end of the tunnel was always blazingly bright and had been since 1963, brighter every day." Yet in late summer, Rostow delivered a thirty-three-page report from CIA director Richard Helms entitled, "Implications of an Unfavorable Outcome in Vietnam," on which Rostow scrawled "Top Secret-Sensitive. Eyes Only—For the President from Walt Rostow." The report, dated September 12, 1967, offered Johnson another way out of the war.

In a two-page cover memorandum to the president, Helms wrote in part, "Since part of my job is to examine contingencies and since our involvement in Vietnam has many facets, I recently asked one of my most experienced intelligence analysts in the Office of National Estimates to attempt to set forth what the United States stake is in that struggle. The device he chose for the purpose was a paper on the 'Implications of an Unfavorable Outcome in Vietnam.' I believe you will find it interesting. *It has not been given, and will not be given, to any other official of the Government*." He continued: "I would emphasize that the paper was not intended as an argument for ending or for not ending the war. We are not defeatists out here. It deals narrowly with the hypothetical question the author put to himself, i.e., what would be the consequences of an unfavorable outcome for American policy and American interests as a whole. It has no bearing on whether the present political-military outlook within Vietnam makes acceptance of such an outcome advisable or inadvisable."

The intelligence officer responsible for the report, who consulted with at least thirty colleagues of diverse views, concluded that the net effect of U.S. withdrawal in Vietnam, while resulting in "a major setback in the reputation of U.S. power," would probably "not be permanently damaging to this country's capacity to play its part as a world power for order and security in many areas." The consequences would be limited to Southeast Asia, where instability, turmoil, and "some realignments might occur," but importantly, "similar effects would be unlikely elsewhere [in the world] or could be more easily contained." The Soviets did not "stimulate Hanoi's aggression," and while U.S. failure in Vietnam might embolden them in other parts of the world, the threat "would probably be manageable if the U.S. played a steady hand and conveyed to others that it was doing so." As for the Chinese, "Communist success in Vietnam would not make overt Chinese aggression in Southeast Asia any more likely."

The worst potential damage, according to the report, would be "the self-inflicted kind: internal dissension which would limit our future ability to use our power and resources wisely and to full effect, and lead to a loss of confidence by others in American capacity for leadership." The report concluded: "If the analysis here advances the discussion [on options in Vietnam] at all, it is in the direction of suggesting that such risks are probably more limited and controllable than most previous argument has indicated."

A cursive *L* written in the hand of one of Johnson's secretaries indicates that the president read the report. Tom Johnson, a close aide who acted as a notetaker for Johnson and attended most of the Tuesday lunches on the war, was unaware of the memorandum's existence at the time. When he learned of it more than four decades after it was written, he couldn't recall any other "quite like that," and maintained that under normal circumstances the president would have consulted with his most trusted advisers on the matter—Rusk, or Rostow, or, for outside counsel, Abe Fortas. But Johnson's reaction to the memo is lost to history. No record or recollection exists of LBJ exploring its contents with anyone inside or outside the administration.

But why? The report, declassified in 1999, almost thirty-two years after Johnson read it, offered him some assurance that he could get out of the conflict in Vietnam without the threat of the dominoes falling beyond Southeast Asia, or any more Communist aggression spurred elsewhere in the world. Nor would there likely be any long-term damage to the reputation of the United States—assuming internal divisions didn't tear the country apart as a consequence of loss of confidence in American leadership. Why, then, didn't he entertain the option of withdrawal? Was it America's obligation to Vietnam through SEATO; fear of a right-wing backlash—or of the implicit admission that he had been wrong on the war and Democratic opponents such as Bobby Kennedy had been right; concern that U.S. troops would see it as desertion; the possible demoralization and division of the American people; refusal to be the first president to lose a war—perhaps a product of the Alamo legend seared into his consciousness; or an inability to see beyond the blinding lights of war? Or did he simply disagree with the report's conclusions? All offer plausible answers; none can be definitive. Here, again, Johnson remains a mystery.

BOB HARDESTY: I always thought that Vietnam for Lyndon Johnson was like a Greek tragedy, and that moment he put his hand up in *Air Force One* to take the oath of office, he was doomed. One way or another, Vietnam was going to do him in. If he had decided it wasn't worth the salt, the right wing would have gone after him and probably tried to impeach him. He knew it was going to destroy him. He thought he was doing the right thing—I imagine at times he didn't think he was doing the right thing. But there it was.

LYNDA JOHNSON ROBB: His great fear on Vietnam was not of the antiwar liberals but of the hawks on the right. He believed that if he didn't stand tough, if he didn't appear strong, if he didn't seem to be in total control, knowing everything, that the conservatives, the far right, would eat us up.

GEORGE MCGOVERN: I take him at his word. He did not want to be the first president to lose a war. I think that's what he said, and I think he was saying exactly what was in his head. And he was going to hold the line, but then discovered that to hold the line he had to keep putting in more people all the time. I think every time he did that it hurt him, I mean hurt him personally.

He grew up in the shadow of the Alamo, where people fought until the last man.

TOM JOHNSON: I know this with certainty: he felt the United States had an obligation under the SEATO treaty to defend South Vietnam. He felt that we needed to do all we could do to enable the people of South Vietnam to live in freedom—where children could have schools, food, safety, homes.

BARRY GOLDWATER: I don't think he had any concept of [tactics and strategy]. His service in World War II was extremely limited. He wasn't exposed to the command level. I wouldn't say that in a critical way, because there are very, very few of us in the Congress that ever had the opportunity to study warfare and to see the studies practiced, or to live through the war games and the theorizing. On the Armed Services Committee today there are probably two of us who have ever had that. But it was obvious that Lyndon didn't understand that. I think this was one of his weaknesses in Vietnam, in that never having been exposed to the command responsibilities, he was reluctant because of shame—[that's] one source—to rely upon men who had. He was afraid that they might be wrong, so he listened to too many people, in my opinion, and got a little confused.

JACK VALENTI: I would sum up Lyndon Johnson in the words of Winston Churchill. He had what Mr. Churchill called "the seeing eye," the ability to discern beneath the surface of things, to see what's on the other side of the brick wall, to follow the hunt three fields before the throng. The only time it failed him, the only time, was in this fungus that we now call Vietnam. But before that, it was a seeing eye of unbelievable perfection. Every great Captain has it.

■ ■ ■

Though American troops would stay in Vietnam, by late autumn Johnson resolved that it was time for his secretary of defense to go. By then, McNamara had voiced his long-standing doubts about U.S. involvement in the campaign, exacerbating Johnson's own doubts about McNamara. McNamara moved on to become president of the World Bank, an appointment Johnson had arranged for him, extricating him from the war from which he—along with Johnson—would forever be linked. Much later, in 1996, McNamara would write in his memoirs, "We of the Kennedy and Johnson administrations who participated in the decisions on Vietnam acted according to what we thought were the principles and traditions of this nation. We made our decisions in light of those values. . . . I truly believe that we made an error not of values and intentions but of judgment and capabilities."

For his part, Johnson never admitted to an error in judgment on the war in his time in office or afterward. He believed in the end—as he had at the beginning—that not defending Vietnam from Communist infiltration would lead to greater aggression and ultimately to greater conflict, just as he had seen when Neville Chamberlain pursued an appeasement strategy with the Nazis that degenerated into World War II. Even seven months after leaving office, he warned, "The enemy is already in Laos, etc. Indonesia might stand but I doubt it. Ten years from now we'll be back in the Philippines, and we'll wonder then—didn't we learn anything? People say there's nothing worse than Vietnam. Well, I think there are lots of things worse than Vietnam. World War III would have been much worse."

However, Johnson did harbor regrets about retaining McNamara—privately at least.

BARRY GOLDWATER: Lyndon came to regret things that people had advised him on. I remember shortly after he was inaugurated I was back here, and I said, "Now, Lyndon, it should be none of my business but it's my country too, and you'd better get rid of Bob McNamara as soon as you can because he's going to hang it right around your neck." He didn't do it. I saw him twice during that period, told him to get rid of McNamara, and finally the day before Nixon's inauguration [in 1969] Lyndon called and said, "Would you stop by for a drink?" I went by the White House and we sat in his little private office and had a few bourbons. He said, "By God, you were sure right about that McNamara. I wish I had done what you told me, because he got to be so heavy around my neck. I felt I couldn't let him go because I would alienate all of the Kennedy people." I said, "You should have gotten rid of all the Kennedy people, and the man who told you to do that—Harry Truman—learned it the hard way." I don't care how loyal they [Kennedy people] are to their country, when they get in a job their feelings run that job. And McNamara was to me the most dangerous man we've ever had in the secretary's job.

■ ■ ■

In March of 1968, McNamara was replaced by Clark Clifford, an old Washington hand and sage lawyer who had served as an adviser to every Democratic president since Truman, and whose views on the war more closely matched Johnson's—at least for a time.

CLARK CLIFFORD: [Johnson] felt that Secretary McNamara was vacillating on Vietnam and was becoming concerned about the efficacy of our bombing and was becoming rather irresolute in our whole posture in Vietnam. I think the President got concerned with that. And when the opportunity opened up for Secretary McNamara to go to the World Bank, it seemed to me there was general agreement that perhaps that was a good move.

I believe one of the reasons the President selected me to succeed McNamara was that he felt I supported his policy strongly. I did support his policy and he had known me for a good many years, and I think what he wanted was a man who would stand there strong and forthrightly and resolutely, and the President wouldn't have to worry about that particular fellow. He'd know right where that man was all the time. I was perfectly prepared to do that.

The trouble with it was that as I went through that inquiry into the whole subject of Vietnam, my opinion changed.

AROUND THE WORLD IN FOUR AND A HALF DAYS

With the option of withdrawal dismissed, the only way out of Vietnam for Johnson, short of victory, was brokering a peace. An honorable peace. It was there that he set his sights.

TOM JOHNSON: I think he hurt deeply about every casualty, every injury, every child killed. He was not the warmonger that many of his critics described. I saw the emotional toll the war took on him. He desperately wanted an honorable peace.

JOHN CHANCELLOR: We were going out to SAC [Strategic Air Command] in Nebraska one night on *Air Force One*, and President Johnson came back and sat at the press table with us. He sort of slid his way in. There was one of those *Air Force One* note pads that people always used to steal and write notes to friends. He was talking about peace in Vietnam. He wrote the word P-E-A-C-E on that as he was talking, and then he kept drawing circles around it. Then he put this down and said, "Y'all come back," because the secretary-general of NATO, Manlio Brosio, was on the plane at that time. He said, "Come on back, because I want you to meet him." I held back because I was going to steal this piece of paper and have it framed and put in my office. What he'd actually said to us in the course of the conversation was, "Peace. Everything else is chicken shit next to peace." I thought that was wonderful, so I held back and held back. They all went in this little cabin in *Air Force One* to meet the secretary-general, and I dashed back to get [the piece of paper]. I reached out for it, and this big hand came down. And he said, "That's mine, thank you very much." He put it in his pocket and walked away.

■ ■ ■

Before 1967 ended, just prior to the Christmas holiday, Johnson was back on *Air Force One* with peace once again on his mind, as he made a whirlwind 28,294-mile, four-and-a-half-day impromptu journey. Its impetus was the death of Australian prime minister Harold Holt, who had drowned in a swimming accident. In addition to attending Holt's memorial service, Johnson would stop in Vietnam to rally U.S. troops, in Pakistan to meet with its president, Ayub Khan, and in Italy to meet with Pope Paul VI at the Vatican. The trip satisfied Johnson's "deep inbred desire to show his respect and friendship to a dear friend, Harold Holt," Mrs. Johnson reflected later, "and he hoped by his presence in Vietnam to give evidence of his special feeling as commander-in-chief for those troops, and he had made one further effort toward peace by meeting with the Pope." Though Mrs. Johnson remained at the White House in anticipation of Johnson's arrival early on Christmas morning, *Air Force One* was filled with White House staffers and members of the press. Also on board were scores of busts of the president, which Johnson ordered to be kept in generous supply and planned to give out freely, without any hint of self-consciousness, to the VIPs he met. The busts were nothing new. They were a staple on board *Air Force One*, as was the case on a seventeen-day trip to Asia he had made in 1966 to meet with U.S. allies in the region.

JAMES SYMINGTON, chief of protocol, State Department, 1966–68: You can't fault a man for wanting to give mementos and gestures of his friendship. But what he wanted to take with him was, I don't remember the exact figure, something like two hundred busts of himself. Some of them were white marblish in appearance and others were bronze-looking. It is, I think, unusual for a man to give a bust of himself in his lifetime, although it's difficult to give it any other time. But to make a mass-production gesture really boggles the mind. . . .

Today there are heads of state all over Asia who are trying to decide what to do with the President's bust. But not just heads of state, because that would have been only a dozen or less. As I say, we had hundreds of them, so many, many people—cabinet ministers and all kinds of functionaries—received one. The President would say, "I want a white one." "I want a bronze one." "I don't want the bronze one—I want the white one." And you never had the one he wanted and you had to go back to get it. And: "Damn it! Can't anyone do anything right?"

■ ■ ■

As he circumnavigated the globe in 1967, Johnson's message to U.S. troops was one of total victory. "We're not going to yield and we're not going to shimmy," he said to his "boys" in Vietnam. But in his meeting with Pope Paul VI, on the day before Christmas Eve, his focus was back on peace. Nearly two years to the day after ordering a pause in the bombing of North Vietnam in the hopes of enticing Hanoi to a peaceful settlement in the war, Johnson appealed to the Pope to lean on Thieu, a member of his flock, to open a dialogue with the Viet Cong. Though Catholics constituted a minority in Vietnam, they were, as Johnson knew, "an influential segment in Vietnam's political life" and "their support or resistance could be a decisive factor." Along with the Pope's assurance that he would study the matter, Johnson also received a gift from His Holiness: a fifteenth-century oil painting depicting a Nativity scene of the Virgin Mary, Joseph, and angels tending to the newborn baby Jesus. Johnson, in return, gave the pontiff his own gift: a bust of himself. A bronze one.

After completing what Mrs. Johnson described as "the fastest, longest, hardest trip any President of the United States had ever taken," Johnson was back at the White House before sunrise on the morning of the twenty-fourth to spend Christmas with his family. As 1967 drew to a close, it remained to be seen in the foreseeable future if a meaningful peace was achievable with the North Vietnamese or just a hopeful sentiment scrawled on a piece of notepaper by the president of the United States.

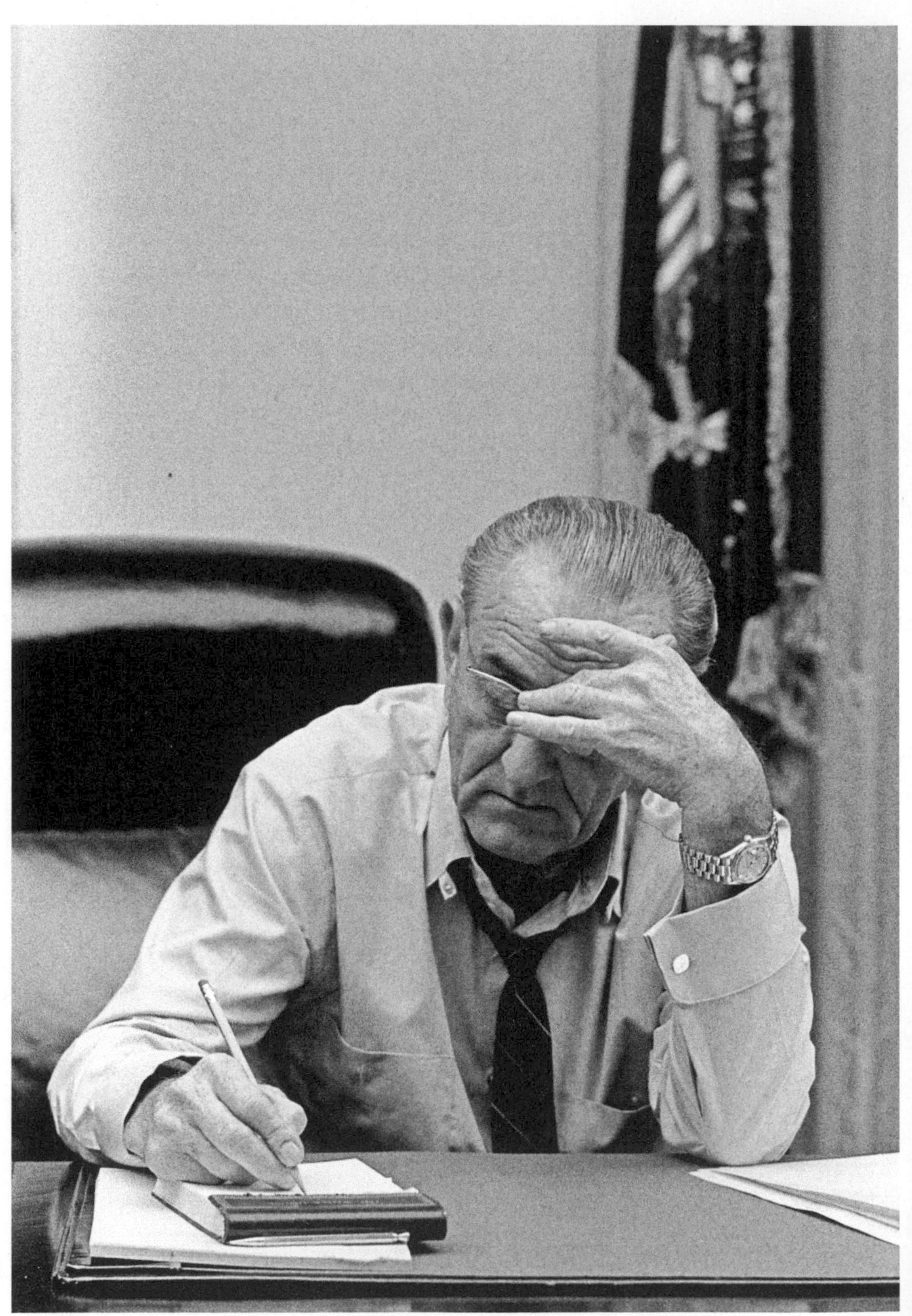

LBJ makes notes in a meeting with his Cabinet, March 27, 1968.

Chapter 10

"THE NIGHTMARE YEAR"

"ONE WAR AT A TIME"

Just before the end of 1967, *Time* magazine, as it had three years earlier, once again named Johnson as its "Man of the Year." This time, though, instead of the artist's portrait of the strong, stolid LBJ that had graced the cover of its 1964 Man of the Year issue, the cover depicted a trouble-worn Johnson caricaturized by artist David Levine as Shakespeare's King Lear, being kicked by Bobby Kennedy, embraced by Hubert Humphrey, and ignored by Everett Dirksen. "More than ever before in an era of material well-being," the cover story began, "the nation's discontent was focused on its president. The man in the White House is at once the chief repository of the nation's aspirations and the supreme scapegoat for its frustrations. . . . Inescapably, he was the Man of the Year." The article went on: "Often, the 36th President called to mind the Duke of Kent's lament for King Lear: 'A good man's fortunes may grow out at the heels.' Whether Johnson was a good man to begin with is disputed by many of his critics, but his tribulations were sufficient to deter any man of lesser fortitude—or obstinacy. . . . An immensely complex, contradictory and occasionally downright unpleasant man, he has never managed to attract the insulating loyalty a Roosevelt or a Truman, however beleaguered, could fall back on. Consequently, when things began to go wrong, he had few defenders and all too many critics."

As 1968 began, it was hard not to argue that Lyndon Johnson's presidency—like his persona—had assumed Shakespearean proportions, just as it was apparent that the press had largely taken leave of him. The barrage of scrutiny and condemnation from the media and the public added to what Johnson would call "the nightmare year," in which he faced a series of crises that amounted to greater anguish than any he had faced earlier in his term—or that had been faced by nearly any other man who had held the office. Increasingly the president appeared wrought physically and emotionally, his weathered face, deeply creviced with worry, aged beyond its fifty-nine years. Leaving the White House became difficult for Johnson in those latter days. Protesters were everywhere, and Johnson kept his distance, fearing that exposing himself to the torrent of dissent would be to diminish the presidency itself. His options limited, presidential appearances were not announced in advance and were principally confined to controlled environments such as military bases. It didn't stop thousands of angry letters from flooding into the White House or preclude the media from lambasting him for his insularity.

The first crisis of the year unraveled all too unexpectedly in the Sea of Japan, off the coast of North Korea, on the twenty-third of January, when the North Korean military seized the U.S.S. *Pueblo*, a navy spy vessel patrolling in international waters. Two sub chasers, four torpedo boats, and two MIG-21 fighter jets were used to commandeer the *Pueblo*, which resisted capture but mounted no counterattack. One U.S. sailor died when the ship was fired on, while the eighty-two remaining crew, blindfolded and beaten, were taken captive along with their ship. "If you're going to play in a pigpen," Johnson had said of the spy game earlier, "you're going to get dirty every now and again." Such was the case when the *Pueblo* was taken by the truculent act of an isolated power, claiming that the vessel had strayed into their territorial waters.

DEAN RUSK: I will never fully understand just why the North Koreans seized the *Pueblo*. It's one of those situations where a small belligerent country can act with a lack of responsibility simply because other countries don't want war. The *Pueblo* was in international waters. It was there to do some listening on communications in North Korea. We had an interest in picking up as much intelligence as [we] could out of North Korea because of the belligerency of North Korea towards South Korea and the increase of infiltration into South Korea, but we were relying upon the high seas, the freedom of the seas.

■ ■ ■

A military response to the seizure was ordered, but never came. Top-secret military documents declassified in 2004 reveal why. According to the report, "There were no suitable armed aircraft immediately available to provide assistance. F-4 aircraft in Korea on nuclear alert could be downloaded and launched unarmed and without air-to-air capability for 'show of force.' F-105 aircraft from Yokota Air Force Base could not reach Wonsan before dark." In other words, the nearest U.S. aircraft, in South Korea, were armed with nuclear munitions that, if stripped of their nuclear payload, would be useful only as airborne paper tigers; F-105 aircraft, capable of engaging in an effective counterattack, were too far from the *Pueblo* to reach her before nightfall. By the time Johnson was awakened with the news of the capture, the *Pueblo* was being dragged impotently into North Korea's east coast port of Wonsan, and the United States was caught flatfooted in the world's view. An immediate armed solution now impossible, Johnson and his staff considered their options, concluding that, as hard as it was to accept, the most prudent course with the North Koreans was diplomacy.

NICHOLAS KATZENBACH: Well, he called in a group of people to look at the recommendations initially on this and I think it's fair to say that nobody advised him—we went into all the possible options that—things that one could do, but there was nobody really who felt that we should do anything more than try through diplomatic means to see whether or not he could get the crew back. Because any efforts at reprisal, or military threats, or things of this kind, they're just too dangerous in a situation with the North Koreans and the South Koreans both absolutely itching to get into a fight with the other one; and if we get involved in that, there would be a fight, and one war at a time is enough.

DEAN RUSK: [Johnson] made a prompt decision to try to get the ship and its men back by diplomatic means rather than by military means. We were faced with the fact that if you tried to use military force to rescue the men, you might pick up dead bodies, but you wouldn't pick up live men and that you might well start a war at a time when we didn't want a war between North and South Korea involving American forces.

So we decided to swallow hard and try to get these men back by diplomatic means, and that took a great deal of doing. We had meeting after meeting that made no progress; and we finally released the men by a device, which I described at the time as being without precedent in international affairs. We signed a statement which the North Koreans insisted we sign, but at the very time we signed it we made a statement saying that we denounced the signature and the statement itself was false.

They knew in advance that we were going to make that statement. This had been worked out in advance. It's as though a kidnapper kidnaps your child and asks for fifty thousand dollars ransom. You give him a check for fifty thousand dollars and you tell him at the time that you've stopped payment on the check, and then he delivers your child to you. I think probably what happened was that the North Koreans came to the conclusion that they had milked the *Pueblo* affair for all that was in it, and that there was no particular point in holding on to these men any further.

■ ■ ■

It would take exactly eleven months before the eighty-two U.S. servicemen, who had been tortured throughout their captivity, were released. On December 23 the crew walked across the "Bridge of No Return" at the DMZ on the Thirty-eighth Parallel to freedom in South Korea, leaving the U.S.S. *Pueblo* behind as a trophy of defiance for North Korean dictator Kim Il Sung.

Less than a week after the *Pueblo* was taken, before the month of January was out, Johnson would face a greater show of defiance, and a greater test of his will—this time from Ho Chi Minh.

NO LIGHT, LONGER TUNNEL

Since the fall of 1967, U.S. intelligence had been picking up chatter among the North Vietnamese and Viet Cong that a major surge in the war was in the offing. Precautions were urgently taken; General Westmoreland and the military brass had put counteroffensive plans into effect to repel enemy forces, troops were put on alert, and leaves were cancelled or postponed. Johnson was hopeful that an American victory against the offensive, a certainty by the estimation of his advisers, would give Ho Chi Minh further impetus to negotiate a peace. What intelligence couldn't predict—and didn't, as it happened—was the timing or intensity of the attack.

Every year since the war had begun, the North and South Vietnamese had observed Tet, their most important holiday—which marks the beginning of a new lunar year and is enjoyed by all Vietnamese regardless of social class, religion, or party affiliation—with a cease-fire. But just one day into the holiday, around midnight on January 30, the North Vietnamese attacked, and the scope of their offensive was breathtaking. The enemy advanced on five of South Vietnam's six largest cities, 36 of its 44 provincial capitals, and nearly a third of its 242 district capitals. In Saigon, the U.S. embassy compound was attacked by Viet Cong forces that blasted a hole in its concrete wall before being killed by U.S. forces, five of whom died in the six-hour standoff.

Robert McNamara, phasing out his responsibilities as defense secretary, gave his assessment of the situation in a phone conversation with Johnson on January 31, 1968:

Robert McNamara: *They have more power than some credit them with. I don't think it's a last gasp action. I do think that it represents a maximum effort, in the sense that they've poured on all of their assets. And my guess is that we will inflict very heavy losses on them both in terms of personnel and materiel and this will set them back some. But after they absorb the losses, they will remain a substantial force. I don't anticipate that we'll hit them so hard that they'll be knocked out for an extended period or forced to drop way back in level of effort against us. I do think that it is such a well-coordinated [effort]—such an obviously advanced-planned operation, that it probably relates to negotiations in some way. . . .*

I don't believe they're going to be successful. I think that in Khe Sahn, where we are going to have the real military engagement, I believe we'll deal them a heavy defeat. I think in the other areas it's largely a propaganda effort and publicity effort and I think they'll gain that way. I imagine that our people across the country will feel that they're much stronger than they had previously anticipated they were. And in that sense, I think they gain.

The question in my mind is how to respond to this. Is there anything we should be doing we're not doing? I've talked to the [Joint] Chiefs about some kind of reciprocal action, in retaliation for their attack on the embassy or in retaliation for their attack across the country. There just isn't anything they've come up with that is worth a damn. . . .

LBJ: *I think that one thing we ought to do is try to keep Westmoreland in the news out there nearly twice a day. . . .*

McNamara: *I quite agree.*

I asked Phil [Goulding] to talk yesterday to our people and have "Westy" make—I said once a day—but I'll make it twice a day. You're quite right.

LBJ: *I think you ought to too. I don't think they get enough information and I think you've become sensitive. And we've all pulled in. I meet with 'em once every two or three months. You meet with them once a month if there's* *something big. But if you'll remember you used to see them every—almost daily—and I think it shows the difference. I think in this campaign year, the other crowd has got two or three committees grinding out things. Their only interest is to find something wrong. People look for something wrong. . . .*

After a fortnight of often intense fighting, the U.S. forces won a lopsided victory while standing nearly all of their ground. An estimated 33,000 to 58,000 Viet Cong or North Vietnamese troops died in the struggle, compared to 1,110 American soldiers (a number that would climb to upward of 4,000 by the end of March). Yet, while the North Vietnamese had largely lost the battles that made up the offensive, the sheer ferocity of Tet meant, in essence, that they were winning the war. Tet demonstrated in clear terms the enemy's extraordinary ability to mount a coordinated attack—despite the enormous losses they had suffered to that point, and the fact that more American bombs had been dropped on Vietnam than during all of World War II—and the will of Ho Chi Minh to win the war, a will unmatched by the American people. McNamara was right: The United States would prevail in Tet, but the American people began realizing that the enemy was "stronger than they had previously anticipated they were," and began asking themselves, is this really worth it?

Already beleaguered before the offensive began, Johnson monitored the developments of Tet at all hours, getting little sleep and wearing himself down further. During the crisis, Richard Russell visited with him privately at the White House, where he watched his former mentee weep over the situation.

CLARK CLIFFORD: Tet had had a very substantial impact on me as it had on others. The first meeting of the senior advisers, I'm almost sure, came after the return visit of Ambassador Bunker and General Westmoreland. They had come back, it seems to me maybe a week, two weeks, or three weeks before the meeting of senior advisers in '67, and those two men had been quite optimistic about our posture in Vietnam. As I recall, Ambassador Bunker said that "we could now see light at the end of the tunnel," and General Westmoreland indicated that he thought it entirely possible that we could begin to bring American boys home in 1968. Well, Tet changed all that. The fact that the enemy could mount a simultaneous offensive against fifty or sixty cities, towns and hamlets at one time and that the effect of such an offensive, even though blunted militarily, could result in our military asking for an additional number of troops amounting to over 200,000, changed the complexion entirely. After Tet, I assure you, there was no suggestion that we could see any light at the end of the tunnel, nor was there any thought of sending any American boys home. The whole thrust was exactly the reverse. After Tet the actual request that was made was that we send over 200,000 more out there to help the 525,000 we already had there.

HARRY MCPHERSON: [H]ere there were competing views and opposing phenomena all over the place. [Our embassy in] Saigon and MACV, the military operation in Saigon, was telling us that we had really beat the hell out of the enemy; that they had taken tremendous casualties. And they had.

The negative was essentially here in this country. It was the feeling on the part of vast numbers of Americans that, particularly after Westmoreland and Bunker had come back in the fall of the year before and said that things were really just looking good—and I believe they used the expression "light at the end of a tunnel"—that after all that and after a tremendous commitment for three years—air power, five hundred and fifty thousand men and all the rest of it—that this crowd was still able to mount a major offensive that smashed into all kinds of cities and secure hamlets and such things, that they were able to hold Hue for a long time while the Marines encircled them, that they were able to get into Saigon and terrorize the population.

The terrible quality of the war in Vietnam came home to people. It appeared that these guys didn't want to quit at all and were never going to quit; that our crowd was as caught off guard as ever.

■ ■ ■

Tet changed the paradigm on Vietnam; support for the war began to erode further, even among those who had been believers earlier. In November of 1967, Johnson's approval rating on Vietnam had climbed upward to 40 percent. Despite a hawkish uptick just after Tet, late February saw his approval rating on the war fall to 32 percent as the public's appetite for war began to sour. The haunting image from Tet, photojournalist Eddie Adams's Pulitzer Prize–winning photograph of the chief of the South Vietnamese military security service summary execution of a Communist guerrilla in a Saigon street, a pistol aimed square at his temple, provided a metaphor for the war's atrocity and senselessness. The sage "Wise Men," many of whom Johnson had first brought together in 1965, reflected the change in the public mood. An early November 1967 Oval Office meeting with Dean Acheson, George Ball, McGeorge Bundy, Clark Clifford, Arthur Dean, Douglas Dillon, Abe Fortas, Averell Harriman, Henry Cabot Lodge Jr., Robert Murphy, and Generals Omar Bradley and Maxwell Taylor had the bulk of the men urging Johnson to stay the course in Vietnam. Their views had mostly changed on March 26, when Johnson again met with the same group, plus Cyrus Vance and General Matthew Ridgway. Acheson spoke for the majority in asserting, "We can no longer do the job we set out to do in the time we have left, and we must begin to take steps to disengage." Only Fortas, Murphy, and Taylor offered opposing views.

DEAN RUSK: I have no doubt about it myself, just as the Tet Offensive made an impression on a lot of people here in this country. Although the Tet Offensive was a military disaster for the North Vietnamese and Vietcong, it had a considerable propaganda and psychological impact, and clearly shocked people here in this country and caused them to feel that the situation was getting to be hopeless. So in the second meeting of these same "Wise Men" there were a number of them who had been so impressed by the Tet Offensive that they were not nearly so sure that we ought to proceed as we were doing, and that we ought to sort of make the best peace we can.

■ ■ ■

Perhaps more significantly, as least as far as the public was concerned, was that Walter Cronkite, whose wisdom Americans seemed to take as an article of faith, had come to a similar conclusion. In February the CBS newsman journeyed to Vietnam himself to get a firsthand view of the war.

WALTER CRONKITE, CBS News anchor: I wanted to see the situation for myself. But in discussing it with [CBS News president Richard] Salant, I suggested that I ought to do a personal report on just what it seemed to me. We had all these conflicting reports coming in on one side and then the other. The American public was utterly confused now because of the Tet offensive. The Vietcong had risen. The North Vietnamese had gotten all the way down into Saigon. Villages we claimed were pacified immediately went back to the Vietcong. We lost them. We hadn't won any "hearts and minds" at all, apparently. I told Salant that it would be a good idea if I did first-person reports: "Why don't I go out there and just try to bring perspective through one person's eyes rather than try to be so unprejudiced and so unbiased?"

■ ■ ■

Upon his return, CBS ran an hour-long prime-time special on February 27, in which Cronkite rendered his verdict on the war: "It seems now more certain than ever that the bloody experience of Vietnam is to end in a stalemate," he told his audience. "To say that we are closer to victory today is to believe, in the face of the evidence, the optimists who have been wrong in the past. To suggest we are on the edge of defeat is to yield to unreasonable pessimism. To say that we are mired in stalemate seems the only realistic, yet unsatisfactory, conclusion. . . . [I]t is increasingly clear to this reporter that the only rational way out then will be to negotiate, not as victors, but as an honorable people who lived up to their pledge to defend democracy, and did the best they could." The writing on the wall on Vietnam became clearer with Cronkite's broadcast. As Johnson told George Christian after the special aired, "If I've lost Cronkite, I've lost the country."

WALTER CRONKITE: I don't think I turned around public opinion on the war at all. I was reflecting it, probably, more than directing it. But I didn't turn Lyndon Johnson around either, but this probably pushed him over. He was beginning to feel misled and misused by the military. I think particularly the Tet offensive had disturbed and alarmed him because, first of all, he later told me that the military said it couldn't happen. And when it did happen, the military claimed it as a great victory for us. As Westmoreland told me, " If they could give me 200,000 more men, I can finish this thing off." I think that Johnson felt just like most of the American people did at that point on: let's just get out of this. But the president couldn't get out himself. He was too deeply committed. So the thing to do was to get out of the job.

THE DECISION

Well before the trials of 1968 came to bear, Johnson, as he had in 1964, considered opting out of the presidency with the completion of the term he was serving. This time there were plenty of precedents. Earlier in the century, Theodore Roosevelt, Calvin Coolidge, and Harry Truman had all been vice presidents who had been catapulted into the presidency with the death of an incumbent, and each, after winning the presidency in his own right, declined a reelection bid. The laconic Coolidge famously announced his intention by publicly stating simply, "I choose not to run for president in 1928." Privately, after an eight-hour session at the Ranch with Mrs. Johnson, John Connally, and Texas congressman Jake Pickle, in September of 1967, Johnson arrived at the same decision for 1968.

The primary factor was health related, the main concern he had raised back in 1964. "The men in my family die early," he continued to point out. Years earlier he had the family's medical history entered into a computer, which spat out a prediction that he would live to be sixty-four, and he had no reason to doubt it. Even if he did, memories of his near-fatal heart attack in 1955 were there to remind him of his fragile hold on whatever life he had left. There were also the images in his mind of Woodrow Wilson, infirm and unable to discharge his duties as president for much of his second term, that haunted him. He didn't want to put the country through that. Mrs. Johnson, who had helped beat back Johnson's doubts about running in 1964, was supportive of her husband's decision for 1968, fearing a "physical and mental incapacitation" that "would be unbearably painful for him to recognize, and for me to watch." Johnson's decision to step down was eased with his hope of using the opportunity of not being involved in a presidential campaign to concentrate on a peaceful settlement in the war.

DEAN RUSK: [H]e talked to me about it [in 1967] and left me with a very clear impression that he was very seriously considering withdrawing from public life at the end of his first full term. He had talked to me about the fact that no vice president had ever succeeded to the presidency and then run for two full terms.

He referred to the tragedy of Woodrow Wilson, who was desperately ill while he was still President. Although President Johnson didn't put it in categorical terms, I had the impression he was concerned about his health as far as running and serving out another full term was concerned.

The idea that he was driven from office by Vietnam is just not true. Long before dissent in Vietnam had become significant he had talked about withdrawing, and I think he had such advice from his wife.

BILLY GRAHAM: He said, "I'm giving serious consideration to not running again." Well, that was before the pressures of the war and Bobby Kennedy and so forth had reached its climax, as it later did, and people thought that he decided not to run on that basis. That could have been contributing factors, but I believe he did feel that he might not serve out his term. He thought a great deal about death, and he talked to me about it several times. I remember that we even prayed about it. So, these things were in his mind.

■ ■ ■

The question became, when should he make the announcement?

GEORGE CHRISTIAN: He had started talking with Mrs. Johnson and me, and I don't know who else, in the summer of 1967 about not wanting to run again. Not knowing how to get out of office was part of that; how do you go about telling people you're not going to run for reelection?

Mrs. Johnson was very supportive of his not running. He sent me to Austin to see [John Connally] because he wanted [his] views and [his] language for a speech announcing it. This was in the fall of 1967.

I was in San Antonio with the White House press while he was at the Ranch. I drove up to Austin on a Saturday afternoon, and [Connally] and I spent the rest of the afternoon at the [Governor's] Mansion while I took down [his] stream of consciousness on what he [LBJ] might say in a withdrawal statement. I took it back to Washington and prepared it for him in a way that he might present it to the Democratic Party, which was his thought at that time because that's what President Truman had done [when he opted not to run again in 1952].

He never could find the right forum and [was] doubtful about what he ought to do. He decided that maybe the best time to do it was in the State of the Union Address in January of 1968. He had me call [Connally] again and ask [his] opinion of his making a withdrawal statement that night, and I'll never forget what [John] said. [He] really [wasn't] that keen on him doing it but [he] said, "Well, tell him he will never have a better audience," so that's what I told [President Johnson].

History records that he decided not to do it that night. Tom Johnson and I made the preparations, but he surprised us by not doing it. I stood in the back of the House chamber waiting for him to make the announcement at the end of his speech, and he didn't do it. As we went back to the White House I said, "I guess you decided not to withdraw tonight."

He said, "It was sort of difficult to lay out a big program and say, 'I want you to pass all of these things,' and then say, 'Okay, so long; I'm checking out.' "

■ ■ ■

The chance to announce his intentions in the State of the Union in 1968 forgone, Johnson rode out the next couple months revealing his impending intentions only to a handful of those close to him—and holding out some possibility, however remote, that he would reenter the political fray. With the tidal change in public opinion on the war, pressure mounted from his own party to change his war policy. As it did, the names of possible challengers for the party's presidential nomination began surfacing. The logical choice was Bobby Kennedy. The dovish Kennedy had come late to the antiwar movement, but quickly rose to become its member of highest standing. Bobby Kennedy, the liberal icon of 1967 and 1968, was substantially different from the one who had been counsel for Joe McCarthy in the fifties, and the Vietnam hawk and hatchet man for his brother the president of earlier in the decade, but he was as contemptuous of Johnson as ever. Despite those feelings, his fervent antiwar crusade, and undeniable presidential ambitions, Kennedy, a good party man, declined to challenge Johnson as the Democratic standard-bearer.

In early March, a week before the New Hampshire primary, Kennedy had lunch with *Time* magazine's Hugh Sidey. "There was no tolerance of Lyndon Johnson," wrote Sidey of the feelings Kennedy expressed. "When the president was mentioned, Kennedy became emotional. He felt like Lyndon Johnson's leadership had collapsed. He was despondent over the new recommendations for more troops. When the question about Kennedy renouncing his candidacy came up, he suddenly looked up and shot us a blunt question: 'Do you think I made a mistake?'"

The challenger who emerged was Eugene McCarthy, a liberal senator from Minnesota, who hadn't made much of a mark in Washington and commanded little name recognition nationally. A December poll revealed that only 40 percent of Americans had heard of him and that Johnson would beat him handily in an election standoff.

LBJ: I always thought of Senator McCarthy as the type of fellow who did damn little harm and damn little good. I never saw anything constructive come out of him. He was always more interested in producing a laugh than a law in the Senate.

■ ■ ■

The results of the New Hampshire primary, held on March 12, came as a surprise to much of America, including Johnson himself. When the votes were tallied, Johnson garnered 49.4 percent versus McCarthy's 42.2 percent—while McCarthy captured twenty of twenty-four convention delegates. The press played the story out as a referendum on the war, and a David-over-Goliath upset. *The New York Times*'s lead front-page story the following morning came with the headline "M'Carthy Gets About 40%, Johnson and Nixon on Top of New Hampshire Voting." (Richard Nixon had won the GOP primary in New Hampshire, which also occurred on March 12.) What the article neglected to mention until its third paragraph was the fact that Johnson's name wasn't on the ballot. He had won the popular vote as a write-in candidate. Though McCarthy's performance was impressive, the primary's result—even the delegate count, where Johnson's vote was divided among a slate of forty-five delegate candidates whereas McCarthy's was divided among only twenty-four—had an apples-to-oranges disparity, with McCarthy leveraging a distinct advantage.

LBJ: I never allowed my name to go on the ticket in New Hampshire. If I had, I have no doubt that I would have won New Hampshire two to one.

I was surprised by McCarthy's vote in New Hampshire. I was surprised that folks all over the country were taken. I was surprised that a man with as little principle as McCarthy could take people from Ivy colleges and make them think they were doing some good.

■ ■ ■

What happened four days later held little surprise for Johnson: Bobby Kennedy, smelling blood in the water, announced his own candidacy for the party's nomination. "That little runt will get in," Johnson had insisted for weeks. "The runt's going to run. I don't care what he says now." Though Kennedy had earlier feared that contesting Johnson for the nomination would split the party "in a damaging way," the results in New Hampshire indicated "that a sizable group of Democrats are concerned about the direction in which the country is going both in the fields of foreign and domestic policy."

Prior to his announcement, Kennedy and Ted Sorensen had proposed through Clark Clifford that Kennedy would refrain from a run at the nomination if Johnson changed his policy on the war. The White House immediately dismissed the notion as blackmail. Kennedy and Sorensen came back with another deal: Kennedy would decline a run if Johnson created a White House commission to study the war. They went so far as to propose the members of the committee—all of whom had expressed opposition to Johnson's war policy. Kennedy's name was also on the list, along with some ambiguity as to whether he expected to be the committee's chairman. In order to ensure that the commission had teeth, they further demanded that upon naming the commission, Johnson would offer some assurance that his policy on the war would change.

DAVID BURKE, friend of the Kennedy family: I do remember thinking that it doesn't happen that way, that you don't go make a deal with Lyndon Johnson, you don't go make a deal on the Vietnam commission. One man is president of the United States; another man wants to be president of the United States. Now, if Robert Kennedy was looking for an out by getting some major concessions from Lyndon Johnson on Vietnam, which I viewed the commission thing to be, then I was somewhat happier that he was looking for the out. But it always occurred to me, just as a single guy, that Lyndon Johnson would smell that fifty miles away and he would not acquiesce to anything like that. Why the hell should he?

■ ■ ■

Johnson shot down Kennedy's proposal as quickly as it was tendered. With what he saw as his noble intention roundly blunted, Kennedy's path and conscience were clear to pursue the nomination. New Hampshire further opened the door.

Not until March 31 did Johnson firmly close the door on pursuing the nomination himself, despite privately indicating to others that his stepping down was more or less a foregone conclusion. Part of leaving his options open was certainly ego—the prospect of the vindication of his policy and the approbation of the American people through another election win, and of taking down Kennedy "the runt" in full view of the body politic. Part of it may have been the uncertainty of what would come next after devoting nearly his entire adult life to politics as a singular pursuit. According to Johnson later, the only reason not to step down was the assurance that he wasn't letting down U.S. troops, two of whom were his sons-in-law.

A nationally televised address scheduled for the evening of March 31, in which Johnson planned to announce limitations on the bombing of

North Vietnam as another good faith gesture to the North Vietnamese toward a peaceful settlement to the war, provided an elegant opportunity to put his cards on the table.

JIM JONES, appointments secretary (chief of staff), 1965–69: On Friday, March 29, the president said at a news conference that he would deliver a televised address the following Sunday evening. Friday evening, he called his press secretary, George Christian, Postmaster General W. Marvin Watson and me into his Oval Office study. The discussion lasted a couple of hours.

"I'm thinking about announcing Sunday that I'm not running. What do you think?" he opened over the first drink. The three of us argued vigorously while he poked holes in each argument. By evening's end, we split two to one. (George was against his running, Marvin and I said it was too late for him to step away from the battle.) We left not knowing what he would do.

Early Sunday morning, he told me to put [speechwriter] Horace Busby back on the "I will not run" peroration. The rest of the day, the main speech, in which Mr. Johnson announced a unilateral halt to the top half of North Vietnam and deployment of only a fraction of the troops General William C. Westmoreland had asked for, went through dozens of revisions before the late night final draft.

MARCH 31

March 31 began for the president in the predawn hours with a family matter relating most directly to the monumental news he would deliver to the nation later that evening.

LBJ: The morning of March 31, Lady Bird came in and woke me up at 5:30. She said, "Lynda is going through a trying period. She just told her husband goodbye and she's an expectant mother. He's going over there by your orders. He doesn't even know what you're going to say or do." She said we ought to meet her at the gate.

Lynda was coming in on the "Red Eye" special. We met her. We went upstairs and had a cup of coffee. She told us everything he had said, every little movement, where she kissed him. She looked at me and she had tears in her eyes and her voice. She said, "Daddy, why does Chuck have to go and fight and die to protect people who don't want to be protected?" It was hard for her to understand.

That night I looked over at Pat who had his orders for Vietnam.

The only doubt I ever had about the March 31 decision—the only thing that could have made me reverse it—was those two boys, or 200,000 more, saying I was a yellow bellied SOB. I would ask Westmoreland about this in some detail—what they would think—I salved my conscience. I became convinced that my [sons-in-law] and the public didn't feel that way. In my own heart, the way I really felt was that I was putting my whole stack in to get them out of there.

LYNDA JOHNSON ROBB: I saw the terrible agony that he went through on Vietnam. And I sometimes contributed to it, without even thinking.

I got married in December; my husband left for Vietnam in March. The day Chuck left, I saw him off in California and waved him goodbye. I was pregnant, thinking, "God, he'll never come back. And then what happens?" I thought the same things that every mother and every wife thought.

I was a constant reminder to [my father] as I sat in that White House, getting bigger and bigger, waiting for that baby to come. He had to listen to my complaints, "Why is my husband over there fighting for people who don't want him to be there?"

It was on that March 31 that I came back from seeing Chuck off. We had talked earlier about Daddy not running, but nothing had been decided. I got on the "hoot owl special" and I arrived about six o'clock in the morning. I went to sleep, and when I got up later in the day on that March 31, they told me that he had decided not to run.

I did everything I could to change his mind. I said, "You can't do this. I've just sent Chuck over there. Who is going to take care of him? How can you do this to me?" I felt he was letting me down, and I let him know it. I'm sure that weighed upon him a bit, too.

■ ■ ■

Mrs. Johnson wrote of the episode in her diary: "When I went back into Lyndon's room, his face was sagging and there was such pain in his eyes as I had not seen since his mother died. But he didn't have time for grief. Today was a crescendo of a day. At nine in the evening, Lyndon was to make his talk to the nation about the war. The speech was not yet firm. There were still revisions to be made and people to see."

Just before 9:00 p.m., the president sat behind his desk in the Oval Office, looked into a television camera, and addressed the nation on the subject of "peace in Vietnam and Southeast Asia." He spoke for approximately forty minutes. One of the revisions he had made to the speech earlier in the day came at the very end:

> *With America's sons in the fields faraway, with America's future under challenge right here at home, with our hopes and the world's hopes for peace in the balance every day, I do not believe that I should devote an hour or a day of my time to my personal partisan causes or to any duties other than the awesome duties of this office—the presidency of our country.*
>
> *Accordingly, I shall not seek, and I will not accept the nomination of my party for another term as your president.*
>
> *But let men everywhere know, however, that a strong, a confident, and a vigilant America stands ready tonight to seek an honorable peace—and stands ready to defend an honored cause—whatever the price, whatever the burden, whatever the sacrifice that duty may require.*

LADY BIRD JOHNSON: I saluted him for being clearheaded enough to see that he wasn't the man at that particular juncture of time who could unite the country.

HORACE BUSBY, special assistant to the president, secretary of the Cabinet, 1963–65: Watching him you could see he was clearly exhausted. When he was making the speech his hands trembled, and some people say they saw tears in his eyes. I wasn't sure he'd say it until he actually did.

I don't think there were any regrets later. That is the invention of the so-called psychohistorians. Not any bitterness. Nor any feeling—well, of course, you always have moments, everybody does, of regrets over something as major as that. But, if you ask me, if he had to do it all over again, in my opinion anyway, he'd have done it all over again.

■ ■ ■

After the speech was over, Johnson got up from his desk and was hugged by his wife and daughters, who sensed his relief. "Nobly done, darling," Mrs. Johnson whispered in his ear.

JIM JONES: Later that night, March 31, after the speech had been delivered, the president bounded from his chair in the Oval Office to join his family in watching the television reviews. His shoulders temporarily lost their stoop. His air was that of a prisoner let free.

■ ■ ■

An hour and a half or so after the historic announcement, the White House extended an invitation to a select group of media outlets to meet with the president informally in the private quarters of the White House. Among the handful of reporters was Carl Bernstein, a twenty-four-year-old reporter from *The Washington Post*, who was temporarily diverted from his Metro beat to the White House to help *Post* reporters Carroll Kilpatrick and Carl Rowan, caught up in the news frenzy Johnson had set off.

CARL BERNSTEIN, Metro reporter, *The Washington Post*: I got to the newsroom, and [Ben] Bradlee yelled at me, "Bernstein, you have a tie on. Go to the White House!" And I think the reason was [that] by that time it must have been close to 9:00 [p.m.], and almost nobody was in the newsroom except some old guys on the [news] desk, wearing paisley shirts and their belts off to the side, literally. So [Bradlee] said, "Bernstein, you've got a tie on. Go to the White House and help out."

So, I ran down to the White House, which is three blocks away. Somehow I had been cleared. And I ran into the pressroom, and Kilpatrick and Rowan were both dictating. And it was a madhouse down there. And all of a sudden, there was an announcement over the P.A. system in the press room saying that the President will meet in the Yellow Oval Room with a pool reporter from NBC, the AP [Associated Press], *The New York Times*, and *The Washington Post*, and maybe one other paper, but that was it. Anyway, so I figured Rowan and Kilpatrick would go up there, but they were both too busy dictating, and they said, "Bernstein, you go up." [So, I went] up to the Yellow Oval Room. [George] Christian was up there, and Lady Bird was there. We asked Christian some questions about who knew, and I believe Christian gave us a little information, but basically said, "The President will tell you about his decision." So we had to wait about ten minutes and during that time there was kind of small talk with Lady Bird. And, she was very gracious.

[A]bout ten minutes later, the president strode through the door. He was wearing a powder blue turtleneck. I assumed it was from Neiman Marcus; it had that Neiman Marcus look. And he was spooning tapioca [pudding] in his mouth from a little clear dish. [T]he first thing he did is he looked at us, and he said, "I fooled y'all, didn't I?" And he laughed. And then he started to say he had been carrying around in his pocket—and he put his hand up, I think, like you put your hand into a jacket pocket—this version of the speech for weeks. There had been several occasions when he thought he might draw this thing out of his pocket and append it to his speech, but it hadn't quite worked, and "Bird" was wondering when he was going to do it, and Christian also, and this was the time to do it. And he did.

[T]hen we asked some questions about the war and what led to his decision, and he talked in very emotional terms about what the war was doing to the fabric of the country and his presence if he continued as President as this terribly divisive issue was [affecting] the country. And he became emotional at that point. I think we were all emotional in the sense of knowing this was an incredible moment in history.

[T]here were questions asked of Mrs. Johnson and how she felt. She was very deferential. And I think she teared up.

I think like many people my age, especially covering the anti-war movement, I had come to revile what [Johnson] was doing with this horrible unending war. I hated the war like a lot of people. And at the same time, I viewed Johnson—even then in some ways, but particularly at this moment, and I continue to—as this tragic figure who had done these unbelievable things. He had assumed the presidency; he had promulgated the Great Society; he had done on Civil Rights what Jack Kennedy was never willing to do; he had passed [an] amazing number of bills that meant a whole new era of domestic initiative in terms of the problems of the country, particularly those affected by race and class. And it was all going to hell because of this war. But you could see that his heart was broken by this.

You know, he was not an unpolished man. He had an aura about him that was big and sophisticated in his own Texas-slash-Washington way. I think what I must've thought at the time is that he could see that he could never be president, and do, from then on, what he wanted to do [for] the country. He had lost his opportunity. It was done, even if he would have pulled the troops out and [sent them] home tomorrow. The country was divided.

When I subsequently have been to the White House, I always remember that night.

END OF A DREAM

A tide of goodwill came in the wake of the president's announcement on March 31. The following day, April 1, Johnson saw a jump in his approval ratings from 36 percent to 49 percent. Those who had come to think of Johnson as power-hungry, warmongering, or deceitful were suddenly willing to give him the benefit of the doubt. Had they misjudged him? Had they been unfair or too harsh? Praise for his selflessness came from unlikely sources.

LBJ: After my announcement March 31, one of the first persons to call me was Bobby Kennedy. He came in [on April 3] and said what a great man I was. He thought of me as a man who had to cling to all of his power. He couldn't conceive of it until after it happened.

That was the last thing that entered Bobby's mind. But I wasn't new to public power. I had it for 38 years.

■ ■ ■

In fact, Kennedy called Johnson "a brave and dedicated man," words that Kennedy found hard to spit out, and that Johnson had to ask him to repeat, because either he hadn't heard them or simply wanted to hear Kennedy force them out of his mouth again. After consenting to Kennedy's request for future presidential briefings, Johnson said, "People try to divide us and we both suffer from it. . . . I feel no bitterness or vindictiveness. I want everybody to get together to find a way to stop the killing." It was a surprisingly convivial meeting between rivals, and the last the two men would have. (Johnson's feelings wouldn't stay warm for long. He had met Kennedy in the Cabinet Room, where he had the proceedings covertly taped. Immediately afterward he ordered them transcribed. When the tapes later came out blank, the likely result of a scrambler that Kennedy or his aide, Ted Sorensen, had carried with them, Johnson exploded, not because he needed to know the content of the meeting, which his aides Walt Rostow and Charles Murphy had dutifully captured through copious notes, but because he had been outflanked.)

Another Johnson adversary, William Fulbright, said that Johnson's stepping down was "an act of a very great patriot." The media also lauded Johnson for his decision as their coverage of him softened. Even Ho Chi Minh seemed moved by Johnson's announcement. Word came from Hanoi indicating a willingness to talk to administration officials that might lead to direct negotiations on the war. Johnson was at peace with the decision he had made, and so, it seemed, was the rest of the world. A kind of calm descended over the White House for the first time in months, belying another storm to come.

Early in the evening of April 4, after attending a meeting with UN secretary-general U Thant in New York to discuss the meaning of Hanoi's overtures, Johnson had returned to the White House. At 7:24 p.m., as he was meeting with former Georgia governor Carl Sanders and Robert Woodruff, chairman of Coca-Cola, he was handed a bulletin by his aide Tom Johnson. Martin Luther King Jr. had been shot and killed by a sniper in Memphis. King's killer, later identified as James Earl Ray, an escaped convict with a long history of criminal activity, was caught two months later after the biggest manhunt in American history.

TOM JOHNSON: LBJ was the most steady and clear thinking man I ever have seen in major crises. He read the wire service flash I brought him and immediately began making the urgent calls and assembling the members of his cabinet and staff to deal with the shooting. He immediately summoned his key White House staffers, FBI director J. Edgar Hoover, the attorney general and others. He went to the two wire service machines in the Oval Office, read the bulletins, and began watching the three network newscasts on the Oval Office TV sets. He asked Mr. Hoover for updates from law enforcement. He made multiple calls to members of Congress, to Reverend King Sr., to Mrs. King and others.

ARTHUR KRIM, chairman, Democratic National Finance Committee, 1966–68: [Johnson] was very depressed, and the thing that was so clear [was] how short-lived the euphoria of the announcement had been. Because the first couple of days, with the Vietnamese making their move, with Bobby Kennedy full of apologies, with editorials and calls and everything, and with his talking about concentrating on the big issues, it had seemed as if it had all paid off. Then to have this happen was a devastating blow to the country and to LBJ.

■ ■ ■

By 1966 the productive partnership between Johnson and King had dissolved as the Great Society withered in the shadow of Vietnam. King first began speaking out against the war in 1965; as it escalated, so did his criticism. One year to the day before he was felled in Memphis, King, whose civil rights efforts had evolved over time into efforts on behalf of the nation's poor, spoke out against the war in a meeting of clergymen at Riverside Church in New York. The speech, entitled "Beyond Vietnam: A Time to Break Silence," laid out his position on the war and, though it didn't mention him by name, why it had resulted in a gulf between him and Johnson. "There is," King said, "a very obvious almost facile connection between the war in Vietnam and the struggle I, and others, have been waging in America."

> *A few years ago there was a shining moment in that struggle. It seemed as if there was a real promise of hope for the poor—both black and white—through the poverty program. There were experiments, hopes, new beginnings. Then came the buildup in Vietnam and I watched the program being broken and eviscerated as if it were some idle political plaything of a society gone mad on war. . . . So I was increasingly compelled to see the war as an enemy of the poor and to attack it as such.*

For King, Vietnam was an all-or-nothing proposition; nothing else Johnson did mattered as long as the war raged. King was a crusader, not an old guard civil rights leader like Roy Wilkins, the executive director of the NAACP, who worked within the system and dealt with the president with a kind of congressional cordiality, careful not to alienate him through sweeping condemnation of his policy. King, on the other hand, felt a moral obligation to actively protest the war, and abandoned Johnson over the cause. Given all that Johnson had strived to do for minorities and the poverty-stricken, he resented it. He also remained concerned about King's alleged Communist ties from reports given to him by FBI chief J. Edgar Hoover (though in May 1965, six months after the presidential election, Johnson ordered a stop to the wire tapping of King that had been put in place by attorney general Bobby Kennedy during the Kennedy administration). But Johnson was deeply troubled and saddened by King's murder. "Martin Luther King['s death] was a tragedy. The President was most adversely affected," Johnson later said, uncharacteristically referring to himself in the third person.

TOM JOHNSON: LBJ and Dr. King had worked together closely to achieve the 1964 and 1965 civil rights laws. LBJ was disappointed, hurt and angry when Dr. King later distanced himself and became an opponent of the war in Vietnam.

BOB HARDESTY: No doubt that LBJ was angry with King, but I think that most of his anger was directed at Bobby Kennedy who was poisoning the well. LBJ's anger toward King was mixed with regret and sadness. He couldn't understand how King could have turned so completely on him after all he had done for civil rights. There were others—like Senator Wayne Morse—who vocally disagreed with the President on Vietnam but who supported his domestic agenda almost 100 percent and were not ashamed to say so. Why couldn't King do the same?

■ ■ ■

As Johnson had foreseen after receiving the news of King's death, any goodwill or political capital he may have accrued after March 31 went up in flames along with that which engulfed much of urban America. "Everything we gained in the last few days we're going to lose tonight," he lamented to his aides. Riots broke out in 125 cities in 28 states. The worst of it was in Washington, where more than 700 fires lit up the capital through the night. Smoke permeated the White House lawn as police sirens wailed throughout the city. All told, the chaos throughout the country would leave between 45 and 60 people—almost all African American—dead, many of them in Washington. Another 2,600 were injured, and 21,000 were arrested.

After considering his options, Johnson ordered the dispatch of federal troops to restore order to the capital and several other cities. But it wasn't an easy decision.

LARRY TEMPLE: It was a turbulent time. I kind of remember thinking it wasn't real; it wasn't a reality. Looking out from the White House, from the second floor of the mansion part of the White House, and seeing fires in Washington. It was really set ablaze.

But there were the issues and problems of the riots, and so President Johnson had to do something, and it was recommended that he declare martial law. He was reluctant to do that, for good and valid reasons. The mayor had asked that martial law be declared and [that] the military come in and restore order.

Abe [Fortas], "Chris" [Warren Christopher], and I worked on that.

I always remember something that occurred that I think is awfully important: At one point, President Johnson came in and said, "Now, you boys, I want to tell you: Don't get me into something until you know how we're going to get me out." And I thought pretty often that's a pretty good standard of government: Don't go into something unless you know how you're going to get out. That probably would have been something that each of us would have thought about somewhere along the line, and would've taken into account. [But] he thought about it instantaneously up front. It was his first reaction. I think it probably typified LBJ as much as anything.

■ ■ ■

The riots made manifest the findings of the National Advisory Commission on Civil Disorders, an eleven-member committee Johnson had named in July of 1967, to look into the urban summer riots that, since 1964, had become as inevitable as Fourth of July fireworks. Released in March 1968, the committee's written conclusions, known as the Kerner Report after the committee's chairman, Illinois governor Otto Kerner, warned that the country was "moving toward two societies, one black, one white—separate and unequal," and of a "system of apartheid" in its cities.

As always, Johnson let no crisis go to waste. Just as he had done with the Civil Rights Act of 1964 in the wake of Kennedy's assassination, he used the King tragedy to enact a piece of civil rights legislation that had up to that point proven elusive: a civil rights bill that included a "fair housing" provision that even the obliging "Fabulous Eighty-ninth Congress" had rejected.

JOSEPH CALIFANO: Johnson had pressed the Congress hard on fair housing for more than two years and he finally had gained Senate approval on March 11, 1968. But there had been little hope of getting the House to pass the Senate bill. Urban representatives, normally civil rights supporters, were besieged by middle-class white constituents who wanted to keep blacks out of their neighborhoods. From the tragedy of King's assassination, Johnson saw an opportunity to salvage a national fair-housing bill—and he was prepared to use the tragedy to get it.

■ ■ ■

Gaining the support of the Senate earlier in the year had been no easy feat. Walter "Fritz" Mondale, junior senator from Minnesota, was the bill's sponsor. Mondale had been one of those moved three years earlier, when Johnson had invoked the phrase "We shall overcome" in his appeal for the Voting Rights Act, calling it "the five most dramatic seconds in my public life." Determined to move a fair housing provision through the Senate, Mondale battled long odds to get the measure out of cloture, where it languished; of thirteen previous civil rights cloture votes, only two had carried. The odds got longer as Mondale saw three votes for cloture for his fair housing measure fail between February 20 and March 1. Senate majority leader Mike Mansfield threatened to kill the bill if it didn't pass after a fourth cloture vote, slated for March 4. At his wit's end, Mondale called his mentor Hubert Humphrey, to solicit his advice on how to save the bill. The vice president advised him to call Johnson.

WALTER MONDALE, U.S. senator, Minnesota (D), 1964–76: I talked to Hubert about it, and he told me to call the president. So I did.

He took the call, and I gave him a rundown and told him we were a few votes shy of cloture. He asked who was on the fence. I told him we could get [Alaska senator] Edward Bartlett if he got $18 million for public housing. *Click.*

The next day, the vote came up and we were close to passing it, but we needed one more. Then, just before it closes, in Bartlett comes and says, "Aye." That was Lyndon.

■ ■ ■

Despite lame duck status that limited his political leverage, Johnson put everything he had into passing the bill through the House.

ROBERT C. WEAVER, secretary of housing and urban development, 1966–68: We got the bill through the Senate largely through the efforts of Fritz Mondale. He was just a newcomer and probably had about 28 black constituents, so it wasn't politically inspired. It was just what he believed in.

So we got the bill through the Senate but then we couldn't get it through the House.

After the President indicated that he wasn't going to run again, he didn't have much leverage, certainly not as much as he would have liked to have. We were getting nowhere in the House when Martin Luther King was assassinated. Within 48 hours [*sic*], the bill passed. He put everything aside. This is it. This is the time. And he knew how to take advantage of whatever cards he had.

■ ■ ■

On April 10, less than a week after King was slain, the Civil Rights Act of 1968, Title VIII of which concerned fair housing, made it through the House by a vote of 250 to 172. Later Johnson wrote, "That legislation might have passed anyway, but it is entirely possible that Martin Luther King bought it with his life." The day after the House passed the bill, Johnson signed it into law in the East Room of the White House. Dedicating the measure to King, he said, "I do not exaggerate when I say that the proudest moments of my presidency have been times such as this when I have signed into law the promises of a century."

Unlike the Civil Rights Act of 1964 and the Voting Rights Act of 1965, however, fair housing would ultimately fall short of its own promise: White homeowners found easy ways to sidestep the law by withholding or misreporting sales information. But it continued to push forward a civil rights agenda at a time when polarization between the races was exacerbated by what a growing number of whites perceived as the chronic lawlessness of many urban blacks. Despite those growing obstacles—and the perception that the social reform Johnson envisioned had been stopped in its tracks by Vietnam—Johnson had succeeded in getting the Federal Jury Reform Act, another landmark civil rights law, through Congress just a few weeks earlier. The legislation, which he signed into law on March 27, allowed for the random selection of juror names based on voter lists from a "cross section of the community." It further prevented jury selection on the basis of race, color, religion, gender, national origin, or economic status.

BOB HARDESTY: An anecdote goes along with that: We were down at the Ranch having dinner, and an old friend of [President Johnson's], a retired judge, was having dinner with us and the President was talking about the speech he was about to give. He said, "Bob, go get it off my desk. I want to read a section of [it]." And then he read a section about one clear [civil rights] violation [of] trying an African American in front of an all-white jury. And the judge objected to it very much.

He said, "I've been a judge all my life and I never tried a black in front of all-white jurors and I don't think you ought to say that." And the President said, "Do you remember Otto So-and-so who we grew up with in Johnson City?" And he said, "Sure." [The president] said, "Well, one night old Otto got all beered up and went over to Fredericksburg to a German dance at the dance hall. He went in and the first thing he did was announce in a loud voice, 'I can lick any Dutch son of a bitch in the house!' At that point this German farm boy with biceps as big as boulders grabs him by the collar and said, 'Vhat you say?' He says, 'I can lick any Dutch son of a bitch in the house. Are you a Dutch son of a bitch?' He said, 'You better believe it.' He said, 'Well, I wasn't talking about you.' "

And [the president] told the judge, "I guess I wasn't talking about you either." And the passage stayed in.

"WHAT IS HAPPENING TO US?"

One of the few major American cities to escape rioting in the wake of Martin Luther King Jr.'s assassination was Indianapolis. Bobby Kennedy had been there that night, a day after his last meeting with Johnson, to begin campaigning for the Indiana Democratic primary, scheduled for May 7. Against the warnings of Indianapolis's chief of police, after learning of the King shooting, Kennedy spoke to a group of African Americans in the heart of the city's ghetto. Addressing the crowd from crumpled notes he had made just before the appearance, Kennedy delivered the "sad news" that King had just been reported dead, before speaking movingly about what was needed in the country in a tempestuous time of senseless violence.

> *What we need in the United States is not hatred. What we need in the United States is not division. What we need in the United States is not violence or lawlessness, but love and wisdom, and compassion toward one another, and a feeling of justice for those who suffer within our country, whether they be white or they be black.*

He then appealed to the crowd to go home and "say a prayer for our country and for our people." The speech—and its quieting effect—showed the moral leadership Kennedy had engendered among many Americans. The man whom Johnson had seen as a pissant and a pretender to the Camelot crown left by his martyred brother had come into his own. By 1968 he had begun to evolve into the kind of inspiring public hero his brother had been.

Kennedy went on to win the Indiana primary handily. As most had expected, Hubert Humphrey had also entered the race, throwing his hat in the ring in late April, but refrained from competing in the primaries, which became nip and tuck battles between Kennedy and Eugene McCarthy. Kennedy won a primary contest in Nebraska, and was then beaten by McCarthy in an upset win in Oregon. On June 4, Kennedy pulled ahead with victories in California and South Dakota. After accepting his California win in the ballroom of Los Angeles's Ambassador Hotel shortly before midnight Pacific Coast Time, Kennedy left through the hotel's kitchen, where he was shot in the head with a .22 caliber pistol by Sirhan Sirhan, a demented Palestinian émigré. Johnson, who had retired for the night at 12:50 a.m., was awakened with the news by Walt Rostow at 3:31 a.m.

LADY BIRD JOHNSON: It was a short night. The phone jarred me awake from a deep sleep. Lyndon was saying tersely, "Will you come in here?" I did not see how it could be morning. I was too tired. And sure enough, I saw that the hands of the clock stood at 4:20.

He was propped up against his pillows, looking as though he had never been asleep, and all of the TV sets were turned on. He was listening intently, and I realized that something serious was happening. I am not sure whether I heard it first from the TV set or from Lyndon. Senator Kennedy had been shot. All three faces of the three TV sets were on and the scene was total confusion. Bobby had been at his headquarters in Los Angeles with Ethel, celebrating his victory in the California primary. Every few minutes the tabulation of the voting would come on the screens. The vote was about 44 or 45 percent for Kennedy and 41 or 42 percent for McCarthy.

The whole terrible event had taken place under the eye of the television cameras, and we saw, over and over, the film of the shooting itself and heard the light crack of the gun. We saw Senator Kennedy lying on the floor, a pool of blood under his head, and heard that he had been taken to the hospital, where he was briefly treated, and then dispatched to another—Good Samaritan. There was an air of unreality about the whole thing—a nightmare quality. It couldn't be true. We must have dreamed it. It had all happened before.

■ ■ ■

Later in the morning, at 6:35 a.m., Johnson placed a call to Ted Kennedy:

LBJ: *Lady Bird and I are terribly shocked and grieved. We're praying with you and hoping for the best and fearing the worst. We have put a detail around* *the families of all the candidates and just wanted to be sure that they didn't think that we were snooping.*

Ted Kennedy: *Oh, Mr. President, you are terribly good to call.*

LBJ: *Well, we are terribly grieved. I don't know what we can do but anything we can we want to. It's a horrible tragic thing.*

We have put a detail around the families and we don't have authority but we're going to ask Congress to give us that authority. In the meantime we're assuming it. We don't want them to think we're snooping though or that MPs around are there for any purpose except to protect them. I wanted to—I placed a call for all of you and if they haven't I told them to get Pierre Salinger or get you or get Steve Smith or to get Ted [Sorensen]. And they got [Ted Sorensen]. And if you'll explain to them here what we are doing so they won't . . . A [S]ecret [S]ervice[ ]man will be in charge. Under the present law they can just cover Mrs. Kennedy, ex-presidents, and the President. We're extending that to all candidates for the Presidency and their families. And the Secret Service will take charge and use Defense and Justice people until we get authority. And we're going to try to get it today.

Johnson spent the balance of the morning trying to determine how to get legal authority to provide Secret Service protection for the candidates and their families as he monitored Bobby Kennedy's condition.

HARRY MCPHERSON: Johnson, as much as he disliked Kennedy—Bob Kennedy—and as much as they despised each other, as a matter of fact, as hipped on the subject of the sedulous Kennedy operation moving about and moving in politics everywhere as he was, Johnson didn't seem to fear in any passionate way the Kennedy Presidency. I think he would have been resigned to it in a curious kind of way. He was terribly agitated after Kennedy's shooting. That day before Kennedy died he would listen to the account in the Ambassador Hotel over and over. He had floods of information coming in from the Justice Department and other places about Kennedy's condition.

■ ■ ■

Later in the evening, as Kennedy lay unconscious in a Los Angeles hospital with little hope of surviving, Johnson spoke to the nation. "At 10:07, Lyndon went on TV," Mrs. Johnson wrote in her diary. "He must have had at most two hours of sleep last night. He did look tired, but strong, commanding, and reassuring. All day long I had heard this cacophony over and over—the reactions of people questioned. 'What is our country coming to? What is happening to us? Are we a sick society?'" The president was mindful of the nation's doubts in his remarks:

> *Tonight this nation faces once again the consequences of lawlessness, hatred and unreason in its midst. It would be wrong, and just as self-deceptive, to conclude from this act that our country itself is sick, that it has lost its balance, that it has lost its sense of direction, even its common decency.*
>
> *Two hundred million Americans did not strike down Robert Kennedy last night any more than they struck down President John F. Kennedy in 1963, or Dr. Martin Luther King in April of this year.*
>
> *But those awful events give us ample warning that in a climate of extremism, of disrespect for law, of contempt for the rights of others, violence may bring down the very best among us.*

At 1:44 a.m. on the sixth, just over a day after he was shot, Kennedy's heart ceased to beat. Back in Washington, less than twenty minutes later, Walt Rostow once again awakened Johnson by phone in his bedroom. "Mr. President, it has just been announced that Senator Kennedy is dead," Rostow said. The news came as no surprise to Johnson, who had been told by the Secret Service the previous evening that it was only a matter of time. "Too horrible for words," Johnson replied.

HARRY MCPHERSON: I'm sure there was a mixture of emotions raging inside him. The year and the times were radical. Life stood on its head—King's assassination, the riots, students taking over universities, then this.

■ ■ ■

The country's flags flew at half staff from June 6 until June 9, which Johnson proclaimed a national day of mourning. The same day, he and Lady Bird flew to New York to attend Kennedy's memorial service at St. Patrick's Cathedral, on Fifth Avenue. It couldn't have been a comfortable situation. Many of those attending the service reviled Johnson as much as Kennedy had. However irrational, some may have blamed him for Kennedy's death, just as some around John Kennedy had after he was slain in 1963—perhaps most of all Bobby. "Always the mind was riveted on the flag-draped coffin in the middle of the aisle with its incredible burden," Mrs. Johnson wrote of the service. "This has been the most shocking, the most unbelievable, event in the nation's life as I have shared it, intensified, made all the more tragic, by President Kennedy's assassination nearly five years ago." After the memorial, the Johnsons returned to Washington to attend Kennedy's burial service at Arlington National Cemetery ahead of the funeral train that would carry Kennedy's body.

ARTHUR KRIM: I think it was very painful for him on several levels. Because certain deep loyalties to Bobby Kennedy came to the surface, like with Bob McNamara and others who stood guard on the coffin. The commentators were cruel enough to imply greater loyalty there than to President Johnson. Of course, there was no way of tying this to President Johnson, and yet there was I believe a feeling on that funeral train—which I didn't go on although I was asked to—of resentment about President Johnson, that he shouldn't have come to the funeral. That he was so antagonistic to Bobby that it was unseemly for him to participate in this. It was dirty, unjustified and dirty, but it was there, and I'm sure he felt it.

■ ■ ■

Once again, Johnson saw an opportunity for reform in the wake of the tragedy. Just after 7:00 the morning after Kennedy was shot, Johnson met with Senate majority leader Mike Mansfield to discuss, among other things, a crime bill that would include a gun control measure. A dozen hours after Kennedy's death the following day, Congress passed legislation prohibiting the interstate shipment and out-of-state purchase of handguns. The law didn't regulate "the deadly commerce in lethal shotguns and rifles" as Johnson would have liked, but, he maintained, it did "more good than harm."

DISAPPOINTMENT

While 1968 was rife with tragedy for the nation, it was also marked by disappointment for its president. Tragedy and disappointment were recurrent throughout the year, and Johnson would find little relief in the later summer months. In June he was successful in getting a 10 percent tax surcharge past Congress, a measure he had been pressing since the previous year. But it was hardly a victory. As part of the bargain, Congress demanded spending cutbacks amounting to $6 billion—a clear indication that the guns of Vietnam would mean increasingly less butter at home.

At least he could strike a deal with Congress. In the Hotel Majestic in suburban Paris, where Johnson had placed so much hope in a settlement of the war, the peace talks had not begun auspiciously. Even before they began, preliminary discussions were delayed for two months over where the peace talks should be held, as each side made suggestions that were just as quickly rejected by the other. Determined to settle on a neutral site, Johnson was at first resistant to Paris due to his fears that France's president, Charles de Gaulle, a vocal critic of the war, would show favoritism toward the North Vietnamese. He soon gave in, however, so that the talks could proceed.

In May the U.S. delegation, headed by Averell Harriman, former governor of New York and veteran diplomat, and his deputy, Cyrus Vance, headed off to Paris, carrying with them Johnson's greatest hopes for peace. But the discussions were still mired. At first the South Vietnamese refused to participate. As Johnson had seen in a mid-July meeting with President Thieu in Honolulu, the South Vietnamese government had no incentive to facilitate agreements that would result in the withdrawal of U.S. troops when they remained incapable of staving off the enemy themselves. Thieu capitulated and sent his delegation to Paris, bringing all sides to the bargaining table at least figuratively. The discussions stalled again when the parties couldn't agree on the table itself; neither side could come to consensus on its shape and on which side would speak first. Throughout the summer the peace talks went on futilely in Paris; so did the war in Vietnam.

CLARK CLIFFORD: We'd worked awfully hard to get the substantive peace talks going. They were the hope. They could end the killing in Vietnam and here now the Saigon government was dragging its feet. First, when we were so anxious for them to send the delegation to Paris so we could get the talks started they delayed day after day, weeks went by, and they wouldn't even send the delegation. And all the time, American boys were dying in Vietnam.

[E]ven after they sent a delegation then they got there and day after day, week after week was spent on the shape of the table.

■ ■ ■

Along with Johnson's unrequited desire for peace in Vietnam was his hope that before the end of his term he could establish détente with the Soviet Union through the reduction in nuclear arms, something he had set his sights on well before. He had hoped to make headway on that front in his summit with Kosygin in Glassboro the previous year. Though nothing had come of the summit, Johnson didn't let the matter end there, doggedly pursuing the prospect of another summit through diplomatic channels. By the summer of 1968, the White House and the Kremlin had come to an agreement that on Wednesday, August 21, they would jointly announce a meeting between the superpowers to be held before the end of the year.

TOM WICKER, Washington bureau, *New York Times*: One of the signal achievements of the Johnson Administration, and for which it has received practically no credit, is that it was the first administration to take seriously the problems of arms control and develop a series of proposals that were seriously meant to be negotiated. Up until the Johnson Administration, I think all arms-control proposals coming out of the Joint Chiefs of Staff were meant to be rejected.

When President Johnson signaled to the Pentagon, as he did, his serious intent on the question of arms control, the word went back. I'm told that John McNaughton said, "Gee, I've got to learn something about arms control." The word went out to the Joint Chiefs of Staff, and a serious proposal came forward to be taken to the Soviets.

CLARK CLIFFORD: The fact is, [arms limitation] was one of the brightest hopes and most eagerly sought goals of [Johnson's] administration. He must have started it back when he was new in the presidency. I would say it goes back surely to 1964. And he began to plan on the development of a basis for talks with the Soviet Union on limitation and ultimate reduction of nuclear weapons. He brought that along as a result of his personal leadership and this driving compulsion that he had to get that accomplished in his administration, which was one of the noblest aims that any president could have. And as a result we had any number of meetings at the Cabinet level, and we had an extraordinarily able second-level group that would meet in between and then meet with the Cabinet level. And finally towards the spring and summer of 1968, we finally had reached an agreement on all the basic principles to be discussed.

■ ■ ■

A little after 8:00 p.m., the evening before the summit was to be announced, the Soviet ambassador to the United States, Anatoly Dobrynin, met in the Cabinet Room with Johnson and Walt Rostow. After exchanging pleasantries, Dobrynin read a statement from the Kremlin informing

Johnson of "the further aggravation of the situation which was created by a conspiracy of the external and internal forces of aggression against the existing social order of Czechoslovakia." The Soviets had invaded Czechoslovakia.

Czechoslovakia's leader, Alexander Dubcek, had actively strayed from Soviet Communist doctrine since assuming the post of first secretary of the nation's Communist Party in January, promising his people "socialism with a human face." His government loosened its grip on industry and the press, paving the way for free speech and freedom of assembly. "Prague Spring," as it became known, was as eagerly embraced by Czechs as it was condemned by Soviet party chairman Leonid Brezhnev. After Dubcek broke from the Warsaw Pact in the face of pressure and veiled threats from the Soviets and Czechoslovakia's Eastern Bloc neighbors, the Soviets mobilized five hundred thousand Warsaw Pact troops that set upon the country. Russian tanks, rolling ominously into Prague on the night of August 20, were met with fierce resistance by student protesters, resulting in a standoff that left more than a hundred dead. After Dubcek surrendered and was taken to Moscow, along with other Czech leaders, the Soviets pulled the reins tighter around the Eastern Bloc nations, claiming the right to intervene when socialist principles were in jeopardy.

JIM JONES: When Soviet Ambassador Dobrynin called me to request a meeting with the president that night at 6:00 p.m., our first thought was that this pertained to the president's proposed trip to Moscow. So although our intelligence material showed Soviet troop movements, Dobrynin's announcement to LBJ that at that moment Soviet troops were crossing the border into Czechoslovakia came as somewhat of a surprise. I think LBJ wanted to make the Moscow trip to further the effort to move the Vietnam peace process along. The Czech invasion was another shoe dropping that worked against a peace agreement.

DEAN RUSK: The Soviets moved into Czechoslovakia on a Tuesday night. It had been agreed between us and the Soviet Union that on the Wednesday morning—the next day—we were both going to launch the SALT [Strategic Arms Limitation Treaty] talks. And one of the first things that we had to do when they moved into Czechoslovakia was to cancel that announcement. [W]e were just on the point of announcing a summit meeting to start the talks on offensive and defensive missiles. So we had gone a long way down that trail.

Now from their point of view, of course, it would have been fine if we had been willing to go ahead. Because we would have put our blessing on what they were doing in Czechoslovakia and [that] would mean that we would not take too much offense to it. But it was perfectly clear that from the point of view of our own people and our allies and the general world situation that we could not announce a summit meeting with the Soviets the morning after they had moved into Czechoslovakia.

■ ■ ■

Despite Johnson's best intentions, plans for the SALT talks dissolved along with the Prague Spring, and the world went back to the way it was.*

Not all of Johnson's disappointments in 1968 related to foreign policy. In June, Earl Warren announced he would be stepping down as the Supreme Court's chief justice after sixteen years at the court's helm. Neither Warren nor Johnson held Richard Nixon, the presumptive Republican presidential nominee, with much regard, and Warren, though active and healthy at seventy-seven, wasn't going to take the chance that Nixon would secure the presidency and be in a position to appoint his successor. He wanted Johnson to name the next chief justice, having little doubt that he would appoint someone with a like judicial philosophy.

It didn't take Johnson long to land on Supreme Court Justice Abe Fortas as Warren's successor as Chief Justice. Johnson had known Fortas, whom he later described as "the most experienced, compassionate, articulate and intelligent lawyer I knew," since their days as young New Deal Democrats in the mid-thirties. As their friendship grew over the years, so did Johnson's reliance on Fortas's counsel, which he sought often in his presidency; Johnson counted him among a core group of confidants whom he "knew best," including Richard Russell, A. W. Moursund, John Connally, and Mrs. Johnson. That confidence in Fortas led to Johnson's naming him to the Supreme Court as an associate justice in 1965 in the wake of the resignation of Arthur Goldberg, who had accepted Johnson's offer to become U.S. ambassador to the United Nations.

The Memphis-born son of a Jewish cabinetmaker, Fortas declined the prospect of serving on the High Court in favor of continuing his lucrative

*It may have given Johnson some satisfaction to know, however, that the SALT proposals drafted by the Joint Chiefs of Staff were the same, more or less, that were later adopted by the Nixon administration, and which resulted in President Nixon's successful SALT negotiations with Leonid Brezhnev in 1972.

practice as a partner at his Washington law firm, Arnold, Fortas and Porter, a view he made clear to the president. Johnson, however, would have none of it. Summoning Fortas to an Oval Office meeting in late June 1965, he exacted the Johnson Treatment. "If your president asks you to do something for your country, can you run out on him?" he asked rhetorically, shortly before adjourning to make his choice known to the press. In the glory days of 1965, Fortas was appointed to the court almost summarily, after securing the approval by a voice vote after only three senators spoke against his confirmation. His fate in 1968 was far less assured.

As the nominee to succeed Fortas, Johnson settled on fellow Texan Homer Thornberry, a longtime family friend who went even further back with Johnson than Fortas. The two had met when Johnson was administrator for the National Youth Administration. In 1948 it was Thornberry who took Johnson's House seat after Johnson advanced to the Senate; in 1965 Johnson appointed Thornberry as a judge on the U.S. Court of Appeals.

JOSEPH CALIFANO: When White House special counsel Larry Temple pointed out that nominating Thornberry invited charges of cronyism, Johnson rebuffed him, as he had on other occasions: "What political office did you ever get elected to? . . . don't come to me as any great knowledgeable political expert until you've run and gotten elected to political office . . . then I'll listen to your political judgment." But at that point, Lady Bird interrupted, "Lyndon, he may be right about that, and that's what worries me about Homer—although I'd love to see him on the Supreme Court."

SAM HOUSTON JOHNSON, LBJ's younger brother: Lyndon decided to name his old friend Abe Fortas as chief justice, and he announced that he was going to appoint an even older friend, Homer Thornberry, as associate justice to take Fortas's place.

I thought it would have been better if Lyndon had submitted the names separately; then when Fortas got approved, he should have sent in Thornberry's name. But he didn't, and the Republicans were just waiting.

■ ■ ■

From the start, Johnson's choices were met with resistance, Fortas's potential nomination with whispers of anti-Semitism—Harry McPherson recalled one southern senator saying to another, "You're not going to vote for that Jew to be chief justice, are you?"—and Thornberry's, indeed, with charges of cronyism.

But Johnson had taken stock of the Senate and took the nominations forward with grudging optimism after securing the support of two pivotal members: Minority Leader Everett Dirksen, and Richard Russell, who respectively brought the Republicans and southern Democrats who would be crucial in getting Fortas and Thornberry passed. At the same time, the president knew that the administration would have to move the nominations quickly through the Senate or risk losing Dirksen. "Just take my word for it," Johnson told Joe Califano presciently, "I know him. I know that Senate. If they get this thing drug out very long, we're going to get beat. . . . Ev will leave us."

Regardless of their support, the nominations soon hit snags when Robert Griffin, a conservative freshman senator from Michigan, announced his refusal to entertain any nominees put forth by a lame duck president.

JIM JONES: We kept telling him that we had the count, we had the votes, and he kept saying, "You gotta move. You gotta button this thing down. We're losing. We're going to get beat. Griffin's going to take over."

■ ■ ■

Here Johnson was right. On the day the Fortas and Thornberry nominations were announced in the Senate, with supportive statements given by Dirksen and Majority Leader Mike Mansfield, Griffin got the support of eighteen of his Republican colleagues to block the nomination, and with them the power to mount a filibuster that would, as Johnson feared, drag out the proceedings. Opposition began to build as senators pointed to the fact that Fortas, as a frequent adviser to the president, had in principle violated the separation of powers inherent in the Constitution, an argument that, as Johnson wrote later, was a "straw man." Members of the Supreme Court had been consulted by presidents, and even been called on to establish policy, nearly since the beginning of the republic; in 1794, President Washington tapped John Jay, the nation's first chief justice, to sail off to London as his emissary in the negotiation of an agreement with England that would ease the threat of war.

Another charge was more damaging. Later it would be revealed that Fortas had accepted $15,000 to teach a nine-week course at American University Law School. Represented as a conflict of interest, this stipend had come from $30,000 that Fortas's former law partner Paul Porter had raised from five businessmen who, opponents claimed, could at some point have business before the court. Most damning for Fortas was his liberal record since joining the Court three years earlier, including his vote with the majority on the 5–4 *Miranda* decision (ensuring legal rights to anyone accused of breaking the law) and his open stand on pornography.

Eventually, as Johnson had predicted, he lost Dirksen's support. More unexpectedly, and more personally, he lost the support of Richard Russell. When Johnson held up the Russell-backed nomination of Alexander Lawrence Jr. for a judgeship in federal district court in Russell's home state of Georgia, as accusations of Lawrence's racism surfaced, Russell broke away from Johnson. In a letter to the president, Russell wrote that he didn't wish to be treated as "a child or a patron-seeking ward healer." The incident permanently severed the twenty-year friendship between Johnson and his former mentor.

In September, after the Senate Judiciary Committee approved Fortas's nomination by an 11–6 vote, Griffin began a filibuster. When Johnson called for its end, a vote in the Senate came up short by fourteen votes. The writing clearly on the wall, Fortas, while retaining his seat as an associate justice on the court, withdrew his name for consideration as its chief justice.

Telephone conversation between LBJ and Abe Fortas, October 1, 1968, 6:06 p.m.

Abe Fortas, associate justice, U.S. Supreme Court, 1965–69: *In my point of view, A) I think this is over, in the sense that it's not possible now to accomplish anything. And B), what I want to do is to put it to rest in some way. . . .*

LBJ: *What do you think; we leave it up to Nixon?*

Fortas: *I don't think we can get anybody through there. . . . Do you?*

LBJ: *. . . I don't want to be just walking off and letting them off of the easy end of it. I want to fight 'em. They're a bunch of sons of bitches. . . .*

LBJ: *I'm just trying to find a good one. That's the point I'm making. . . .*

I think we've got to be satisfied with less than the best, because we've tried the best and that hasn't gone with them. But I don't think we have to take the worst. That's my feeling. . . .

LBJ: *Now then the Senate has refused and turned us down. I agree with you A) It is over. I agree with you, B) we ought to put it to an end just as quick as we can, tomorrow, I'd think. Third, C) I think we ought to say, "Alright. What are we going to do?" That can be do nothing; just withdraw it and say we'll wait til next; or say withdraw it and you write the President a letter and just stand up like men to each other, and I write you back and say I'm very sorry, and then send another name up. . . .*

Fortas: *I don't want this filibuster to continue. . . .*

What I'll do is time my request for withdrawal. . . .

LBJ: *I think this is going to be a pretty important decision. We've made a lot of important ones but I don't know of any more vital than this one. I want to try to be sure we're right. I wish you'd get all the judgments you can from the Chief [Warren] and all that you can think of overnight. And I will try to think about it some.*

But I think we're in agreement now that all we need is a name—a good name. And I don't know any good ones.

Fortas: *Unless we find a good name, I don't know, I guess let things go to Nixon.*

LBJ: *I don't think I* can *do that. I've got to be President. I can't . . . Hell I've got other people to name every day. And, I just can't say that I just know one man in America that I would recommend to Chief Justice. I mean that's the position I think I would be in. . . .*

I think it ought to be a progressive Republican. . . .

LBJ: Abe Fortas is as good, fine, patriotic and courageous a human as I have ever known. He [was] victimized in a terrible way. We're cruel people. I made him take the [associate] justiceship. In that way I ruined his life.

JOSEPH CALIFANO: [Fortas's defeat] was a disappointment but not a surprise. We simply didn't have the juice at that stage. [Johnson] did insist on a vote to show Abe he could get a majority, though he couldn't kill a filibuster.

■ ■ ■

Mrs. Johnson attributed the episode to "the rising anger against Lyndon and mostly the rising anger against liberalism." For her husband, it represented "a final blow to an unhappy, frustrating year."

HHH

On the last day of March, when Johnson announced to the nation that he would not pursue the presidency in 1968, one of the few people to get advance warning was his vice president, Hubert Horatio Humphrey.

JIM JONES: Early Sunday morning, [March 31, Johnson] summoned me to the White House to accompany him and his daughter Luci to mass at St. Dominic's Church. Luci had converted to Roman Catholicism and Mr. Johnson took great solace in these church services. He often visited St. Dominic's, where the priests, whom he referred to as "the little monks," would often conduct a private service. During the service he whispered to me to ask the Secret Service to get his speech from his bedroom and to call Vice President Hubert Humphrey, who was scheduled to leave that morning for Mexico City.

At the Vice President's apartment in southwestern Washington, Mrs. Humphrey and Luci visited while the President gave Mr. Humphrey the speech. When he got to the final paragraph, the Vice President's face flushed, his eyes watered and he protested that Mr. Johnson should not step down. Mr. Johnson pressed his right forefinger to his lips and admonished: "Don't mention this to anyone until Jim calls you in Mexico tonight. But you'd better start planning your campaign for President."

Mr. Humphrey's facial expression was pathetic at that moment. Shoulders hunched, he said softly, "There's no way I can beat the Kennedys."

■ ■ ■

The Kennedys were one of the few things that daunted Humphrey. Affable and loquacious, the "Happy Warrior," as he was aptly known, had been a liberal beacon in Washington since Minnesota had sent the former Minneapolis mayor there as its junior senator in 1948. The same year, Humphrey came to prominence nationally with an impassioned speech at the Democratic National Convention in which he urged his party to "get out of the shadow of states' rights and walk forthrightly into the bright sunshine of civil rights." Initially held at arm's length by many of his Senate colleagues for what they saw as Humphrey's self-righteousness, especially southern Democrats, over time they came to accept him as a respected member of the body, in part due to the tutelage of his friend and fellow senator Lyndon Johnson. In 1961, Humphrey became majority whip, and went on to play a key role in helping President Johnson gain passage of the Civil Rights Act of 1964.

GEORGE MCGOVERN: I remember one night, when I was presiding [over the Senate], Hubert Humphrey and [Mississippi senator] John Stennis were debating a filibuster. It was when those filibusters weren't entirely empty of content. The southerners made rather thoughtful statements against civil rights and why they were opposed to it, and why they didn't want to extend the long arm of Washington into every relationship and so on.

Stennis was making a rather eloquent defense, and it was Hubert's turn to be on the floor in a leadership role; he was the logical person. It was about three o'clock in the morning, and Stennis said, "We had an old Negro mammy that worked in our home. She reared our children as much as their mother, and I loved that old black lady. So did my wife, so did my children. When she got cancer, I myself took her from Mississippi to the Mayo Clinic in the senator's home state in Minnesota and I stayed with that old lady until I was assured that she had the best doctors in the Mayo Clinic. I loved her like I did a member of my family."

Tears came down [his cheeks], and he said, "Excuse me," and he dabbed at his eye. And Hubert says, "Well, if the senator will yield to me, I want to say that that's a very moving story that he has just told you. It shows the big heart that the senator from Mississippi has. I know he loved that old black lady. I know that we all know that he is a kind and decent man.

"But that old black lady can't go to a restaurant and have a cup of coffee with the senator. She can't drink out of the same drinking fountain. She can't take her grandchildren to the public park. She can't see her children enrolled in the University of Mississippi—No Blacks Allowed. And that is what we are trying to change. We love that old lady, too, but we want her treated like a human being."

Those two men, you know, a couple of old political jocks—it was so touching to see the two of them there. I wouldn't take anything for that experience [of seeing] two men so opposite, but both of them such warm-hearted, patriotic Americans. It was quite a lesson to me.

■ ■ ■

When Humphrey became vice president in 1965, the position, unfilled since Johnson had relinquished it upon Kennedy's assassination, remained largely unchanged—the Twenty-fifth Amendment to the Constitution allowing for the presidential appointment of a vice president would not be adopted until 1967. It was, as Johnson's fellow Texan John "Cactus Jack" Garner once described it, the original, unsanitized version of his famous statement, "a bucket of warm piss." Garner had found it that way under FDR; so had Johnson under JFK; and it was no different for Humphrey under LBJ. Whatever limitations inherent in the position, Humphrey made it more difficult for himself by his natural gregariousness—and his incapacity for discretion.

WALTER MONDALE: He treated Hubert terribly. I used to tell Hubert that all the time. But Hubert was an optimist, and didn't see a lot of it. I think [with Johnson] it was a lot like the child who was beaten and who grows to beat his children himself. He was treated horribly [as vice president] by Kennedy, and [Johnson] did the same to Hubert.

TOM JOHNSON: LBJ genuinely loved Humphrey, but he was convinced that he could not trust him with secrets. He felt that the vice president was so open, so talkative, and so indiscreet. LBJ rarely included Humphrey in the most secret Tuesday luncheon meetings for that reason. On reflection, I think LBJ should have pulled the vice president closer to him, consulted with him more, and provided him with a relationship more like Vice President Mondale had with President Carter, and like Vice President Biden has with President Obama. It was too bad that LBJ felt Humphrey could not be trusted with secrets. Yet there is no doubt that LBJ had genuine affection for him.

LARRY TEMPLE: I know that at one time, somebody had said—I don't think it was LBJ—that the problem with Hubert is he agrees with the last person that talks to [him]. But I think that was part of the issue with Hubert. LBJ liked Humphrey—loved Humphrey. He just didn't always have confidence that Humphrey could keep a confidence or stay hitched.

LBJ: Humphrey believed in everything I believed, until I announced I wouldn't run. You can't be all over the court. He's a wonderful human being. But you can't be all things to all people. Humphrey doesn't like to face cold decisions. Well, neither do I. Neither does anyone.

■ ■ ■

Despite any reservations Johnson may have had, Humphrey, with Bobby Kennedy tragically out of the presidential race, emerged as the party's lead candidate to head the Democratic ticket in 1968. Though nothing was guaranteed, his nomination was all but certain. He had secured more than enough delegates with the support of minorities, labor groups, and southern Democrats, all who lined up in his favor. But questions about where Johnson stood on Humphrey loomed over the latter's campaign as he rode into the Democratic National Convention, which would take place in Chicago on August 25–30. Vietnam was the issue that divided the president from his vice president as Humphrey's views on the war deviated from Johnson's—and Vietnam was the issue that hung balefully over Chicago in the last, hot days of the summer of 1968.

There was another question, too. Regardless of his announcement on March 31, did Johnson want the nomination himself?

CHICAGO

In early August, prior to the 1968 Democratic National Convention in Chicago, the Grand Old Party gathered in Miami Beach and elected Richard Nixon as the Republican presidential nominee on its first ballot. It would have seemed unlikely just a few years before, but Nixon was nothing if not resilient. He had survived a failed presidential bid in 1960, a bitter loss in California's gubernatorial race two years later, and several years in the political wilderness before reinventing himself. As a "New Nixon," he fended off challenges from a spate of formidable hopefuls—Ronald Reagan, Nelson Rockefeller, and George Romney—to capture the nomination. Nodding to the South, whose support he would need to win in the general election, Nixon named Spiro Agnew, the little-known governor of Maryland—a "law and order" man—as his running mate. Nixon's nomination speech further aimed at appealing to moderate southern voters as he exacted a direct hit on the Johnson White House. "America's in trouble today not because her people have failed but because her leaders have failed," he told his party.

> *When the strongest nation in the world can be tied up for four years in a war in Vietnam with no end in sight, when the richest nation in the world can't manage its own economy, when the nation with the greatest tradition of the rule of law is plagued by unprecedented lawlessness, when a nation that has been known for a century for equality of opportunity is torn by unprecedented racial violence, and when the President of the*

United States cannot travel abroad or to any major city at home without fear of a hostile demonstration—then it's time for new leadership for the United States of America.

The Republicans' convention played out as smoothly and easily as the summer breezes blowing into Miami Beach from the Atlantic, giving Nixon a campaign bounce that positioned him well for the fall.

Things were different in Chicago. Along with the Democratic Party faithful who crowded into the city between August 25 and 30 were thousands of young protesters determined to make heard their voices against the war—a war they associated with President Johnson and, by extension, his vice president. The city, under the iron fist of its veteran mayor, Richard Daley, had planned for the convention expecting the worst. With the eyes of the nation on his city, Daley was taking no chances that chaos would reign: All of Chicago's nearly twelve thousand police were on duty throughout the convention week, assigned to rotating twelve-hour shifts, while fifteen thousand Illinois National Guardsmen and U.S. Army troops stood by, armed for whatever might happen. Additionally, barbed wire was incongruously laid down around the exterior of the convention hall where the Democratic Party's business, and the business of democracy, would be conducted. Tensions in the city were palpable.

WALTER CRONKITE: We anticipated trouble. Before we even got there the Grant Park encampment was taking place there at Lake Michigan right outside the Hilton Hotel, which was the Democratic headquarters. That's where the Weatherman and the SDS and the hippie, anti–Vietnam War people camped out. They were permitted to camp there by the police. Senator Eugene McCarthy and Hubert Humphrey were in the same hotel. But anyway, we anticipated trouble. We were geared up for it. There had already been some police raids in Grant Park, some ugliness. So it began right on schedule.

■ ■ ■

Clashes between demonstrators and the police lasted throughout the week in scenes of violence that became a backdrop for the convention—police in riot gear wielding nightsticks and billy clubs, young people shouting obscenities, tear gas billowing on unruly crowds—all of it captured by television cameras and beamed into living rooms across the country. By week's end, 100 protesters and 119 police would sustain injuries, and 589 people would be taken into custody. Those who had disbelievingly asked, "What is happening to us?" in the wake of the assassinations of Martin Luther King Jr. and Bobby Kennedy and their violent aftermath were posing the question again as the riots played out in Chicago, further draining the idealism inherent in the American spirit.

LAWRENCE O'BRIEN: The [Hilton Hotel] became a battle area. People were urinating in the lobby and throwing things out the windows. It was known to be the headquarters hotel for Humphrey. We didn't have any incidents in the actual headquarters area. As you moved from the hotel to the convention hall or from the hotel to another hotel, you observed a great deal of activity, much of it peaceful. But eruptions escalated dramatically. And Grant Park became a scene of considerable violence. Depending on your point of view the violence was caused by the youth movement or the police overreacting. There were elements of the youth movement intent upon violence. The fact is that the Chicago police had a reputation for being tough. So I think you could find fault on both sides.

The majority of the police probably tried to act in a professional manner and, certainly, the vast majority of the youth movement similarly tried to act [peacefully]. You had a lot of young people who had no desire whatsoever to be involved in any violent acts. But you can't have thousands and thousands where you're not going to have some problems. The record has been pretty well established by those who have reported the convention as overreacting on the part of the police. But what I observed outside the hotel and in the lobby and in the immediate environs was not the result of police actions.

■ ■ ■

Eventually, the brutality made its way into the convention hall. When CBS reporter Dan Rather was roughed up by police while reporting from the convention floor, Walter Cronkite remarked, "Dan, I think we've got a bunch of thugs out there."

WALTER CRONKITE: Daley had two or three motives for trying to keep tight control on that convention. One was purely crowd control, with all these demonstrators around. He didn't like them in the first place, you know. These "unpatriotic, dirty, unwashed people" just weren't his kind of people. Another was civic pride. He didn't like the idea of all this being seen on the air from his city of Chicago.

The third was, though, strictly political. I'm not sure about this but I think Daley had the impression that Lyndon was hoping for a draft from that convention. Daley was doing everything he could to manipulate the convention. He packed the galleries with sympathizers, who he could order to do anything he wanted. By doing so, he hoped to perhaps control the convention by public demonstrators in the galleries. He could either silence people on the floor or he could support them by packing the gallery.

■ ■ ■

Johnson was one of many Americans who watched the convention on television, horrified at the scenes unfolding in Chicago. He had declined to attend, opting instead to sit it out at the Ranch, ostensibly so as not to steal thunder from Humphrey. But despite stating his intention not to seek the nomination, Johnson had indeed entertained the notion that party leaders would come to the conclusion that he was the only candidate who could lead the party forward, and that a "Draft LBJ" movement would sweep over convention delegates. Johnson surrogates patrolled the convention floor, getting a read on whether such a scenario was plausible.

LARRY TEMPLE: I was at the Ranch during the entirety of the convention in 1968. I've always said he was the Edgar Bergen and I was the Charlie McCarthy, because he wanted deniability. He wanted—as a matter of fact, he told George Christian that he could tell the press that he, Lyndon Johnson, had not talked to anybody in Chicago at the Democratic National Convention, and technically, that was right. But John Connally was there, and Marvin Watson was there. I would be with the president in his office at the Ranch. I would get on one phone and he would get on the other, and he'd put his hand over the receiver and say, "[A]sk John what Mayor Daley is doing about X." Everybody we talked to—there wasn't more than three or four—knew what was going on, but he could say he had not talked to anybody up there.

JOHN CONNALLY: I personally was asked to go to meet with the governors of the southern delegations, with Buford Ellington, Farris Bryant, and that group, to see if they would support President Johnson in a draft movement in 1968. Whether or not he really intended there to be a draft, who knows? Maybe it was a ploy to force Hubert Humphrey to support his Vietnam policy. But I believed it strongly enough that I went before all those southern governors and asked them if they would support Johnson in a draft, and they said, "No way."

■ ■ ■

Did Johnson have second thoughts? Did he really want another term in office?

LARRY TEMPLE: [T]here was always the rumor of, well, he might get drafted; the convention might draft him. There was always a contingency plan to go to Chicago, plain and simple; it was a contingency plan. That was under wraps. [There weren't] a lot of people who knew about that, but it could be done in pretty short order.

I have been asked multiple times, "Did LBJ want to be drafted?" And I have a very strong view about that, maybe wrong, but a strong view. And that is, I think LBJ wanted to be drafted. He wanted to be wanted—he wanted some approbation for who he was and what he had done. And I think he wanted there to be a draft and [he] wanted the convention to say, "We would like to draft you and give you the nomination." And I'm 100 percent sure he would've turned it down. He didn't want the nomination; he just wanted them to want him to have the nomination.

GEORGE CHRISTIAN: He had fantasized that the convention would be such a mess that he would go in on a flying carpet and be acclaimed as the nominee. I think he knew it was a fantasy. I think it was one of these things where he watched the disintegration of the Democratic Party about that time. He didn't like it, didn't think anybody had his act together, didn't think Humphrey was really going to be the consensus candidate, and was having second thoughts. I also was convinced that he didn't want the nomination . . . because this health matter was so deep in everything he was doing from the very beginning, and he looked for a way to get out of the presidency and get the best he could out of it. And that's why he chose the Vietnam peace effort as his reason for getting out.

TOM JOHNSON: He would have loved for the Democratic National Convention in Chicago to re-nominate him, but he was a realist—and he knew it would not.

■ ■ ■

Realism aside, "Chicago hurt," LBJ said a year after the fact. "Of course it did." But if not being summoned by his party for a command performance left his ego bruised, he consoled himself with the certainty that if he had sought the nomination he would have gotten it—and that if he had, he would have handily beaten Nixon in November.

LBJ: In 1968, I thought whoever I was for, for the nomination, would get it. I have not the slightest doubt that if I'd wanted to, I could have been reelected. I believe I would have been nominated by that convention and that I would have won over Nixon by a substantial margin.

■ ■ ■

Instead, the Democrats cast their lot with Humphrey, who captured the nomination just before midnight on Wednesday the twentieth. Johnson logged a congratulatory call into Humphrey, and the following day the two talked at greater length during two late morning conversations in which Johnson dispensed advice on whom Humphrey should choose as his running mate. Hoping to break down another barrier, at least indirectly, Johnson lobbied hard for Hawaii senator Daniel Inouye, a second-generation Japanese American who, heroically, had lost an arm in combat in World War II. He also voiced support for Maine senator Edmund Muskie.

Telephone conversation between LBJ and Hubert Humphrey on August 29, 1968, 11:45 a.m.

LBJ: *The only thing—one thing I want to emphasize, and I don't think you've given enough credit to it. And I know everybody around you is shoving and peddling something. I think you ought to give one thing positive of who is going to be* really *loyal to you and with you when nobody else is.*

Hubert Humphrey: *Well, I'm thinking hard about that.*

LBJ: *Inouye, in my judgment, would be the most politically appealing and would knock Nixon on his tail and would be the most loyal to you. . . .*

Experience, judgment, sitting down with you and saying, "I just wouldn't do that, Mr. President." I would think it would be Muskie. He's been a governor and he's been a Senator. He's balanced, he's got good judgment, and so on and so forth.

If I had to pick them, I would give awfully close consideration to Muskie and Inouye. . . .

LBJ: *What I would do then, just make up my mind whether I wanted to answer Nixon on Vietnam, and every other thing that he might raise on you, and Civil Rights, and West . . . with Inouye or with Muskie. You're the only judge, and any of them are for me. . . .*

LBJ: *I like the fact that Muskie stood up yesterday [at the convention]. You couldn't have improved him an inch in his platform appearance. You just have to be sure you and Muriel—I love his wife; I like her—you just have to be sure of that personal relationship three years from now before your nomination whether he's gonna say Humphrey did make a mistake or I wasn't quite responsible for it or I didn't do it—*

I know what Inouye will do. I know what that veteran will do. I know what that color will do for this ticket. And I know it's not obnoxious to the South; it would get 'em hot. And I know what it'll do for the Spanish American. And I know you would be the boss; you'd be the man. You'd never have anybody going in the back door and getting any reason from anybody else. You would be there.

But it maybe . . . if you'd be more comfortable, you ought to get who you know would be more loyal to you and your wife and your kids and your fellows. The standard you set is just what I'd do.

Describing himself oxymoronically to Johnson as "old conservative Humphrey," Humphrey concluded that Inouye would take him "a little too far, too fast." He chose Muskie to round out the ticket. Happy to leave the ugly events of Chicago behind them, the delegates disbanded on August 30, their party more divided than unified after their convention, as Humphrey and Muskie began what would be an uphill race; a September 3 Gallup poll had them trailing Nixon and Agnew by 12 percent with just over two months until voters cast their ballots.

"NIXON'S THE ONE"

Though Chicago hadn't resulted in the curtain call Johnson was hoping for, his political influence, even at a distance, was felt throughout its proceedings.

JOHN BARTLOW MARTIN: I was at the convention and the Johnson presence there was overwhelming. There were a few of us dissidents. But Johnson had control. He was trying to get a plank that would justify his Vietnam policy and get his candidate Humphrey nominated on the theory that Humphrey would not break with him during the campaign.

■ ■ ■

Humphrey would soon show that he had his own decidedly dovish mind on Vietnam, a fact that would drive a wedge in the relationship between him and Johnson, while dividing their respective camps. Still desperate to make headway in the Paris peace talks, Johnson didn't want Humphrey to send the signals to the North and South Vietnamese that might adversely affect them. The differences between Johnson and Humphrey on the war gave rise to speculation that Johnson supported not his vice president but Nixon, whose views on Vietnam were closer to his own.

At least on the surface, Humphrey agreed with Johnson's views on the danger of breaking with Johnson on the war while peace was at issue across the Atlantic.

HUBERT HUMPHREY: I remember what he said to me. "Hubert, anybody can make a headline, and you can get a headline by some proposal that you make that's different from what this administration is pursuing, but I can get you peace. And if we get peace, you have won the election!" Well, that was pretty hard, you know, to resist and I knew he was struggling for peace. Averell Harriman and Cyrus Vance were in Paris, two of our best people, and I had to be very careful that I didn't say anything during that critical period that would jeopardize their efforts, that would show a break in the administration.

■ ■ ■

But he did break with Johnson. In late September the vice president's lackluster campaign gained unlikely momentum during a swing through the South, where Nixon and Alabama governor and Independent Party candidate George Wallace, who was polling nationally at just under 20 percent, enjoyed widespread support. As Humphrey's campaign progressed on firmer ground, encouraged by his staff, he was eager to bring his position on the war front and center. On September 30 he stood on a platform in Salt Lake City, devoid of the vice-presidential flag or seal that would link him to Johnson, and spoke in a nationally televised address as simply "Hubert H. Humphrey, candidate for president." There he delivered what amounted to a declaration of independence, a public departure from Johnson's hard-line policy on the war:

> *As President, I would stop the bombing of North Vietnam as an acceptable risk for peace because I believe it could lead to success in the negotiations and thereby shorten the war. In weighing that risk, and before taking action, I would place key importance on evidence—direct or indirect—by word or by deed—of Communist willingness to restore the Demilitarized Zone between North and South Vietnam. If the government of North Vietnam were to show bad faith, I would reserve the right to resume the bombing.*

Additionally, he called for an immediate bombing halt—holding out no contingency that North Vietnam offer a reciprocal olive branch as a gesture of good faith—and the subsequent withdrawal of U.S. troops from South Vietnam in his first year in office.

LARRY O'BRIEN: The Vietnam speech in Salt Lake turned the corner. The Muskie candidacy was a major plus in the campaign. We were able to play catch-up ball, not nearly all we would have liked to. We did stay in the fight with Nixon, pretty evenly matched in terms of media exposure and campaign effort over the last two or three weeks of the campaign.

■ ■ ■

The president was not pleased. As Joe Califano put it later, "the cooling relationship between Johnson and Humphrey dropped into a deep freeze."

JIM JONES: LBJ had high hopes that peace could be reached before he left office. He soon came to realize how difficult the North Vietnamese could be at the negotiating table. He felt that politics within the U.S. influenced the North Vietnamese as well as the overall prospects for a peace agreement. So he was very sensitive to domestic criticisms from U.S. political figures, because he felt that such would be magnified in the foreign press and would be misinterpreted by the North Vietnamese and their patrons, making it harder to achieve an agreement. He was particularly sensitive to Humphrey's Salt Lake City speech, because that would be interpreted that LBJ no longer had the power to deliver on a peace agreement.

ARTHUR KRIM: The president wanted Hubert to win the election. I have no qualification on that. But he wanted Hubert to be under his control until he was president, and he wanted that control to be on every level, financially, his own public endorsements, and for Hubert to need it enough so that he wouldn't cross him on the big issues of the day, particularly Vietnam. He had no confidence in Hubert's ability to make a commitment to him and keep it. And he had no confidence in the people around Hubert in relation to himself and his policies.

[O]n the one hand there are people who insist that he was out to scuttle Hubert's candidacy and secretly wanted Nixon to win because Nixon would be tougher on Vietnam. On the other hand, there were the people in the Humphrey camp who wanted to go all the way in soliciting the atmosphere that Johnson wanted Hubert to lose. In other words, they felt that was a gain to Hubert's candidacy. They wanted it to appear that Hubert was not Johnson's candidate. If you think of that background you can make sense of a lot of things that happened in the campaign.

Now, what the president wanted me to convey to Hubert was that there was only one president at a time and that the best way for Hubert to be elected was for him to say just that, "There is only one president and I'm not about to issue pronouncements of what I'm going to do when I'm president until I am president." And to stay out of anything that would dilute the president's negotiation postures. And Johnson wanted me to convey to Hubert that if Hubert would conduct himself that way, he—Johnson—was convinced that he would have the Vietnamese make the right moves at the table before the election. That he could establish a peace but only if Hubert didn't foul it up and cause a confusion in the minds of the North and South.

Hubert got the absolutely diametrically opposed view from the people around him. . . . [M]ost of the people around him wanted him to repudiate LBJ, to make his stand known on the Vietnam situation, and a few of them advised him to resign from the vice presidency so he could be his own man. Johnson knew every facet of this.

ORVILLE FREEMAN: I would like to put down one criticism from some of the people who were very close to Hubert Humphrey, and that is that Johnson did not really support Hubert Humphrey in 1968. If he had, they say, Humphrey would have won the election.

I can attest that was not true. There were great sensitivities between the two at that time. I was very, very close to Humphrey and his campaign, and I also enjoyed a very close relationship with President Johnson. I thought that President Johnson was right about Vietnam, and I tried to get Humphrey to follow the administration line where Vietnam was concerned. He did not do that.

So the staffs of the respective men started hacking away at each other, which tends to happen under those circumstances. I got to be a kind of contact man running back and forth between them, explaining things. I would go into President Johnson's office, and he would take after Humphrey something fierce, almost a tirade. Then he would grab me by the arm and say, "Now don't tell him I said that. I don't really mean that. But I've got to get it out of my system. Tell him I want to help him." And that went back and forth. . . .

There had been friction, inevitably, but President Johnson supported Humphrey every way he could, and I think that has not been understood.

■ ■ ■

Those in Humphrey's camp didn't see it that way, except Humphrey himself.

HUBERT HUMPHREY: Most of my people felt that Johnson would be more of a liability than an asset. I think they were dead wrong.

I know a lot of people say that he didn't help me as much as he should, but I never went right to him and said, "Mr. President, I need you—I want you to speak for me—I want you to get out there and help me. You've got to do it."

And when we did ask him, at the end of the campaign, he moved heaven and earth. He delivered crowds, he raised money. He did a hell of a lot more than people who were criticizing him.

■ ■ ■

Overcoming whatever reservations he may have had, Johnson took to the stump for Humphrey toward the end of the campaign, restating his support for his vice president in Texas, a swing state in the contest that had evolved into a dead heat between Nixon and Humphrey, with Wallace trailing well behind.

In mid-October, Johnson began setting the stage for a total bombing halt on the condition that the North Vietnamese de-escalate military operations, an action made as a Hail Mary to catalyze the fruitless Paris peace talks. Both sides also dropped objections to dealing directly with the Vietcong and South Vietnamese respectively. In Saigon, President Thieu gave every indication that he was willing to negotiate on those terms. Then, just before Johnson announced the halt in bombing, Thieu backed off unexpectedly. Despite pressure exerted on Thieu by the administration, he stood his ground, prompting Johnson to go ahead with the bombing halt anyway, a move he announced on October 31. By then, days before Americans went to the polls to determine their next president, the White House got a bead on Thieu's sudden change of heart—and it pointed to the Nixon campaign.

Intelligence reports showed that Madame Anna Chennault, co-chair of Republican Women for Nixon and the wealthy widow of General Claire Chennault, the famed World War II aviator who attained hero status by leading the Flying Tigers squadron, had urged Nixon to reach out to the South Vietnamese to assure them that they would get more favorable terms from him than those Johnson was proposing. Though no evidence linked Nixon directly to Chennault, Nixon and she had broached the subject of Vietnam at a meeting in his New York apartment in which he asked her to be his "channel to Mr. Thieu."

An October 27 wiretap revealed that Chennault had forwarded a message from "apparently authoritative Republican" sources urging "Mr. Thieu to abort or cripple the [Paris] deal by refusing to participate." Johnson strongly suspected that Nixon had sanctioned the communication, which, in effect, hedged the Republican candidate's bets against the probability of a galvanized peace process having a positive rub-off effect on Humphrey in the neck-and-neck presidential race.

Nixon, campaigning under the slogan "Nixon's the One," dangled the notion of his "secret plan for peace" in Vietnam compellingly before the American people on the hustings, with the candidate pledging to unveil its details after his election. As the contest wound down to its final days, the Johnson White House wrestled with what to do with potentially explosive implications that the Nixon campaign had, in fact, *derailed* the peace process.

ARTHUR KRIM: Nixon, on the record, was saying, "I have a plan [for peace] but I won't announce it until after I'm president." Now, as far as Nixon's connection with that is concerned, I do not know how far it went. LBJ, of course, suspected it and probably knew more about it than he would tell me, but I'm referring to those famous cables.

Just before the weekend of the election, there was a lot of movement in Paris about their finally sitting down for serious negotiations with the South Vietnamese, at a time when the momentum was moving tremendously toward Hubert. The fact that they were going to have a real peace conference was a big factor in the momentum. The president told me very much off the record that they had this cable that Madame Chennault had sent to, I guess it was Thieu or somebody in South Vietnam saying, "Don't cooperate in Paris. It will be helpful to Humphrey."

■ ■ ■

In a direct exchange with Johnson, Nixon denied having any part in the Chennault affair. Johnson, upon getting wind of the Chennault cables, called Everett Dirksen demanding to know whether Nixon was at fault. In turn, Dirksen phoned Bryce Harlow, a Washington power broker and adviser to Nixon, who placed an early morning call to Nixon while he was campaigning in California.

BRYCE HARLOW, senior adviser and counselor to Richard Nixon, 1968–71, 1973–74: I told [Nixon], "You've got to talk to LBJ. Someone has told him that you're all over the South Vietnamese to keep them from doing something about peace and he's just about to believe it. If you don't let him know quickly that it's not so, then he's going to dump. At least he says so. Ev is just beside himself. He says that Lyndon is simply enraged and we ought to do something . . . you've got to do it." And so he did. He called him. He got him on the phone and said there was absolutely no truth to it as far as he knew.

I'm not convinced it was not true. It was too tempting a target. . . .

But at any rate, Nixon told him no and Johnson put down his pistol, except probably Johnson didn't believe it. But he probably couldn't prove it, I suppose.

ARTHUR KRIM: [Johnson] said at that time that he had no evidence of how much Nixon had to do with this but rather suspected that he had. And he said he was going to call Hubert and at least give him the information, let him decide what to do with it.

LARRY O'BRIEN: [W]hen this information finally developed into something assumed meaningful with the Anna Chennault situation, it was very late in the campaign. Should you go or not go? You don't have the documentation, but it's clearly beyond the point of thinking wishfully of being suspicious. There is clearly something there. We were convinced of that. But

I didn't focus on that until, I'll have to say probably 48, 72 hours before the election.

What happened was I went to California. I had our close-out meetings with our California people, trying to utilize my time over those last couple of days as effectively as I could. Humphrey came into Los Angeles very upbeat. I'll have to say I was upbeat because the reports I received on the Texas venture were upbeat. Humphrey was the old Humphrey with all his enthusiasm. This campaign was coming to a great upbeat climax. Now, in that atmosphere, there was a brief discussion on [the Chennault] matter. I recall it was hasty. He's going somewhere, I'm going somewhere. It probably didn't last more than a few minutes, and I must say that my focus wasn't total. But it did penetrate enough for me to realize that Humphrey had sufficient evidence to consider going public. But it was clear that he really didn't want to discuss it in detail with me. Not that he was keeping me out of the circle, but he was wavering and leaning toward leaving it alone.

He expressed deep concern, made a couple of references to Nixon personally: "What kind of a guy could engage in something like this?" He was, I guess you'd have to say, shocked.

But now, in the context of what knowledge he had, I think what came across to me was his concern about utilizing it—whether it was justified, whether there was enough evidence so he could hold his head high and not be accused of playing cheap politics at the end of a desperation effort to win an election.

■ ■ ■

In the late 1970s, after Humphrey's death in 1978, Abe Fortas and Clark Clifford informed Mrs. Johnson about the Chennault affair, asserting that Humphrey sat on the information because he believed that the country had suffered enough throughout the course of the last several years, and that going forward would only divide it further. Mrs. Johnson's only response was "Poor Hubert."

TOM JOHNSON: I thought the actions by those associated with the Nixon campaign to convince the South Vietnamese government to wait until Nixon was in office were reprehensible. I remain amazed that LBJ and Humphrey did not publicize the actions taken by the Nixon side in this ultra-sensitive matter. It is my belief that Nixon would not have been elected if the public had learned of the efforts to sabotage, or at least to delay, the peace talks until Nixon was president. This was kept as a very closely guarded secret.

■ ■ ■

Regardless of Nixon's denials, Johnson remained convinced that he had been complicit in sabotaging the peace process toward his own political ends and the betrayal of his country. Chennault herself put the question to rest nearly three decades later, revealing in a 1997 interview with Nixon biographer Anthony Summers that Nixon had been in the loop on all of her exchanges with the South Vietnamese leadership. Nixon had been "conspiratorial" since asking Chennault for advice on Vietnam as he geared up for the campaign in 1967. "They worked out this deal to win the campaign," Chennault said of the assurances she gave the South Vietnamese on Nixon's behalf. "Power overpowers reason. It was all very, very confidential."

The episode, while escaping public attention in 1968, remained a portent for Nixon. In a Memorandum for the Record dated May 14, 1973, Walt Rostow, who along with Clark Clifford and Dean Rusk had recommended to Johnson that he refrain from going public with the Chennault revelations, outlined the chronology of events surrounding the Chennault matter. At the time of the memo's writing, a year and a half before Nixon's resignation from office, *The Washington Post* had broken the Watergate story but lacked a "smoking gun" implicating Nixon. "I am inclined to believe the Republican operation of 1968 relates in two ways to the Watergate affair of 1972," Rostow wrote:

> *First, the election of 1968 proved to be close and there was some reason for those involved on the Republican side to believe their enterprise with the South Vietnamese and Thieu's recalcitrance may have sufficiently blunted the impact on U.S. politics of the total bombing halt and agreement to negotiate to constitute the margins of victory.*
>
> *Second, they got away with it. Despite considerable commentary after the election, the matter was never investigated fully.*
>
> *Thus, as the same men faced the election of 1972, there was nothing in their previous experience with an operation of doubtful propriety (or even legality) to warn them off; and there were memories of how close an election could get and the possible utility of pressing the limit—or beyond.*

As it stood, on November 5, 1968, America, by the slightest margin, invested its trust in Nixon to lead the nation forward. He took the election with 43.4 percent of the vote versus 42.7 percent for Humphrey, a difference of half a million votes. Nixon was the one.

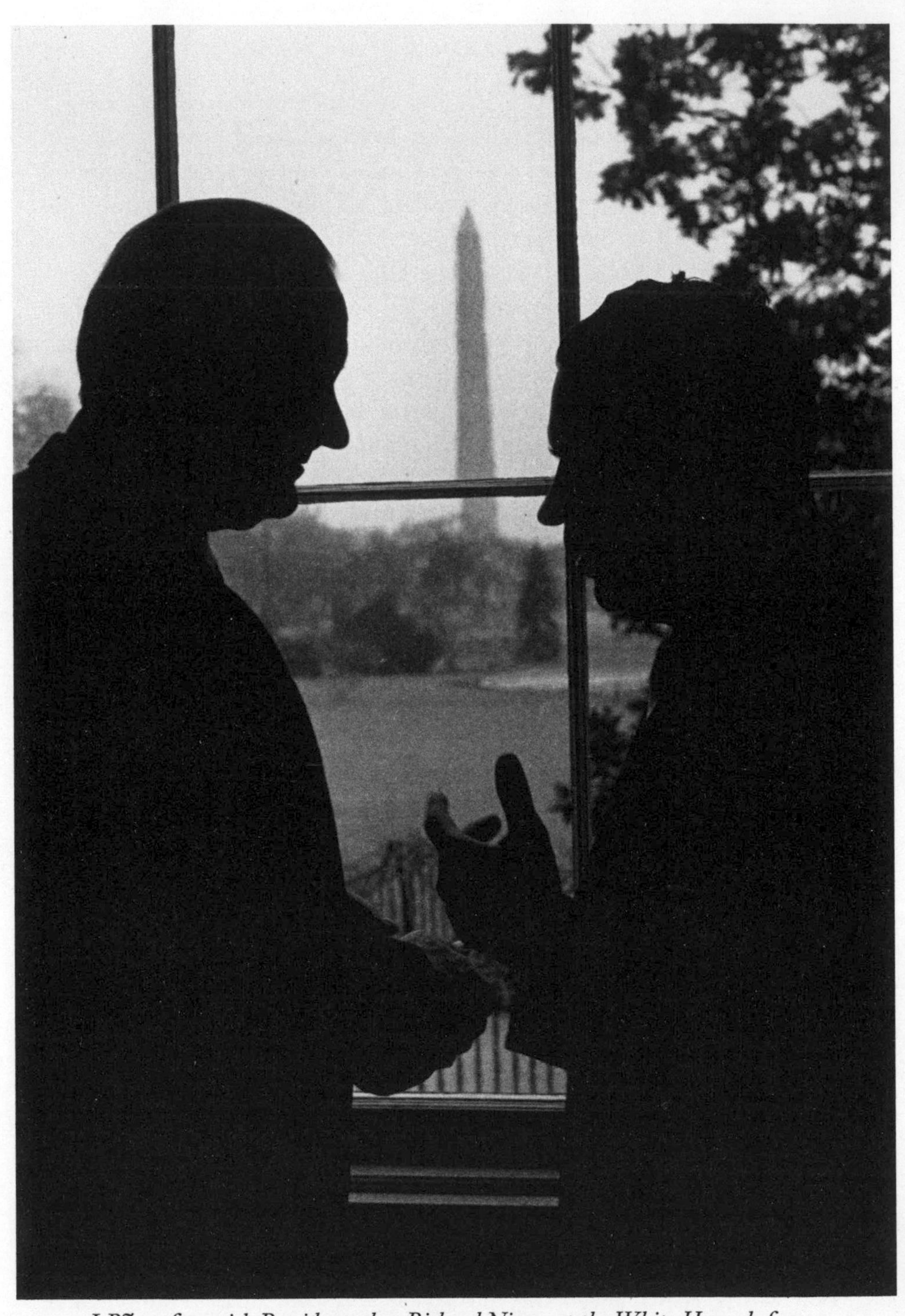

LBJ confers with President-elect Richard Nixon at the White House before Nixon's inauguration, January 20, 1969.

Chapter 11

"THE GOLDEN COIN IS ALMOST SPENT"

A SMOOTH TRANSITION

Upon past White House Christmases Lyndon Johnson had held out hope, however remote, that an honorable peace in Vietnam might be soon in coming. He had ordered the first and longest bombing pause on Christmas Eve of 1965, as emissaries were dispatched across the world to enlist nations in the cause, and assurances were given that the president set "no arbitrary limits to our search for peace." Over a dozen bombing pauses followed, all pulled back when the overture failed to bring a reciprocal response from Ho Chi Minh. The day before Christmas Eve 1967, Johnson once again had designs on peace when he visited Pope Paul VI at the Vatican to make a direct appeal for his help in the process.

Now, with 1968 almost at its end and talks with the North Vietnamese stalled in Paris, hope of leaving office with peace at hand in Vietnam had all but faded. "The golden coin is almost spent," Mrs. Johnson wrote in her diary just before leaving the White House. For LBJ the golden coin had bought much—monumental change and progress that would have seemed inconceivable for most who came before him—but regardless of his best intentions, peace remained beyond his grasp. Five hundred and thirty-five thousand American troops were in Vietnam at the end of 1968, and the death toll stood at just over thirty-six thousand. *The Washington Post* wrote that peace was "the President's abiding preoccupation as his days in office slip away." Not achieving it was certainly his biggest regret, one he carried through his remaining days in office. Billy Graham recalled Johnson's disposition during a White House visit with the president shortly before the end of his term:

BILLY GRAHAM: I remember that he and I alone late at night walked up to the East Room and we stood there where all those mirrors are. I said, "Mr. President, could we pray?" [He was] remembering what had happened while he was president, the good things that had happened primarily and asking God to bless the situation in Vietnam and help the new president to steer a right course, and that the killing could stop and so forth and so on, because President Johnson at that time felt strongly that way himself. He had stopped the bombing and all that, and I think he was trying to wind it down before Mr. Nixon ever got in there.

I think he had come to the point to realize that mistakes had been made. He hadn't been able to keep the country with him, and this was a great, of course, I think disappointment to him. He felt that maybe it interfered with many of the great social achievements that he wanted to do. And of course he did take a great many of these things that President Kennedy found difficult to get through Congress, and he was able to get them through.

TOM JOHNSON: LBJ so wanted an honorable peace, especially after five years of trying everything that had not worked—back-channel messages to Hanoi, bombing pauses, continually increasing troop levels, a promise to rebuild Vietnam if Hanoi would agree to a peace. There were periods when he was asked to use military force much more aggressively, and he did. There were periods when he was asked to restrain the use of military force, and he did. Hawks in Congress wanted him to be far more assertive: bomb the dikes, bomb the cities, mine the harbors. Doves in Congress and elsewhere wanted him to do less: stop the war—get out.

His anguish level with his inability to get Ho to meet was exceptionally high. He placed great faith in Averell Harriman and the Paris peace talks, but peace eluded him.

■ ■ ■

Additionally, Johnson's plan for reestablishing negotiations toward détente with the Soviet Union, which had been derailed after the Soviet invasion of Czechoslovakia, was scrapped when Nixon withdrew his support for participating in a joint conference.

ARTHUR KRIM: The President during this period was full of frustrations. He hadn't been able to move either the relationship with the Soviet Union or the peace process in Vietnam to the results he had hoped to achieve by the end of his presidency. We had many conversations about that. I remember that in November, probably during the Thanksgiving period, he was still talking about the hope of going to the Soviet Union to have the meeting that had been aborted by the Czechoslovakian invasion. . . . I remember he said that he had asked [Robert] Murphy to explore the possibility of Nixon joining him in such a meeting and indicated the Russians were still very much interested in having the meeting.

Then I remember around Christmastime he said Murphy had brought back a very strong negative reaction, that Nixon wasn't interested in any joint meeting. Johnson had visualized it as something of unprecedented historic proportions, for the present president to be joined by the incoming president from another party in such a conference. He was disappointed that Nixon had taken the other point of view. But Nixon's ground, according to [Robert] Murphy, was that he wasn't prepared and he wasn't ready to speak for his coming administration. This was a period when there were a lot of ongoing difficulties between Nixon and Johnson, on who spoke for whom in foreign affairs. Nixon made an unwise public statement that whereas there's only one president, that President Johnson had agreed not to move without talking to him. Johnson wasn't about to allow that kind of a distortion of the Constitution to be in place, because who would know, if there was an emergency, to what that kind of an alleged commitment to Nixon could lead? So he repudiated that. But as a result, maybe not as a result of this, but as part of the dynamics of the situation at that time, the Russians decided to withdraw the invitation to Johnson, as I recall. In other words, seeing all this they felt that nothing could be served by having a lame duck president there without being able to commit the next president of the United States. So that was a disappointment.

■ ■ ■

Yet Johnson's last Christmas in the White House brought with it some hope even if war raged unabated. The eighty-two sailors of the U.S.S. *Pueblo*, released by the North Koreans on December 23 after eleven months in captivity, would return home to their families in time for the holiday, the reward of Johnson's patient pursuit of diplomacy over military action. As they arrived back on American shores, the astronauts of Apollo 8—Frank Borman, Jim Lovell, and Bill Anders—became the first human beings to break the hard bounds of earth. On December 21, Apollo 8 lifted off from Kennedy Space Center in Florida en route to the moon. By Christmas Eve the capsule had journeyed almost a quarter of a million miles, where it was pulled into lunar orbit and hovered sixty miles from the moon's face, capturing the attention and imagination of the world.

The space program had slowly recovered from the setbacks of Apollo 1 almost two years earlier, but that recovery hadn't come easily. Ongoing technical problems with the *Saturn V* rocket and lunar spacecraft put the goal of reaching the moon by the decade's end—a lingering piece of unfinished business from Kennedy's presidency—in jeopardy. With those problems came reports from the CIA that the Soviet space program—also hampered by setbacks, including the crash of its Soyuz spacecraft, which killed a cosmonaut—was gaining ground. In August 1968, NASA revised its plans for Apollo by scheduling a flight with the goal of entering into lunar orbit and looping around the moon, not of landing on it. A circumlunar mission would achieve the public relations dividend of Americans getting to the moon, even if an American flag weren't planted in its surface, while setting the stage for the probability of a lunar landing before the end of 1969—and the attainment of Kennedy's goal. As it set its sights on the Apollo 8 mission, NASA regained its footing.

On Christmas Eve night, half a billion people watched a live broadcast of the Apollo 8 crew as they revolved around the moon, providing a guided tour of the barren terrain below. Then, just prior to the end of the broadcast, each of them read movingly from the book of Genesis—"In the beginning, God created the heavens and the earth. . . ."—before signing off with "And from the crew of Apollo 8, we close with good night, good luck, a Merry Christmas, and God bless you all, all of you on the good earth."

Earlier in the flight, after they had entered lunar orbit, the crew was struck not by the lifeless pockmarked moon they had studied meticulously in preparation for their flight, but by looking back at the planet they had left behind rising in the distance: a blue-and-white sphere as striking in its beauty as it was in its fragility suspended against the black void of space. "The earth coming up," said Bill Anders as he looked out of the spacecraft's small windows before spontaneously capturing it through the lens of his camera. "*Wow*, is that pretty." Along with their mission, Anders's photograph, *Earth Rising*, provided a welcome contrast to the images of violence and turmoil that had pervaded the nation's consciousness throughout the "nightmare year" of 1968. Shortly after returning to earth on December 27, Borman, the flight's commander, received a telegram that reflected the feelings of many. It read simply, "You saved 1968."

For Johnson, who since his days as Senate majority leader had been as invested as anyone in Washington in America's space efforts, the mission was a final triumph.

Telephone conversation between LBJ and the wives of the Apollo 8 astronauts—Susan Borman, Marilyn Lovell, and Valerie Anders—December 27, 1968, 11:15 a.m.:

LBJ: *When [S]putnik came over the Ranch many, many years ago, we had dreams of something like this, but we never thought it could be so perfect. I talked to Dr. Payne, and everyone in NASA, wherever they're located is just jumping up and down. But I know no one is as proud as the three girls who did more than anybody else to help bring it about.*

Susan Borman, Marilyn Lovell, and Valerie Anders: *Thank you, Mr. President. Thank you for your thoughtfulness. Thank you very much, Mr. President. . . .*

LBJ: *Give all of your children our best regards. And we're going to be seeing you before long. It's just the finest declaration I know how to devise, and I'm so very proud of all of you.*

As 1969 rolled in, Johnson and his people wound down. Any ill feelings the outgoing president may have had toward his successor were put aside in the interest of transitioning the office without travail or political wrangling getting in the way. He owed it to the American people and the Constitution he'd sworn to uphold. "Nixon's a son of a bitch," he told Jim Jones. "But he's the only SOB president we have." Anything on the table was handled in deference to the incoming administration.

WALT ROSTOW: [The transition] was a magnificent performance to observe. But I think it goes back to a strand in President Johnson that I think is important and hasn't been caught much, which is that he is a man of government—politics. Out of all the presidents of the century he had the longest and widest experience in government and politics. The image that some have, of a swashbuckling Southwesterner shooting from the hip, is exactly the opposite—[he was] an extremely careful man, careful about the correct way to do things. There never was a president more scrupulous about avoiding scandal in his administration and keeping the rules kept. There never was a president who respected the institutions of government and the permanent civil servants, or promoted them more.

GEORGE DAVIS, Washington, D.C., pastor and personal friend of LBJ: The White House years softened Johnson to some extent. They made him more understanding. They deepened his spiritual life. One of his greatest contributions was [the] tremendous way he relinquished office.

[Nixon inherited] the easing of tensions [in the peace talks] in France, but it's because Johnson stayed silent in the face of criticism. . . .

He got [the North Vietnamese] to the peace table. One reason that [it happened] is because we stood so steadfast as long as we did in spite of all the criticism on the part of the people in the United States and the press.

I think he [was] mindful of his mistakes and errors. He made some. It did a lot in deepening him, but I think it was tremendous the way he let go of his office and moved out of it and the way he turned it over. I don't know of anything in American history that equals it.

NICHOLAS KATZENBACH: President Nixon got so much credit for opening the door to China, and that was something that LBJ wanted to do. Indeed, the first proposals that were made by President Nixon were developed for President Johnson.

After the 1968 election, President Johnson had us go to President Nixon and say, "If you want me to start this process, I'll be happy to do it and take the political flak for doing it, and there will be some from the right [wing]. But if you want to do it, I'll hold off."

Nixon said he wanted to do it. So we did hold off. It was fascinating: I had worked on it, and Nixon's proposal was word for word what we had developed.

■ ■ ■

Johnson also demanded of his staff that any initiative that couldn't be carried out by the end of his term be put to a stop. "We don't need to be putting something in play to leave it to the next administration," he told his aides. "I know you think you've got a lot of these ideas that need to be done, but if they're really good ideas, those people are smart enough—they'll pick up on them, too." Perhaps presciently, he also warned that they make no mistakes that could be exploited by Nixon or the members of his administration in a spiteful use of their own executive power.

LARRY TEMPLE: [LBJ] wasn't a fan of Richard Nixon. Certainly, once Nixon became president, he was respectful of the office of the presidency, but not of Nixon. And I know from the time of the election in '68, in addition to the rush to do a bunch of things, he frequently said, "Well, tell everybody they need to do everything right. We've been doing it right for [five years], but you tell everybody they'll indict us and send us to prison and they'll be out to find some way to get us. Tell everybody they need to do it right, because that Nixon crowd, they'll try to send you to prison."

"EVERYTHING THAT WAS IN ME"

The last days were spent on big things and small. If there was still urgency in Johnson's agenda, it was to make sure those who had made the journey with him through the presidency would be taken care of after he left office.

LARRY TEMPLE: The [last days there was] buttoning up of things that had been done. [A]t one time he gave me a handful of people and he said, "I want you to be sure these people are taken care of." And he wanted to look after the least of the people around him. [One was] Zephyr [Wright], his cook. He wanted to be sure she was covered by Social Security, to be sure she was getting her Social Security check and if she wanted a job, he wanted to make sure she had a job. He wanted to look after her. He assumed that some people could look after themselves. But those that might not be in a position to look after themselves, he wanted to do it.

W. DEVIER PIERSON, special counsel, 1967–69: The one story that I remember and will always carry my affection for President Johnson to the grave was in December of 1968—when he and we were lame ducks and all of us were trying to determine what we were going to do next in life.

And I had an overture from a large California law firm to consider, opening a Washington office for them. And I sent a note into President Johnson, and I told him that I would like to go to Los Angeles that I'd only be gone two days but I'd like to go out and have a meeting with them.

And, as he always did with things that went into him in a night reading, he would just check off and he checked off approved. And, off I went to Los Angeles.

I was meeting with the board of directors of the firm in their fine paneled conference room when a secretary came in all atwitter and said, "Mr. Pierson, the President is on the phone and he says he really needs to talk to you right now."

The senior partners of this firm said, "Look, we'll just clear out of this office and you use it as long as you need and let us know when you're ready to resume the talk." Well, I was sure of it: He'd forgotten that I was in Los Angeles and had just called for me.

And so I came on the phone, and sure enough the President was on the line. And, I said, "Mr. President, I'm, I'm not in Washington. I'm in Los Angeles." And he said, "Oh, I, I know that." He said, "I know that. I remembered you were going out to Los Angeles." And I said, "Well, then, Mr. President, what can I do for you?"

And he said, "Oh, I didn't have anything. I just thought the call might be helpful."

HARRY MCPHERSON: The day before he left the White House the Johnsons held a little party for those who had served in the administration, and since I had been with him longest, I gave a little speech as the senior member of the team. And it was all very nice.

The next morning, I slept in because I wasn't going to rush in there [to the White House] with Nixon taking over. And it's early in the morning and I'm in bed and the phone rings, and it's Johnson. And he says, "Nice talk last night." And I said, "Thanks." And he says, "Someone like you is a big success in Washington. So what are the kinds of things you want to do next?" He says, "You like the Kennedy Center. How would you like to be on the board?" I said, "Sure." He says, "Maybe vice chairman." I could hear him writing it down on the other end of the line with the intent of helping to make it happen.

Scratch, scratch, scratch.

"And what about being on the board of the Woodrow Wilson [International] Center . . ."

Scratch, scratch, scratch.

■ ■ ■

McPherson was among a number of aides Johnson had asked to return with him to Texas after his presidency. Many of those in the White House would be heading to Austin, including Liz Carpenter, George Christian, Tom Johnson, Bob Hardesty, Harry Middleton, Walt Rostow, Larry Temple, and several of Johnson's secretaries. Resisting the Johnson treatment, McPherson declined, choosing instead to emerge from Johnson's formidable shadow. "After my years in the White House and being around so much power," McPherson told his boss, "nobody intimidates me—heads of state, captains of industry, celebrities. Nobody except you." Johnson paused before responding, "I guess I do understand power better than most people." Oversize in every way, LBJ was still capable of understatement.

Johnson had insisted to his staff that there were "several words I have cut from my vocabulary. Among them are 'last' and 'goodbye.'" But there were many farewells in those last days. On January 14, 1969, at 9:00 p.m., Johnson gave his final State of the Union address to the nation, speaking before members of Congress, some of whom teared up at the prospect of his leaving Washington after thirty-five years. In an even voice, soft and unemotional, he said:

> *My term of office has been marked by a series of challenges, both at home and throughout the world. In meeting some of those challenges, the nation has found new confidence. In meeting others, it knew turbulence and doubt, and fear and hate. . . .*
>
> *Now, it is time to leave. I hope it may be said, a hundred years from now, that by working together we helped to make our country more just, more just for all its people, as well as to insure and guarantee the blessings of all of our posterity.*
>
> *That is what I hope. But I believe that at least it will be said that we tried.*

For those foreign leaders with whom the United States had diplomatic relations, Johnson's parting correspondence was a personalized letter along with copies of the *Earth Rising* photograph Bill Anders had taken from the Apollo 8 spacecraft. In each letter was a fixed passage that read:

> *As the enclosed photographs of our recent lunar flight suggest, this shrinking globe is rapidly becoming a single neighborhood. Even the most distant nations now live closer to each other than villages in a single nation did only a few centuries ago. Countries are learning that they must work together for common ends, if any are to survive and prosper in the new world of interdependence which science and technology are helping to create.*
>
> *We have made some progress to this end in recent years. New forms of international cooperation are evident in many areas. I believe that this progress will continue, and that one day an international community will*

come into [being,] which is as solidly grounded in common interest and common institutions as national communities are today.

For those leaders with whom the United States did not have diplomatic relations, Johnson opted to have the *Earth Rising* photograph sent along with his personal card. One of the responses he received was sent by airmail to

A Son Excellence
M. le President Lyndon B. Johnson
Washington
(USA)

Postmarked from Hanoi on March 13, 1969, and sent via Berlin, the mailing was forwarded to Austin, where it has received on May 10 and given to former President Johnson. Inside was a personal card with the embossed name of "Ho-Chi-Minh" and a typed message below it in French that read in translation, "[T]hank you for sending pictures of the moon taken by Apollo 8."

At his last Cabinet meeting, on January 17, Johnson, who was joined by Mrs. Johnson, waxed sentimental: "It has been a high excitement to have been associated with people like you—a great adventure," he told those assembled. "I have loved every minute of it, every hour of it, and I have learned a lot, I think. . . . I am just so proud of you, every one, and so glad my country has had your services and I have had you as friends." The previous October, the president's Cabinet gave him a document entitled "Landmark Laws of the Lyndon B. Johnson Administration." A massive counterweight to the colossus of Vietnam, it chronologically enumerated the profusion of legislation realized during Johnson's presidency: the profusion of laws passed in the first two years of his tenure—Civil Rights Act of 1964, Voting Rights Act of 1965, the War on Poverty, Elementary and Secondary Education, Higher Education, Fair Immigration, Medicare, Clean Air, Water Pollution Control, Highway Beautification, Arts and Humanities, Kennedy Cultural Center—and, though slowed by the war, the swift current of activity seen throughout the balance of his term—Fair Housing, Federal Jury Reform, Outer Space Treaty, Public Broadcasting, Gun Controls, Scenic Rivers, Scenic Trails, Highway Safety, and on and on. All told, the kept promises of the Great Society.

On January 19, the Johnsons' last night in the White House, the First Couple threw a small party in the residence for the White House staff and their spouses.

LARRY TEMPLE: Maybe my most vivid memory about the end was the most melancholy evening I can remember spending. On Sunday, January 19, the President and Mrs. Johnson had a dinner party at the White House, and I'm going to say maybe there were twenty people there. Could've been less, could've been more. Staff and spouses, and [the President] was very relaxed, not at all unhappy. Of course, Mrs. Johnson, she was always outstanding, but it was really a melancholy evening in some ways. He reminisced about some things, talked about his time in Washington, how much he loved Washington and his time in the presidency. Nobody was on show. Of course, the President was [on show] in any kind of group like that—the President's staff, I mean—he's the central one. He's not only controlling the conversation, he *is* the conversation. Which, you know, [was] what we wanted. But it was a grand, grand evening. He knew he was leaving Washington, but it was just a wonderful evening.

■ ■ ■

In what was almost certainly a metaphor for the tenure she and her husband had spent in the White House, Mrs. Johnson wrote later of the evening, "At last it was time to go home and everybody began to drift away. The mood of the party perceptibly changed. We had all come in at a high key, tense, emotional, but I felt that everybody, me included, was leaving with the feeling that we were played out, numb, all passion spent, ready for it to be over."

The Johnsons awoke the next day to temperatures in the mid-thirties and a pewter sky that portended rain. At 10:30 a.m. sharp, Richard and Pat Nixon arrived by limousine at the North Portico of the home that would soon be theirs, for the traditional coffee between the outgoing and incoming first couples in the mansion's Red Room. Thirty-five minutes later, the Johnsons and Nixons boarded limousines that would take them two miles up Pennsylvania Avenue to the Capitol, where Richard Nixon would become the thirty-seventh president. As they left the White House for the last time as its chief occupants, Mrs. Johnson whispered in her husband's ear that she had no regrets.

LADY BIRD JOHNSON: I wouldn't trade anything for the experience. But not for anything would I pay the price of admission again.

LBJ: "So help me God" were the happiest words I heard. When Nixon took the oath, I was no longer responsible for Vietnam or the Middle East. . . .

One thing about the job of president—it's a wonderful job—the American people are good—the people of the United States were better to me than the press would ever have you believe. They were understanding and tolerant.

■ ■ ■

After Nixon's inauguration, the Johnsons attended a small luncheon at the Georgetown home of Clark Clifford, then boarded *Air Force One*, on loan from Richard Nixon, which took them to Austin. From there they went by JetStar to the Ranch, back to the Hill Country where it had all begun.

LBJ: That warm night, before retiring, I went outside and stood in the yard, looking up at the moon in the broad, clear Texas sky. My thoughts went back to that October night in 1957 when we had walked along the banks of the Pedernales River and looked for the Soviet Sputnik orbiting in the sky overhead. I thought of all that happened in the years between. I remembered once again a story I had heard about one of the astronauts from the crew of Apollo 8, which a month ago had circled the moon only a few miles above the surface. Soon after his return to earth the astronaut had stepped into his backyard at home and had looked up at the moon. He had wondered if it really could be true that he had been there. I had recounted this story to a group of friends. Perhaps, I told them, the time would come when I would look back on the majesty and the power and splendor of the presidency and find it hard to believe I had actually been there.

But on this night I knew I had been there. And I knew that I had given it everything that was in me.

■ ■ ■

Three months before leaving office, Johnson sat in the Oval Office behind the standard-issue Senate desk he had brought with him from his days as majority leader, looked into a television camera, and spoke words not for broadcast during his presidency or for the Americans of the day, but for the ages.

No president ever came to this office on a platform of doing what was wrong. Most of us have made decisions that were wrong. But every man who ever occupied this office, or sat at this desk, or reclined in this chair, has been dedicated to doing what he believed was for the best interest of the people of this country. I am utterly convinced that any man who takes the oath of office as president is determined to do right, as God gives him the wisdom to know the right.

Most people come into office with great dreams and they leave it with many satisfactions and some disappointments, and always some of their dreams have not come true. I'm no exception. But I am so grateful and so proud that I have had my chance. And as to how successful we've been in doing the greatest good for the greatest number, the people themselves, and their posterity, must ultimately decide.

Lady Bird and Lyndon Johnson walk among the wildflowers at the LBJ Ranch, July 5, 1968.

Chapter 12

SUNSET

After battling problems relating to angina throughout his post-presidency, Lyndon Johnson succumbed to heart failure while taking an afternoon nap in his bedroom at the Ranch on January 22, 1973. He was sixty-four. The death of the thirty-sixth president four years and two days after he left office came as a shock to the nation, leaving Richard Nixon the only living man to have taken the presidential oath of office, the first time the nation had been without a living former president since Herbert Hoover was in his final weeks in the White House four decades earlier.

Death hovered around Johnson in his last months, lying in wait. His friend Hale Boggs, a Louisiana congressman, died in an October plane crash in Alaska; the following month, a busload of schoolchildren from working-class Austin were killed in an accident on the way to a church outing; and Harry Truman expired stubbornly at age eighty-eight on Christmas Day. Against doctor's orders, his heart weak and writhing, Johnson insisted on attending each of the memorial services. "When I die," he told Mrs. Johnson after Boggs's funeral, to which the wealthy and powerful flocked to pay their respects, "I don't want just the people coming in their private jets; I want the men in their pickup trucks and the women whose skirts hang below their dresses."

A day after his own death, as his body laid in state in the Great Hall of the Lyndon Baines Johnson Presidential Library in Austin, twenty thousand filed past his flag-draped coffin, a pageant of Americans echoing myriad voices as rich as their nation's promise: a black man well into his eighties, hobbling on a cane, who insisted on climbing the hall's grand marble staircase to bid farewell to "the man who gave me my freedom"; several of the Mexican American students who had been Johnson's pupils in Cotulla, well into middle age now, making their way in a kinder world; a University of Texas library school graduate student in her mid-twenties named Laura Welch—twenty-eight years later to be the First Lady of the United States—whose professor had wept upon learning of Johnson's death, saying, "President Johnson made it possible for me to get the money to go to graduate school."

HARRY MIDDLETON: Lady Bird Johnson [stood] vigil by her husband's casket as his body laid in state in the Great Hall, accepting the murmured condolences of the endless stream of mourners. Many of them seemed, surprisingly to those of us watching, to be reminders of those who had marched against him while he lived. One young man stood before her silently and then, out of whatever emotions he was feeling, said: "I'm sorry." "It's all right," she told him. "He wanted to change things too."

■ ■ ■

At the Ranch in early evening, Johnson would often tell visitors, "I'm going to show you the greatest thing you ever saw, the greatest treasure that no money in the world can buy—sunset on the Pedernales." He was buried on the Ranch grounds, just shy of the river's banks, under the shade of a giant oak, in the earth he had trod upon as a boy and that had helped to sustain him after he left to scale unimaginable heights. He was part of it now. He was home.

Notes

Introduction

1 *"withered little Apple John":* Washington Irving description of James Madison.

2 *"Television never really caught":* Robert Hardesty, *The Difference He Made* (Austin, Texas: Lyndon Baines Johnson Library, 1993), 184.

3 *"I shall not seek":* Lyndon Johnson television address, March 31, 1968.

3 *"Allowing for shades of subtlety":* Hardesty, *The Difference He Made*, ix.

3 *"There is no adjective":* Merle Miller, *Lyndon: An Oral Biography* (New York: Putnam, 1980), xvi.

3 *"I think [Johnson] did monogram":* Hardesty, *The Difference He Made*, 174.

4 *"Martin Luther King understood":* "Media and the Voting Rights Act of 1965." The Paley Center for Media, October 20, 2008.

4 *"The baton had been passed":* David Hume Kennerly et al., *Barack Obama: The Official Inauguration Book* (New York: Five Ties Pub., 2009), introduction.

4 *"one of":* Ibid.

5 seeing *was believing:* Joseph A. Califano Jr., "Seeing Is Believing: The Enduring Legacy of Lyndon Johnson," keynote address at the Centennial Celebration for President Lyndon Baines Johnson, Washington, D.C., May 19, 2008.

5 *"This man makes the":* Robert Hardesty, "The LBJ the Nation Seldom Saw" (1983), *Office of the President Publications*, Paper 2, 7, available at ecommons .txstate.edu/presopub/2.

5 *"People, not TV studios":* Hardesty, *The Difference He Made*, 29.

5 *"Vietnam, of course":* Ibid., 174.

5 *"I knew from the start":* Doris Kearns Goodwin, *Lyndon Johnson and the American Dream* (New York: St. Martin's, 1991), 251.

5 *"Lincoln: He freed the slaves":* Recounted by Ronald Reagan in his speech "Address to the Nation on the Situation in Nicaragua," March 16, 1986, www.reagan.utexas.edu/archives/speeches/1986/31686a.htm.

6 *"deepest apologies":* Apology by Dan Davids, History Channel Executive vice president, printed in *The Washington Post*, April 5, 2004.

6 *"Every time you could":* Hardesty, *The Difference He Made*, 141.

6 *"I don't really believe"*: Walter Cronkite, *Conversations with Cronkite* (Austin, Texas: Dolph Briscoe Center for American History, University of Texas at Austin, 2010).

6 *2010 Gallup Poll:* Lydia Saad, "Kennedy Still Highest-Rated Modern President, Nixon Lowest: Jimmy Carter's retrospective approval rating and rank drop from 2006," for Gallup.com (www.gallup.com/poll/145064/kennedy-highest-rated-modern-president-nixon-lowest.aspx).

Chapter 1: "A MAN WHO REMAINS A MYSTERY"

9 *"How can you capture"*: Hardesty, *The Difference He Made*, ix.

9 *"I frankly didn't understand"*: Ibid., 163.

9 *"There have been good"*: Harry Middleton to author, 1/29/10.

9 *"I've known or interviewed"*: Hardesty, *The Difference He Made*, 175.

10 *"He was a complex"*: Harry Middleton, *LBJ: The White House Years* (New York: H.N. Abrams, 1980), 24.

10 *"Lyndon Johnson was the"*: Hugh Sidey, *A Very Personal Presidency: Lyndon Johnson in the White House* (London: Deutsch, 1968), 43.

10 *"He was an extremely"*: Hardesty, *The Difference He Made*, 148.

10 *"Johnson got his kicks"*: Ibid., 194.

10 *"The Lyndon Johnson I"*: Joseph A. Califano, *The Triumph and Tragedy of Lyndon Johnson: The White House Years* (College Station, Texas: Texas A&M University Press, 2000), 10.

11 *"I think Lyndon Johnson"*: Miller, *Lyndon: An Oral Biography*, 342.

11 *"[Johnson] was a man"*: Marie Fehmer Chiarodo to author, April 2010.

11 *"He was a young man"*: Hardesty, *The Difference He Made*, 128.

11 *"On the question of his ambition"*: Ibid., 156.

12 *"In my book, President"*: Ibid., 31.

12 *"Looking back on LBJ"*: Ibid., 30.

12 *"It was no secret"*: Lee C. White, Southwest Texas State University Oral History Project, www.eeoc.gov/eeoc/history/35th/voices/oral_history-lee_white-stacey_petersen.wpd.html.

12 *"[A]nyone who knew him"*: Hardesty, *The Difference He Made*, 34–35.

Chapter 2: LOOKING AT THE LIVING, WISHING FOR THE DEAD

15 *"Dallas has always been"*: Lyndon B. Johnson Oral History Collection, 8/9/69, by Bob Hardesty and Harry Middleton, LBJ Library.

15 *"[Lyndon Johnson] arrived center"*: Hardesty, *The Difference He Made*, 28.

15 *"God, how well I remember"*: Ibid., 18.

15 *"We left Fort Worth"*: Lyndon B. Johnson Oral History Collection.

16 *"Through it all Lyndon"*: Johnson, Mrs. Lyndon B. "Lady Bird." "Statement of Mrs. Lyndon B. Johnson." In *Investigation of the Assassination of President John F. Kennedy: Hearings Before the President's Commission on the Assassina-*

tion of President Kennedy, Vol. 5. 564-67. Washington, D.C.: U.S. Government Printing Office, 1964.

17 *"[Johnson] was very sober"*: Jack Brooks, Oral History Interview I, February 1, 1971, interviewed by Joe B. Frantz, transcript, Internet copy, LBJ Library.

17 *"[S]omewhere in my mind"*: Lyndon B. Johnson Oral History Collection.

18 *"Mrs. Kennedy came on"*: Homer Thornberry, Oral History Interview I, 12/21/70, transcript, Internet copy, LBJ Library.

18 *"Deputy Attorney General Mr. [Nicholas] Katzenbach"*: Lyndon Johnson Oral History Collection.

18 *"We get on this"*: Transcript, Kenneth O' Donnell, Oral History Interview I, July 23, 1969, by Paige Mulhollan, LBJ Library.

19 *"I walked into the"*: Sarah T. Hughes, Oral History Interview I, 10/7/68, by Joe B. Frantz, transcript, Internet copy, LBJ Library.

20 *"No question about it"*: Lyndon Johnson Oral History Collection.

20 *"There weren't any rumors"*: Ibid.

20 *"If it existed, it"*: Ibid.

20 *"Bill Manchester reported"*: Hardesty, *The Difference He Made*, 172–73.

20 *"It was a peculiar situation"*: Lyndon B. Johnson Oral History Collection.

21 *"Yes, Mrs. Kennedy"*: Michael R. Beschloss, ed., *Taking Charge: The Johnson White House Tapes, 1963–1964* (New York: Simon and Schuster, 1997), 17–18.

21 *"Where's Jackie?"*: Miller, *Lyndon*, 321.

22 *"[The flight was] uneventful"*: Marie Fehmer Chiarodo Oral History Interview II, 8/16/72, by Joe B. Frantz, 60, Internet copy, LBJ Library.

22 *"I was a little disappointed"*: Jack Brooks Oral History Interview I.

22 *"It seemed like minutes"*: Elizabeth (Liz) Carpenter Oral History Interview I, 12/3/68, by Joe B. Frantz, Internet copy, LBJ Library.

22 *"This is a sad time"*: Lyndon B. Johnson, "Remarks Upon Arrival at Andrews Air Force Base," November 22, 1963, John T. Woolley and Gerhard Peters, The American Presidency Project [online], Santa Barbara, Calif., available at www.presidency.ucsb.edu/ws/?pid=25976.

23 *"Twelve hours later"*: Hardesty, *The Difference He Made*, 18–19.

23 *"What we wanted"*: Lyndon B. Johnson Oral History Collection.

Chapter 3: "LET US CONTINUE"

"He Knew Instinctively What to Do"

25 *All I have I would:* President Lyndon B. Johnson's Address Before a Joint Session of the Congress, November 27, 1963.

27 *"What I wanted to do"*: Lyndon B. Johnson, *The Vantage Point: Perspectives of the Presidency, 1963–1969* (New York: Holt, Rinehart and Winston, 1971), 35.

27 *Others, such as aides:* Theodore Sorensen resigned in February 1964; Kenneth O'Donnell left the Johnson administration on January 16, 1965;

and the former president's brother, Attorney General Robert Kennedy, left on September 3, 1964.

27 *"Many people told him"*: Barry Goldwater Oral History Interview I, June 26, 1971, by Joe B. Frantz, transcript, Internet Copy, LBJ Library.

27 *"Do it now!"* Califano, "Seeing Is Believing."

28 *"I told [*New York Times *journalist] Scotty Reston"*: LBJ to Harry Middleton, Lyndon Johnson Oral History transcript.

28 *"One of the things about the White House"*: Miller, *Lyndon*, 352.

28 *"[T]here wasn't a human"*: Recording of Telephone Conversation Between Lyndon B. Johnson and Katharine Graham, December 2, 1963, 11:10 a.m., Tape K6312.01, PNO: 19, Recordings and Transcripts of Conversations and Meetings, LBJ Library.

29 *"I had problems"*: Transcript, Lyndon B. Johnson, CBS interview conducted by Walter Cronkite on September 23, 1969, and aired on May 2, 1970, *A CBS News Special, LBJ: Tragedy and Transition*, page 10, LBJ Library.

29 *"Kennedy became much more"*: Miller, *Lyndon*, 345–46.

30 *"They say Jack Kennedy had style"*: Noted in James MacGregor Burns, *Running Alone: Presidential Leadership from JFK to Bush II: Why It Has Failed and How We Can Fix It* (New York: Basic Books, 2006), 84.

30 *"What would Lyndon Johnson"*: Hardesty, *The Difference He Made*, 16.

30 *"Johnson knew how to woo"*: Hubert H. Humphrey Oral History Interview III, 6/21/77, by Michael L. Gillette, transcript, Internet copy, LBJ Library.

30 *"I have always thought"*: Miller, *Lyndon*, 345.

31 *"Johnson in my judgment"*: Ibid., 34.

Big as Texas

31 *The Texas Hill Country:* Ibid., 4.

31 *"Now the light came"*: Rebekah Baines Johnson, *A Family Album* (New York: McGraw-Hill, 1965), 17.

31 *While his great-great-grandfather:* Sidey, *Personal Presidency*, 22–23.

32 *"My father was outgoing"*: Lyndon B. Johnson Oral History Collection.

32 *"came out into the hills"*: Ibid.

32 *"At last I realized that"*: Johnson, *Family Album*, 31.

32 *"I was three months"*: Lyndon B. Johnson Oral History Collection.

33 *"One of the first things I remember"*: Goodwin, *American Dream*, 22–23.

33 *"I wanted to copy"*: *The Hill Country: Lyndon Johnson's Texas*, narrator and interviewer, Ray Scherer [LBJ Library serial number #MP211], aired May 9, 1966.

33 *Lyndon began his formal education:* Ibid.

33 *"For days after I quit"*: Goodwin, *American Dream*, 25.

34 *"I was not going to be the victim"*: Miller Center biography of LBJ, available at millercenter.org/academic/americanpresident/lbjohnson/essays/biography/2.

34 *"To think that my eldest"*: Baines Johnson, *Family Album*.

34 *"My mother tried to"*: *The Hill Country: Lyndon Johnson's Texas*, narrator and interviewer, Ray Scherer [LBJ serial number MP211], aired May 9, 1966.

34 *it was she who talked him into going to college:* Lyndon B. Johnson Oral History Collection.

34 *the latter of which his mother would ensure:* Ibid.

35 *"just worse than you'd treat"*: Julie Leininger Pycior, *LBJ and Mexican Americans: The Paradox of Power* (Austin: University of Texas Press, 1997), 18.

35 *"We will soon have 250"*: Letter to Rebekah Baines Johnson, October 17, 1928.

35 *"[H]e would ask questions"*: Miller, *Lyndon*, 33.

35 *"pretty girl"*: Ibid., 34.

36 *"I think in one sense"*: Hardesty, *The Difference He Made*, 147.

37 *"I was elected to the"*: Lyndon B. Johnson Oral History Collection.

37 *"active duty with the Fleet"*: Letter from LBJ to Franklin Roosevelt, December 8, 1941, in Miller, *Lyndon*, 91.

38 *"I heard [President Johnson] say"*: Larry Temple to the author, March 30, 2011.

38 *"Every time somebody calls it a chateau"*: "The Home: Ormes & the Man," *Time*, November 17, 1961, at www.time.com/time/magazine/article/0,9171,939326,00.html.

39 *"I'd rather cut my"*: Frank Oltorf Oral History Interview I, 8/3/71, by David G. McComb, transcript, Internet copy, LBJ Library.

39 *"our heart's home"*: Miller, *Lyndon*, 402.

39 *"The sun is indomitable"*: Sidey, *Personal Presidency*, 18.

39 *"Here the sun seems"*: Miller, *Lyndon*, 403.

39 *"aged before their time"*: Sidey, *Personal Presidency*, 19.

39 *"Poverty was so common"*: PBS, *American Experience: The Presidents: Lyndon B. Johnson*, WGBH-Boston, 1991, www.pbs.org/wgbh/amex/presidents/video/lbj_01.html#v226, "Part One: Beautiful Texas," "Part Two: My Fellow Americans." Written and produced by David Grubin. Copyright 1991; Robert Dallek, *Lone Star Rising: Lyndon Johnson and His Times, 1908–1960* (New York: Oxford University Press, 1991), 13.

40 *"I was thinking about a story"*: LBJ's toast at a White House state dinner for Maurice Yaméogo, president of Upper Volta, March 29, 1965.

41 *"were teachers and lawyers"*: Dallek, *Lone Star*, 14.

41 *"Lyndon Johnson has been fighting"*: Hardesty, *The Difference He Made*, 203.

41 *"I think that there are times"*: Round table discussion, with Harry Middleton, Dean Rush, John Gronouski, Wilbur Cohen, Robert Hardesty, George Christian, and Larry Temple, April 17, 1984, LBJ Library.

41 *"[T]he British Prime Minister"*: Ibid.

41 *"[Johnson had] an inferiority complex"*: Hardesty, *The Difference He Made*, 203.

42 *"I gave a long interview"*: Round table discussion, April 17, 1984.

42 *"He had to have people"*: Miller, *Lyndon*, 420.

42 *"The greatest bigots in"*: Lyndon B. Johnson Oral History Collection.

43 *"I think he tended to exacerbate"*: Round table discussion, April 17, 1984.
43 *"I doubt that President"*: Ibid.
43 *"If he wasn't the wisest man"*: Harry McPherson to the author, March 8, 2011.
44 *"Mr. Haggar?"*: Recording of Telephone Conversation Between Lyndon B. Johnson and Joe Haggar, August 9, 1964, 1:17 p.m., citation no. 4851, Recordings and Transcripts of Conversations and Meetings, LBJ Library.
45 *convertible model that a prankish Johnson:* Hardesty, *The Difference He Made*, 304.
46 *"I had no regrets"*: Lyndon B. Johnson Oral History Collection.
46 *"the one thing they can't take away"*: Goodwin, *American Dream*, 357.
46 *"In Johnson City the"*: Reminiscences of Lyndon B. Johnson, August 9, 1969, Oral History Collection, LBJ Library.

Seeking the Ultimate to Do the Possible

46 *"a high caliber, top flight"*: Recording of Telephone Conversation Between Lyndon B. Johnson and Everett Dirksen, November 29, 1963, 11:40 a.m., Tape K6311.04, PNO 8, Recordings and Transcripts of Conversations and Meetings, LBJ Library.
47 *"If they're with you"*: *Newsweek*, May 5, 2010, 32.
47 *"I had no question"*: Lyndon B. Johnson Oral History Collection.
47 *"I had a call from"*: Earl Warren Oral History Interview I, 9/21/71, by Joe B. Frantz, transcript, Internet copy, LBJ Library.
49 *"I called every man"*: Lyndon B. Johnson Oral History Collection.
49 *"Now, Mr. President"*: Recording of Telephone Conversation Between Lyndon B. Johnson and Richard Russell, November 29, 1963, 8:55 p.m., Tape K6311.06, PNO 14, 15, 16, Recordings and Transcripts of Conversations and Meetings, LBJ Library.
50 *"I can't honestly say"*: Transcript, Lyndon B. Johnson, Interview, September 23, 1969, by Walter Cronkite, "CBS Interview: 'Tragedy and Transition' (Dallas)," Special Files, CBS Interviews, Box 1.
50 *"I've tried to figure"*: Earl Warren Oral History Interview I.
50 *"Can you imagine"*: Lyndon B. Johnson Oral History Collection.

"An American Bill"

50 *"We can pass the tax bill"*: Recording of Telephone Conversation Between Lyndon B. Johnson and Everett Dirksen, November 29, 1963, 11:40 a.m., Tape K6311.04, PNO 8, Recordings and Transcripts of Conversations and Meetings, LBJ Library.
51 *"Well it might amaze you"*: Johnson, *Speech to Students at Lyndon B. Johnson School of Public Affairs*, 12/2/1972, Video, LBJ Library and Museum.
52 *"Now every person that"*: Recording of Telephone Conversation Between Lyndon B. Johnson and Katharine Graham, December 2, 1963, 11:10 a.m.,

Tape K6312.01.19, PNO 19, Recordings and Transcripts of Conversations and Meetings, LBJ Library.

53 *"I voted for the"*: Hardesty, *The Difference He Made*, 36–37.

54 *"resist to the bitter end"*: Richard Russell, March 3, 1964.

54 *"watered-down, ineffective"*: Johnson, *Vantage Point*, 158.

54 *"I was visiting with"*: Hardesty, *The Difference He Made*, 149.

54 *"Occasionally, when LBJ got lonesome"*: Ibid.

54 *"[H]e called to the White House"*: Ibid., 19.

55 *"I talked to Dick [Russell]"*: Recording of Telephone Conversation Between Lyndon B. Johnson and Everett Dirksen, May 13, 1964, 4:30 p.m., citation no. 3437, Recordings and Transcripts of Conversations and Meetings, LBJ Library.

56 *"After that piece of legislation"*: Luci Johnson, in Recollections of LBJ, 2010, Lyndon Baines Johnson Library and Museum, produced by the Technical Services Department of the LBJ Library, TSV 0258, at glifos.lbjf.org/gsm/index.php/Recollections_of_LBJ.

56 *"The night that the Civil"*: Hardesty, *The Difference He Made*, 32.

57 *"Look, I'm gonna get this Civil Rights Bill passed"*: James Davis, in Recollections of LBJ.

57 *"No one understood better"*: Hardesty, *The Difference He Made*, 27.

57 *"To me no greater example"*: Califano, "Seeing Is Believing."

The Kennedys

58 *"Kennedy was pathetic"*: Lyndon Johnson interview with Robert Hardesty and Harry Middleton.

58 *"One curious thing reflecting"*: Round table discussion, April 17, 1984.

58 *"Bobby's story on the missile"*: Lyndon B. Johnson Oral History Collection.

59 *"On civil rights, I recommended"*: Ibid.

59 *"[Johnson] made a point"*: Hardesty, *The Difference He Made*, 135.

60 *"great public hero"*: Transcript, Lyndon B. Johnson, CBS interview conducted by Walter Cronkite on September 23, 1969, and aired on May 2, 1970, *A CBS News Special, LBJ: Tragedy and Transition*, page 10, LBJ Library.

60 *"[President Kennedy and I] were not like"*: Ibid.

60 *"I think in the first"*: Barry Goldwater Oral History Interview I.

60 *"[Johnson] had a difficulty"*: Hardesty, *The Difference He Made*, 188–89.

60 *"I always was under"*: Edward M. Kennedy Oral History Interview III, 1/21/70, by Joe B. Frantz, LBJ Library.

61 *"I thought I was dealing"*: Reminiscences of Lyndon B. Johnson, August 9, 1969, Oral History Collection, LBJ Library.

61 *"I think there were"*: Edward M. Kennedy Oral History Interview III.

61 *"Bobby had too much"*: George McGovern Oral History, interview with author, February 3, 2011.

61 *"It would have been difficult"*: Barry Goldwater Oral History Interview I.

62 *"[Johnson] would have liked"*: Harry Middleton interview with author, March 29, 2011.
62 *"At the 1960 convention"*: Hardesty, *The Difference He Made*, 135–36.
63 *"[M]aybe President Kennedy and"*: Ibid., 136.
63 *"[Bobby] said Jack wanted"*: Lyndon B. Johnson Oral History Collection.
64 *"Bobby elbowed me out"*: Ibid.
64 *"I'm really quite confident"*: Hardesty, *The Difference He Made*, 137.
64 *"It must have given"*: Ibid., 134.
64 *"[Robert Kennedy's] mood during"*: Edward M. Kennedy Oral History Interview III.
65 *"[Bobby] volunteered to LBJ"*: Round table discussion, April 17, 1984.
65 *"This is ma boy"*: Irwin Unger and Debi Unger, *LBJ: A Life* (New York: Wiley, 1999), 397.
65 *"It must have been very difficult"*: Harry McPherson to the author, March 8, 2011.
66 *"My first real direct contact"*: Edward M. Kennedy Oral History Interview III.
66 *"I remember [Johnson's] name"*: Edward M. Kennedy Oral History Interview III.
66 *"With Joe and Rose"*: Lyndon B. Johnson Oral History Collection.
67 *"mushy"*: Harry Middleton to the author. 1/29/10.
67 *"Mr. President?"*: Recording of Telephone Conversation Between Lyndon B. Johnson and Jacqueline Kennedy, December 2, 1963, 2:42 p.m., Tape K6312.01, PNO 24, Recordings and Transcripts of Conversations and Meetings, LBJ Library.
69 *"[Y]ou know what's going"*: Jacqueline Kennedy Onassis, Arthur M. Schlesinger, and Michael R. Beschloss, *Jacqueline Kennedy: Historic Conversations on Life with John F. Kennedy, Interviews with Arthur M. Schlesinger, Jr., 1964*, ed. Caroline Kennedy. (New York: Hyperion, 2011), 273.

Chapter 4: THE JOHNSON TREATMENT

"Bird"

71 *"I remember one time"*: Transcript, Claudia "Lady Bird" Johnson Oral History Interview I, 8/12/77, by Michael L. Gillette, Internet Copy, LBJ Library.
72 *"We wound up spending"*: Miller, *Lyndon*, 52.
72 *"Some of the best trades"*: Ibid.
73 *"[Mrs. Johnson] told me"*: Bill Moyers's eulogy for Lady Bird Johnson, July 15, 2007.
73 *Johnson's "North Star"*: Jake Pickle, in Recollections of LBJ.
73 *become more than she "would have been"*: Jan Jarboe Russell, *Lady Bird: A Biography of Mrs. Johnson* (New York: Scribner, 1999), 20.

73 *"He was marvelous, contradictory":* Lady Bird Johnson, in *Among Friends*, January 2003 (publication LBJ Library and Museum).

74 *"She never cried":* Lynda Johnson Robb to the author, March 9, 2011.

74 *"I always thought that [Johnson]":* John Chancellor Oral History Interview I, 4/25/69, by Dorothy Pierce McSweeny, transcript, Internet copy, LBJ Library.

74 *"He was, as the expression":* William S. White Oral History Interview II, 3/10/69, by Dorothy Pierce McSweeny, transcript, Internet copy, LBJ Library.

75 *"I feel like I am":* Miller, *Lyndon*, 351.

75 *"Early in the White House":* Bill Moyers's eulogy for Lady Bird Johnson, July 15, 2007.

75 *"You want to listen":* Recording of Telephone Conversation Between Lyndon B. Johnson and Lady Bird Johnson, March 7, 1964, 4:10 p.m., citation no. 2395, Recordings and Transcripts of Conversations and Meetings, LBJ Library.

76 *"LBJ trusted Lady Bird":* Tom Johnson to the author, March 2011.

76 Lady Bird Express*:* Lady Bird Johnson, *A White House Diary* (New York: Holt, Rinehart and Winston, 1970), 198.

77 *"The thing that I liked about Lyndon":* Hardesty, *The Difference He Made*, 158.

77 *"To me as to you":* Johnson, Mrs. Lyndon B. ("Lady Bird"), "Remarks by Mrs. Lyndon B. Johnson, Alexandria, Virginia, Tuesday, October 6, 1964," Reference File, Press Release Copies of Mrs. Johnson's Speeches—1964 [1/11/64–10/27/64], page 3 (of 3), LBJ Library.

77 *Her joy was not shared:* Bill Moyers's eulogy for Lady Bird Johnson, July 15, 2007.

77 *"[In] one little town":* Bess Abell Oral History Interview II, 6/13/69, by T. H. Baker, transcript, Internet copy, LBJ Library.

77 *"This is a country of":* Bill Moyers's eulogy for Lady Bird Johnson, July 15, 2007.

78 *Thinking back on that:* Johnson, *White House Diary*, 199.

78 *"impossible"* man: Moyers's eulogy for Lady Bird Johnson, July 15, 2007.

78 *"Why darlin'":* Miller, *Lyndon*, 355–56.

"The Summertime of Our Lives"

79 *"Before I first went up":* Hardesty, *The Difference He Made*, 164–65.

79 *"The notion that Lyndon":* Ibid., 130–31.

80 *"I'm going to try":* Recording of Telephone Conversation Between Lyndon B. Johnson and George Reedy, January 25, 1964, 2:25 p.m., citation no. 1544, Recordings and Transcripts of Conversations and Meetings, LBJ Library.

81 *"Why don't you have":* Arthur Gelb, A. M. Rosenthal, and Marvin Siegel,

New York Times Great Lives of the Twentieth Century (New York: Times, 1988), 303.

81 *"As a human being"*: Middleton, *LBJ: White House Years*, 24.

81 *"That's just him"*: Charles Peters, *Lyndon B. Johnson: The American Presidents Series: The 36th President, 1963–1969*, ed. Arthur M. Schlesinger and Sean Wilentz (New York: Times, 2010), 161.

81 *"Why don't you use your head?"*: "The Funny Feminist: Liz Carpenter knew how to wield a joke," *Houston Chronicle*, March 24, 2010.

81 *Jumbo:* Robert Caro, *The Years of Lyndon Johnson: Volume I: The Path to Power* (New York: Vintage, 1990), 155.

81 *"He was very much like"*: Ervin Duggan, in Recollections of LBJ.

82 *"I never had an unkind word"*: Round table discussion, April 17, 1984.

82 *"I certainly never felt"*: Ibid.

82 *"In all honesty"*: Ibid.

82 *"I don't think you can characterize"*: Ibid.

83 *"I think there are several reasons"*: Betty Hickman Oral History Interview I, 4/10/84, by Mike Gillette, transcript, Internet copy, LBJ Library.

83 *"He never said, 'I'm sorry' "*: Bill Foster to the author, February 18, 2011.

83 *That desire to make amends:* Unger and Unger, *LBJ*, 336.

83 *"One day I came"*: Phyllis Bonanno, in Recollections of LBJ.

84 *"He was just so wonderful"*: Bob Hardesty to the author, February 20, 2011.

84 *"[O]ne time John Kenneth Galbraith"*: Jack Valenti, in Recollections of LBJ.

85 *made sure she "walked behind him"*: Lynda Johnson Robb to the author, March 9, 2011.

85 *Even Richard Nixon recalled:* Richard M. Nixon, *The Memoirs of Richard Nixon* (New York: Grosset and Dunlap, 197), 272–73.

85 *"spirit of family"*: Hardesty, *The Difference He Made*, 130–31.

85 *"I want someone who will kiss"*: Robert A. Caro, *The Years of Lyndon Johnson, Volume 2: Means of Ascent* (New York: Vintage, 1991), 111.

85 *"He always talked about"*: Larry Temple to the author, March 30, 2011.

85 *"LBJ told me to"*: Ben Barnes to the author, September 27, 2011.

86 *"The facts are that"*: Recording of Telephone Conversation Between Lyndon B. Johnson and Clark Clifford, October 14, 1964, 8:20 p.m., citation no. 5880, Recordings and Transcripts of Conversations and Meetings, LBJ Library.

86 *"I would like to do"*: Recording of Telephone Conversation Between Lyndon B. Johnson and Lady Bird Johnson, October 15, 1964, 9:12 a.m., citation no. 5895, Recordings and Transcripts of Conversations and Meetings, LBJ Library.

89 *"The problem with Walter"*: Jack Valenti Oral History Interview III, February 19, 1971, by Joe B. Frantz, transcript, Internet copy, LBJ Library.

89 *"He knew he drove"*: Lynda Johnson Robb to the author, March 9, 2011.

90 *"For all the tragedy"*: Hardesty, *The Difference He Made*, 54.

90 *"[W]e were part of"*: Ibid., 17.

90 *"[C]haracter is something that"*: Middleton, *LBJ: White House Years*, 16.

Finishing Franklin Roosevelt's Revolution

90 *"out of the ditch"*: Richard N. Goodwin, *Remembering America: A Voice from the Sixties* (Boston: Little, Brown, 1988), 269.

90 *"It was February or"*: Hardesty, *The Difference He Made*, 65–66.

91 *"We've got to use the"*: Goodwin, *Remembering America*, 270–71.

92 *approval rating of 77 percent:* Unger and Unger, *LBJ: A Life*, 314.

92 *the university's 120th commencement ceremony:* Miller, *Lyndon*, 376.

92 *"For a century we labored"*: LBJ's commencement speech at the University of Michigan, May 22, 1964. www.presidency.ucsb.edu/ws/index.php?pid=26262

92 *Imploring the 4,943 graduates:* Miller, *Lyndon*, 376.

92 *"Knowledge of human nature"*: Henry Adams, *The Education of Henry Adams* (Boston: Houghton Mifflin, 1973).

92 *"He studied individuals with"*: Hardesty, *The Difference He Made*, 148.

93 *"LBJ's mastery in achieving"*: Lee White Oral History, by Stacey Petersen, Southwest Texas State University Oral History Project, transcript at www.eeoc.gov/eeoc/history/35th/voices/oral_history-lee_white-stacey_petersen.wpd.html.

93 *"Johnson was like a psychiatrist"*: Hubert Humphrey Oral History Interview III.

93 *"I was invited"*: John Brademas, in Recollections of LBJ.

94 *"Lyndon Johnson just towered"*: Robert Dallek, *Flawed Giant: Lyndon Johnson and His Times, 1961–1973* (New York: Oxford University Press, 1998), 5.

94 *"Its tone could be supplication"*: Rowland Evans and Robert Novak, *The Exercise of Power* (New York: New American Library, 1966), 104.

94 *"Way back when he"*: Hardesty, *The Difference He Made*, 174.

95 *"This mastery of debate"*: George Reedy Oral History Interview III, 6/7/75, by Michael L. Gillette, transcript, Internet copy, LBJ Library.

95 *"That's the difference when"*: Thurgood Marshall Oral History Interview I, 7/10/69, by T. H. Baker, transcript, Internet copy, LBJ Library.

95 *"Lyndon on a couple of occasions"*: Gerald R. Ford, in Recollections of LBJ.

95 *"[One] time he called"*: Hardesty, *The Difference He Made*, 37.

96 *"I was leaving home"*: Ibid., 90–91.

96 *"He was guilty of"*: Ibid., 131.

96 *"His favorite saying was"*: Hardesty, *The Difference He Made*, 145.

96 *"I never could quarrel"*: Barry Goldwater Oral History Interview I.

97 *"Johnson was a doer"*: George McGovern Oral History, interview by author, February 3, 2011.

97 *"My view is that"*: George H. W. Bush to the author, March 22, 2006.

97 *"He would be very":* Tom Johnson to the author, January 3, 2011.
98 *Johnson got 58 percent:* "Man of the Year 1964," *Time*, January 3, 1965.
98 *"There is planning money":* Recording of Telephone Conversation Between Lyndon B. Johnson and Everett Dirksen, June 24, 1964, 6:22 p.m., citation no. 3856, Recordings and Transcripts of Conversations and Meetings, LBJ Library.
99 *"You can't ask a man":* Larry Temple to the author, 6/28/10.
99 *"I remember once asking":* Dallek, *Flawed Giant*, 5.

No Men with Umbrellas

100 *"They had just . . . assassinated":* Lyndon B. Johnson Oral History Collection.
100 *"Those first few days":* Ibid.
101 *"The only thing new":* Merle Miller, *Plain Speaking: An Oral Biography of Harry S. Truman* (New York: Berkley Publishing/Putnam, 1974), 26.
101 *"I think we ought to have stopped Castro":* Lyndon B. Johnson Oral History Collection.
102 *"What American wants to go to bed by the light of a Communist moon?":* *Time*, Friday, May 31, 1963.
102 *"We shall pay any price":* John F. Kennedy, "Inaugural Address," January 20, 1961, in Woolley and Peters, The American Presidency Project, at www.presidency.ucsb.edu/ws/?pid=8032.
102 *"We're not going":* Sidey, *Personal Presidency*, 218.
102 *"[I]n February and March":* Hardesty, *The Difference He Made*, 65–66.
103 *"Every President since President":* Dean Rusk Oral History Interview II, 9/26/69, by Paige E. Mulhollan, transcript, Internet copy, LBJ Library.
103 *"There are a great many":* Clark M. Clifford Oral History Interview II, 7/2/69, by Paige Mulhollan, transcript, Internet copy, LBJ Library.
104 *"first and foremost a contest":* Johnson, "Remarks at the 96th Charter Day Observance of the University of California at Los Angeles," February 21, 1964, in Woolley and Peters, The American Presidency Project, at www.presidency.ucsb.edu/ws/?pid=26079.
104 *"send[ing] American boys nine":* Johnson, "Remarks in Memorial Hall, Akron University," October 21, 1964, in Woolley and Peters, The American Presidency Project, at www.presidency.ucsb.edu/ws/?pid=26635.
104 *"get tied down to":* Johnson, "Remarks in Oklahoma at the Dedication of the Eufaula Dam," on September 25, 1964, in Woolley and Peters, The American Presidency Project, at www.presidency.ucsb.edu/ws/?pid=26528.
105 *"I guess those were":* Clark M. Clifford Oral History Interview II.
105 *"That was a good vote":* Recording of Telephone Conversation Between Lyndon B. Johnson and John McCormack, August 7, 1964, 3:01 p.m., citation nos. 4807 and 4808, Recordings and Transcripts of Conversations and Meetings, LBJ Library.
106 *Gallup polls showed that 66 percent of Americans:* Miller, *Lyndon*, 419.

106 *"Kennedy never said anything"*: Ibid., 380.
107 *"We have to remember"*: Hardesty, *The Difference He Made*, 205.
107 *"In January of 1965"*: Ibid., 41.

The Public Man

107 *"a nervous bow to"*: "The Book L.B.J. Should Write," *Time*, November 8, 1971.
107 *"The prose had to be"*: Round table discussion, April 17, 1984.
107 *"forcing himself"*: Ibid.
108 *"He used to say"*: Ibid.
108 *"I just think the television"*: Ibid.
108 *"Unfortunately, I don't think he"*: Transcript, Claudia "Lady Bird" Johnson Oral History Interview XXI, 8/10–11/81, by Micahel L. Gillette, Internet Copy, LBJ Library.
109 *"When he would meet"*: Ibid.
109 *"I don't know how many"*: Middleton, *White House Years*, 121.
109 *"I want a Gettysburg"*: Round table discussion, April 17, 1984.
109 *"[He spoke to us] about the brevity"*: Jack McNulty, in Recollections of LBJ.
110 *"He had a rapport"*: Round table discussion, April 17, 1984.
110 *"I watched him particularly"*: Ibid.
111 *"One of the things"*: Hardesty, *The Difference He Made*, 173.
111 *"Sometimes in the midst"*: Middleton, *White House Years*, 118.
112 *"He was certainly the most"*: Hardesty, *The Difference He Made*, 181.
112 *"[H]e failed in press"*: Ibid., 182–83.
112 *"I'm sure no president"*: Ibid., 179.
112 *"Everything was overdeveloped"*: George Reedy Oral History Interview III.
113 *"[The White House press corps was] fascinated"*: Ibid.
113 *"[W]hen Lyndon Baines Johnson wanted to make a point"*: Walter Cronkite, in Recollections of LBJ.
114 *"The press was a target"*: Hardesty, *The Difference He Made*, 200.
114 *Occasionally, Johnson's challenges:* Hugh Sidey, "The Presidency: Thoughts on the State of the Man," *Life*, January 26, 1968.
114 *"As Johnson's presidency became"*: Hardesty, *The Difference He Made*, 188.

Chapter 5: "ALL THE WAY WITH LBJ"

Foreboding

117 *"[O]ne time we were flying"*: Hugh Robinson, in Recollections of LBJ.
118 *"I had just started"*: Bob Hardesty to the author, May 6, 2011.
118 *"[W]e need to remember"*: Hardesty, *The Difference He Made*, 41.
119 *"I never got the feeling"*: Barry Goldwater Oral History Interview I.
119 *"In 1960, Mr. Rayburn called"*: Lyndon B. Johnson Oral History Collection.
119 *"We know that in 1964"*: Hardesty, *The Difference He Made*, 41.

119 *"I did have reason":* Miller, *Lyndon*, 391.
119 *"I fear I must bid":* Richard Norton Smith, *Patriarch: George Washington and the New American Nation* (Boston: Houghton Mifflin, 1993), xix.
120 *The difference was that Johnson:* Yokimoto speaking to the National Press Photographers Association, 1970.
120 *Johnson expressed his reservations:* George Reedy Oral History Interview III.
120 *"To [the liberals] my name":* Miller, *Lyndon*, 390.
120 *"the men in my family die young":* Larry Temple to the author, June 28, 2010.
120 *"The best way I know":* Lyndon B. Johnson Oral History Collection.
121 *"The fact is that Lyndon":* Hardesty, *The Difference He Made*, 32.
121 *"Beloved—You are as brave a man":* Lady Bird's letter to LBJ, received on August 25, 1964, Johnson, *Vantage Point*, 96–98.
123 *Just 6 percent of black:* Dallek, *Flawed Giant*, 212.
123 *"What you better do is":* Recording of Telephone Conversation Between Lyndon B. Johnson and Hubert Humphrey, August 14, 1964, 11:05 a.m., citation no. 4918, Recordings and Transcripts of Conversations and Meetings, LBJ Library.
124 *"You know [getting two seats for the MFDP] wasn't nothing":* Fannie Lou Hamer Oral History, University of Southern Mississippi.
125 *Harry McPherson, who worked closely:* Harry McPherson to the author, March 8, 2011.

"In Your Heart You Know He Might"

125 *"Extremism in the defense":* Goldwater acceptance speech at Republican National Convention, July 16, 1964, San Francisco, Calif., at www.washingtonpost.com/wp-srv/politics/daily/may98/goldwaterspeech.htm.
126 *"When Kennedy was shot":* Barry Goldwater Oral History Interview I.
126 *"Come on down to the speakin'":* Gelb, Rosenthal, and Siegel, *Great Lives*, 303.
126 *The candidates established one ground rule:* Jeremy D. Mayer, "LBJ Fights the White Backlash: The Racial Politics of the 1964 Presidential Campaigns," *Prologue Magazine* 33, no. 1 (Spring 2001): National Archives and Records Administration.
126 *"[Johnson] asked me if":* Barry Goldwater Oral History Interview I.
127 *"[Goldwater] came in":* Recording of Telephone Conversation Between Lyndon B. Johnson and Nicholas Katzenbach, July 25, 1964, 10:15 a.m., citation no. 4337–4339, Recordings and Transcripts of Conversations and Meetings, LBJ Library.
127 *"We can't let Goldwater":* Sidey, *Personal Presidency*, 219.
127 *"I had a movie":* Barry Goldwater Oral History Interview I.
128 *Tennessean Andrew Johnson was never:* "Man of the Year," *Time*, January 3, 1965.
128 *"I remember the nomination":* Johnson, *White House Diary*, 198.
128 *"I just never fooled myself":* Barry Goldwater Oral History Interview I.

The Loophole

129 *"When he won in 1964"*: Hardesty, *The Difference He Made*, 194.
129 *Johnson held that when:* Sidey, "The Presidency: Thoughts on the State of the Man."
129 *"Now, look . . . I've just"*: Gelb, Rosenthal, and Siegel, *Great Lives.*
129 *"[Johnson] said, when he came back"*: Round table discussion, April 17, 1984.
129 *"He would say, 'I want ideas' "*: Hardesty, *The Difference He Made*, 19–20.
130 *"President Johnson was very conscious"*: Ibid., 81.
130 *"He referred to his popularity"*: Round table discussion, April 17, 1984.
130 *"It was Johnson's landslide"*: Hardesty, *The Difference He Made*, 76.

Chapter 6: POWER AND GLORY

"We Shall Overcome"

133 *"There is a tide of affairs"*: "Man of the Year," *Time*, January 3, 1965.
134 *A record 1.2 million people:* Michael E. Ruane and Aaron C. Davis, "DC Inauguration Head Count: 1.8 Million," *The Washington Post*, January 22, 2009.
134 *"Johnson used to tell me"*: Hubert Humphrey Oral History Interview III.
134 *"every remaining obstacle to"*: Johnson, "State of the Union Address," January 4, 1965, www.presidency.ucsb.edu/ws/index.php?pid=26907.
135 *"the lowest form of humanity"*: Dallek, *Flawed Giant*, 213.
135 *"make it clear to the nation"*: Michael R. Beschloss, *Reaching for Glory: Lyndon Johnson's Secret White House Tapes, 1964–1965* (New York: Simon and Schuster, 2001), 160.
135 *"Just got down here"*: Recording of Telephone Conversation Between Lyndon B. Johnson and Martin Luther King Jr., January 15, 1965, 12:06 p.m., citation nos. 6736 and 6737, Recordings and Transcripts of Conversations and Meetings, LBJ Library.
138 *"We saw ourselves"*: "Media and the Voting Rights Act of 1965," October 20, 2008, Robert M. Batscha University Seminar Series, Paley Center for Media, New York.
138 *The attack was picked up by national television:* Ibid.; Peters, *Lyndon B. Johnson*, 107.
138 *"[T]he campaigners marched over"*: Miller, *Lyndon*, 429.
139 *"Television news came"*: "Media and the Voting Rights Act of 1965," The Paley Center for Media, New York, October 20, 2008.
139 *"This was a piece of history"*: Ibid.
139 *"People wanted action"*: Ibid.
139 *"Wallace sent a telegram"*: PBS, *American Experience: LBJ*, "Part Three: We Shall Overcome," WGBH-Boston, 1991.
140 *"That was the most amazing"*: Ibid.

141 *"I speak tonight for the dignity of man"*: Johnson, "Special Message to the Congress: The American Promise," March 15, 1965, in Woolley and Peters, The American Presidency Project, at www.presidency.ucsb.edu/ws/?pid=26805.

142 *"I never was suspected"*: LBJ's speech to students at LBJ School of Public Affairs, December 2, 1972.

143 *"[Johnson] wasn't a good orator"*: Hardesty, *The Difference He Made*, 85.

143 *"I was in the home"*: "Media and the Voting Rights Act of 1965," The Paley Center for Media, New York, October 20, 2008.

144 *"A president born in the South"*: Martin Luther King Jr., "Our God Is Marching On!," March 25, 1965, Montgomery, Ala., www.mlkonline.net/ourgod.html.

144 *By 1968, African American registration:* Dallek, *Flawed Giant*, 220–21.

144 *In 1964 there were only 79 elected:* Joseph A. Califano, "What Was Really Great About the Great Society: The Truth Behind the Conservative Myths," *Washington Monthly*, October 1999; statistics from "Black Elected Officials" from the Joint Center for Political and Economic Studies, Washington, D.C.

A War for the Poor

144 *"going through a garbage pile"*: Pycior, *LBJ and Mexican Americans*, 18.

145 *"My students were poor"*: Johnson, "Special Message to the Congress: The American Promise," March 15, 1965.

145 *"The biggest mistake that"*: "Media and the Voting Rights Act of 1965."

145 *"In the first place"*: Roy Wilkins Oral History Interview I, 4/1/69, by Thomas H. Baker, transcript, Internet copy, LBJ Library.

146 *"my kind of undertaking"*: Johnson, *The Vantage Point*, 71.

146 *"[Johnson] embraced the concept"*: Lawrence F. O'Brien Oral History Interview VII, 2/12/86, by Michael L. Gillette, transcript, Internet copy, LBJ Library.

147 *The difference was that Kennedy's program:* Michael Gillette, *Launching the War on Poverty: An Oral History* (Oxford: Oxford University Press, 2010), xvii.

147 *"I realized that a program"*: Johnson, *The Vantage Point*, 75.

147 *"During the Christmas holidays"*: Hardesty, *The Difference He Made*, 20.

147 *"an unconditional war on poverty"*: Johnson, "Annual Message to the Congress on the State of the Union," January 8, 1964, in Woolley and Peters, The American Presidency Project, at www.presidency.ucsb.edu/ws/?pid=26787.

147 *He made the lifting of the poor:* Gillette, *Launching the War on Poverty*, xi.

147 *"He thought of the War on Poverty"*: Miller, *Lyndon*, 363.

148 *"As far as I can see"*: Ramsey Clark Oral History Interview V, 6/3/69, by Harri Baker, transcript, Internet copy, LBJ Library.

148 *By comparison, the New Deal's work appropriations:* Gillette, *Launching the War on Poverty*, xviii.

148 *"give every American community"*: Johnson, "Special Message to the Congress Proposing a Nationwide War on the Sources of Poverty," March 16, 1964, in Woolley and Peters, The American Presidency Project, at www.presidency.ucsb.edu/ws/?pid=26109.

149 *"I'm going to rewrite your poverty program"*: Recording of Telephone Conversation Between Lyndon B. Johnson and Bill Moyers, August 7, 1964, 8:35 p.m., citation nos. 4815, 4816, 4817, Recordings and Transcripts of Conversations and Meetings, LBJ Library.

150 *"I think he gave me the job"*: Gillette, *Launching the War on Poverty*, 35.

150 *"[T]here have been situations"*: Recording of Telephone Conversation Between Lyndon B. Johnson and Eunice Kennedy Shriver, December 18, 1966, 6:55 p.m., citation no. 11155, Recordings and Transcripts of Conversations and Meetings, LBJ Library.

150 *"a few choice words"*: Dallek, *Flawed Giant*, 108.

151 *"I don't know if I'll pass"*: Gillette, *Launching the War on Poverty*, xi.

151 *"Madison Avenue publicity stunt"*: Miller, *Lyndon*, 363.

151 *"OEO was set up"*: Gillette, *Launching the War on Poverty*, 412.

151 *In the wake of riots in Watts: American Experience: RFK*, WGBH-Boston, 2004.

152 *"poverty won"*: Ronald Reagan, "State of the Union Address," January 25, 1988.

152 *According to U.S. Census Bureau data:* U.S. Bureau of the Census, Current Population Survey, Annual Social and Economic Supplements, Table 2: Poverty Status of People by Family Relationship, Race, and Hispanic Origin: 1959 to 2009.

153 *"Johnson's relationship with his pet project"*: Califano, "Seeing Is Believing."

153 *"I see a society learning"*: Miller, *Lyndon*, 361.

"All the Education They Can Take"

153 *He then outlined the crisis:* Johnson, *The Vantage Point*, 206.

154 *"[His speech] was an impressive"*: Hardesty, *The Difference He Made*, 25.

154 *The reason that no president:* Unger and Unger, *LBJ: A Life*, 344.

154 *"The kids is where the money ain't"*: Johnson, *The Vantage Point*, 206.

154 *"He was a nut on education"*: Miller, *Lyndon*, 407.

155 *Aware of the formidable challenges:* Johnson, *The Vantage Point*, 206.

155 *"educationally deprived children"*: Unger and Unger, *LBJ: A Life*, 345.

155 *The cost of putting the bill into effect:* Press release on January 2, 1968, "Facts About the Elementary and Secondary Education Amendments of 1967."

155 *"entire power and prestige"*: Johnson, *Vantage Point*, 209.

155 *"Is that with* our *Billy?"*: Ibid., 210.

155 *"we have been trying to do"*: Dallek, *Flawed Giant*, 200.

155 *"the most significant education bill"*: Johnson, "Remarks Upon Signing the Higher Education Facilities Act," December 16, 1963, in Woolley and

Peters, The American Presidency Project, at www.presidency.ucsb.edu/ws/?pid=26387.

155 *"hyperbole was to Lyndon"*: Miller, *Lyndon*, 441.

156 *Nearly three years later: Public Papers of the President: Lyndon B. Johnson, 1968–69*, Vol. 1 (Washington, D.C.: Government Printing Office, 1970), 15–17; Educational Attainment of the Population 25 Years and Over: 1940 to 2000, U.S. Census Bureau, Statistical Abstract(s) of the United States for 1964, 1969, and 2011.

156 *"This guy's committed to quality"*: Lawrence F. O'Brien Oral History Interview XIV, 9/11/86, by Michael L. Gillette, transcript, Internet copy, LBJ Library.

156 *In 1940, before the bill went into effect:* Educational Attainment of the Population 25 Years and Over: 1940 to 2000, U.S. Census Bureau.

157 *Mulling over the two dozen education bills:* "President's Talk in Texas on Higher Education Act," *New York Times*, November 9, 1965.

157 *$785 million annual price tag:* Unger and Unger, *LBJ: A Life*, 382.

157 *"It's hard to remember"*: Ramsey Clark Oral History Interview V.

157 *"These laws [passed by Johnson]"*: Sidey, *Personal Presidency*, 102–3.

157 *"My creed was simple"*: Johnson, speech to LBJ School of Public Affairs, December 4, 1972.

Making Harry Truman's Dream Come True

158 *"number one priority"*: Dallek, *Flawed Giant*, 205.

158 *"be spared the darkness"*: Johnson, "Statement by the President on His Message on the Nation's Health," January 7, 1965, in Woolley and Peters, The American Presidency Project, at www.presidency.ucsb.edu/ws/?pid=27351.

158 *missed passage in the Senate by a few votes:* King-Anderson Bill, July 17, 1962, 52–48 votes.

158 *"socialized medicine"*: Unger and Unger, *LBJ: A Life*, 363.

158 *"invade every area of freedom in this country"*: Dallek, *Flawed Giant*, 209.

158 *"the times had caught up with the idea"*: Johnson, *The Vantage Point*, 213.

159 *"work something out"*: Dallek, *Flawed Giant*, 205; Johnson, *The Vantage Point*, 214.

159 *"When are you going"*: Recording of Telephone Conversation Between Lyndon B. Johnson and Wilbur Mills and Wilbur Cohen, March 23, 1965, 4:54 p.m., citation no. 7142, Recordings and Transcripts of Conversations and Meetings, LBJ Library.

160 *Mills had approved a $500 million:* Miller, *Lyndon*, 410.

160 *"I told [Wilbur] about the test"*: Johnson, *The Vantage Point*, 216.

160 *"the villain of [Medicare]"*: Ibid.

160 *95 percent of American doctors would follow suit:* Miller, *Lyndon*, 412.

160 *"watch out for trains"*: Johnson, *The Vantage Point*, 216.

161 *"all do their utmost"*: Ibid., 217.

161 *"These men are going to get doctors":* Dallek, *Flawed Giant*, 210.
161 *AMA would formally endorse Medicare:* Johnson, *The Vantage Point*, 218.
161 *"He had started it all":* Ibid., 219.
161 *"make Harry Truman's dream come true":* Hardesty, *The Difference He Made*, 20.
161 *"Medicare made an enormous":* Ibid., 24.

Nature Was My Companion

162 *"My poor baby":* Luci Johnson to the author, April 29, 2011.
162 *"Nature was my first":* Ibid.
162 *"My deepest attitudes":* Johnson, *The Vantage Point*, 336.
162 *"would have been content":* Ibid., 336.
162 *Theodore . . . who increased the protected land:* "Grand Canyon Becomes National Monument, January 11, 1908," Miller Center, at millercenter .org/president/events/01_11.
162 *"unimaginative name":* Middleton, *White House Years*, 212.
163 *In sum, beautification means:* Johnson, *White House Diary*, 234.
163 *"beauties of their country":* Harry J. Middleton, *Lady Bird Johnson: A Life Well Lived* (Austin, Texas: Lyndon Baines Johnson Foundation, 1992), 109.
163 *"We started at an Indian reservation":* Ibid., 102.
163 *"When we were going down":* Ibid.
163 *"She was the greatest salesman":* Ibid.,109.
164 *"She was one of the more influential":* Ibid., 116.
164 *"I never see you around anymore":* Recording of Telephone Conversation Between Lyndon B. Johnson and Phil Potter, August 6, 1965, 7:12 p.m., citation no. 8525, Recordings and Transcripts of Conversations and Meetings, LBJ Library.
165 *"Just before the first session":* Bob Hardesty to the author, May 19, 2011.
166 *amendment to . . . replace the title "Secretary of Commerce":* *The Washington Post*, October 9, 1965.
166 *"Our goal was the city":* Middleton, *Lady Bird Johnson*, 106.
167 *By 1966 she was receiving two hundred letters a week:* Sidey, *Portrait of a President*, 86.
167 *"Where flowers bloom, so does hope":* Mrs. Johnson. Bob Bryant and Bonnie L. Harper-Lore, "Where Flowers Bloom, So Does Hope," *Public Roads* 61, no. 3. www.fhwa.dot.gov/publications/publicroads/97novdec/p97nov38 .cfm.

"What Can You Do for Our Country?"

167 *"The national origins quota system":* Lawrence F. O'Brien Oral History Interview XII, 7/25/86, by Michael L. Gillette, transcript, Internet copy, LBJ Library.

168 *Johnson had helped Jewish refugees:* Interview with Claudia Anderson, supervisory archivist, LBJ Library and Museum, November 23, 2010.
168 *"In establishing preferences":* Johnson, "Annual Message to the Congress on the State of the Union," January 8, 1964, LBJ Library.
168 *"a matter of common sense":* Sidey, *Personal Presidency*, 54.
169 *"I know this":* Recording of Telephone Conversation Between Lyndon B. Johnson and Ted Kennedy, March 8, 1965, 9:10 p.m., citation no. 7043, Recordings and Transcripts of Conversations and Meetings, LBJ Library.
170 *"The first speech John McCormack":* Carl Albert Oral History Interview III, 7/9/69, by Dorothy Pierce McSweeny, transcript, Internet Copy, LBJ Library.

"The Fabulous Eighty-ninth Congress"

170 *Sixty-nine percent of the 469 proposals: Congress and the Nation 1965–68* (Washington, D.C.: Congressional Quarterly Press, 1969), 625.
170 *Of the 115 bills:* Unger and Unger, *LBJ: A Life*, 382.
171 *"The monumental record of": Congress and the Nation*, 1965–68, 625.
172 *"I thought [the signing ceremony]":* Recording of Telephone Conversation Between Lyndon B. Johnson and John McCormack, August 6, 1965, 6:35 p.m., citation no. 8517, Recordings and Transcripts of Conversations and Meetings, LBJ Library.
172 *"[Johnson] would never rest":* Carl Albert Oral History Interview III.
173 *"I came in at the time":* Hardesty, *The Difference He Made*, 36.
173 *"The achievements of President":* Edward M. Kennedy Oral History Interview III.
173 *"It was a very creative":* George McGovern Oral History, interview with author, February 3, 2011.
173 *"History will be the final judge":* Hardesty, *The Difference He Made*, 77.

"Nearly Every Person in the World Is Good"

174 *"When he argued":* George Reedy Oral History Interview III.
174 *"The devil with a pitchfork":* Hardesty, *The Difference He Made*, 35–36.
175 *"I have read a great":* Ibid., 22–23.
175 *"I think that [there]":* Billy Graham Oral History, Special Interview, 10/12/83, by Monroe Billington, transcript, Internet copy, LBJ Library.
176 *"Roosevelt didn't have any":* Lyndon B. Johnson Oral History Collection.
176 *"There were times when":* Hardesty, *The Difference He Made*, 149.
176 *I remember one incident:* Claudia Taylor Johnson Oral History Interview XVIII, 9/26–27/80, by Michael L. Gillette, transcript, Internet copy, LBJ Library.
177 *"I'll tell you this":* Miller, *Lyndon*, 19.
178 *"The Ku Klux Klan was":* Ibid., 20.

178 *"Now, listen here, you"*: Ibid.
178 *"My father fought the"*: Ibid.
178 *"where folks care when"*: Tom Johnson to the author, April 2011.
179 *"Lyndon had the most"*: Miller, *Lyndon*, 55.
179 *"[H]e started in a"*: *American Experience: LBJ*, "Part Four: The Last Believer," WGBH-Boston, 1991.
180 *recalled with*: Lynda Johnson Robb to the author, September 4, 2011.
180 *"If you're President"*: Lawrence F. O'Brien Oral History Interview VIII, 4/8/86, by Michael L. Gillette, transcript, Internet copy, LBJ Library.
180 *"He intended to be"*: Thurgood Marshall Oral History Interview I.
181 *"They have babylike faith"*: *Time* magazine, May 1, 1964.
181 *"My father would go"*: Nancy Gibbs and Michael Duffy, *The Preacher and the Presidents: Billy Graham in the White House* (New York: Center Street, 2007), 122.
182 *"[Daddy] was religious"*: Lynda Johnson Robb to the author, October 3, 2011.
182 *"If you really trust"*: Lyndon B. Johnson Oral History Collection.
182 *"For all his realism"*: Ramsey Clark, in Recollections of LBJ.

Chapter 7: COMMANDER IN CHIEF

"What the Hell Is Vietnam Worth to Me?"

185 *"What do you think about"*: Recording of Telephone Conversation Between Lyndon B. Johnson and Richard Russell, May 27, 1964, 10:55 a.m., citation no. 3519, Recordings and Transcripts of Conversations and Meetings, LBJ Library.
186 *"I'll tell you, the more"*: Recording of Telephone Conversation Between Lyndon B. Johnson and McGeorge Bundy, May 27, 1964, 11:24 a.m., citation no. 3522, Recordings and Transcripts of Conversations and Meetings, LBJ Library.
187 *"They want what we've"*: Lyndon B. Johnson Oral History Collection.
188 *The "Who Lost China?" debate:* Peters, *Lyndon B. Johnson*, 127.
188 *"Lyndon Johnson quoted"*: Round table discussion, April 17, 1984.
188 *"I don't know whether"*: Ibid.
189 *At the beginning of 1965:* Gelb, Rosenthal, and Siegel, *Great Lives*, 306.
189 *"They are killing our"*: Johnson, *The Vantage Point*, 125.
189 *With the dispatch of two:* Miller Center biography of LBJ, at millercenter.org/president/lbjohnson/essays/biography/5.
189 *"If I don't go in"*: *American Experience: LBJ*: "Part Two: My Fellow Americans," WGBH-Boston, 1991.
190 *"[Johnson] once said"*: Hardesty, *The Difference He Made*, 209.
190 *"If they get 150"*: Randall B. Woods, *LBJ*: *Architect of American Ambition* (Cambridge, Mass.: Harvard University Press, 2007), 611.
190 *"[Johnson] did have what"*: Hardesty, *The Difference He Made*, 209.

190 *"Westmoreland was a protégé"*: Ibid.
190 *"I didn't see [Johnson]"*: Ibid., 162.
191 *"Lest we forget"*: Ibid., 209.
191 *"[I] thought that the balloon"*: *American Experience: LBJ*, "Part Two: My Fellow Americans," WGBH-Boston, 1991.
192 *"George Ball was the only"*: Round table discussion, April 17, 1984.
192 *"We had a series"*: Harry McPherson to the author, December, 15, 2010.
192 *"The problem for President"*: Round table discussion, April 17, 1984.
192 *"[M]any of us felt"*: Ibid.
193 *"It was April 6"*: Hardesty, *The Difference He Made*, 180–81.

"Another Cuba"?

194 *"dangerous demagogue"*: Dallek, *Flawed Giant*, 262.
194 *"another Cuba"*: Miller, *Lyndon*, 425.
194 *"hundreds" of American lives were "in danger"*: Johnson, "Statement by the President Upon Ordering Troops into the Dominican Republic," April 28, 1965, in Woolley and Peters, The American Presidency Project, at www.presidency.ucsb.edu/ws/?pid=26922.
195 *"The Castro forces are"*: Recording of Telephone Conversation Between Lyndon B. Johnson and Mike Mansfield, April 30, 1965, 11:51 a.m., citation no. 7410, Recordings and Transcripts of Conversations and Meetings, LBJ Library.
195 *"signs that people trained outside"*: Johnson, "Statement by the President on the Situation in the Dominican Republic," April 30, 1965, *Presidential Papers*: 1965, 465–66.
195 *"at stake are the lives . . . Communist conspirators"*: Johnson, "Radio and Television Report to the American People on the Situation in the Dominican Republic," May 2, 1965, in Woolley and Peters, The American Presidency Project, at www.presidency.ucsb.edu/ws/?pid=26932.
196 *"The President ran the"*: John Bartlow Martin Oral History Interview I, 1/30/71, by Paige E. Mulhollan, transcript, Internet copy, LBJ Library.
196 *"some 1,500 innocent people"*: Johnson, "The President's News Conference," June 17, 1965, at www.presidency.ucsb.edu/ws/index.php?pid=27040&st=Some+1%2C500+innocent+people+were+murdered+and+shot&st1=#axzz1HFGWtzoW.
196 *"Johnson was fundamentally dishonest"*: Miller, *Lyndon*, 424.
197 *"What astounded me about"*: Ibid., 427.
197 *"Our policy seemed more"*: Ibid., 428.
197 *"an outstanding act of democratic purity"*: OAS Statement. Yves Beigbeder, *International Monitoring of Plebiscites, Referenda and National Elections: Self-Determination and Transition to Democracy* (New York: Springer Publishing, 1994), 233.
198 *"He can have anything"*: Frank Cormier, *LBJ: The Way He Was* (Garden City, N.Y.: Doubleday, 1977), 190.

Lyndon Johnson's War

198 *"What I would like"*: Peters, *Lyndon B. Johnson*, 120.

199 *"I'm having a meeting"*: Recording of Telephone Conversation Between Lyndon B. Johnson and Dwight Eisenhower, July 2, 1965, 11:02 a.m., citation no. 8303, Recordings and Transcripts of Conversations and Meetings, LBJ Library.

200 *"When Jack was killed"*: George McGovern Oral History, interview with author, February 3, 2011.

201 *"No More War" and "We Want Peace Now"*: *The Washington Post*, September 27, 1999.

201 *Vietnam "must be stopped"*: *The New York Times*, July 3, 1965.

202 *"Now there's one other point"*: Recording of Telephone Conversation Between Lyndon B. Johnson and Dr. Martin Luther King Jr., July 7, 1965, 8:05 p.m., citation nos. 8311–8313, Recordings and Transcripts of Conversations and Meetings, LBJ Library.

202 *"[O]ur national honor is"*: Johnson, "Remarks to the National Rural Electric Cooperative Association," July 14, 1965, in Woolley and Peters, The American Presidency Project, at www.presidency.ucsb.edu/ws/?pid=27082.

203 *"ordered to Vietnam the air"*: Johnson, "The President's News Conference," July 28, 1965, in Woolley and Peters, The American Presidency Project, at www.presidency.ucsb.edu/ws/?pid=27116.

203 *"not allow" his domestic goals:* Ibid.

203 *"[M]ost certainly [Johnson] did"*: Ted Gittinger, ed. *The Johnson Years: A Vietnam Roundtable* (Austin, Texas: Lyndon Baines Johnson Library, 1993), 69–70.

203 *"From November 23[, 1963] until"*: LBJ to Harry Middleton, Lyndon B. Johnson Oral History transcript.

204 *"A great part of our"*: Ibid.

204 *"The procedure as far"*: Gittinger, *Vietnam Roundtable*, 79.

205 *"We recommended an increase"*: Robert S. McNamara Oral History Interview I, 1/8/75, by Walt W. Rostow, transcript, Internet copy, LBJ Library.

206 *troop levels stood at 184,000:* Middleton, *The White House Years*, 118.

206 *McNamara maintained . . . guarantee success:* Peters, *Lyndon B. Johnson*, 128.

206 *"The Paul Reveres are"*: Johnson, *White House Diary*, 347.

207 *diplomatic overtures were written off . . . as "deceptive" and "a trick"*: Middleton, *White House Years*, 117.

Chapter 8: HAWKS AND DOVES

Fissures

209 *"most admired man in America"*: *The Washington Post*, January 2, 1966.

209 *Other polls by Gallup:* Joseph Carroll (Gallup poll assistant editor), "The

Iraq-Vietnam Comparison," Gallup online, June 15, 2004, at www.gallup.com/poll/11998/iraqvietnam-comparison.aspx.

209 *71 percent of the public approved:* Miller, *Lyndon*, 453.

209 *Reading the newspapers and:* Letter from Bobby Kennedy, in Miller, *Lyndon*, 419–20.

210 *"When you think of enemies":* Hardesty, *The Difference He Made*, 200.

210 *"There was a reception":* Ibid., 193.

211 *"Well, as I recall it": American Experience: LBJ*, "Part Two: My Fellow Americans," WGBH-Boston, 1991.

211 *After discovering their mistakes:* Regina Greenwell, "In August 1964 North Vietnamese Forces Twice Attacked American Destroyers in the Gulf of Tonkin. Not So Much." *The Alcalde* (University of Texas), Nov./Dec. 2009, 32.

211 *"PT Boat personnel":* Recording of Telephone Conversation Between Lyndon B. Johnson and Robert McNamara, February 19, 1968, 12:29 p.m., citation no. 12724, Recordings and Transcripts of Conversations and Meetings, LBJ Library.

213 *Johnson retaliated by putting: American Experience: LBJ.* "Part Three: We Shall Overcome." WGBH-Boston, 1991.

213 *"I remember Mr. Rayburn":* LBJ to Harry Middleton, Lyndon B. Johnson Oral History transcript.

213 *"[H]e called Senator Fulbright":* Round table discussion, April 17, 1984.

Guns and Butter

213 *Johnson considered it a portent:* Middleton, *White House Years*, 128.

213 "[Toward the end of 1965,] The Washington Post *had the temerity":* Gittinger, *Vietnam Roundtable*, 71.

214 *"mighty enough, its society healthy":* Johnson, "Annual Message to the Congress on the State of the Union," January 12, 1966, in Woolley and Peters, The American Presidency Project, at www.presidency.ucsb.edu/ws/?pid=28015.

214 *Around the same time:* Miller, *Lyndon*, 460.

214 *Its cost, which stood:* Gelb, Rosenthal, and Siegel, *Great Lives*, 306.

214 *"You ask for a billion here":* Middleton, *White House Years*, 118.

214 *"Now, I would have":* Miller, *Lyndon*, 455.

215 *After three days of looting:* Unger and Unger, *LBJ: A Life*, 398.

215 *"[R]iots in the street":* Johnson, "Remarks in Indianapolis at a Luncheon with Indiana Business, Labor, and Professional Leaders," July 23, 1966, in Woolley, The American Presidency Project, at www.presidency.ucsb.edu/ws/?pid= 27734.

215 *"I want a fair housing":* Joseph A. Califano, *Inside: A Public and Private Life* (New York: Public Affairs, 2004), 153.

216 *"continuing tendency toward managed":* Thomas Blanton, ed., "Freedom of Information at 40," The National Security Archive [online], at www.gwu.edu/~nsarchiv/NSAEBB/NSAEBB194/index.htm.

216 *"if we don't stop"*: Johnson, "Remarks at the Signing Ceremony for Seven Conservation Bills," October 15, 1966, in Woolley and Peters, The American Presidency Project, at www.presidency.ucsb.edu/ws/?pid=27929.
216 *This would not only benefit:* Unger and Unger, *LBJ: A Life*, 401.
216 *"for that little charwoman"*: Middleton, *White House Years*, 132.
216 *"quiet man"*: *Ebony* magazine, April 1966.
217 *"It was one of those"*: Johnson, *White House Diary*, 353.
217 *"is about two-thirds"*: Ibid., 362.
217 *According to Gallup:* Carroll, "The Iraq-Vietnam Comparison," Gallup online, June 15, 2004.
217 *"Down to June of 1966"*: Hardesty, *The Difference He Made*, 163.
218 *"At every Cabinet meeting"*: Round table discussion, April 17, 1984.
218 *"I think he sort of sensed"*: Ibid.
218 *"I think it is absolutely true"*: Ibid.
219 *"I think he used"*: Ibid.
219 *"It is unbearably hard to"*: Johnson, *White House Diary*, 469.
219 *"Now [in] World War II"*: Barry Goldwater Oral History Interview I.
220 *"My God, I've offered Ho"*: Miller, *Lyndon*, 466.
220 *"LBJ had no particular grasp"*: Ibid.
220 *"President Johnson was marvelous"*: Hardesty, *The Difference He Made*, 90.
221 *"His weakness was that"*: Ibid., 189–90.
221 *"no reluctance about those two men"*: Lyndon B. Johnson Oral History Collection.

A Question of Credibility

222 *"the imagination of people"*: Unger and Unger, *LBJ: A Life*, 405.
222 *"I never wanted to get"*: Middleton, *White House Years*, 152.
222 *"the public was deceived"*: *Congress and the Nation, 1965–68*, 641.
222 *"How do you know when Lyndon"*: Dallek, *Flawed Giant*, 280–281.
222 *"Of course Johnson was"*: Hardesty, *The Difference He Made*, 177.
223 *"The Vietnam War obviously"*: Ibid., 188.
223 *"[One question] is to ask"*: Gittinger, *Vietnam Roundtable*, 139.
223 *Johnson's approval rating had fallen to 43 percent:* Carroll, "The Iraq-Vietnam Comparison," Gallup online, June 15, 2004.

Chapter 9: UNDER FIRE

"We're Burning Up!"

225 *"an assembly of hope"*: Johnson, *The Vantage Point*, 270.
225 *"This is an inspiring moment"*: Johnson, "Remarks at the Signing of the Treaty on Outer Space," January 27, 1967, in Woolley and Peters, The American Presidency Project, at www.presidency.ucsb.edu/ws/?pid=28205.
225 *"commit itself to achieving"*: John F. Kennedy, "Special Message to the Con-

gress on Urgent National Needs," May 25, 1961, in Woolley and Peters, The American Presidency Project, at www.presidency.ucsb.edu/ws/?pid=8151.

226 *There were nearly as many:* Andrew Chaikin, *A Man on the Moon: Lunar Explorers* (Alexandria, Va.: Time-Life, 1999), 11.

226 *"I remember once riding":* Hardesty, *The Difference He Made*, 177.

226 *"The U.S. can, if it will":* Vice President Johnson's memorandum to the president evaluating the space program, April 28, 1961, at www.jfklibrary.org/Asset-Viewer/DjiWpQJegkuIlX7WZAUCtQ.aspx; Johnson, *Vantage Point*, 281.

227 *"Kennedy said that in":* Hardesty, *The Difference He Made*, 16.

227 *"Mr. President . . . James Webb just reported":* Johnson, *The Vantage Point*, 290.

227 *"I watched him as":* Johnson, *White House Diary*, 482–83.

227 *After the fire broke out:* Chaikin, *A Man on the Moon*, 24.

"The Hot Line Is Up"

228 *"When the phone rings":* Lyndon B. Johnson Oral History Collection.

228 *Johnson was awakened:* Johnson, *The Vantage Point*, 287.

228 *"[T]he battle has come":* Radio Cairo, at mideastweb.org/briefhistory.htm.

228 *"The danger implicit":* Johnson, *The Vantage Point*, 288.

229 *"[T]he United States strongly": The Washington Post*, May 24, 1967.

229 *"In 1967 we became":* Dean Rusk Oral History Interview IV, 3/8/70, by Paige E. Mulhollan, transcript, Internet copy, LBJ Library.

229 *"The facts were, I think":* Robert S. McNamara Oral History, Special Interview I, 3/26/93, by Robert Dallek, transcript, Internet copy, LBJ Library.

230 *"Mr. President . . . the hot line is up":* Johnson, *The Vantage Point*, 287.

230 *"Yeah?"* Recording of Telephone Conversation Between Lyndon B. Johnson and Robert McNamara, June 5, 1967, 7:57 a.m., citation no. 11903, Recordings and Transcripts of Conversations and Meetings, LBJ Library.

231 *The attack, which the Israelis:* U.S. Naval Court of Inquiry of June 1967, at www.thelibertyincident.com/docs/CourtOfInquiry.pdf.

231 *"unconditionally":* Miller, *Lyndon*, 481.

232 *"My last message to":* Miller, *Lyndon*, 481.

232 *Later in the month:* Sherwin J. Markman, "Some Aspects of Lyndon Johnson's Personality," in *Lyndon Johnson Remembered: An Intimate Portrait of a Presidency*, ed. Thomas W. Cowger and Sherwin Markman (Lanham, Md.: Rowman and Littlefield, 2003), 47–50.

233 *"I wanted to call":* Recording of Telephone Conversation Between Lyndon B. Johnson and Dwight Eisenhower, June 25, 1967, 9:44 p.m., citation nos. 11914–11916, Recordings and Transcripts of Conversations and Meetings, LBJ Library.

234 *"Nothing really concrete came":* Gelb, Rosenthal, and Siegel, *Great Lives*, 308.

Justice and Lawlessness

235 *"He called one day"*: Thurgood Marshall Oral History Interview I.
236 *"[H]e asked me who"*: Larry Temple to the author, March 30, 2011.
237 *"Nigger, nigger, nigger"*: Califano, *The Triumph and Tragedy*, 178.
237 *"[T]he American struggle for"*: Johnson, *Vantage Point*, 179.
237 *In Newark, New Jersey:* David Hartman and Barry Lewis, *A Walk Through Newark*, Thirteen WNET, New York Public Media, at www.thirteen.org/newark/history3.html.
237 *"How is it possible"*: Gelb, Rosenthal, and Siegel, *Great Lives*, 316.
238 *"He reacted badly"*: *American Experience: LBJ*, "Part Three: We Shall Overcome," WGBH-Boston, 1991.
238 *"Lyndon Johnson could not"*: Ibid.
238 *By August, Johnson would see:* Carroll, "The Iraq-Vietnam Comparison," Gallup online, June 15, 2004.

"Hey, Hey, LBJ . . ."

239 *"One of the things that people don't realize"*: Luci Johnson to the author, February 2011.
239 *In mid-April, more than 250,000 people came together:* "This Day in History: Vietnam War: April 15, 1967," at www.history.com/this-day-in-history/antiwar-protests-held-in-new-york-and-san-francisco.
240 *"The enemy is Lyndon Johnson"*: *Time* magazine, October 27, 1967.
240 *"There is no greater importance"*: Norman Mailer, *The Armies of the Night: History as a Novel, the Novel as History* (New York: New American Library, 1968).
241 *"I think [Johnson's] downfall"*: George Reedy Oral History Interview III.
241 *"You saw those protesters"*: Middleton, *White House Years*, 104.
241 *"The young people I've"*: LBJ to Harry Middleton, Lyndon B. Johnson Oral History transcript.
242 *"He was [not concerned] so"*: Hardesty, *The Difference He Made*, 165–66.
242 *"My heart was with"*: Middleton, *White House Years*, 104–5.
243 *"[The protesting] was very"*: Lynda Johnson Robb to the author, March 9, 2011.
243 *"[Daddy] would be watching"*: Luci Johnson to the author, February 2011.

"Eyes Only—For the President"

244 *"Are we going to"*: Middleton, *White House Years*, 178.
244 *"almost never brought bad"*: Miller, *Lyndon*, 480–81.
244 *"Since part of my job"*: Richard Helms, CIA Report on "Implications of an Unfavorable Outcome in Vietnam," September 11, 1967, National Security

File Vietnam Country File Folder "Vietnam, Outcome (CIA Study)" Box 259.

245 *No record or recollection exists:* Tom Johnson to the author, March 22, 2011.

246 *"I always thought that":* Bob Hardesty to the author, February 2011.

246 *"His great fear on":* Hardesty, *The Difference He Made*, 165–66.

246 *"I take him at his":* George McGovern Oral History, interview with the author, February 3, 2011.

246 *"I know this with certainty":* Tom Johnson to the author, April 2011.

247 *"I don't think he":* Barry Goldwater Oral History Interview I.

247 *"I would sum up":* Hardesty, *The Difference He Made*, 165.

247 *"We of the Kennedy":* Robert McNamara, *In Retrospect: The Tragedy and Lessons of Vietnam* (New York: Times, 1995), xvi.

248 *"The enemy is already":* LBJ to Harry Middleton, Lyndon B. Johnson Oral History transcript.

248 *"Lyndon came to regret":* Barry Goldwater Oral History Interview I.

248 *"[Johnson] felt that Secretary":* Clark M. Clifford Oral History Interview III, 7/14/69, by Paige Mulhollan, transcript, Internet copy, LBJ Library.

Around the World in Four and a Half Days

249 *"I think he hurt deeply":* Tom Johnson to the author, January 2011.

249 *"We were going out":* Hardesty, *The Difference He Made*, 204.

250 *"deep inbred desire to":* Johnson, *White House Diary*, 606.

250 *"You can't fault a":* Miller, *Lyndon*, 455–56.

251 *"We're not going to yield":* Johnson, "Remarks to Senior Unit Commanders, Cam Ranh Bay, Vietnam," December 23, 1967, in Woolley and Peters, The American Presidency Project, at www.presidency.ucsb.edu/ws/?pid=28634.

251 *"an influential segment in":* Johnson, *The Vantage Point*, 380.

251 *"the fastest, longest, hardest trip":* Johnson, *White House Diary*, 605.

Chapter 10: "THE NIGHTMARE YEAR"

"One War at a Time"

253 *"More than ever before":* "Man of the Year," *Time*, January 5, 1968.

254 *His options limited:* Sidey, *Personal Presidency*, 291.

254 *"If you're going to play":* Ibid., 289.

254 *"I will never fully":* Dean Rusk Oral History Interview III, 1/2/70, by Paige E. Mulhollan, transcript, Internet copy, LBJ Library.

254 *According to the report:* Richard Helms, CIA Report. See also: www.vietnam.ttu.edu/virtualarchive/items.php?item=04109127006.

255 *"Well, he called in":* Nicholas D. Katzenbach Oral History Interview III, 12/11/68, by Paige E. Mulhollan, transcript, Internet copy, LBJ Library.

255 *"[Johnson] made a prompt":* Dean Rusk Oral History Interview III.

256 *U.S.S.* Pueblo: Now harbored in the Taedong River in North Korea's west coast capital of Pyongyang, the ship, described as an "armed spy ship of the U.S. imperialist aggression forces," is a tourist attraction.

No Light, Longer Tunnel

257 *"They have more power":* Recording of Telephone Conversation Between Lyndon B. Johnson and Robert McNamara, January 31, 1968, time unknown, citation no. 12617, Recordings and Transcripts of Conversations and Meetings, LBJ Library.

258 *An estimated 33,000:* Dallek, *Flawed Giant*, 504.

258 *Tet demonstrated in clear terms:* Robert Dallek, *Lyndon B. Johnson: Portrait of a President* (New York: Oxford University Press, 2004), 322.

258 *weep over the situation:* Dallek, *Flawed Giant*, 527.

258 *"Tet had had a very":* Clark M. Clifford Oral History Interview III.

259 *"[H]ere there were competing":* Harry McPherson Oral History Interview IV, 3/24/69, by T. H. Baker, transcript, Internet copy, LBJ Library.

259 *approval rating on Vietnam:* Carroll, "The Iraq-Vietnam Comparison," Gallup online, June 15, 2004.

260 *Only Fortas, Murphy, and Taylor offered opposing views:* Andrew Glass, "Johnson Meets with 'The Wise Men,' March 25, 1968," *Politico* (March 25, 2010): at www.politico.com/news/stories/0310/34945.html.

260 *"I have no doubt":* Dean Rusk Oral History Interview II.

260 *"I wanted to see":* Cronkite, in Walter Cronkite and Don E. Carleton, *Conversations with Cronkite*, Dolph Briscoe Center for American History, University of Texas at Austin, 2010, 210.

261 *"It seems now more":* Ibid., 212.

261 *"I don't think I":* Ibid., 213.

The Decision

262 *Years earlier he had: Time*, February 5, 1973.

262 *"physical and mental incapacitation":* Johnson, *White House Diary*, 567.

262 *"[H]e talked to me":* Dean Rusk Oral History Interview II.

262 *"He said, 'I'm giving'":* Billy Graham Oral History, Special Interview.

263 *"He had started talking":* Hardesty, *The Difference He Made*, 155–56.

264 *"There was no tolerance":* Sidey, *Personal Presidency*, 291.

264 *A December poll revealed:* Dallek, *LBJ: Portrait of a President*, 330.

264 *"I always thought of":* Lyndon B. Johnson Oral History Collection.

265 *"I never allowed my":* Ibid.

265 *"That little runt will":* Miller, *Lyndon*, 506.

265 *"in a damaging way":* "M'Carthy Gets About 40%, Johnson and Nixon on Top of New Hampshire Voting," *The New York Times*, March 14, 1968.

266 *Kennedy's name was also:* Sidey, *Personal Presidency*, 294.

266 *"I do remember thinking":* Miller, *Lyndon*, 507.
267 *"On Friday, March 29":* Jim Jones, *The New York Times* op-ed, April 16, 1988.

March 31

267 *The morning of March 31:* Lyndon B. Johnson Oral History Collection.
268 *"I saw the terrible agony":* Hardesty, *The Difference He Made*, 165.
268 *"When I went back":* Johnson, *White House Diary*, 642.
269 *"With America's sons in":* Johnson, "President Lyndon B. Johnson's Address to the Nation Announcing Steps to Limit the War in Vietnam and Reporting His Decision Not to Seek Reelection," March 31, 1968, in *Public Papers of the Presidents of the United States: Lyndon B. Johnson, 1968–69*, vol. 1, entry 170, pp. 469–76.
269 *"I saluted him":* Guggenheim Papers, Sync 20, pg. 2
269 *"Watching him you could":* Miller, *Lyndon*, 513.
269 *"After the speech was":* Lynda Johnson Robb to the author, March 22, 2011.
269 *"Nobly done, darling":* Miller, *Lyndon*, 513.
269 *"Later that night":* Jim Jones, *New York Times* op-ed, April 16, 1988.
270 *"I got to the newsroom":* Carl Bernstein to the author, June 2011.

End of a Dream

272 *April 1, Johnson saw a jump in his approval ratings:* Sidey, *Personal Presidency*, 297.
272 *"After my announcement March 31":* Lyndon B. Johnson Oral History Collection.
272 *"a brave and dedicated man":* Evan Thomas, *Robert Kennedy: His Life* (New York: Simon and Schuster, 2000), 365.
272 *"People try to divide":* Johnson, *The Vantage Point*, 540.
272 *Johnson's feelings wouldn't stay:* Larry Temple to the author, March 30, 2011.
272 *"an act of a very":* Dallek, *Flawed Giant*, 530.
273 *"LBJ was the most":* Tom Johnson, e-mail to the author, March 16, 2011.
273 *"[Johnson] was very depressed":* Arthur Krim Oral History Interview IV, 11/9/1982, by Michael L. Gillette, transcript, Internet copy, LBJ Library.
274 *"There is . . . a very obvious":* Martin Luther King Jr., "Beyond Vietnam: A Time to Break Silence," April 4, 1967, at www.hartford-hwp.com /archives/45a/058.html.
274 *He also remained concerned:* Califano, *The Triumph and Tragedy*, 276–77.
274 *"Martin Luther King['s death]":* LBJ to Harry Middleton, Lyndon B. Johnson Oral History.
274 *"LBJ and Dr. King had":* Tom Johnson, e-mail to the author, March 16, 2011.
275 *"No doubt that LBJ":* Bob Hardesty, e-mail to Tom Johnson, March 16, 2011.
275 *"Everything we gained":* Califano, *The Triumph and Tragedy*, 274.

275 *The worst of it:* Johnson, *White House Diary*, April 1968.

275 *All told, the chaos:* Melissa Ware, "39 Years Later: Lyndon Johnson and the Civil Rights Act of 1968," Hauenstein Center for Presidential Studies, online at www.gvsu.edu/hauenstein/lyndon-johnson-and-fair-housing-446.htm.

275 *"It was a turbulent":* Larry Temple to the author, March 30, 2011.

276 *"Johnson had pressed the":* Califano, *The Triumph and Tragedy*, 276.

277 *Mondale had been one:* Steven M. Gillon, *The Democrats' Dilemma: Walter F. Mondale and the Liberal Legacy* (New York: Columbia University Press, 1992), 88.

277 *"I talked to Hubert":* Walter Mondale interview with author, January 27, 2011.

277 *"We got the bill through":* Miller, *Lyndon*, 515.

278 *"That legislation might have":* Johnson, *The Vantage Point*, 538.

278 *"I do not exaggerate":* Johnson, "Remarks Upon Signing the Civil Rights Act," April 11, 1968, in Woolley and Peters, The American Presidency Project, at www.presidency.ucsb.edu/ws/?pid=28799.

278 *"cross section of the community":* Johnson, "Remarks Upon Signing the Jury Selection and Service Act of 1968," March 27, 1968, in Woolley and Peters, The American Presidency Project, at atwww.presidency.ucsb.edu/ws/?pid=28758.

278 *"An anecdote goes along":* Bob Hardesty to the author, February 20, 2011.

"What Is Happening to Us?"

279 *"What we need":* Robert Kennedy, April 4, 1968, at www.americanrhetoric.com/speeches/rfkonmlkdeath.html.

280 *Johnson, who had retired:* President's Daily Diary, at www.lbjlibrary.org/collections/daily-diary.html, 6/5/68.

280 *"It was a short night":* Johnson, *White House Diary*, 679–80.

280 *"Lady Bird and I are":* Conversation Between Lyndon B. Johnson and Ted Kennedy, June 5, 1968, 6:35 a.m., citation no. 13104, Recordings and Transcripts of Conversations and Meetings, LBJ Library.

281 *"Johnson, as much as he":* Harry McPherson Oral History Interview X, 5/13/86, by Michael L. Gillette, transcript, Internet copy, LBJ Library.

281 *"At 10:07, Lyndon went":* Johnson, *White House Diary*, 681.

282 *"Tonight this nation faces":* Johnson, "Address to the Nation Following the Attack on Senator Kennedy," June 5, 1968, in Woolley, The American Presidency Project, at www.presidency.ucsb.edu/ws/?pid=28908.

282 *"Mr. President, it has just":* Johnson, *White House Diary*, 682.

282 *"Too horrible for words":* Unger and Unger, *LBJ: A Life*, 468.

282 *"I'm sure there was":* Harry McPherson to the author, March 8, 2011.

282 *"Always the mind was riveted":* Johnson, *White House Diary*, 684.

283 *"I think it was very":* Arthur Krim Oral History Interview IV.

283 *"the deadly commerce in":* Unger and Unger, *LBJ: A Life*, 470.

Disappointment

283 *As part of the bargain:* Middleton, *White House Years*, 248.
284 *"We'd worked awfully hard":* Clark Clifford Oral History Interview III.
285 *"One of the signal achievements":* Hardesty, *The Difference He Made*, 89.
285 *"The fact is":* Clark M. Clifford Oral History Interview V.
286 *"the further aggravation of the situation":* Recording of Cabinet Room Meeting Between Lyndon B. Johnson and Anatoly Dobrynin, Walt Rostow, August 20, 1968, 8:17–8:42 p.m., Tape SC.01, PNO: 3, Recordings and Transcripts of Meetings Conducted in the Cabinet Room, LBJ Library.
286 *"When Soviet Ambassador Dobrynin":* Jim Jones to the author, May 4, 2011.
286 *"The Soviets moved into":* Dean Rusk Oral History Interview IV.
287 *"the most experienced":* Johnson, *The Vantage Point*, 545.
287 *As their friendship grew:* Lyndon B. Johnson Oral History Collection.
288 *"If your president asks":* Miller, *Lyndon*, 483.
288 *"When White House special":* Califano, *The Triumph and Tragedy*, 308.
288 *"Lyndon decided to name":* Miller, *Lyndon*, 483.
288 *"You're not going to vote":* Ibid., 485.
289 *"Just take my word":* Califano, *The Triumph and Tragedy*, 308.
289 *"We kept telling him":* Miller, *Lyndon*, 484.
289 *"straw man":* Johnson, *The Vantage Point*, 546.
290 *"a child or a patron-seeking ward healer":* Unger and Unger, *LBJ: A Life*, 479.
290 *"In my point of view":* Recording of Telephone Conversation Between Lyndon B. Johnson and Abe Fortas, October 1, 1968, 6:06 p.m., citation no. 13509, Recordings and Transcripts of Conversations and Meetings, LBJ Library.
291 *"Abe Fortas is as good":* Lyndon B. Johnson Oral History Collection.
291 *"[Fortas's defeat] was a disappointment":* Joe Califano to the author, May 6, 2011.
291 *"the rising anger against Lyndon":* Unger and Unger, *LBJ: A Life*, 473.
291 *"a final blow":* Johnson, *The Vantage Point*, 547.

HHH

292 *"Early Sunday morning":* Jim Jones, *The New York Times* op-ed, March 31, 1988.
292 *"get out of the shadow":* Hubert Humphrey, 1948 Democratic National Convention, at www.americanrhetoric.com/speeches/huberthumphey1948dnc.html.
293 *"I remember one night":* George McGovern Oral History, interview with author, February 3, 2011.
294 *"He treated Hubert terribly":* Walter Mondale interview with the author, January 27, 2011.
294 *"LBJ genuinely loved Humphrey":* Tom Johnson to the author, March 2011.

294 *"I know that at one time"*: Larry Temple to the author, March 30, 2011.
294 *"Humphrey believed in everything"*: LBJ to Harry Middleton, Lyndon B. Johnson Oral History.

Chicago

295 *"America's in trouble today"*: Richard Nixon, Presidential Nomination Acceptance Speech, Republican National Convention, Miami Beach, Florida, August 8, 1968, at www.4president.org/speeches/nixon1968acceptance.htm.
296 *With the eyes of the nation:* Unger and Unger, *LBJ: A Life*, 480.
296 *"We anticipated trouble"*: Cronkite, *Conversations with Cronkite*, 215.
296 *By week's end:* CNN [online], at www.cnn.com/ALLPOLITICS/1996/conventions/chicago/facts/chicago68/index.shtml.
297 *"The [Hilton Hotel] became"*: Lawrence F. O'Brien Oral History Interview XXIII, 7/21/87, by Michael L. Gillette, transcript, Internet copy, LBJ Library.
297 *"Daley had two or three"*: Cronkite, *Conversations with Cronkite*, 215.
298 *"I was at the Ranch"*: Larry Temple to the author, March 30, 2011.
298 *"I personally was asked"*: Hardesty, *The Difference He Made*, 157.
299 *"[T]here was always the rumor"*: Larry Temple to the author, March 30, 2011.
299 *"He had fantasized that"*: Round table discussion, April 17, 1984.
299 *"He would have loved"*: Tom Johnson, e-mail to the author May 2011.
300 *"Chicago hurt"*: Lyndon B. Johnson Oral History Collection.
300 *"In 1968, I thought"*: Ibid.
300 *"The only thing"*: Recording of Telephone Conversation Between Lyndon B. Johnson and Hubert Humphrey, August 29, 1968, 11:45 a.m., citation no. 13337, Recordings and Transcripts of Conversations and Meetings, LBJ Library.
301 *"old conservative Humphrey"*: Recording of Telephone Conversation Between Lyndon B. Johnson and Hubert Humphrey, August 29, 1968, 10:41 a.m., citation no. 13330, Recordings and Transcripts of Conversations and Meetings, LBJ Library.

"Nixon's the One"

302 *"I was at the convention"*: Miller, *Lyndon*, 523.
302 *"I remember what he said"*: Ibid., 522.
302 *In late September:* Gallup, September 30, 1968, "Election Polls—Presidential Vote by Groups," Gallup online, at www.gallup.com/poll/139880/Election-Polls-Presidential-Vote-Groups.aspx#6.
302 *On September 30 . . . "As President, I would"*: "Some Forward Motion For H.H.H.," *Time*, Friday, Oct. 11, 1968, at www.time.com/time/magazine/article/0,9171,902365,00.html.

303 *"The Vietnam speech"*: Lawrence F. O'Brien Oral History Interview XXV, 8/25/87, by Michael L. Gillette, transcript, Internet copy, LBJ Library.
303 *"the cooling relationship between"*: Califano, *The Triumph and Tragedy*, 325.
303 *"LBJ had high hopes"*: Jim Jones to the author, May 4, 2011.
304 *"The President wanted Hubert"*: Arthur Krim Oral History Interview V, 4/7/83, by Michael L. Gillette, transcript, Internet copy, LBJ Library.
304 *"I would like to put"*: Hardesty, *The Difference He Made*, 153–54.
305 *"Most of my people"*: Miller, *Lyndon*, 524.
306 *Though, no evidence linked:* Dallek, *Portrait of a President*, 356.
306 *"apparently authoritative Republican"*: Ibid., 356.
306 *"Nixon, on the record"*: Arthur Krim Oral History Interview V.
307 *"I told [Nixon]"*: Arthur Bryce Harlow History Interview II, 5/6/79, by Michael L. Gillette, transcript, Internet copy, LBJ Library.
307 *"[Johnson] said at that"*: Arthur Krim Oral History Interview V.
307 *"[W]hen this information"*: Lawrence F. O'Brien Oral History Interview XXVI, 8/26/87, by Michael L. Gillette, transcript, Internet copy, LBJ Library.
308 *"Poor Hubert"*: Harry Middleton to the author, May 14, 2011.
308 *"I thought the actions"*: Tom Johnson to the author, April 2011.
309 *Regardless of Nixon's denials:* Anthony Summers, *The Arrogance of Power: The Secret World of Richard Nixon* (New York: Viking, 2000), 222.
309 *"I am inclined to believe"*: Walt Rostow, memorandum for the record, May 14, 1973, Anna Chennault, Reference File, LBJ Library.

Chapter 11: "THE GOLDEN COIN IS ALMOST SPENT"

A Smooth Transition

311 *"The golden coin"*: Johnson, *White House Diary*, 770.
311 *Five hundred and thirty-five thousand:* Gelb, Rosenthal, and Siegel, *Great Lives*, 306.
311 *peace was "the President's abiding preoccupation"*: Unger and Unger, *LBJ: A Life*, 497.
312 *"I remember that he"*: Billy Graham Oral History, Special Interview.
312 *"LBJ so wanted an honorable"*: Tom Johnson to the author, April 26, 2011.
312 *"The President during this period"*: Arthur Krim Oral History Interview VI, 10/13/83, by Michael L. Gillette, transcript, Internet copy, LBJ Library.
314 *"The earth coming up"*: Chaikin, *A Man on the Moon*, 112.
314 *It read simply, "You saved 1968"*: Ibid., 134.
315 *"When [S]putnik came over"*: Recording of Telephone Conversation Between Lyndon B. Johnson and the Wives of the Apollo 8 Astronauts—Susan Borman, Marilyn Lovell, and Valerie Anders—December 27, 1968, 11:15 a.m., citation no. 13825, Recordings and Transcripts of Conversations and Meetings, LBJ Library.
315 *"Nixon's a son of a bitch"*: Jim Jones to author, May 4, 2011.

315 *"[The transition] was a magnificent":* Walt W. Rostow Oral History Interview I, 3/21/69, by Paige E. Mulhollan, transcript, Internet copy, LBJ Library.
316 *"The White House years":* George R. Davis Oral History Interview I, 2/13/69, by Dorothy Pierce McSweeny, transcript, Internet copy, LBJ Library.
316 *"President Nixon got so much":* Hardesty, *The Difference He Made*, 89.
316 *"We don't need":* Larry Temple to the author, March 30, 2011.
316 *"[LBJ] wasn't a fan":* Ibid.

"Everything That Was in Me"

317 *"The [last days there was] buttoning":* Larry Temple to the author, March 30, 2011.
317 *"The one story that":* DeVier Pierson, in Recollections of LBJ.
318 *"The day before he left":* Harry McPherson to the author, March 8, 2011.
318 *"After my years":* Harry Middleton to the author, March 8, 2011.
319 *"several words I have":* Miller, *Lyndon*, 529.
319 *"My term of office":* Johnson, "Annual Message to the Congress on the State of the Union," January 14, 1969, in Woolley and Peters, The American Presidency Project, at www.presidency.ucsb.edu/ws/?pid=29333.
319 *"As the enclosed photographs":* Calling card from President Ho Chi Minh of the Democratic Republic of Vietnam to President Lyndon B. Johnson, March 13, 1969, Special Head of State Correspondence, North Vietnam Folder, National Security File Collection, Box 59, LBJ Library.
320 *"It has been a high":* Miller, *Lyndon*, 529.
321 *"Maybe my most vivid":* Larry Temple to the author, March 30, 2011.
321 *"At last it was time":* Johnson, *White House Diary*, 774.
321 *As they left the White House:* Russell, *Lady Bird*, 304.
322 *"I wouldn't trade anything":* Middleton, *White House Years*, 237.
322 *"That warm night":* Johnson, *The Vantage Point*, 568–69.
323 *"No president ever came":* 1968 White House Tour with Lady Bird Johnson, at www.c-spanvideo.org/videoLibrary/clip.php?appid=555257392.

Chapter 12: SUNSET

325 *"When I die":* Harry Middleton to the author, April 26, 2011.
325 *A day after his own death:* Luci Johnson to the author, April 28, 2011; Laura Bush, *Spoken from the Heart* (New York: Scribner, 2010), 92.
326 *"Lady Bird Johnson [stood] vigil":* Harry Middleton, in *Among Friends*, January 2011.
326 *"I'm going to show":* Miller, *Lyndon*, 403.

Sources

Adams, Henry, Ernest Samuels, and Jayne N. Samuels. *The Education of Henry Adams.* Boston: Houghton Mifflin, 1973.

American Experience: The Presidents: Lyndon B. Johnson. WGBH-Boston, 1991. www.pbs.org/wgbh/amex/presidents/video/lbj_01.html#v226.

Beschloss, Michael R., ed. *Reaching for Glory: Lyndon Johnson's Secret White House Tapes, 1964–1965.* New York: Simon and Schuster, 2001.

———. *Taking Charge: The Johnson White House Tapes, 1963–1964.* New York: Simon and Schuster, 1997.

Bolger, Major Daniel P. *Scenes from an Unfinished War: Low-Intensity Conflict in Korea, 1966–1969.* Leavenworth Paper No. 19. www.cgsc.edu/carl/resources/csi/content.asp#scenes.

Burns, James MacGregor. *Running Alone: Presidential Leadership from JFK to Bush II: Why It Has Failed and How We Can Fix It.* New York: Basic Books, 2006.

Busby, Horace. *The Thirty-first of March: An Intimate Portrait of Lyndon Johnson's Final Days in Office.* New York: Farrar, Straus and Giroux, 2006.

Califano, Joseph A. Jr. *Inside: A Public and Private Life.* New York: Public Affairs, 2004.

———. *The Triumph and Tragedy of Lyndon Johnson: The White House Years.* College Station: Texas A&M UP, 2000.

Caro, Robert A. *The Years of Lyndon Johnson, Volume 1: The Path to Power.* New York: Vintage, 1990.

———. *The Years of Lyndon Johnson, Volume 2: Means of Ascent.* New York: Vintage, 1991.

———. *The Years of Lyndon Johnson, Volume 3: Master of the Senate.* New York: Vintage, 2003.

Chaikin, Andrew. *A Man on the Moon: Lunar Explorers.* Alexandria, Va.: Time-Life, 1999.

Congress and the Nation, 1965–68. Washington, D.C.: Congressional Quarterly Press, 1968.

Cormier, Frank. *LBJ: The Way He Was.* Garden City, N.Y.: Doubleday, 1977.

Cowger, Thomas W., and Sherwin Markman, eds. *Lyndon Johnson Remembered:*

An Intimate Portrait of a Presidency. Lanham, Md.: Rowman and Littlefield, 2003.

Cronkite, Walter, and Don E. Carleton. *Conversations with Cronkite*. Dolph Briscoe Center for American History, University of Texas at Austin, 2010.

Dallek, Robert. *Flawed Giant: Lyndon Johnson and His Times, 1961–1973*. New York: Oxford University Press, 1998.

———. *Lone Star Rising: Lyndon Johnson and His Times, 1908–1960*. New York: Oxford University Press, 1991.

———. *Lyndon B. Johnson: Portrait of a President*. New York: Oxford University Press, 2004.

Evans, Rowland, and Robert D. Novak. *Lyndon B. Johnson: The Exercise of Power*. New York: New American Library, 1966.

Forslund, Catherine. *Anna Chennault: Informal Diplomacy and Asian Relations*. Wilmington, Del.: Scholarly Resources, 2002.

Gelb, Arthur, A. M. Rosenthal, and Marvin Siegel. *New York Times Great Lives of the Twentieth Century*. New York: Times, 1988.

Gilbert, Marc Jason, and William Head, eds. *The Tet Offensive*. Westport, Conn.: Praeger, 1996.

Gillette, Michael L. *Launching the War on Poverty: An Oral History*. Oxford: Oxford University Press, 2010.

Gillon, Steven M. *The Democrats' Dilemma: Walter F. Mondale and the Liberal Legacy*. New York: Columbia University Press, 1992.

Gittinger, Ted, ed. *The Johnson Years: A Vietnam Roundtable*. Austin, Texas: Lyndon Baines Johnson Library, 1993.

Goodwin, Doris Kearns. *Lyndon Johnson and the American Dream*. New York: St. Martin's, 1991.

Goodwin, Richard N. *Remembering America: A Voice from the Sixties*. Boston: Little, Brown, 1988.

Hardesty, Robert L. "The LBJ the Nation Seldom Saw" (1983). *Office of the President Publications*. Paper 2. ecommons.txstate.edu/presopub/2.

Hardesty, Robert L., ed. *The Johnson Years: The Difference He Made*. Austin, Texas: Lyndon Baines Johnson Library, 1993.

Johnson, Lady Bird. *A White House Diary*. New York: Holt, Rinehart and Winston, 1970.

Johnson, Lyndon B. *The Vantage Point: Perspectives of the Presidency, 1963–1969*. New York: Holt, Rinehart and Winston, 1971.

Johnson, Rebekah Baines. *A Family Album*. New York: McGraw-Hill, 1965.

Kennerly, David Hume, Robert McNeely, Pete Souza, and Matthew Naythons. *Barack Obama: The Official Inaugural Book*. New York: Five Ties Publishing, 2009.

Mailer, Norman. *The Armies of the Night: History as a Novel, the Novel as History*. New York: New American Library, 1968.

McNamara, Robert S., and Brian VanDeMark. *In Retrospect: The Tragedy and Lessons of Vietnam*. New York: Times, 1995.

"Media and the Voting Rights Act of 1965." October 20, 2008. Robert M. Batscha University Seminar Series. Paley Center for Media, New York City.
Middleton, Harry J. *Lady Bird Johnson: A Life Well Lived*. Austin, Texas: Lyndon Baines Johnson Foundation, 1992.
———. *LBJ: The White House Years*. New York: H.N. Abrams, 1980.
Miller, Merle. *Lyndon: An Oral Biography*. New York: Putnam, 1980.
———. *Plain Speaking: An Oral Biography of Harry S. Truman*. New York: Berkley Pub/Putnam, 1974.
Nixon, Richard M. *The Memoirs of Richard Nixon*. New York: Grosset and Dunlap, 1978.
Oberdorfer, Don. *Tet! The Turning Point in the Vietnam War*. New York: Doubleday, 1971. Rep. 1984 with new foreword.
Parmet, Herbert S. *Richard Nixon and His America*. Boston: Little, Brown, 1990.
Peters, Charles. *Lyndon B. Johnson: The American Presidents Series: The 36th President, 1963–1969*. Ed. Arthur M. Schlesinger and Sean Wilentz. New York: Times, 2010.
Pycior, Julie Leininger. *LBJ and Mexican Americans: The Paradox of Power*. Austin: University of Texas Press, 1997.
Round table discussion, with Harry Middleton, Dean Rusk, John Gronouski, Wilbur Cohen, Robert Hardesty, George Christian, and Larry Temple. April 17, 1984. LBJ Library.
Russell, Jan Jarboe. *Lady Bird: A Biography of Mrs. Johnson*. New York: Scribner, 1999.
Schulzinger, Robert D. *A Time for War: The United States and Vietnam, 1941–1975*. New York: Oxford University Press, 1997.
Shenk, Joshua Wolf. *Lincoln's Melancholy: How Depression Challenged a President and Fueled His Greatness*. Boston: Houghton Mifflin, 2006.
Sidey, Hugh. *A Very Personal Presidency: Lyndon Johnson in the White House*. London: Deutsch, 1968.
———. *The Presidency*. West Stockbridge, Mass.: Thornwillow, 1991.
Sidey, Hugh, and Fred Ward. *Portrait of a President*. New York: Harper and Row, 1975.
Smith, Richard Norton. *Patriarch: George Washington and the New American Nation*. Boston: Houghton Mifflin, 1993.
Summers, Anthony, and Robbyn Swan. *The Arrogance of Power: The Secret World of Richard Nixon*. New York: Viking, 2000.
Thomas, Evan. *Robert Kennedy: His Life*. New York: Simon and Schuster, 2000.
Unger, Irwin, and Debi Unger. *LBJ: A Life*. New York: Wiley, 1999.
White, Theodore H. *The Making of the President 1968*. New York: Atheneum Publishers, 1969.
Wirtz, James J. *The Tet Offensive: Intelligence Failure in War*. Ithaca, N.Y.: Cornell University Press, 1991.
Woods, Randall B. *LBJ: Architect of American Ambition*. Cambridge, Mass.: Harvard University Press, 2007.

Oral Histories

Arthur Bryce Harlow History Interview II, 5/6/79, by Michael L. Gillette. Transcript. Internet copy. LBJ Library.

Arthur Krim Oral History Interview IV, 11/9/82, by Michael L. Gillette. Transcript. Internet copy. LBJ Library.

Arthur Krim Oral History Interview V, 4/7/83, by Michael L. Gillette. Transcript. Internet copy. LBJ Library.

Arthur Krim Oral History Interview VI, 10/13/83, by Michael L. Gillette. Transcript. Internet copy. LBJ Library.

Barry Goldwater Oral History Interview I, 6/26/71, by Joe B. Frantz. Transcript. Internet copy. LBJ Library.

Bess Abell Oral History Interview II, 6/13/69, by T. H. Baker. Transcript. Internet copy. LBJ Library.

Betty Hickman Oral History Interview I, 4/10/84, by Mike Gillette. Transcript. Internet copy. LBJ Library.

Billy Graham Oral History Interview, Special Interview, 10/12/83, by Monroe Billington. Transcript. Internet copy, LBJ Library.

Carl Albert Oral History Interview III, 7/9/69, by Dorothy Pierce McSweeny. Transcript. Internet copy. LBJ Library.

Clark M. Clifford Oral History Interview II, 7/2/69, by Paige Mulhollan. Transcript. Internet copy. LBJ Library.

Clark M. Clifford Oral History Interview III, 7/14/69, by Paige Mulhollan. Transcript. Internet copy. LBJ Library.

Dean Rusk Oral History Interview II, 9/26/69, by Paige E. Mulhollan. Transcript. Internet copy. LBJ Library.

Dean Rusk Oral History Interview III, 1/2/70, by Paige E. Mulhollan. Transcript. Internet copy. LBJ Library.

Dean Rusk Oral History Interview IV, 3/8/70, by Paige E. Mulhollan, Transcript. Internet copy. LBJ Library.

Earl Warren Oral History Interview I, 9/21/71, by Joe B. Frantz. Transcript. Internet copy. LBJ Library.

Edward M. Kennedy Oral History Interview III, 1/21/70, by Joe B. Frantz, LBJ Library.

Elizabeth (Liz) Carpenter Oral History Interview I, 12/3/68, by Joe B. Frantz. Internet copy. LBJ Library.

Fannie Lou Hamer Oral History, University of Southern Mississippi. digilib .usm.edu/cdm4/document.php?CISOROOT=/coh&CISOPTR =2957&REC=16.

Frank Oltorf Oral History Interview I, 8/3/71, by David G. McComb. Transcript. Internet copy. LBJ Library.

George McGovern Oral History, interview with author, February 3, 2011.

George R. Davis Oral History Interview I, 2/13/69, by Dorothy Pierce McSweeny. Transcript. Internet copy. LBJ Library.

George Reedy Oral History Interview III, 6/7/75, by Michael L. Gillette. Transcript. Internet copy. LBJ Library.
Harry McPherson Oral History Interview IV, 3/24/69, by T. H. Baker. Transcript. Internet copy. LBJ Library.
Harry McPherson Oral History Interview X, 5/13/86, by Michael L. Gillette. Transcript. Internet copy. LBJ Library.
Homer Thornberry Oral History Interview I, 12/21/70. Transcript. Internet copy. LBJ Library.
Hubert H. Humphrey Oral History Interview III, 6/21/77, by Michael L. Gillette. Transcript. Internet copy. LBJ Library.
Jack Brooks Oral History Interview I, 2/1/71, by Joe B. Frantz. Transcript. Internet copy. LBJ Library.
Jack Valenti Oral History Interview III, 2/19/71, by Joe B. Frantz. Transcript. Internet copy. LBJ Library.
John Bartlow Martin Oral History Interview I, 1/30/71, by Paige E. Mulhollan. Transcript. Internet copy. LBJ Library.
John Chancellor Oral History Interview I, 4/25/69, by Dorothy Pierce McSweeny. Transcript. Internet copy. LBJ Library.
Kenneth O'Donnell Oral History Interview I, 7/23/69, by Paige Mulhollan. LBJ Library.
Lawrence F. O'Brien Oral History Interview VII, 2/12/86, by Michael L. Gillette. Transcript. Internet copy. LBJ Library.
Lawrence F. O'Brien Oral History Interview VIII, 4/8/86, by Michael L. Gillette. Transcript. Internet copy. LBJ Library.
Lawrence F. O'Brien Oral History Interview XII, 7/25/86, by Michael L. Gillette. Transcript. Internet copy. LBJ Library.
Lawrence F. O'Brien Oral History Interview XIV, 9/11/86, by Michael L. Gillette. Transcript. Internet copy. LBJ Library.
Lawrence F. O'Brien Oral History Interview XXIII, 7/21/87, by Michael L. Gillette. Transcript. Internet copy. LBJ Library.
Lawrence F. O'Brien Oral History Interview XXV, 8/25/87, by Michael L. Gillette. Transcript. Internet copy. LBJ Library.
Lawrence F. O'Brien Oral History Interview XXVI, 8/26/87, by Michael L. Gillette. Transcript. Internet copy. LBJ Library.
Lee White Oral History, by Stacey Petersen. Southwest Texas State University Oral History Project. Transcript at www.eeoc.gov/eeoc/history/35th/voices/oral_history-lee_white-stacey_petersen.wpd.html.
Lyndon Johnson Oral History Collection, 8/9/69, by Bob Hardesty and Harry Middleton. LBJ Library.
Marie Fehmer Chiarodo Oral History Interview II, 8/16/72, by Joe B. Frantz, 60. Internet copy. LBJ Library.
Nicholas D. Katzenbach Oral History Interview III, 12/11/68, by Paige E. Mulhollan. Transcript. Internet copy. LBJ Library.
Ramsey Clark Oral History Interview V, 6/3/69, by Harri Baker. Transcript. Internet copy. LBJ Library.

Robert S. McNamara Oral History Interview I, 1/8/75, by Walt W. Rostow. Transcript. Internet copy. LBJ Library.
Robert S. McNamara Oral History, Special Interview I, 3/26/93, by Robert Dallek. Transcript. Internet copy. LBJ Library.
Roy Wilkins Oral History Interview I, 4/1/69, by Thomas H. Baker. Transcript. Internet copy. LBJ Library.
Sarah T. Hughes Oral History Interview I, 10/7/68, by Joe B. Frantz. Transcript. Internet copy. LBJ Library.
Thurgood Marshall Oral History Interview I, 7/10/69, by T. H. Baker. Transcript. Internet copy. LBJ Library.
Walter Mondale interview with author, January 27, 2011. Transcript.
Walt W. Rostow Oral History Interview I, 3/21/69, by Paige E. Mulhollan. Transcript. Internet copy. LBJ Library.
William S. White Oral History Interview II, 3/10/69, by Dorothy Pierce McSweeny. Transcript. Internet copy. LBJ Library.

Conversations

Recording of Cabinet Room Meeting Between Lyndon B. Johnson and Anatoly Dobrynin, Walt Rostow, August 20, 1968, 8:17–8:42 p.m. Tape SC.01, PNO: 3. Recordings and Transcripts of Meetings Conducted in the Cabinet Room. LBJ Library.
Recording of Telephone Conversation Between Lyndon B. Johnson and Abe Fortas, October 1, 1968, 6:06 p.m. Citation no. 13509. Recordings and Transcripts of Conversations and Meetings. LBJ Library.
Recording of Telephone Conversation Between Lyndon B. Johnson and Bill Moyers, August 7, 1964, 8:35 p.m. Citation nos. 4815, 4816, 4817. Recordings and Transcripts of Conversations and Meetings. LBJ Library.
Recording of Telephone Conversation Between Lyndon B. Johnson and Clark Clifford, October 14, 1964, 8:20 p.m. Citation no. 5880. Recordings and Transcripts of Conversations and Meetings. LBJ Library.
Recording of Telephone Conversation Between Lyndon B. Johnson and Dr. Martin Luther King, Jr., July 7, 1965, 8:05 p.m. Citation nos. 8311–8313. Recordings and Transcripts of Conversations and Meetings. LBJ Library.
Recording of Telephone Conversation Between Lyndon B. Johnson and Dwight Eisenhower, July 2, 1965, 11:02 a.m. Citation no. 8303. Recordings and Transcripts of Conversations and Meetings. LBJ Library.
Recording of Telephone Conversation Between Lyndon B. Johnson and Dwight Eisenhower, June 25, 1967, 9:44 p.m. Citation nos. 11914–11916. Recordings and Transcripts of Conversations and Meetings. LBJ Library.
Recording of Telephone Conversation Between Lyndon B. Johnson and Eunice Kennedy Shriver, December 18, 1966, 6:55 p.m. Citation no. 11155.

Recordings and Transcripts of Conversations and Meetings. LBJ Library.

Recording of Telephone Conversation Between Lyndon B. Johnson and Everett Dirksen, November 29, 1963, 11:40 a.m. Tape K6311.04, PNO 8. Recordings and Transcripts of Conversations and Meetings. LBJ Library.

Recording of Telephone Conversation Between Lyndon B. Johnson and Everett Dirksen, May 13, 1964, 4:30 p.m. Citation no. 3437. Recordings and Transcripts of Conversations and Meetings. LBJ Library.

Recording of Telephone Conversation Between Lyndon B. Johnson and Everett Dirksen, June 24, 1964, 6:22 p.m. Citation no. 3859. Recordings and Transcripts of Conversations and Meetings. LBJ Library.

Recording of Telephone Conversation Between Lyndon B. Johnson and George Reedy, January 25, 1964, 2:25 p.m. Citation no. 1544. Recordings and Transcripts of Conversations and Meetings. LBJ Library.

Recording of Telephone Conversation Between Lyndon B. Johnson and Hubert Humphrey, August 14, 1964, 11:05 a.m. Citation no. 4918. Recordings and Transcripts of Conversations and Meetings. LBJ Library.

Recording of Telephone Conversation Between Lyndon B. Johnson and Hubert Humphrey, August 29, 1968, 10:41 a.m. Citation no. 13330. Recordings and Transcripts of Conversations and Meetings. LBJ Library.

Recording of Telephone Conversation Between Lyndon B. Johnson and Hubert Humphrey, August 29, 1968, 11:45 a.m. Citation no. 13337. Recordings and Transcripts of Conversations and Meetings. LBJ Library.

Recording of Telephone Conversation Between Lyndon B. Johnson and Jacqueline Kennedy, December 2, 1963, 2:42 p.m. Tape K6312.01, PNO 24. Recordings and Transcripts of Conversations and Meetings. LBJ Library.

Recording of Telephone Conversation Between Lyndon B. Johnson and Joe Haggar, August 9, 1964, 1:17 p.m. Citation no. 4851. Recordings and Transcripts of Conversations and Meetings. LBJ Library.

Recording of Telephone Conversation Between Lyndon B. Johnson and John McCormack, August 7, 1964, 3:01 p.m. Citation nos. 4807, 4808. Recordings and Transcripts of Conversations and Meetings. LBJ Library.

Recording of Telephone Conversation Between Lyndon B. Johnson and John McCormack, August 6, 1965, 6:35 p.m. Citation no. 8517. Recordings and Transcripts of Conversations and Meetings. LBJ Library.

Recording of Telephone Conversation Between Lyndon B. Johnson and Katharine Graham, December 2, 1963, 11:10 a.m. Tape K6312.01, PNO: 19. Recordings and Transcripts of Conversations and Meetings. LBJ Library.

Recording of Telephone Conversation Between Lyndon B. Johnson and Lady Bird Johnson, March 7, 1964, 4:10 p.m. Citation no. 2395. Recordings and Transcripts of Conversations and Meetings. LBJ Library.

Recording of Telephone Conversation Between Lyndon B. Johnson and Lady

Bird Johnson, October 15, 1964, 9:12 a.m. Citation no. 5895. Recordings and Transcripts of Conversations and Meetings. LBJ Library.

Recording of Telephone Conversation Between Lyndon B. Johnson and McGeorge Bundy, May 27, 1964, 11:24 a.m. Citation no. 3522. Recordings and Transcripts of Conversations and Meetings. LBJ Library.

Recording of Telephone Conversation Between Lyndon B. Johnson and Robert McNamara, June 5, 1967, 7:57 a.m. Citation no. 11903. Recordings and Transcripts of Conversations and Meetings. LBJ Library.

Recording of Telephone Conversation Between Lyndon B. Johnson and Robert McNamara, January 31, 1968, Time Unknown. Citation no. 12617. Recordings and Transcripts of Conversations and Meetings. LBJ Library.

Recording of Telephone Conversation Between Lyndon B. Johnson and Robert McNamara, February 19, 1968, 12:29 p.m. Citation no. 12724. Recordings and Transcripts of Conversations and Meetings. LBJ Library.

Recording of Telephone Conversation Between Lyndon B. Johnson and Martin Luther King Jr., January 15, 1965, 12:06 p.m. Citation nos. 6736 and 6737. Recordings and Transcripts of Conversations and Meetings. LBJ Library.

Recording of Telephone Conversation Between Lyndon B. Johnson and Mike Mansfield, April 30, 1965, 11:51 a.m. Citation no. 7410. Recordings and Transcripts of Conversations and Meetings. LBJ Library.

Recording of Telephone Conversation Between Lyndon B. Johnson and Nicholas Katzenbach, July 25, 1964, 10:15 a.m. Citation nos. 4337–4339. Recordings and Transcripts of Conversations and Meetings. LBJ Library.

Recording of Telephone Conversation Between Lyndon B. Johnson and Phil Potter, August 6, 1965, 7:12 p.m. Citation no. 8525. Recordings and Transcripts of Conversations and Meetings. LBJ Library.

Recording of Telephone Conversation Between Lyndon B. Johnson and Richard Russell, November 29, 1963, 8:55 p.m. Tape K6311.06, PNO 14, 15, 16. Recordings and Transcripts of Conversations and Meetings. LBJ Library.

Recording of Telephone Conversation Between Lyndon B. Johnson and Richard Russell, May 27, 1964, 10:55 a.m. Citation no. 3519. Recordings and Transcripts of Conversations and Meetings. LBJ Library.

Recording of Telephone Conversation Between Lyndon B. Johnson and Ted Kennedy, March 8, 1965, 9:10 p.m. Citation no. 7043. Recordings and Transcripts of Conversations and Meetings. LBJ Library.

Recording of Telephone Conversation Between Lyndon B. Johnson and the Wives of the Apollo 8 Astronauts—Susan Borman, Marilyn Lovell, and Valerie Anders—December 27, 1968, 11:15 a.m. Citation no. 13825. Recordings and Transcripts of Conversations and Meetings. LBJ Library.

Recording of Telephone Conversation Between Lyndon B. Johnson and Wilbur Mills and Wilbur Cohen, March 23, 1965, 4:54 p.m. Citation no. 7142. Recordings and Transcripts of Conversations and Meetings. LBJ Library.

Video Recollections

Recollections of LBJ. Video. Lyndon Baines Johnson Library and Museum. Produced by the Technical Services Department of the LBJ Library. TSV 0258. glifos.lbjf.org/gsm/index.php/Recollections_of_LBJ.

Interviews

Lyndon Johnson interviewed by Walter Cronkite, "An Assessment of Harry S. Truman, the Man: An Interview with President Lyndon B. Johnson." KTBC-TV Studios, Austin, Texas. May 7, 1971.

Lyndon Johnson interviewed by Walter Cronkite. "Lyndon Johnson Talks Politics." Aired January 27, 1972.

Lyndon Johnson interviewed by Walter Cronkite. "The Decision to Halt the Bombing." Aired February 6, 1969.

Lyndon Johnson interviewed by Walter Cronkite. "The Last Interview." Aired February 1, 1973.

Lyndon Johnson interviewed by Walter Cronkite. "Tragedy and Transition." Aired May 2, 1970.

Lyndon Johnson interviewed by Walter Cronkite. "Why I Chose Not to Run." Aired December 27, 1969.

The Hill Country: Lyndon Johnson's Texas. Narrator and interviewer Ray Scherer. [LBJ Library serial no. MP211]. Aired May 9, 1966.

Photo Credits

All photos are courtesy of the **LBJ Presidential Library—Yoichi Okamoto,** except for those indicated below.

Courtesy of the LBJ Presidential Library—Cecil Stoughton
"LBJ with Lady Bird and Jacqueline Kennedy," "LBJ addressing Congress," "LBJ greets crowds," "LBJ takes oath of office on *Air Force One*," "LBJ signs the Civil Rights Act of 1964," "LBJ visits Appalachia"

Courtesy of the JFK Presidential Library—Cecil Stoughton
"John Connally, LBJ, and JFK in Fort Worth, Texas"

Courtesy of the LBJ Presidential Library—Frank Wolfe
"LBJ confers with President-elect Richard Nixon," "The Johnsons at LBJ Ranch," "Vietnam War protests," "LBJ and Lady Bird walking among wildflowers"

Courtesy of the LBJ Presidential Library—Jack Kightlinger
"LBJ listens in anguish to recording of son-in-law in Vietnam"

Courtesy of the LBJ Presidential Library—Mike Geissinger
"LBJ surrounded by well-wishers"

Courtesy of the LBJ Presidential Library—Robert Knudsen
"Anti-war protests outside the White House"

Courtesy of the U.S. Department of Defense
"U.S. troops of the Twenty-fifth Infantry Division in Vietnam"

Index

Abbreviations: LBJ stands for Lyndon Baines Johnson; JFK stands for John F. Kennedy
Page numbers of photographs appear in italics.